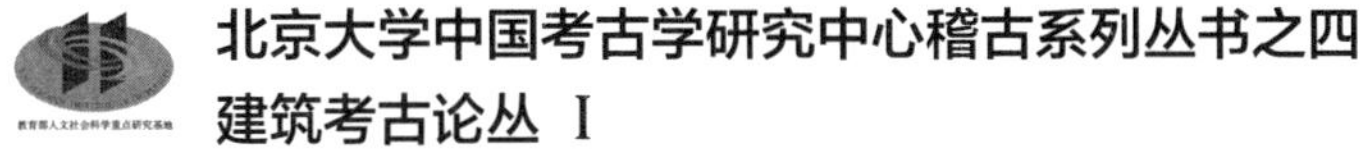

北京大学中国考古学研究中心稽古系列丛书之四

建筑考古论丛 I

建筑考古学的体与用

Essence and Applications of Building Archaeology in China and Europe

北京大学中国考古学研究中心
北京大学考古文博学院
鲁汶大学工学院
徐怡涛　[比]高曼士　张剑葳　主编

中国建筑工业出版社

图书在版编目（CIP）数据

建筑考古学的体与用 / 徐怡涛，（比）高曼士，张剑葳主编 . 北京：中国建筑工业出版社，2019.3
（建筑考古论丛 I）
ISBN 978-7-112-23157-7

Ⅰ.①建… Ⅱ.①徐…②高…③张… Ⅲ.①建筑学－考古学－文集 Ⅳ.①K869.1-53

中国版本图书馆CIP数据核字（2019）第006083号

责任编辑：陈海娇 李 鸽
责任校对：芦欣甜

北京大学中国考古学研究中心稽古系列丛书之四
建筑考古论丛 I

建筑考古学的体与用
北京大学中国考古学研究中心
北京大学考古文博学院
鲁汶大学工学院
徐怡涛 [比] 高曼士 张剑葳 主编
*
中国建筑工业出版社出版、发行（北京海淀三里河路9号）
各地新华书店、建筑书店经销
北京雅盈中佳图文设计公司制版
北京缤索印刷有限公司印刷
*
开本：889×1194 毫米 1/20 印张：12 字数：332 千字
2019 年 6 月第一版 2019 年 7 月第二次印刷
定价：67.00 元
ISBN 978-7-112-23157-7
（33245）
版权所有 翻印必究
如有印装质量问题，可寄本社退换
（邮政编码 100037）

本书编委会

徐怡涛　[比]高曼士　张剑葳　杭　侃

徐天进　雷兴山　孙庆伟　张　敏

序

中、欧建筑考古的体与用

[比] 高曼士　徐怡涛　张剑葳

在中国，研究历史建筑的学科包括建筑历史学与考古学。这两个学科有着不同的研究方法、问题和研究目标。一方面，建筑学院中的建筑历史与理论专业为新建筑设计和既有建筑更新提供学术支撑；另一方面，在考古学院中的教学科研，则基于田野发掘技术、方法与理论，以及对建筑遗产的调查记录、历史研究，文物分析与修复而展开。虽然考古学家与建筑史家都对历史建成环境有兴趣，但他们实际上缺乏合作。

我们需要一门学问来联结建筑历史与考古，对发掘所见的建筑遗存和地面以上的历史建筑都开展研究，以跨学科的视角来打破“地平线”的限制。建筑考古正是这样一门学问，因为它不仅是建筑历史学与考古学科的简单结合。

建筑考古的目标与方法

建筑考古的目标在于发现建筑的历史，其方法可以在即使没有考古发掘和文献信息的情况下，也能通过建筑本体的史料确定建筑年表，辨识与解读建筑的使用历程，从而通过建筑本体的物质性信息来理解人和社会。

建筑考古以考古学的方法来观察、分析现存建筑，尤其是要发现隐藏于建筑物质本体中的历史信息（图 1）。建筑考古关注建筑的一切组成部分，包括建筑的材料、结构、构造技术、改建过程，以及建筑装饰、建筑设备、使用功能，等等。

建筑考古可综合运用测绘技术、科技考古、材料分析技术、科学测年等来自自然科学领域的各种分析技术，同时也从考古发掘和历史文献研究中获得支撑。

欧洲、中国建筑考古研究的源与流

建筑考古学在大多数欧洲国家已经是既有的学科，例如英国的“Building archaeology”，德国的“Bauforschung”，意大利的“archeologia dell’architettura”，法国的“archéologie du bâti”，西班牙的“arqueologia de la architectura”，荷兰的“bouwhistorie”，等等。建筑考古从业者有着不同的学术背景：考古学、建筑学、艺术史

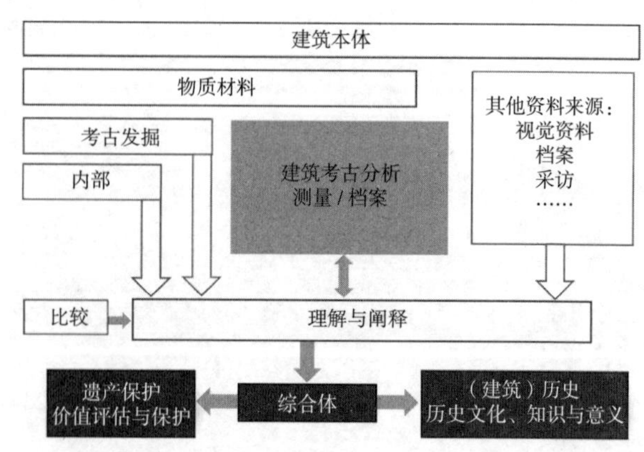

图 1　建筑考古方法的技术路线图（高曼士）

学、历史学、工程学、地理学，等等。其中一部分是科研院所的学者，而大部分是专业实践者。从本质上说，建筑考古学具有跨学科的特征。建筑考古学家从实践和田野中不断获取经验，这是最好的教育。然而作为一个学科来说，建筑考古学也已建立了自身的理论、思辨、方法以及学术教育体系。

欧洲各国的建筑考古方法各有自身传统，意大利、法国、英国、德国、瑞士、荷兰各有自身特点。有些更多受到考古地层学的影响，以专门研究层累发展的历史建筑；有些则来自对于中世纪建筑修复的预研究。建筑考古的起源可上溯自 19 世纪中叶，受到考古学运动的古物学家和第一代理性主义中世纪建筑修复建筑师的影响，其代表人物是维奥莱 · 勒 · 杜克（1814—1879）。

第二次世界大战对历史城镇中心的大量破坏，引发了战后大规模考古和建筑考古研究，遗产保护方面的新知识和进展相应唤起了人们对于历史建筑的兴趣。近年来，建筑考古研究则受到历史学家关于社会经济领域，以及人类学家关于生产周期等新问题的影响。

1970 年代以来，一些高校成立了专门的研究中心，开设了专门课程；遗产保护管理部门推动建筑考古与考古学的协同发展；建筑考古工作者则不断开展个人实践。今天，建筑考古已经是有独立研究问题和方法的既有学科，涵盖了历史建筑的各个物质性层面。近二十年来科技考古以及计算机辅助设计与数字记录等科技手段的快速发展，也大大促进了建筑考古的发展。

在中国，建筑考古研究至今也已开展了八十余年——沿着梁思成（1901—1972）和刘敦桢（1897—1968）的足迹，相关学者们常常自称为建筑史学家而没有意识到他们开展的工作实际上是建筑考古。诚然，建筑考古学在中国尚未被清晰地界定并形成共识的专门学科。

首届中欧建筑考古国际研讨会

2015 年，我们萌生了在北京组织一次建筑考古国际会议的想法。这一想法来自两个层面的观察：首先，建筑考古自梁思成、刘敦桢以来，在中国有着长久的优秀传统，但主要关注历史时期的古建筑，而对更早的（例如新石器时代）和更晚近的（例如近代）建筑关注有限；其次，建筑考古研究的成果常常未被保护与修复工作者充分了解吸收。这两点观察既面向历史建筑研究，也在于提高对古代建筑和近代建筑的保护水平。

建筑考古如何促进中国的建筑遗产保护？反映在 2014 年以来北京大学考古文博学院与鲁汶大学建筑系及雷蒙德·勒迈尔国际保护中心的一系列合作研究中，包括：为更好地理解建筑考古领域的不同经验与方法而组织的建筑考古国际会议；推动建筑考古作为一种跨学科研究方法；在考古学者、建筑学者、工程师、建造史学者、历史学者和建筑史学者之间搭建沟通桥梁；以及探讨如何以建筑考古的、更深入的物质性研究来提升未来的保护与修复水平。

2016 年 5 月 13~15 日，首届中欧建筑考古国际研讨会在北京成功举办。此次会议有三个主要目标：首先，邀请中国和欧洲考古、建筑史、艺术史、建造史、工程等方面的相关杰出学者，聚首于学科交叉的十字路口，以展现当前论题、方法和挑战的多样性；其次，讨论建筑考古本身作为一门学科的定义，或至少作为促进学科间合作的平台；再次，为未来的发展打下基础。

本次会议的主旨并不在于探讨测绘技术、建筑史、建造史、遗产保护、考古发掘、实验室分析、历史建筑结构鉴定分析、三维数字建模等具体问题。这些领域都已有系列会议，建立了成熟的学术网络。当然，在本次建筑考古的各个会议报告中，多少也涉及上述专业领域的少数内容。

本次会议由 11 场议程、37 个报告组成，每个报告长 20 分钟（见附录 2）。会议论文为中文或英文，现场同声传译。年轻学者是学科与事业的未来，我们认为吸纳年轻学者参与会议，以共享对于建筑遗产事业的热情尤为重要。因此我们专门在晚上设置了青年论坛，由 8 个平行论坛共 33 篇论文组成，每篇发表 12 分钟（见附录 3）。青年论坛用中文发表，在第二天由青年论坛主持人总结并向大会报告。

研讨会的第二天我们发布了两本新书。这是我们近年在中国开展建筑考古研究的实际成果，它们是：

- 高曼士，徐怡涛 . 舶来与本土——1926 年法国传教士所撰中国北方教堂营造之研究 [M]. 北京： 知识产权出版社，2016.
- 徐怡涛等 . 山西万荣稷王庙建筑考古研究 [M]. 南京： 东南大学出版社，2016.

关于本书

本书遴选了 14 篇来自中国和欧洲学者的论文，经过作者修订，每篇自成一章。文章主题和研究对象丰富，且有较大的时空跨度，从 11 世纪到 20 世纪的中国、英国、意大利、德国、荷兰和比利时。

本书正文由三部分组成，各篇为中文或英文，摘要则均为中、英双语。

第一部分“理论与文化”的五篇，其中三篇分别为陵墓建筑（陈同滨、李敏、刘翔宇），城市形态（韦正），以及早期佛教构筑物（梅晨曦），它们作为物质性研究资料，其变迁都反映了中国文化的发展；另外两篇分别关于英国的建筑考古理论（Adam MENUGE）和德国的建筑考古理论（Elke NAGEL and Manfred SCHULLER）。

第二部分“遗址与建筑”的六篇为建筑考古的代表性研究案例，包括：建筑基址（汪盈），屋顶结构与树轮测年的应用（Vincent DEBONNE），仿木构墓（俞莉娜、徐怡涛），木构斗栱（徐新云），城市住宅（Gabri VAN TUSSENBROEK），以及中国的哥特拱顶（高曼士）。

第三部分“保护研究”的三篇反映了建筑考古如何在遗产保护实践中发挥重要作用，例如对意大利的历代层叠型建筑演变研究的推动（Carolina DI BIASE），修缮工程过程中的勘察与研究（赵元祥、李林东、蔡宇琨），以及历史上石灰砌砖的方法研究（Koenraad VAN BALEN）。

本书附件包括三部分：

一、北京大学文物建筑专业与中国的建筑考古学

二、2016 中欧建筑考古国际学术研讨会议程 · 主论坛

三、2016 中欧建筑考古国际学术研讨会议程 · 青年论坛

致谢

首届中欧建筑考古国际研讨会于 2016 年 5 月 13~15 日在北京大学成功举办。比利时大使马怀宇（Michel MALHERBE）阁下、北京大学副校长李岩松教授、北京大学考古文博学院杭侃教授、鲁汶大学建筑系主任 Krista DE JONGE 教授到会致开幕词。对此我们表示诚挚的谢意。

感谢所有参会嘉宾，以及促成本次会议成功举办的各位学者。北京大学中国考古学研究中心主任徐天进教授为本次会议提供了大力支持。北京大学考古文博学院魏正中（Giuseppe VIGNATO）教授为本次会议提供了帮助并赐稿。王书林博士从初始就参与组织了本次会议。本次会议的合办单位有：中国建筑设计研究院有限公司、成都博物院、故宫研究院古建筑研究所、清华大学建筑学院和中国社会科学院考古研究所等国内知名学术机构合办。谨此表示感谢。

最后，向所有参与会议组织、翻译和会务的学生志愿者和同声传译员表示诚挚的谢意。大型国际会议的会务工作十分繁杂，翻译工作时间紧、任务重，他们以出色的能力圆满完成了这项任务。志愿者包括：刘绎一、吴煜楠、杨兆凯、朱柠、陈彦运、梁源、黄青岩、李敏、卢亚辉等研究生，以及北京大学考古文博学院文物建筑专业 2012 级、2014 级本科生。担任同声传译工作的有：李光涵、左拉拉、张剑葳、王舜泽、陈豪、崔金泽、刘洋、陈昊迪、赵东旭、章亿安、吴筱、黄华、王音等青年学者与学生。2018 级研究生席雅卿、杨佳帆、高勇、马青龙协助翻译了本书英文论文的中文摘要。鲁汶大学舒畅雪博士，本书

责任编辑李鸽博士、陈海娇女士亦为本书的翻译和编辑提出了诸多宝贵意见，谨此一并致谢。

以上难免挂一漏万，谨此向所有为本书出版贡献力量的同仁们表示衷心感谢。

延伸阅读

Bauforschung und ihr Beitrag zum Entwurf[M]//Building archaeology and its contribution to Design. Zurich: Instituts für Denkmalpflege，ETH Zürich，1993.

Boato Anna. L' archeologia in architettura. Misurazioni，stratigrafie，datazioni，restauro [M]//Archaeology in architecture. Measurements，stratigraphy，dating，restoration. Venice: Marsilio，2008.

Brogiolo Gian Pietro (ed.). Archeologia dell' Architettura. Archaeology of architecture[J]. supplement to Archeologia medievale 22，Florence，1996.

De Jonge Krista and Van Balen Koen (eds). The Role of Preparatory Architectural Investigation in the Restauration of Historical Buildings[M]. Leuven: Leuven University Press，2002.

Hassler Uta (ed.). Bauforschung: Zur Rekonstruktion des Wissens[M]//Building archaeology: towards reconstructing knowledge. Zurich: ETH Zurich，2010.

Menuge Adam. Understanding Historic Buildings: A Guide to Good Recording Practice[M]. London: Historic England，2016.

Parron-Kontis Isabelle and Reveyron Nicolas (eds). Archéologie du bâti. Pour une harmonisation des methods[M]//Building archaeology: towards a methodological harmonisation. Paris : Errances，2005.

Schuller Manfred. Building Archaeology (Series Monuments and Sites，7)[M]. Paris-Munich : ICOMOS，2002.

Stenvert Ronald and van Tussenbroek Gabri (eds). Inleiding in de bouwhistorie. Opmeten en onderzoeken van oude gebouwen[M]// Introduction to building archaeology. Measuring and investigating ancient buildings，2nd ed.. Utrecht: Matrijs，2015.

Preface

Essence and Applications of Building Archaeology in China and Europe

Thomas COOMANS, XU Yitao, ZHANG Jianwei

In China, architectural history and archaeology currently share the field when it comes to the study of historic buildings. Both disciplines have different methods, research questions and aims. On the one hand, architectural history and theory depend on the schools of architecture and contribute to supporting both the design of new buildings and the renovation of existing buildings. On the other, teaching in the schools of archaeology is based on excavation techniques and methods, history and theory of excavations, architectural heritage investigations, architecture and art history, as well as the analysis and restoration of excavated relics. Despite a shared interest in the built environment from the past, archaeologists and architectural historians rarely work together.

There is a need for a specific discipline that would bridge architectural history and archaeology and be able to contribute, in an interdisciplinary sense, to the understanding of both excavated structures and those in elevation, instead of being limited to above or under 'level zero'. Building archaeology could be that discipline because it is more than an interface between architectural history and archaeology.

Aims and Methods of Building Archaeology

Building archaeology aims at reconstructing the history of buildings, defining chronologies, identifying transformations and interpreting evolving use. It contributes to an understanding of people and societies through material architectural evidence, even if there is no information from excavations or archives.

Building archaeology adapts methods of archaeology in order to observe and analyse structures in elevation and unravel the information hidden in the building itself, the 'material source' *par excellence*(Fig. 1).

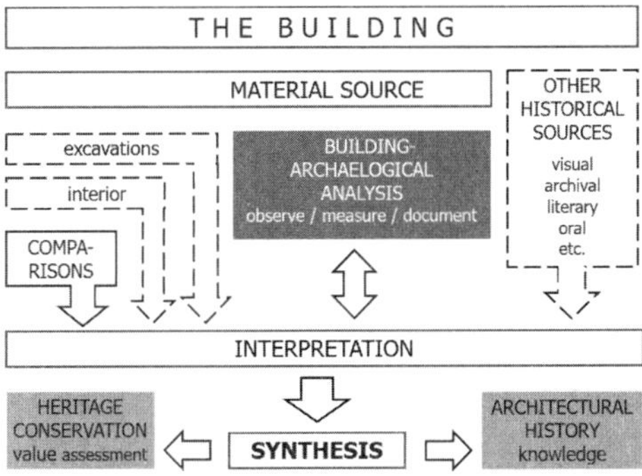

Fig. 1 Sources and steps of the building archaeological method (Thomas COOMANS)

Attention is paid to all components: from the building materials, structures, construction techniques and transformations to the decoration, equipment and use.

Building archaeology uses recording methods, archaeometry, material-technical analysis and other analysis from the field of natural sciences, including dating methods. It can benefit from the results of excavations as well as from historical research in archives.

Origins and Development of Building Archaeology in Europe and China

Building archaeology exists as a recognised discipline in most European countries: 'Building archaeology' (English), 'Bauforschung' (German), 'archeologia dell' architettura' (Italian), 'archéologie du bâti' (French), 'arqueologia de la architectura' (Spanish), 'bouwhistorie' (Dutch), etc. Building archaeologists have different backgrounds: archaeology, architecture, (art) history, engineering, geology, etc. Some are academics; most are not. This intrinsically gives building archaeology a multidisciplinary character. Building archaeologists, however, gain experience through fieldwork and practice, which is the best education. However, as a discipline, building archaeology has developed its own theory, debates, methodology and academic education.

Building archaeological approaches vary according to national traditions: Italian, French, British, German, Swiss, Dutch, etc. Some are more influenced by the archaeological stratigraphy of buildings transformed through the ages; others by preliminary studies of the restoration of medieval architecture. The origins of building archaeology date from the mid-19th century, with the antiquarians of the Archaeological Movement and the first generation of rationalist restoration architects of medieval buildings led by Eugène-Emmanuel Viollet-Le-Duc (1814-1879).

Massive damage to historical centres during World War II was at the origin of large-scale archaeological and building archaeological investigations, which contributed to reviving interest in historical architecture by generating new knowledge and new reflexions on conservation. More recently, building archaeological research has been influenced by new questions from historians on social and economic contexts, as well as from anthropologists on production cycles.

From the 1970s, universities started specific courses and founded research centres, heritage administrations promoted building archaeology in synergy with archaeology, and individual building archaeologists developed private practice. Today, building archaeology is an established discipline with its own research questions and methods applied to all material aspects of historical building. It benefits from the technological evolutions of archaeometry, CAD and recording methods, two fields that have evolved considerably during the last twenty years.

When it comes to China, building archaeological investigations have also been carried out for more than eighty years now - in the footsteps of LIANG Sicheng (1901-1972) and LIU Dunzhen (1897-1968) - by scholars who often consider themselves architectural historians but do not realise that what they are doing is in fact building archaeology. Building archaeology has, indeed, never been clearly defined as a specific discipline in China.

The First International Forum on Sino-European Building Archaeology

In 2015, we had the idea of organising an international conference on building archaeology in Beijing. This idea resulted from two observations. Firstly, building archaeology has a long tradition of excellence in China, going back to LIANG Sicheng and LIU Dunzhen, but with a primary focus on Middle Ancient Chinese architecture rather than earlier (e.g. Neolithic) or more recent architecture (e.g. early modern). Secondly, the results of building archaeological research are often not fully understood or used by those carrying out the restorations. These two observations deal with the material knowledge of ancient buildings, as well as aiming for the better conservation of ancient and early modern architecture.

How could building archaeological knowledge improve conservation in China? Since 2014, this reflexion has formed part of the research collaboration on building archaeology between Peking University, School of Archaeology and Museology, and KU Leuven, Department of Architecture and Raymond Lemaire International Centre for Conservation. This includes the organisation of international forums on building archaeology, with the aim of better understanding the different experiences and methods in the field of building archaeology; promoting building archaeology as a transdisciplinary method; building a bridge between the disciplines of the archaeologists, architects, engineers, construction historians, historians and architectural historians; and seeing how better material knowledge based on building archaeology could improve conservation and restoration in the future.

The International Forum on Sino-European Building Archaeology, held in Beijing on 13-15 May 2016, had three main aims. Firstly, to show the diversity of present issues, methods and challenges - at the cross-roads between different disciplines of archaeology, architectural history, art history, construction history, engineering, etc. - by bringing together outstanding scholars in all these fields from China and Europe. Secondly, to define building archaeology as a discipline in its own right, or at least as an interface between disciplines that could better collaborate. And thirdly, to set up future developments.

This forum was thus not about measurement techniques, architectural history, construction history, heritage conservation, excavations, laboratory analysis, stability and structural analysis of historic buildings, modelling and 3D reconstructions, etc. All these fields are well established and have outstanding networks and conferences. Building archaeology, however, includes a little from all these specialised fields, which were present, to a lesser or greater extent, in the forum's lectures.

The forum was structured as eleven plenary sessions with a total of thirty-seven papers of twenty minutes each (see Annex 2). The papers were in English and Chinese, with simultaneous translation. Because young scholars are the future of all our sciences and disciplines, we believed it to be of prime importance to involve them in the forum and to share our common enthusiasm for architectural heritage. Evening sessions were organised for young scholars, with a total of thirty-three papers of twelve minutes each, presented in eight parallel sessions of ten papers (see Annex 3). The evening sessions were in Chinese and reported to the conference assembly.

After the last evening session, two new books were presented. They are the tangible results of our recent building archaeological research in China:

- Thomas COOMANS, XU Yitao. *Building Churches in Northern China*[M]//*A 1926 Handbook in Context*. Beijing: Intellectual Property Rights Publishing House, 2016: 449 .
- XU Yitao et al. Building Archaeological Study of Wanrong Jiwang Temple in Shanxi Province[M]. Nanjing: Southeast University Press, 2016: 208.

The Book

This publication is a selection of fourteen Chinese and European papers, which have been improved in order to become full book chapters. The editors based their selection on a diversity of research questions and objects, combined with a broad time-space scope that spans eras from the Song Dynasty to the 20th century in China, England, Italy, Germany, Holland and Belgium.

The book is structured in three parts and the chapters are in Chinese and English, with abstracts in both languages:

- Part one: 'Theory and culture' contains three chapters on cultural changes in China that resulted in material shifts in funerary architecture (by CHEN Tongbin, LI Min and LIU Xiangyu), urban form (by WEI Zheng) and early Buddhist architecture (by Tracy MILLER), as well as two chapters on building archaeological theory in England (by Adam MENUGE) and Germany (by Elke NAGEL and Manfred SCHULLER).
- Part two: 'Archaeological sites and buildings' presents eight representative applications of research methodologies adapted to specific cases, such as foundations (by WANG Ying), roof structures and the use of dendrochronology (by Vincent DEBONNE), wood-imitating funerary architecture (by YU Lina and XU Yitao), wooden bracket sets (by XU Xinyun), urban houses (by Gabri VAN TUSSENBROEK) and Gothic vaults in China (by Thomas COOMANS).
- Part three: 'Conservation studies' reflects on how building archaeology can play an im-

portant role in conservation practices, as in the enhancement of the 'palimpsest' layering approach in Italy (by Carolina DI BIASE), the investigation and study during conservation projects (by ZHAO Yuanxiang, LI Lindong and CAI Yukun) and the historic use of lime mortar in brickwork (by Koenraad VAN BALEN).

Three appendixes complete the book with information on:

- The architectural heritage major at Peking University and building archaeology in China.
- The thirty-seven papers delivered at the main forum, May 2016.
- The eighty papers delivered at the youth forum, May 2016.

Acknowledgements

The International Forum on Sino-European Building Archaeology was held at Peking University on 13-15 May 2015. It was opened with a welcome from Prof. LI Yansong, Vice-President of Peking University; His Excellency Michel MALHERBE, Ambassador of Belgium; Prof. HANG Kan, Dean of the School of Archaeology and Museology, Peking University; and Prof. Krista DE JONGE, President of the Department of Architecture, KU Leuven. We are very grateful to them.

We would like to warmly thank all the speakers and those who made this forum possible, especially Prof. XU Tianjin, Director of the Centre for the Study of Chinese Archaeology at Peking University, Prof. Giuseppe VIGNATO, who supported our project and gave a paper, WANG Shulin, who was involved in the practical organisation from the outset. The forum was sponsored by the China Architecture Design Academy: Institute of Architectural History, Chengdu Museum, the Institute of Archaeology of the Chinese Academy of Social Sciences, and the Institute of Heritage Architecture of the Palace Museum, who welcomed the foreign guests at the Forbidden City.

Last but not least, we would like to express our sincere thanks to all the students who helped us with translations and numerous other tasks - often decided at the last minute - as required by such an international conference.

Further Reading

Bauforschung und ihr Beitrag zum Entwurf[M]// Building archaeology and its contribution to Design. Zurich: Instituts für Denkmalpflege, ETH Zürich, 1993.

Boato Anna. L' archeologia in architettura. Misurazioni, stratigrafie, datazioni, restauro [M]//Archaeology in architecture. Measurements, stratigraphy, dating, restoration. Venice: Marsilio, 2008.

Brogiolo Gian Pietro (ed.). Archeologia dell' Architettura. Archaeology of architecture[J]. supplement to Archeologia medievale 22, Florence, 1996.

De Jonge Krista and Van Balen Koen (eds). The Role of Preparatory Architectural Investigation in the Restauration of Historical Buildings[M]. Leuven: Leuven University Press, 2002.

Hassler Uta (ed.). Bauforschung: Zur Rekonstruktion des Wissens[M]//Building archaeology: towards reconstructing knowledge. Zurich: ETH Zurich, 2010.

Menuge Adam. Understanding Historic Buildings: A Guide to Good Recording Practice[M]. London: Historic England, 2016.

Parron-Kontis Isabelle and Reveyron Nicolas (eds). Archéologie du bâti. Pour une harmonisation des methods[M]//Building archaeology: towards a methodological harmonisation. Paris: Errances, 2005.

Schuller Manfred. Building Archaeology (Series Monuments and Sites, 7)[M]. Paris-Munich: ICOMOS, 2002.

Stenvert Ronald and van Tussenbroek Gabri (eds). Inleiding in de bouwhistorie. Opmeten en onderzoeken van oude gebouwen[M]// Introduction to building archaeology. Measuring and investigating ancient buildings, 2nd ed.. Utrecht: Matrijs, 2015.

目 录

CONTENTS

导言　为什么研究建筑考古学

徐怡涛

建筑是人类从蒙昧进入文明的标志，她承载着人类在科学、技术、艺术、文化、宗教、经济、习俗等方面所取得的成就，始终随人类文明的发展而演变，随人类的足迹而散播。透过建筑，我们可以认识文明；透过文明，我们又可以理解建筑。正所谓，有什么样的文明，就有什么样的建筑，让我看你的建筑，我就能了解你的文明。所以，古罗马的政体与古罗马的广场相互呼应，择中而居的宫殿与华夏王朝互为表里。既然建筑是认识文明的线索，文明是建筑产生的依据，那么，当我们将这一规律运用于历史研究时，建筑就成为承载历史的“史料”，而不再仅仅是建造的材料与方法。

建筑考古学，就是一门以建筑史料为研究对象，以还原建筑史料所承载的历史为目标的学科，其核心价值是历史真实性，其研究范畴包括，任何与建筑史料有关的物质或非物质遗存，如现存建筑、考古遗址、绘画、雕刻、器物、文献、工具、匠系，等等。

在中国，建筑考古学发端于营造学社对古代建筑的调查、测绘和断代，但由于梁思成等早期研究者多以服务建筑创作为建筑历史研究的最大目的，所以，还原历史之旅，在建筑史学的语境下，止于半途。其后，虽有如杨鸿勋提出“建筑考古的核心是建筑遗址复原”等多种关于建筑考古学的阐释，但均有失于建筑与文明的整体互证，不能进行全面的历史还原研究。

1998 年，北京大学与国家文物局联合办学，时任北京大学考古系主任的李伯谦先生，于考古学内增设了文物建筑专业方向，专业设立以来，我们在宿白先生所开创的运用历史时期考古学理念和方法研究古代建筑的基础上，创新了建筑考古学的内涵、理论与方法，通过多年实践探索，掌握了提升建筑史料时间精度的方法，从而可以从建筑史料上揭示出更多、更准确的历史信息。同时，我们建立了“中国建筑的科学认知”本科课程体系、“建筑考古学理论与实践”研究生课程体系，初步建立了建筑考古学的学科体系和培养机制，推动了中国建筑考古学的发展。

在推进中国建筑考古学发展的进程中，我有幸结识了比利时鲁汶大学高曼士教授，基于对建筑考古学的共同认识，我们很快克服了文化和语言上的障碍，彼此认同。2014 年，北京大学考古文博学院和鲁汶大学工学院、雷蒙德勒麦尔国际保护中心（RLICC），签署了共同推进建筑考古学发展的合作协议。协议内容主要包括：共同发展建筑考古学的学术理念、

作者简介：
徐怡涛，北京大学考古文博学院，教授。

开展联合教学、开展中国共享建筑遗产的案例研究、建立广泛的建筑考古学合作沟通平台等。2016 年 5 月在北京大学举办的中欧建筑考古国际研讨会，即是这一合作协议的产物。

中欧有各自引以为傲的历史与建筑，虽有明显的差异，但其建筑都是自身文明的产物和见证，正是基于这一共同点，我们达成了对建筑考古学的共识，即运用考古学、建筑学等多学科的研究手段，揭示建筑的历史信息，还原建筑的历史过程及历史背景，让建筑成为历史的时空隧道，使建筑成为沟通过去、现在与未来的纽带。

建筑考古学的基础是建立建筑形制演变的精细时空框架，在具体建筑上解析出历史层叠，求解出历史刻印在建筑上的时间线索，从而科学地还原建筑与历史的共存关系，发现建筑的历史价值。在这一过程中，多学科的研究方法必不可少，只有多学科、多维度的研究，才能准确、全面、立体地还原建筑的历史，同时，由于建筑史料价值的提升，与建筑考古研究相关的学科也将从中受益。例如，随着建筑考古的发展，未来当建筑的整体性知识被运用于田野发掘时，田野考古剖析建筑遗址、发现建筑史料的能力将得以全面提升，田野考古的操作规程，也将因之而完善。

总之，建筑考古学的价值，就是释放建筑中所蕴含的真实历史信息。历史的价值基于真实性，发现越多的真实信息，历史的价值也就越高。所以，研究建筑考古学的根本意义在于，提升历史的整体价值，提升一切和建筑史料相关的学科的研究价值，最终提升文明的价值。

基于以上意义的中国建筑考古学，尚在发展初期，需要多学科、跨国界的共同努力推动，2016 中欧建筑考古国际研讨会，即是这样一次尝试。或许，本论文集的论文研究目标和方法并不一致，但是，作为建筑考古学理念的推动者和本次会议的组织方，我们认为，有必要在与会学者自愿的前提下，尽量收录论文，保持会议多元探索的原貌。因为，只有开放多元的态度，探索自由的精神，才是孕育学术森林的土壤，或许，若干年后，当建筑考古学在中国日趋成熟时，再回头看这本论文集时会发现，某篇论文富于远见，抑或某篇论文不是将来的热点。但，正如建筑的多样性所反映的文明的多样性，建筑考古学未必是单一或一成不变的，今天的多元和开放，正是为后世留下发展的契机。

谁能读懂砖石土木书写的历史？谁能揭示建筑历史中蕴含的价值？谁能提取历史建筑中的文明基因？不是建造者，而是研究者，这是建筑考古学家的学术使命和社会责任。

Introduction Why Study Building Archaeology?

XU Yitao

Architecture is a symbol of human beings entering civilisation from obscurity. It carries with it the achievements of mankind in science, technology, art, culture, religion, economics, customs, etc. It never ceases to evolve with the development of human civilisation and spreads with the footprints of mankind. Through architecture, we can learn about civilisation. Through civilisation, we can understand architecture. As the saying goes: 'Like civilisation, like architecture. Show me your architecture so I can understand your civilisation'. In this sense, the ancient Roman forum echoes the ancient Roman political system, as the centrally-seated palaces convey the Chinese dynasties. Because architecture is a clue to understanding civilisation and civilisation is the basis of the creation of architecture. It is for this reason that architecture becomes the 'historical sources' that witnessed history when we carry out research, no longer just the materials and methods of construction. It tells us about much more than just building materials and methods of construction; it tells us about history and people.

Building archaeology is a discipline that takes historical sources as the object of its research and aims to restore the history carried by them. Its core value is historical authenticity. Its research scope includes any material and non-material remains, such as existing buildings, archaeological sites, paintings, sculptures, artefacts, literature, tools and craftsmanship systems, etc.

Building archaeology in China originated from the investigation, mapping and dating of ancient architecture by the Society for the Study of Chinese Architecture. However, since early researchers such as LIANG Sicheng carried out architectural history research primarily with the purpose of assisting architectural design, the 'journey' of historical restoration, in the context of architectural historiography, ends half way. Later, although researchers like YANG Hongxun proposed that 'the essence of architectural archaeology is the conceptual reconstruction of archaeological sites' - in addition to many other interpretations of building archaeology - due to their lack of awareness of the mutual-evidence relationship between

Author:
XU Yitao, Professor, School of Archaeology and Museology, Peking University

architecture and civilisation, they could not conduct comprehensive historical restoration studies.

In 1998, Peking University and the State Administration of Cultural Heritage jointly organised the School of Archaeology. At that time, LI Boqian, Dean of the school, added the specialised profession of heritage architecture. Since then, based on SU Bai's initiative of using the theory and method of historical archaeology for ancient architecture research, we have set out the aim, theory and method of building archaeology. Through years of explorative practice, we have shaped the method for improving the precision of the dating of historical sources so that more and accurate historical information can be revealed. At the same time, we have established the undergraduate programme of 'Scientific Cognition of Chinese Architecture' and the postgraduate course programme of 'Theory and Practice of Building Archaeology'. We have also promoted the development of Chinese building archaeology by preliminarily founding its discipline system and training mechanism.

In the process of advancing the development of Chinese building archaeology, I had the privilege of meeting Thomas COOMANS, professor at KU Leuven, Belgium. Based on a shared understanding of this field, we quickly overcame cultural and linguistic obstacles and endorsed each other. In 2014, the School of Archaeology and Museology of Peking University and the Department of Architecture of the Faculty of Engineering Science, KU Leuven / Raymond Lemaire International Centre for Conservation (RLICC) signed a cooperation agreement to jointly promote the development of building archaeology. The contents of this agreement primarily included: jointly developing the academic concepts of building archaeology, carrying out joint education, initiating case studies of China's shared built heritage and establishing a wide-ranging platform for building archaeology cooperation and communication, etc. The Sino-European International Symposium on Building Archaeology, held at Peking University in May 2016, is one of the results of this cooperation agreement.

Europe and China both proudly have their own history and architecture. Though with obvious differences, architecture is the product and witness of both civilisations. It is on the basis of this point that we have reached a consensus on building archaeology, namely, using multidisciplinary methods such as archaeological and architectural research to reveal the historical information of architecture, restore the historical process and background of the building, and make the building a historical 'space-time tunnel', a link between the past, present and future.

The foundation of building archaeology is to establish a detailed space-time framework of the evolution of architectural forms before analysing the historical layers of a particular building and discovering the time clues imprinted on it by history. This aims to scientifically restore the coexistence between the building and its history in order to discover its historical values. A multidisciplinary and multi-angled research approach is indispensable to this process because it is the only way to restore the history of architecture accurately and comprehensively. At the same time, because of the improvement of the value of architecture as a historical source, disciplines related to architectural archaeology will also benefit from it. For example, with the development of building archaeology - when a holistic knowledge of architecture is applied to field excavation in the future - the ability to analyse architectural sites and discover historical sources in field archaeology will be comprehensively improved and its operational rules perfected.

In short, the value of building archaeology is the releasing of the real historical information contained in buildings. The value of history is based on authenticity. The more authentic information discovered, the higher the value of history. Therefore, the fundamental significance of building archaeology is to enhance the overall value of history, the research value of all disciplines related to architectural historical sources, and ultimately, the value of civilisation.

Based on the above significance, Chinese building archaeology is still in its infancy and requires the joint efforts of multidisciplinary and multi-international circles. The 2016 Sino-European International Symposium on Building Archaeology is such an attempt. The research purposes and methods of the papers may be inconsistent, but, as the promoter of the building archaeology concept and organiser of this conference, we believe that it is necessary to include as many papers as possible - with the participating scholars' consent as a precondition - so that the conference's appearance of original pluralistic exploration can be kept. Because only an open and pluralistic attitude and a spirit of free exploration can be the 'soil' for cultivating an 'academic forests'. Perhaps, in a few years' time, when building archaeology has gained maturity in China, people will look back at this collection of papers and see one as visionary, while another as irrelevant. However, just as the diversity of civilisations is reflected by the diversity of architecture, building archaeology may not be monistic or static. Today's pluralism and openness offer development opportunities for future generations.

Who can read and understand the history written in masonry, stone, earth and wood? Who can reveal the values of architectural history? Who can extract the genes of civilisation from historical buildings? Not builders, but researchers. This is the academic mission and social responsibility of building archaeologists.

(Translated by CUI Jinze
and Laura BENNETT)

理论与文化

Theory and Culture

西夏陵所体现的亚欧大陆文化交流与融合

Cultural Changes in Western Xia Mausoleums

陈同滨 李敏 刘翔宇 | CHEN Tongbin，LI Min，LIU Xiangyu

摘要：西夏陵是以西夏王朝（1038—1227 年）建立前后的历代统治者陵墓为主体的大型墓葬群，以其在选址、格局、形制、建造技术等方面，展现出 11~13 世纪在这一地区所产生的跨区域的多种文明与文化的融会与影响，不仅受到中原农业文明中心唐宋王朝的突出影响，也反映出受到周边诸多民族不同程度的文化影响，在亚洲文明史上具有不可替代的地位。本文受世界文化遗产研究理论的启发，从广泛的欧亚大陆文化交流的角度出发，分析其民族迁徙和地理文化特征，从选址、格局、建筑特征等方面，对这个独特的建筑遗产进行条分缕析、探本溯源式的重新解读。

关键词：西夏陵；文化交流

Abstract：Western Xia mausoleums are the tombs of the rulers of Western Xia Dynasty（1038—1227 years）. The location，plan，pattern，construction technology and other aspects，show the integration and influence of various civilizations and cultures of the 11~13 century in this area，not only by the prominent influence of the Central China Agricultural Civilization Center in Tang Dynasty and Song Dynasty，but also the cultural influence by other nationalities in different degree，playing an irreplaceable role in the history of civilization in Asia. Inspired by the theory of world cultural heritage studies，the writers start from a wide range of Eurasian cultural exchange perspective，analyze the cultural characteristics of people migration and geography to study the Western Xia mausoleums from the aspects of location，pattern and architectural features，the unique architectural heritage.

Keywords：Western Xia Mausoleum；Cultural Changes

作者简介：
陈同滨，中国建筑设计院建筑历史研究所，研究员；李敏，中国建筑设计院建筑历史研究所，副研究员；刘翔宇，中国建筑设计院建筑历史研究所，建筑师。

西夏陵是以西夏王朝（1038—1227 年）建立前后的历代统治者陵墓为主体的大型墓葬群，位于宁夏回族自治区银川市西夏区和永宁县境内的贺兰山脚下，东北距银川市兴庆区（西夏都城兴庆府所在地）直线距离约 25 公里。陵区南起贺兰山榆树沟，北至泉齐沟，西至贺兰山脚，东至 110 国道，南北长 10 余公里，东西宽约 4 公里，分布范围 37.69 平方公里。遗产整体由分布在贺兰山中段南侧东麓洪积扇上的 9 座王陵及其附属设施、255 座陪葬墓、北端建筑遗址、防洪工程遗址以及陵区内各类出土遗物组成。①

西夏陵的建筑历来以其独特的形制成为中国建筑历史上的一个特例，其陵墓格局和建筑形制的来源也有各种各样的解读和探讨。尤其是对其中心建筑——陵塔的形制探讨，有学者认为其以夯土为台、外架木构的做法是学习中原土木建筑传统的结果，有认为是仿照佛塔的，种种不一而足。② 本文受世界文化遗产研究理论的启发，从广泛的欧亚大陆文化交流的角度出发，分析其民族迁徙和地理文化特征，从选址、格局、建筑特征等方面，对这个独特的建筑遗产进行条分缕析、探本溯源式的重新解读。③

一、陵区和陵墓选址

西夏陵区和陵墓选址所体现的山水格局蕴涵着中国传统汉文化中的风水观念。

西夏陵西枕贺兰山，东面黄河水，其选址总体体现了汉族“背山面水”的墓葬选址理念。王陵和陪葬墓的分布既不在山上，也远离河滩地，而是位于山前洪水冲积扇地带，正是汉族不近卑湿、不在高山的选址理念的应用。西夏陵区 9 座王陵，各自的主轴线都在视线或概念上对应贺兰山的一座山峰，其中尤以其最为宏大的 3 号陵所对的山峰最为雄伟。这种与山水环境的密切关系都符合汉族城市与墓葬选址的理念，甚至可以在古老的“风水”理论中找到依据。④

二、陵寝制度

西夏陵展现了西夏对唐宋以来中原陵寝制度的继承、吸收与改造的过程；在陵园格局上更是受到了北宋帝陵深厚的影响，并且融合了唐、辽帝陵中的某些布局要素。

依山为陵的西夏陵采用了陵塔的形式，融合了中原传统帝陵中的两大主要形式：以汉陵、宋陵为代表的“积土为陵”和以唐陵、辽陵为代表的“因山为陵”。整个陵区一直延伸至贺兰山脚，有“因山为陵”之意；而每个王陵陵园的主体建筑——陵塔系夯土而成，与“积土为陵”的汉陵、宋陵之覆斗形封土有类似之处。但西夏陵并非完全沿袭，而是介乎两者之间，有所创新。西夏陵是整体如宋陵式的集中布局、整体依山而建，不同于唐陵的分散、每座陵单独有其山；西夏陵的陵塔虽然也是陵园主体并大致在玄宫上方，但变陵台为陵塔，并且位于玄宫上方偏后。这些方面都体现了西夏对唐宋以来中原陵寝制度的继承、吸收与改造。

西夏陵采用每个王陵单独有陵园的形式，单独陵园的平面布局虽不尽相同，但都包含了类似于唐宋以来帝陵中的陵城、阙台、月城、神道、碑亭、献殿、陵台（塔）等布局要素，以及轴线式的大致对称的布局特征。同时，西夏陵的陵园布局也明显体现出党项族本民族的特征，有浓郁的游牧民族色彩。首先，每座帝陵并非方向完全一致，而是略有偏差，打破以往宋陵严格划一的规制，表现出游牧民族不拘一格的民族特点和追求；其次，陵园主要建筑陵塔、献殿等并非沿革居中设置而是在中轴线偏西侧，且与中轴线成一定夹角，表现出党项族的原始崇拜中“鬼神居中”，人应予以避让的思想[⑤]。其神道缩短并置于月城，两重陵墙，以及对唐宋辽陵要素综合吸收等特征，都是不同于任何一个模仿原型的本地创新。

三、陵塔建筑形式

西夏陵以其独特的陵塔建筑形式展现了西藏地区塔葬传统及其塔形墓冢、辽代密檐佛塔以及西北地区生土建筑传统的交互影响与融合再创新。

党项民族起源于青藏高原东北缘，在民族上属于羌族，在语言上属于藏缅语族的羌语支。在起源和文化上深受西藏文化的影响。西夏陵陵塔的建筑形式，是在西藏地区塔葬的基础上再创造和发挥而来的。塔葬是兴起于吐蕃时期（7~9 世纪）、流行于青藏高原的墓葬形式，来源于苯教，后期受佛教影响得以强化。[⑥]在吐蕃王朝时结合佛教影响，形成了用于佛教高僧和笃信佛教的贵族的一种墓葬形式。此后，塔葬作为一种高等级的墓葬形式，一直在西藏地区流传至今。墓塔的建筑外观，也逐渐演变成藏式喇嘛塔的样子。在西夏陵开始建造的 11 世纪初，藏传佛教已经成熟，并且为西夏贵族所接受。因此，这种地域性和宗教性合为一体的墓葬建筑形式为西夏贵族继承。

在物质层面，则借鉴了当时更为发达的宋辽佛塔的外观，并结合西北地区土建筑地域性，遂形成了这种土台、木构外檐的陵塔建筑。宋辽时期在北方发达的六角、八角楼阁式木结构塔，以及砖仿木的密檐塔为西夏陵的建筑外观提供了直接的借鉴素材。西夏陵 1 号陵塔的底边直径和山西辽代应县木塔、辽上京皇家寺院 1 号佛塔的基础直径均为 40 米左右，在尺度上也是相当的。[⑦]不同于宋辽佛塔的砖、木材料为主，西夏陵陵塔采取了西北地区（亚洲内陆地区）特有的生土建筑材料，以夯土形成塔身主体，仅以木、瓦构成外观。因此西夏陵陵塔在建成之初，与宋辽地区的木构楼阁式佛塔外形接近；而在变为遗址的今天，则与河西走廊及以西地区的土筑佛塔相似，显示出其材料和建筑技术的内在一致性。

四、木构建筑遗迹

西夏陵土木结合的建筑形式和木构建筑，以及大量砖、瓦、脊饰等建筑构件等，反映了中原同期建筑样式对西夏的影响。

从西夏陵陵塔表面的木构件留下的孔洞，塔身上仍旧保存的层层垮塌的瓦屋檐遗存，可以推断出陵塔曾经仿照中原地区木构建筑的外观。其献殿、碑亭、陵城大门、三出阙等建筑台基和遗存，其平面和柱洞，经推断为中原木构殿堂建筑的模仿，并有对移柱、减柱等同期建筑构造的吸收。陵塔及陵区其他建筑周围出土的与同期中原地区高度类似的陶、瓷、琉璃建筑构件，包括板瓦、筒瓦、滴水、鸱尾、脊饰等，在工艺和造型上，与中原同期木构建筑的砖瓦构件高度相似。这些特征都见证了中原传统建筑样式及相关的构造技术和装饰艺术在中原北方和西夏等地的传播与影响。

五、陵园阙体造型

西夏三号陵园阙体造型独特的圆弧形，揭示了西亚建筑元素的影响。

西夏陵现存最完好、规模最大的 3 号陵，其陵园内围墙多采用三出阙的造型，这符合中原文化传统中关于帝王的宫殿、都城、陵寝使用最高等级三出阙的传统。以此作为帝王权威的象征和天宫的模拟。在阙台的造型上，却采用了中原地区不多见的圆弧造型，具有明显的外来影响，与源于西亚地区的圆弧形城垛十分类似。

六、佛教因素

西夏陵所体现的佛教丧葬理念，以及建筑、构件和出土物所具有的佛教因素，展现了明显的佛教影响。

佛教在西夏社会拥有崇高的地位，尤其获得统治阶层的信奉。现存西夏艺术中，有大量的佛教石窟寺、佛塔、佛像、经卷、佛教绘画、雕塑等。这些佛教因素在西夏陵中有非常多的体现。如前所述，首先，每座王陵在理念上吸收藏区受佛教影响至深的塔葬理念，创造性地使用陵塔作为主体建筑替代宋陵中的陵塔封土；其次，在建筑外观上直接模仿宋辽木构佛塔，在建筑装饰上使用了迦陵嫔伽、莲花等佛教意味浓郁的因素；最后，北区建筑基址出土的僧人及佛像残块等，都是佛教对西夏社会深刻影响的体现。

西夏陵在选址、格局、形制、建造技术等方面，展现出 11~13 世纪在这一地区所产生的跨区域的多种文明与文化的融汇与影响，不仅受到中原农业文明中心唐宋王朝的突出影响，也反映出受到周边诸多民族不同程度的文化影响，在亚洲文明史上具有不可替代的地位。

注释：

① 宁夏文物考古研究所，许成，杜玉冰．西夏陵 [M]．北京：东方出版社，1995．宁夏文物考古研究所，银川西夏陵区管理处．西夏三号陵：地面遗迹发掘报告 [M]．北京：科学出版社，2007．宁夏文物考古研究所，银川西夏陵区管理处．西夏陵六号陵 [M]．北京：科学出版社，2013．

② 前者为北京大学考古文博学院方拥教授于 2012 年口述，后者见：韩小忙．西夏陵塔建筑形制探讨 [J]．宁夏学刊，1991（1）．后在各种讨论会中，也有多位学者持上述观点。

③ 世界文化遗产突出普遍价值的评价标准（ii）：展现了在一段时期内或世界某一文化区域中人类价值观念的相互交流，体现于建筑、技术、纪念性艺术、城市规划或景观设计之发展。见：联合国教科文组织世界遗产中心．世界遗产公约操作指南 [M]．2015．

④ 北宋《地理新书》，“西北高，东南下，水流出巽，如天地之势也。故宜西山之东，西来之地，南北相望而远东有流水，吉。”

⑤《西夏陵》引述沈括《梦溪笔谈》，“盖西戎之俗，所居正寝，常留中间以奉鬼神，不敢居之……”。许成，杜玉冰 . 西夏陵 [M]. 北京：东方出版社，1995.

⑥ 霍巍．西藏古代墓葬制度史 [M]．成都：四川人民出版社，1995. 第五章第一节“特殊的封土形制——塔形墓丘”，第十章“西藏的塔葬与灵塔——肉身制度”；夏吾卡先．吐蕃塔形墓的起源与原始塔葬 [J]．西藏大学学报（社会科学版），2011（4）．根据该文研究中得知，现存塔形墓葬 50 余座，分属七处吐蕃时代的墓葬遗址，在拉萨、日喀则、林芝地区都有分布。吐蕃时期的塔形墓葬底边长 10~30 米，残高 1~5 米，3~5 级不等，平面有梯形、长方形、方形、曼荼罗形四类，其中最具藏传佛教特征的曼荼罗形不足 5%。研究者认为，吐蕃墓葬中塔形墓的总体佛塔特征并不

明显。研究者进一步在西藏的史前岩画和苯教垛（to）文化中发现了这种层层升起的、阶梯金字塔状的墓塔原型，认为是从苯教祭坛发展而来。

⑦ 董新林，陈永志，汪盈．内蒙古辽上京遗址探微 [J]. 中国文化报，2013-06-07；内蒙古文物考古研究所. 辽上京城址勘察报告 [A]．见：李逸友，魏坚主编；内蒙古文物考古研究所编．内蒙古文物考古文集 第一辑 [M]．北京：中国大百科全书出版社，1994.

参考文献：

[1] 宁夏文物考古研究所，许成，杜玉冰．西夏陵 [M]. 北京：东方出版社，1995.

[2] 宁夏文物考古研究所，银川西夏陵区管理处．西夏三号陵：地面遗迹发掘报告 [M]．北京：科学出版社，2007.

[3] 宁夏文物考古研究所，银川西夏陵区管理处．西夏陵六号陵 [M]．北京：科学出版社，2013.

[4] 韩小忙．西夏陵塔建筑形制探讨 [J]．宁夏学刊，1991（1）.

[5] 联合国教科文组织世界遗产中心．世界遗产公约操作指南 [M]．2015.

[6] 霍巍．西藏古代墓葬制度史 [M]．成都：四川人民出版社，1995.

[7] 夏吾卡先．吐蕃塔形墓的起源与原始塔葬 [J]．西藏大学学报（社会科学版），2011（4）.

[8] 董新林，陈永志，汪盈．内蒙古辽上京遗址探微 [J]. 中国文化报，2013-06-07.

[9] 内蒙古文物考古研究所. 辽上京城址勘察报告 [A]. 见：李逸友，魏坚主编；内蒙古文物考古研究所编．内蒙古文物考古文集 第一辑 [M]．北京：中国大百科全书出版社，1994.

追随福尔摩斯的脚步？
英国遗产实践的调查传统

In the Footsteps of Sherlock Holmes?
The Investigative Tradition in UK Heritage Practice

Adam MENUGE

摘要：在英国，遗产的记录手段有着悠久的历史，并且与国家机构、专业机构和学会以及后来的商业组织的实践密切相关。最近的技术进步带来了日益复杂且引人注目的数据采集方法，这在遗产领域内外都备受关注，但是在对数据进行有效分析和理解中缺乏对于相关专业知识和调查实践作用的讨论。结果，这些不太容易可视化、往往是低技术、意会式的方法难以被少数从业人员之外的人群理解。甚至在业界和学术界，对其认识论的推敲也很少开展。

为了产出深入细致又兼具叙事性和分析性的阐释，如何采纳编排个体的观察资料，如何评估研究素材的不同属性特征？在学术视野不断扩大的时代，这种阐释性的研究方式本身的局限到底又是什么？现代数字记录方法捕捉的数据达到了无法想象的范围、数量和精度，这是否预示了传统调查方法将变得多余？本文将基于最近的一个备受瞩目的保护项目，简要地分析笔者眼中的调查传统的起源及其在英国的开展，从而进一步探讨其在解释零碎的或者难解的数据方面的作用。

关键词：建筑考古；专业实践；英格兰

Abstract：Approaches to the documentation of heritage have a long history in the United Kingdom and are prominently associated with the activities of state agencies，professional bodies and learned societies as well as，latterly，the commercial sector. Recent technical advances have made available increasingly sophisticated and eye-catching methods of data-capture，giving rise to justifiable excitement in the heritage community and beyond，but there is a surprising lack of discussion of the role of expert knowledge and investigative practice in underpinning effective analysis and understanding. As a result，these less easily visualised，often low-tech，cerebral methods are poorly understood beyond a small circle of practitioners；even in professional and academic circles they are rarely subjected to epistemological scrutiny.

How are individual observations assembled and sequenced in order to produce robust and

作者简介：
Dr. Adam MENUGE，University of Cambridge，UK，Department of Architecture，Course Director for MSt Building History.

nuanced interpretations, both narrative and analytic? How should differing qualities of evidence be evaluated? What, indeed, are the limits of interpretation itself in an era of ever-expanding scholarly horizons? Do modern digital recording methods, which capture a hitherto undreamt-of range, quantity and precision of data, foreshadow a time when traditional investigative methods will become redundant? This paper will briefly consider the origins of what I have termed the investigative tradition and its operation in the UK, and will then explore its role in elucidating often fragmentary or recalcitrant data, with a particular focus on a recent high-profile conservation project.

Keywords: Building archaeology; Expert practice; England

This title refers to heritage practice in the United Kingdom and I should begin by qualifying my terms of reference for a Chinese readership. British identities, like Russian dolls, are sometimes nested one within another, sometimes more sharply and antagonistically defined. Geographers talk of the British Isles — a physical entity or archipelago off the north-western coast of continental Europe, inhabited by several different peoples. The English, Welsh, Scots and Irish generally see themselves as distinct nations regardless of the political arrangements under which they have at different times been governed. Their heritage is distinctive in all sorts of ways, and because heritage is inseparable from national (as well as regional and local) identity, it has long been a devolved matter in domestic affairs. There are separate heritage administrations in England, Scotland, Wales and Northern Ireland, another for the Isle of Man, and no less than two for the Channel Islands. Nevertheless, from a global perspective there is much commonality in the built heritage of the British Isles — in materials, styles, building types and (in very broad terms) underlying social structures. Our fluctuating internal borders have usually been permeable zones of transition rather than cultural cliff-edges. The vernacular buildings of Ireland bear comparison, in their various forms, with those of several parts of mainland Britain; the architectural expression of 18th-century Dublin echoed that of London and Liverpool; and the country house with its landscape garden, one of the defining elements of the English landscape, is dispersed across a larger area of the British Isles, even though the feelings it evokes vary considerably from one part to another. So I hope I may be excused when I refer primarily in what follows to English buildings and English heritage practice.

The Investigative Tradition

I can offer only the most summary account of the emergence of the investigative tradition in Britain. English antiquarianism is generally traced back to John Leland (*c.* 1503-1552), whose long-unpublished *Itinerary*, undertaken at the end of the 1530s, focused especially on the passing of the monasteries in the wake of the English Reformation.[1] Leland feared the imminent losses of sublime medieval architecture — the 'bare ruined choirs, where late the sweet birds sang' of Shakespeare's sonnet, [2]— and richly endowed libraries of English monasticism, and imparted to the antiquarian tradition a mood of melancholy and regret that it has never wholly lost. *Britannia* by William Camden (1551-1623), first published in Latin in 1586, attempted the first systematic account of the nation's heritage. It aimed to 'restore Britain to its Antiquities and its Antiquities to Britain' and remained a standard text for two centuries.[3] Camden was succeeded by numerous county historians who transcribed monumental inscriptions and pedigrees, and charted the descent of property, and by more archaeologically inclined antiquaries such as William Stukeley (1687-1765), who recorded earthworks and other monuments through field observations, measured drawings and illustrations.[4]

With growing urbanisation and industrialisation from the late 18th century the pace of destruction of antiquities quickened, and during the 19th century figures such as the art critic John Ruskin (1818-1900) and the designer and socialist William Morris (1834-1896) called for a more sympathetic appreciation of the legacy of the past, and its value for generations to come. The Society for the Protection of Ancient Buildings (SPAB), nicknamed 'Anti-Scrape' because of its opposition to aggressive church restorations in which old plaster and often medieval wall-paintings were stripped to reveal bare masonry, was founded in 1877, four years after the Ancient Monuments Act extended legal protection to a small number of monuments for the first time. Bodies devoted to recording and protecting heritage proliferated from the 1890s with the founding of the Survey of London (1894) and the National Trust (1895), and in 1908 Royal Commissions were established in England, Scotland and Wales to compile inventories of historic buildings at public expense, employing teams of professional investigators.[5] Effective legal protection for large numbers of buildings — what we term 'listed buildings' — had to overcome considerable opposition from property owners. It developed progressively from 1932, first acquiring real teeth in 1968 as a wave of post-war reconstruction swept through Britain's towns and cities.

Following so soon after the damage inflicted by aerial bombing during the Second World War, widespread redevelopment triggered an increasingly deep and widespread feeling of loss. Protocols for the recording of heritage assets threatened with destruction were an important result. Publicly sanctioned rescue excavations became routine for buried remains, whilst the Royal Commissions undertook 'emergency recording' of buildings threatened with demolition or significant alteration.

More recently, governmental disinclination to fund research directly, coupled with a tendency to favour 'free market' solutions, has altered the heritage landscape considerably, and in ways that have prompted serious concern in some quarters. The protections, processes and accumulated documentation of the historic environment nevertheless represent a considerable (if not infallible) defence against irresponsible action. England has around 500,000 listed buildings, nearly 20,000 scheduled monuments and more than 8,000 conservation areas, as well as a planning system that acknowledges that the historic environment is seamless and not comprised merely of statutorily designated assets. The National Planning Policy Framework, introduced in 2011, defines the historic environment in commendably broad terms as comprising "All aspects of the environment resulting from the interaction between people and places through time, including all surviving physical remains of past human activity, whether visible, buried or submerged, and landscaped and planted or managed flora".[6]

I have stated that my theme is the investigative tradition, and this raises two immediate questions: what does the word 'investigative' imply and why do I draw attention to its traditional nature? I have also invoked the name of Sherlock Holmes, the fictional London detective who resided at the equally fictional 221B Baker Street, London. Holmes was introduced to the reading public by Arthur Conan Doyle (1859-1930) in his 1887 novel *A Study in Scarlet* and sustained through a series of novels and short stories until the 1920s. Holmes's deductive powers are legendary, but he also relied upon research data, and he describes himself as the author of a monograph, *Upon the Distinction Between the Ashes of the Various Tobaccos*, which proved useful in solving a number of cases.[7] In a memorable put-down to Watson, his practical but unperceptive assistant, he states, "You see, but you do not observe".[8] This seems to me to encapsulate the dilemma of field-based research in the era of digital manumission. Digital methods have enormously enhanced our ability to capture data. We talk now of 'mass data capture' rather than the human selection of points and their more laborious collection. We have been liberated from the stranglehold of conventional, orthogonal representations of structure and space. But while digital techniques have extended the visible (and non-visible) spectrum to a horizon that outstrips human capacity they remain stubbornly anchored, one way or another, to physical form and the incidental occlusions to which it gives rise: what you see is what you get. The English-language acronym 'WYSIWYG' (pronounced 'wiz-ee-wig'), used to describe the technical accomplishment of rendering digital outputs faithfully on the computer screen, can also be used to argue the emptiness of merely descriptive data-capture. I would assert, by way of corrective, that the way in which we investigate the material remains of the past — that movement, sometimes laborious and slow, sometimes instantaneous, from observation to understanding — is as much an art as a science, and relies on thought processes which resist digitisation.

By the 'investigative tradition', then, I mean an approach to the historic built environment that is rooted in the forensic examination of the skeleton, skin, interstitial fabric and spaces of buildings, as well as their physical (or landscape) setting. I have no wish to suggest, by such anatomical analogies, that the contingent and non-corporeal evidence of documentary and visual sources, or the ideal realm of conceptualisation, are not also valuable and often wonderfully fruitful. Here again, however, I would turn to Holmes for the trenchant observation that "It is a capital mistake to theorize before one has data. Insensibly one begins to twist facts to suit theories, instead of theories to suit facts".[9] And by 'tradition' I wish to imply a body of knowledge — what in the guilds or trade fraternities of medieval England would have been termed a 'mystery' — refined through long practice and passed down as it were from master to apprentice, often without much thought being given to documenting it. This is reflected in the general paucity of good pedagogical works instructing novices in their task. What we have in their place are recording standards, manuals and methodologies, and guides to dating and nomenclature, but these seldom do more than touch upon the processes through which data are interpreted.[10] Overwhelmingly ours is a time-served profession, in which apprentice-like attention to the accumulated wisdom of others, coupled with the careful amassing of a personal store of empirical data, are decisive in promoting the advance of collective as well as individual knowledge.

The operation of this master-and-apprentice relationship was not always straightforward, and not, indeed, always inspiring. Mortimer Wheeler (1890-1976), who became one of the foremost British archaeologists of the 20th century, began his career uncertainly as a junior investigator helping to compile the Essex inventory of the English Royal Commission (RCHME) . His account of his first experience of fieldwork cheerfully explodes the myth:

"On a frosty morning of late autumn in 1913, I cycled across London to Liverpool Street station for my first day's probationary fieldwork in Essex. There I was to meet the commission's senior investigator, Murray Kendall, under whom I was to begin my tutelage. Kendall was already pacing up and down the platform, blowing upon his fingers. He greeted me with 'Still a quarter of an hour to go, my boy. What a morning like this requires is a Little Reinforcement. Come along.' He strode away to the upstairs refreshment-room, and briskly ordered: 'Two double whiskies in new milk.' [...] My eyes stood out of my head. [...] An hour later Dunmow station received us with a cold, inhospitable look about it, and Kendall again sniffed the frosty air. 'My boy,' he said parentally, 'what we need before we set out down the road is a Little Reinforcement'; and he led the way to an adjacent inn where the startling ceremony was repeated." [...]

[After a cycle ride of three or four miles they reach Stebbing church, their destination.] "Let me here repeat that my education had been strangely neglectful of the niceties of English medieval architecture, and, in spite of reinforcement, my heart was by now slipping steadily in the direction of my boots. We looked inside the building, and to my unskilled eye there seemed to be a great deal of involved stonework and quite an array of decorative shields. [At length Wheeler painfully confesses his utter ignorance of church architecture and associated heraldry.] 'Hum,' said Kendall, and reflected. Then he looked up brightly. 'I know what we want,' he was saying. 'What we want is a ...' But I was already following him mechanically up the village street towards the Red Lion" [...].[11]

On this occasion the amount of knowledge and experience imparted by the senior partner in the relationship seems to have been inversely proportionate to the quantity of whisky consumed. But there is a deeper truth underlying Wheeler's affectionate anecdote, for it is on such shared endurance and experiences of adversity, later fashioned and refined into amusing recollections, that close working relationships and their lasting power are often built.

The Gothic Tower, Wimpole, Cambridgeshire

In order to explore the operation of the investigative process I will focus on a single case study: a building in the landscaped garden of Wimpole Hall, roughly 16 km west of Cambridge and about 80 km north

Fig.1 The Gothic Tower, forming part of the larger Gothic Folly, viewed from the south [© Adam Menuge].

of central London. The building is currently known as the Gothic Tower [Fig. 1], though it forms part of a larger ensemble, sometimes referred to as the Gothic Folly or, formerly, 'Wimpole Ruins' or 'Wimpole Castle', principally comprising three round towers and intervening lengths of curtain wall so as to give the impression of a defensive castle enclosure. This larger entity is a 'sham-castle', a building type popular with landscape designers during much of the 18th century as a way of punctuating sightlines within, and sometimes beyond, country house parks and evoking a consciousness of antiquity. The Gothic Tower is the dominant, roughly central element of the composition, ashlar-faced to the south, but less neatly finished in a mixture of brick and stone to the north, where an ungainly corbelled-out section spans between the two adjoining lengths of curtain wall. My discussion is based on detailed investigative and recording work undertaken there some years ago, and is prompted by a more recent opportunity to revisit that work in a more reflective mode.[12] It is very materially supported by documentary research published by David Adshead and by his *catalogue raisonné* of the visual sources for Wimpole.[13]

Wimpole Hall is a substantial country house, a product of the growing wealth of 17th, 18th and 19th-century England, but also of the disproportionate concentration of that wealth in a few hands. The house dates from the 17th century, but was substantially rebuilt in the mid-18th century to a neo-Palladian design by the architect Henry Flitcroft (1697-1769). It was the subject of important work by John Soane (1753-1837) in the 1790s and was considerably enlarged in the mid-19th century by Henry Edward Kendall (1776-1875).[14] Kendall's work fell out of favour during the 20th century, when the size of the household also contracted sharply, and much of it was demolished in the 1950s.[15] The Hall and the associated landscape park have belonged to the National Trust since 1976.[16] The Gothic Tower, abandoned and deteriorating for many years, was recently the subject of a conservation programme, culminating in the 2016 *Europa Nostra Grand Prix* award.[17] This programme entailed a series of additional research and recording, including further documentary research, the excavation of below-ground remains, and analyses of historic paint and wallpaper fragments, tending mainly to amplify knowledge of the later 19th-century and 20th-century occupation of the site.[18]

The Gothic Tower occupies a prominent position on a rise at the northern end of what originated as a late 17th-century avenue, depicted in a Kip and Knyff view of 1707.[19] It had a curiously protracted genesis. The scheme originated in 1749 in correspondence between the then owner of Wimpole, Philip Yorke (1690-1764), later 1st Earl of Hardwicke, and the gentleman-architect Sanderson Miller (1716-1780), who belonged to Yorke's circle of cultivated gentry landowners.[20] Miller had established a reputation for designing mock-ruins or 'sham castles' in the Gothick style pleasingly rugged, three-dimensional eye-catchers to adorn a landscaped park and hint at the lineage and venerable antiquity of the park's owner. Yorke wanted such a building to cement his hold on Wimpole, an old-established property which he had newly acquired in 1739. His initial request, relayed in a letter by his friend Lord Lyttleton, was simple: a building with "no House or even room in it, but merely the Walls and Semblance of an old castle to make an object from his House. At most [···] a staircase carried up one of the Towers, and a leaded gallery half round it to stand in, and view the Prospect".[21] As the discussion continued even the stair was dropped: "As my Lord designs it merely for an Object he would have no Staircase nor Leads in any of the Towers, but merely the Walls so built as to have the appearance of a Ruined Castle".[22] Miller prepared a series of sketch designs which are reproduced fully elsewhere.[23] They show his characteristically vigorous way with Gothic forms and the semblance of old decay. At the centre of his composition rises a bold, three-storey round tower [Fig. 2]. The scheme seems to have found approval; in 1750 Miller staked out the site and the following year he was considering stone sources for the project, but in the end Yorke did not proceed with it, and it lapsed.[24]

Fig.2 One of Sanderson Miller's perspective design sketches for the Gothic Folly [© National Trust, WIM/D/455].

The project was revived by Yorke's son (1720-1790), the 2nd Earl of Hardwicke, in the late 1760s during landscaping works to the park by Lancelot 'Capability' Brown (1716-1783). The Cambridge architect James Essex (1722-1784) was appointed and was clearly instructed to adhere in key respects to Miller's design of 1749-1750 though, as we shall see, the building emerged in a somewhat different form. We know that ground works began in 1767, that these proceeded slowly enough to cause friction between Yorke and Essex, and that late in the day Brown imposed some modifications to the design.[25] Graffiti on the lower courses of the masonry survive from as early as 1772 and a convincing *terminus ante quem* for the finished building is provided by an engraving published in 1777[26] [Fig. 3]. Thereafter we hear little of the Gothic Tower until 1801, when another distinguished landscape gardener, Humphry Repton (1752-1818), presented one of his 'Red Books' proposing modifications to Wimpole's landscape and buildings. Since the 1770s many of England's country house estates had embraced the shooting, for sport and the table, of partridge, pheasant and other game. But the exclusive — and expensive — management of estates for sport was hotly resented by many English labourers and tenant farmers at a time of growing agricultural unrest, compelling landowners to invest in teams of gamekeepers to maintain stocks of game birds and deter poachers.[27] Repton recommended that the Gothic Tower be made "more useful, by adding floors… and outbuildings in the yards behind to form a [game] keeper's lodge, a purpose for which from its lofty and central situation it is admirably calculated".[28] We do not know when the work was put into effect; the fact that the work adhered to Repton's advice might suggest that it was not delayed for long — but then we should recall that Miller's earlier design was executed, still recognisably, some twenty years after his initial proposal. Thereafter, the documentation of the building is miserably thin, and the first resident gamekeeper of which we can be certain is not recorded until the 1871 census. The building remained occupied until the 1930s and appears to have been pressed into service as a fire-watching post during the Second World War before being left to decay.[29]

Fig.3 The anonymous 1777 engraving of the Gothic Folly, entitled 'Gothic Tower at Wimple' [© National Trust, WIM/D/559].

This story, baldly told, is quite tightly defined by the contemporary documents, which provide key dates and names and even motivations. In the absence of other data the documentary record is apt to resemble a reassuring bridge spanning a temporal void of uncertainty. Even where that bridge is interrupted by gaps in knowledge, by chasms of unbridged space, we feel that, knowing the larger arc of the narrative, we are justified in extrapolating lines across the void, like the continuous cables and deck of a suspension bridge. In such situations, we may feel, the structural integrity of the historical narrative is only slightly impaired by the acknowledged gaps.

However, at the most basic level, the documentary record tells us at best what *was*, not what *is*. Sometimes it tells us only what *might have been*. It is no guide to present-day management and conservation, with their requirement for a clear understanding of significance, not only of the building as a whole but of its constituent parts. The investigation and survey of the Gothic Tower quickly demonstrated that most of the fabric of the building designed by Miller, and executed by Essex subject to Brown's modification, survived; that Repton's work also survived little altered and clearly differentiated, both stratigraphically and stylistically; hence that the main phases of work could be characterised and their extent determined with some precision. An unlooked for discovery was that the only inhabitants of the building for the past half-century had been pigeons, who had left a considerable legacy.[30]

Fig.4 The rear of the Gothic Tower, showing the principal entrance (formerly served by a stair and landing approaching from the right) raised above the cellar entrance [©Adam Menuge].

Investigation also began to clarify the use and experiential history of the Gothic Tower. Like most garden buildings, it was a multi-purpose conception, designed to provide an intellectually charged visual interest and delight in the course of movement — probably along carefully prescribed routes — around the park, whilst also affording accommodation of several sorts. In its simplest form it served as an eye-catcher, axially aligned on the central window of the first-floor saloon in the centre of the north side of Wimpole Hall, but it was also visible from many other points within the park and at least glancingly from the Great North Road (the high road linking London with York and Edinburgh) just a kilometre to the west. Consequently in the interests of verisimilitude the curtain walls had not only to convey an impression of depth, but also to baffle sight of the 'unprotected' and unadorned rear of the structure.[31] In this the strictly architectural elements were assisted by judicious use of relief and careful tree-planting. The principal approach was from the south, probably by the Chinese Bridge, surviving only in facsimile but illustrated on the so-called Frog Service of Catherine the Great of Russia.[32] The visitor is drawn towards a tall gateway, emblazoned with blank shields. Once inside the 'ruins' visitors were led to the rear wall of the Gothic Tower and to an entrance raised above a humble cellar doorway; in other words, they entered at a level equivalent to the *piano nobile* of the Hall [Fig. 4].

Inside the Tower [Fig. 5], visitors faced a stair rising clockwise on plan around the inner skin of the drum. They would have noted, in passing, the provision of a fireplace large enough for cooking (provisioned from the cool cellar beneath); also, perhaps, cupboards with delicate door furniture of the period, and perhaps a servant in attendance; and would have recognised in these signs the promise of comfort and civility. But the stair attracted the eye, picking up in its balustrade the dominant saltire motif of the Chinese Bridge [Fig. 6]. The timber stair rose dizzily through the equivalent of two high storeys and with a flagrant disregard for a series of two-centred arched windows and mock arrow loops, some of which it cut with apparent artlessness. After completing a full revolution it rested at a landing — a landing with no view, and at the rear of the tower — before depositing the visitor in an enclosed stair in the corbelled-out brick structure on the rear. Only at the top of this stair, which is sparsely lit from the north, did the visitor emerge into a well-appointed Gothic prospect room or belvedere and, advancing into the room, take in the key views to east, west and especially south, towards the Hall. The stair, then, is a piece of structural virtuosity, framed around a tall empty space in imitation of a cantilevered stair, and the space is amply lit by windows so placed as to cheat the viewer of any satisfying views outwards, thereby focusing attention on the geometry of the stair itself, and perhaps on the vertiginous drop to the kitchen below. Expectations of the view are repeatedly thwarted, so that the entrance to the prospect room represents a kind of deliverance.

Fig.5 The ground floor of the Gothic Tower from the south, showing the fireplace (left) and the floor of the stair rising to the right [© Adam Menuge].

But now a problem presents itself. The

Tower as depicted in 1777 and as surviving has four stages; Miller's design had only three. And our prospect room is in the top storey of three. Surely one would place a prospect room on the topmost storey, not one floor down? Here the documents supply only a hint of an explanation. In 1772 there is mention of Brown raising the Gothic Tower as part of a range of modifications, apparently to increase its visibility from various points on the estate.[33] It is unclear whether the structure was complete according to the original plans before the modifications took place. The building evidence, on the other hand, is clear. The Gothic Tower was completed as a structure of three stages before Brown's decision to alter the design; indeed his intervention has something of a botched character. It does not appear that the added storey was put to any use, nor even that it was rendered accessible in the normal way. The evidence for this is as much stylistic as stratigraphic, and relies heavily on what we may call reasonable inferences. The prospect room was designed as a perfect circle, and we can prove this because behind the canted screen or lobby which now intrudes into the room we can see an earlier (by inference, original) pattern of shallow-recessed pointed Gothic arches continuing around the circumference [Fig. 7]. We can also identify the original doorway position between the stair and the prospect room from the vestigial survival of the pointed arched head beneath which it was placed [Fig. 8].

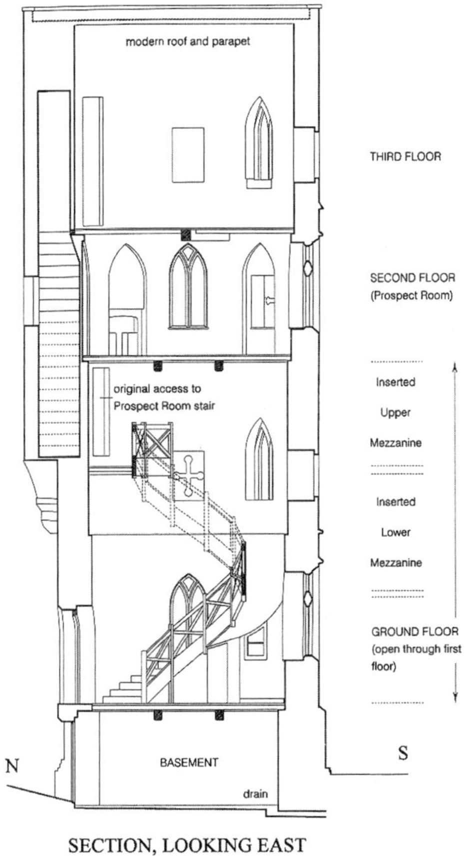

Fig.6 The author's sectional drawing through the Gothic Tower. Secondary features, including Repton's inserted floors, are indicated only schematically [© Historic England].

But how do we know that Brown's top floor was just a shell? The screen I referred to becomes necessary only when a continuation of the stair is called for. A new, steeper stair in the corbelled-out structure was needed to provide access to the added top floor, and the screen was needed to pro-

Fig.7 The prospect room from the south, showing the screen inserted when a stair to the floor above was inserted [© Adam Menuge].

vide a circulation space where the two flights met in order that traffic should not intrude on the prospect room. The top-floor room cannot make a satisfactory prospect room because it is unheated, and therefore unfit for polite recreation, but a fireplace could easily have been provided. More important to our argument, then, is the underlying design principle of rotating the fenestration through 45 degrees between alternate stages of the Tower, which means that the top floor has no south-facing window, and therefore cannot deliver the all-important axial

Fig.8 Diagonal cuts and a portion of the two-centred arched frame indicate the position of the original doorway to the prospect room, removed when the screen in Fig.7 was inserted. Viewed from the south [©Adam Menuge].

view back to the Hall. There was no obvious function for such a room. We can also compare the screen with the original room scheme, and determine that it is more simply built, with unmoulded recesses instead of the beaded originals, and with door furniture of simpler form and later date. These observations suggest that a more plausible context for the changes is the creation of Repton's lodge, in which the prospect room seems to have been adapted to serve as the keeper's drawing room; [34] and when we look at the door to the top-floor room we see a vernacular plank affair with a humble latch — quite out of keeping with the simple but refined character of the original furnishings. So we conclude that Brown added the top storey, but that its purpose was purely to enhance the eye-catching qualities of the Tower, and that it remained unused, and probably inaccessible, until Repton's scheme was implemented.

Is this interpretation a merely rhetorical *coup de théâtre*? My account presents, in abbreviated form, the key pieces of evidence, and I have constructed a narrative that seems to me to fit them. In so doing I have selected what I consider to be the most relevant data, and I have not knowingly suppressed any contrary evidence. The data take the form of physical characteristics and relationships, and they are interpreted in the light of a series of preconceptions about the structural properties of the building, the stylistic evolution of forms, and the social use of space, bearing in mind the prevailing social hierarchy and the nature of cultivated leisure in the period, to mention only the most obvious circumstances. These preconceptions, being the accumulated but not definitive professional wisdom of the investigator, are not immutable by any means; they can be corrected or fine-tuned in the light of new experience; on occasions they may be more extensively redefined; but on the whole they set out the parameters within which the evidence is expected to fall into place. Yet this complex epistemology of building investigation has seldom been exposed to detailed enquiry in its own right. Much of it seems to outsiders, perhaps, to proceed intuitively, almost arbitrarily, through adroit selection, juxtaposition and even special pleading.

On what, then, do we base our interpretations, and to what tests or rules do we subject our evidence? Certainly we rely on documents and visual sources when we can find them, though the dating and interpretation of these sources is often far from straightforward. We depend more than we sometimes acknowledge on the paradigms and expectations that we bring to each subject from our accumulated observation and experience. If we are not careful there is a danger that paradigms may exert a normative pressure, distorting our interpretations so that they conform to what we have grown to expect, but in principle we assert that they merely prompt hypotheses which we then test against the evidence. We rely heavily on stratigraphic observations, which we invest with a special importance because stratigraphy has an objective basis founded in the physical nature of the universe. Materials, unlike writers and artists, cannot lie, though they can be accomplices to a lie when, as frequently happens, they are used to disguise or dissimulate. But stratigraphy alone supplies only a sequence, not a chronology, and it pitches us into longitudinal modes of analysing change. Just as important are the lateral explorations of form at any given time and an understanding of how this form translated into patterns of use and perception — in other words, how contemporaries interpreted it as a system of functional and social indicators. For this kind of understanding we draw upon an almost bewildering variety of data: metric and non-metric, visual and haptic, material and spatial, present and absent, observed and inferred, localised and comparative. Though some subjugate thought processes to what might be termed orthogonal reasoning, in which data are amassed in grids or matrices for subsequent analysis, others proceed serendipitously in real time, following a trail of clues or diagnostics to find the solution at —

to return to my initial analogy — the scene of the crime. And this, it is important to acknowledge, is an iterative, recursive process. Often we resist an interpretation until we can corroborate it from another location or with a different type of evidence. Far from being haphazard, the range and diversity of the evidence on which we draw generates a mesh-like strength and resilience in our interpretations. At that point we can begin to rebuild the bridge across the void, not as a simple arc with occasional supports, but as a fully engineered structure. Or, to give Holmes the last word: '…observation and inference. Therein lies my *métier*'.[35]

notes

① Toulmin Smith, Lucy (ed.), *The Itinerary of John Leland*, 5 vols, London: George Bell & Sons, 1906-10 (reprinted London: Centaur Press & Carbondale, IL: Southern Illinois UP, 1964).

② Shakespeare, William, 'Sonnet 73', in *The Sonnets and Narrative Poems*, ed. by William Burto, London: Everyman, 1992, p. 39.

③ Camden, William, *Britannia: or, a Chorographical Description of the Flourishing Kingdoms of England, Scotland, and Ireland, and the islands adjacent; from the earliest antiquity*, ed. Gough, Richard, 2nd ed., 4 vol., London: John Stockdale, 1806 (reprinted Hildesheim and New York: Georg Olms, 1974), vol. 1, Preface.

④ On the development of antiquarian and archaeological thought and writing, see (among many others): Parry, Graham, *The Trophies of Time: English Antiquarians of the Seventeenth Century*, Oxford: Oxford University Press, 1995; Simmons, Jack (ed.), *English County Historians*, East Ardsley: EP Publications, 1976; Currie, C.R.J. & Lewis, C.P. (eds), *English County Histories: A Guide*, Stroud: Alan Sutton, 1994; Schnapp, Alain, *The Discovery of the Past: The Origins of Archaeology*, London: British Museum, 1996; Sweet, Rosemary, *Antiquaries: The Discovery of the Past in Eighteenth-Century Britain*, London: Hambledon and London, 2004; Piggott, Stuart, *William Stukeley: An Eighteenth-Century Antiquary*, revised ed., London: Thames & Hudson, 1985.

⑤ The titles of the different Royal Commissions varied significantly: Royal Commission on the Historical Monuments of England (RCHME), but Royal Commissions on the *Ancient and* Historical Monuments of Scotland and Wales (RCAHMS and RCAHMW). 'Ancient' seems to have been an acknowledgement of the stronger bond between prehistoric monuments and Scottish and Welsh identities. RCHME and RCAHMS were merged with other agencies in 1999 and 2015 respectively and are now absorbed in Historic England and Historic Environment Scotland. RCAHMW remains a precariously independent body.

⑥ Department for Communities and Local Government (CLG), *National Planning Policy Framework*, London: CLG, 2018, p. 67—available at <https: //www.gov.uk/government/uploads/system/uploads/attachment_data/file/6077/2116950.pdf>.

⑦ Conan Doyle, Arthur, *The Sign of Four*, London: Penguin, 1982, p. 10-11 (first published 1890).

⑧ Conan Doyle, Arthur, 'A Scandal in Bohemia', in *The Adventures of Sherlock Holmes and The Memoirs of Sherlock Holmes*, ed. Glinert, Ed, London: Penguin, 2001, p. 5 (first published in *The Strand Magazine*, July 1891).

⑨ Conan Doyle, 'A Scandal in Bohemia'…, as in note 8, p. 6. Earlier, in *A Study in Scarlet* (1887), Holmes remarks in the same vein but less memorably: "It is a capital mistake to theorize before you have all the evidence. It biases the judgement" (Conan Doyle, Arthur, *A Study in Scarlet*, ed. Glinert, Ed & Sinclair, Iain, London: Penguin, 2001, p. 27).

⑩ The most widely recognised historic building recording standard in England was first issued as: *Recording Historic Buildings: A Descriptive Specification*, London: RCHME, 1990. In its original form it leant heavily towards the physical (archival) properties of recording media, and convention sets such as those employed for architectural drawings. The revision of this document was the first to highlight investigation as a specific topic, albeit briefly, and this section retains its place in the latest revision: Menuge, Adam, *Understanding Historic Buildings: a guide to good recording practice*, Swindon: English Heritage, 2006 (last edition: London: Historic England, 2016) available at https://historicengland.org.uk/images-books/publications/understanding-historic-buildings/.

⑪ Wheeler, Mortimer, *Still Digging: Interleaves from an Antiquary's Notebook*, London: Michael Joseph, 1955, p. 35-36. Wheeler's work between 1913 and 1920 was contributory to RCHME, *An Inventory of the Historical Monuments in Essex*, 4 vols., London: HMSO, 1916-23). His most famous achievement was the excavation, in the 1930s, of the Iron Age hill-fort known as Maiden Castle, Dorset.

⑫ Menuge, Adam & Cooper, Anwen, 'The Gothic Folly, Wimpole Park, Wimpole, Cambridgeshire', English Heritage Architectural Investigation Report, 2001; Menuge, Adam, 'The Gothic Tower, Wimpole: A survey of recent research', unpublished report to the National Trust, 2016. I am grateful to David Adshead, Angus Wainwright and Dr Wendy Monkhouse for these opportunities to work at Wimpole.

⑬ Adshead, David, 'The design and building of the Gothic Tower at Wimpole, Cambridgeshire', *Burlington Magazine*, February 1998, p. 76-84; Adshead, David, *Wimpole: Architectural drawings and topographical views*, London: NT, 2007. Adshead's work extends earlier research published in: Jackson-Stops, Gervase, *An English Arcadia: Designs for Gardens and Garden Buildings in the Care of the National Trust 1600-1990*, London: NT, 1992, *passim*.

⑭ RCHME, *An Inventory of Historical Monuments in the County of Cambridge*, *Vol.1: West Cambridgeshire*, London: HMSO, 1968 (Wimpole monument 2, p. 223).

⑮ Carnwath, Deborah, 'The Work of Henry Edward Kendall (1776-1875) at Wimpole: His Influence on the Appearance and Character of the Estate from 1840', unpublished MSt Building History dissertation, University of Cambridge Faculty of Architecture & History of Art, 2017.

⑯ Souden, David, *Wimpole Hall*, London: NT, 1991. < https://www.europanostra.org/grand-prix-2016-presented-wimpole-halls-gothic-tower-local-award-ceremony-uk/>, consulted 21 February 2017. The project was managed by Paul Coleman, the curator was Dr Wendy Monkhouse and the archaeologist was Angus Wainwright.

⑰ Various reports are summarised in: Menuge, 'The Gothic Tower…', as in note 12, p. 11-18. Though I do not discuss their findings at length in this paper I should particularly acknowledge the work of James Edgar and Anthony Breen (documentary research), Lesley Hoskins (wallpaper), Karen Morrissey (paint) and Tam Webster et al. (excavation).

⑱ Kip, Johannes & Knyff, Leonard, *Britannia Illustrata*, vol. 1, London: David Mortier, 1707, pl. 32.

⑲ Dickins, Lilian & Stanton, Mary (eds), *An Eighteenth-Century Correspondence*, London: John Murray, 1910, p. 270-273; Hawkes, William (ed.), *The Diaries of Sanderson Miller of Radway, together with his Memoir of James Menteath*, Dugdale Society vol. 41, Stratford-upon-Avon: Dugdale Society in association with Shakespeare Birthplace Trust, 2005, p. 172-175 and 410; Meir, Jennifer, *Sanderson Miller and his Landscapes*, Chichester: Phillimore, 2006, p. 141-143.

⑳ Lyttleton to Miller，June 1749，quoted in Adshead 'The design and building…' as in note 13，p. 77. I have modernised the spelling of the original.

㉑ Lyttleton to Miller，13 June 1749，quoted in Meir，*Sanderson Miller*…，as in note 19，p. 141.

㉒ Adshead，*Wimpole*…，as in note 13，p. XX.

㉓ Meir，*Sanderson Miller*…，as in note 19，p. 141.

㉔ Adshead，'The design and building…'，as in note 13，p. 80-81.

㉕ Adshead，*Wimpole*…，as in note 13，p. XX.

㉖ Thompson，F.M.L.，*English Landed Society in the Nineteenth Century*，London：Routledge & Kegan Paul and Toronto：University of Toronto，1963，p. 136-50；Robinson，John Martin，*The English Country Estate*，London：Century，1988，Chapter 6.

㉗ Repton，Humphry，'Wimpole in Cambridgeshire，a Seat of Earl Hardwicke'（Wimpole 'Red Book'），unpublished dis-bound MS，1801（in the possession of the National Trust，with modern pagination），p. 25. Repton compiled his Red Books，containing 'before-and-after' views of the landscape and accompanying notes，as proposals for his clients. Naturally，the extent to which his proposals were adopted varied from client to client.

㉘ Menuge，'The Gothic Tower…'，as in note 12，p. 14-15，based on unpublished research by Anthony Breen for the National Trust.

㉙ The quantity of pigeon guano inside the building at the commencement of the 2014-15 restoration was sufficient to warrant commercial disposal.

㉚ "As the Back View will be immediately closed by the Wood there is no regard to be had to it，nor to the Left side but only to the Front and Right side as you look from the House"（Lyttleton to Miller，13 June 1749，quoted in Meir，*Sanderson Miller*…，as in note 19，p. 141）.

㉛ Adshead，*Wimpole*…，as in note 13，cat. 95.

㉜ Adshead，'The design and building…'，as in note 14，p. 81.

㉝ No room uses are specified in Repton's proposal in his Wimpole 'Red Book'（as in note 27）.

㉞ Conan Doyle，Arthur，'The Boscombe Valley Mystery'，in *The Adventures of Sherlock Holmes*…，as in note 8，p. 73（first published in *The Strand Magazine*，October 1891）.

舍圆用方
——中国城市形态的历史选择

Replacing ‘Round’ with ‘Square’:
The Historical Adoption of Urban Form in China

韦正 | WEI Zheng

摘要：像世界其他地区一样，古代中国最初也有圆形聚落和城市，后来由于天圆地方思想的影响，中国逐渐放弃了圆形城而采用了方形城。

关键词：圆形城；方形城；哲学基础

Abstract: As other areas in the world, there were round settlements and cities in ancient China too. Due to the thought of round-heaven and square-earth, China adopted the square instead of round city.

Keywords: Round City; Square City; Philosophical Foundation

作者简介：
韦正，北京大学考古文博学院，教授。

《考工记·匠人》说："匠人营国，方九里，旁三门。国中九经九纬，经途九轨。左祖右社，前朝后市。"这段关于古代营国制度的文字后世聚讼不已，赞成者与反对者均从书籍流传、考古资料两方面提出证据。反对者代表人物如郭沫若、闻人军、王仲殊、许宏，赞成者如张光直、芮沃寿、贺业矩、曲英杰。但双方多不将话讲死，如王仲殊说："也许是由于《考工记》的规制在西汉初年受到重视而在设计首都长安城时被充分参照，相反，也可能是由于汉儒从长安城的实际情况出发，增改了《考工记》的'匠人营国'部分。"①张光直则说："《周礼·考工记》所记'匠人营国……'这套规矩是来源久长的，虽然规矩的细节自三代到汉一直是在变化着的。"②中国古代文明是延续不断的，中国古代城市的发展有其内在的连续性和规律性，《考工记》的成书年代和流传过程可能存在不少疑问，其中所表达的思想也有理想化倾向，但对城市基本形态和布局的叙述不会凭空而来。不是否定《考工记》，而是利用它来帮助我们理解中国古代城市发展史不失为一个客观科学的选择。如果对中国各地自然条件的差异性、对中国各区域文明发展的不平衡性、对《考工记·匠人》这段文字的针对性有比较充分的理解和估计，"匠人营国"制度将体现出很高的价值。

依据"匠人营国"制度，从聂从歧、戴震到贺业矩所作的复原大同小异，方形外城中央为方形的宫城是基本框架，并由此规定了方格状的路网和各功能区。③如果能够证明大小相套的两个方形城框的存在，那么，"匠人营国"这段文字的可靠性基本就得到确认。《管子·乘马》说："凡立国都，非于大山之下，必于广川之上。高勿近旱而水足用，下勿近水而沟防省。因天材，就地利，故城郭不必中规矩，道路不必中准绳。"这段文字说规矩、准绳是规划建设城市时首先需要考虑的，但由于环境因素的影响，也需要一定的变通，这提醒我们在理解"匠人营国"制度时不可过分拘泥于文字的表面，而可适当变通。按照这种理解，本文认为方形包括正方形，也包括近似的方形和长方形；"左祖右社，前朝后市"是说这几类建筑集中在一起且有一定的位置关系，但不一定那么死板④。

本文即按照上述理解进行考察，考察结果将显示"匠人营国"制度是大体存在的，但方形城之外，中国历史上还存在其他形态的城市，特别是存在与方形城一样经过强烈的人为规划的圆形城，舍"圆"用"方"是历史选择的结果，这一种选择受制于中国传统的宇宙思想和宗教观念。

一、两重套合的方形城

据信《考工记》成书于春秋晚或战国早期，这个时代属于周代，周代城市与"匠人营国"制度是否相符首先值得检讨。

对"匠人营国"制度持否定意见的学者多从两个角度入手进行论述。

其一，集中对"左祖右社，前朝后市"进行否定性讨论。许宏的意见比较明确："……《考工记》所述'左祖右社'的营国制度根本不存在于先秦时期"⑤"《考工记》所载'面朝后市，左祖右社'的制度，与考古发现及较为可靠的文献记载所见先秦时期都城的实际格局完全不合"⑥。许宏对于"左祖右社"的否定是基于将庙寝移出都城的考虑，他说："战国时期的秦、楚等国已把先王之庙寝由都城移至王陵陵园，秦汉时期更使其制度化。……朝廷宫殿不仅是皇帝议政理事的场所，还取代宗庙成为举行国家重要典礼和宣布决策的地方，宗庙的作用则仅限于祭祀祖先和王室内部举行传统礼仪。因此可以说，以宫为主的宫庙格局的形成，是封建君主集权政治发展的必然结果，宫、庙地位的这种变化昭示着中国古代社会结构上的一次划时代的变革。"⑦许宏没有给出战国秦、楚等国将先王庙寝由都城移至王陵陵园的例证，反而在同一节还说道："汉初尚依旧制将太上皇和高祖庙建于长安城中"。其实，战国秦、楚至西汉将庙寝逐步移出都城，正说明庙寝原来在都城中，而且这有考古学上的证据，如在凤翔秦都雍城马家庄发现的秦宗庙遗址，"左祖右社"的制度不是根本不存在，而是有可能存在于先秦时期。许宏对"面朝后市"的否定基于对凤翔秦都雍城遗址北部发现的被认为是战国时期市的遗迹遗物的怀疑，此外并没有有力的证据。曲英杰举出了支持市位于城北的其他证据：汉河南县城北墙夯土中发现带"河市"字样的陶片，这里相当于东周王城宫城的北部，所以符合"面朝后市"之说。⑧如众所知，迄今为止的考古工作没有对先秦都城内部布局给出全面明确的说明，因此，用已有的发现去否认和肯定"左祖右社，前朝后市"的条件都不成熟，而且具体布局如何并不影响"匠人营国"的总体原则。

其二，利用考古发现否认"匠人营国"制度，这与对东周城市考古材料的总体把握有关，其中代表的观点是"西城东郭制"和"两城制"。"西城东郭制"认为："……可知春秋战国时代中原各诸侯国的国都，都推行着西'城'连接东'郭'的布局。这种布局是周公建设东都成周的时候开创的。"⑨"两城制"对"西城东郭制"进行了修正，认为"根据考古学的发现，东周列国都城的普遍形制是'两城制'，即以宫庙为主的宫城和以平民居住区工商业为主的'郭城'。"⑩这两种观点都是深刻的，但是都将大小二城视为一个整体，自然会得出《考工记·匠人》所载"回字形的方正的城郭布局……无考古学上的依据"⑪这个认识。

实际上，大小城制度并非不存在疑问，曲英杰就认为："由于周王倡导'大聚'，周初所封诸侯大国多筑大城，而中、小诸侯的都城规模较小，由城址可见其因等级不同而大小有别。战国时期，七国争雄，其都城的规模又空前扩大。这一时期都城的基本形制为内城外郭式，不存在所谓宫城与郭城两城并列的结构。今所见两城并列等状，皆由后补加筑外郭城所致。"⑫这个认识注重城市的扩张过程，同样是深刻的。

本文认为，大小城的形成过程可能不一，大小城在一定时间内共存也是客观事实，⑬但不是讨论"匠人营国"制度的关键所在。"匠人营国"制度针对的是国君所居的那个小城。在大、小城相套的情形下，两者是作为一个整体考虑的，直接体现"匠人营国"思想，如鲁故城（图 1），齐临淄城等；在小城偏于一隅的情形下，小城体现"匠人营国"思想，与大城无关。无论大小城是哪种关系，小城都是城市的中心，宫殿区又居小城的中心是一致的，这才是"匠人营国"制度的最紧要部分，也与从聂从歧到贺业矩的复原相符。⑭以下即按对两类情况对"匠人营国"制度的实际存在予以说明。⑮

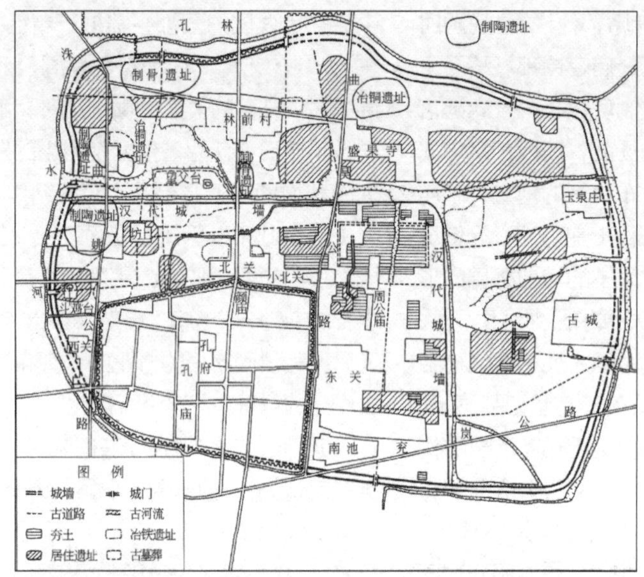

图1 曲阜鲁故城

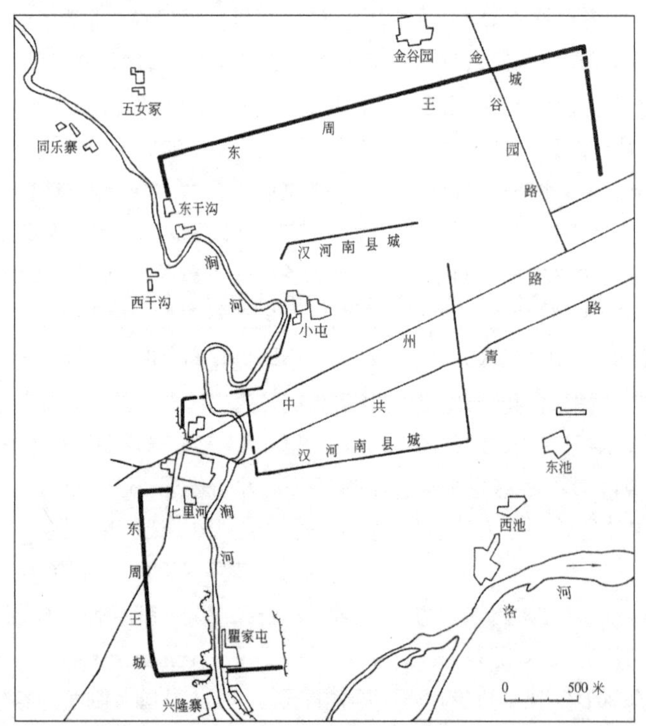

图2 东周王城

大小城相套者除鲁故城、齐临淄城外，还有东周王城、秦雍城、楚纪南城、魏安邑城、薛城、荥阳娘娘寨城等。鲁故城被认为是最接近“匠人营国”制度的周代城址，其宫城遗址在今周公庙一带，恰位于城市中部，城中的道路也呈大致的方格网状（图 1）。齐临淄城考古勘探的结果是小城位于大城的西南角，但《左传 · 襄公十八年》载：晋师伐齐，十二月“己亥，焚雍门及西郭、南郭。刘难、士弱率诸侯之师焚申池之竹木。壬寅，焚东郭、北郭。范鞅门于扬门，州绰门于东闾，左骖迫，还于门中，以枚数阖”。曲英杰据此认为：“晋师焚四郭而临淄城仍可守，是知郭（大城）内有宫城，且位于中心地带。战国时期，田氏代齐，很可能另择西南部‘金銮殿’一带营建宫城，遂有拓展外郭城西南部之举，将‘桓公台’即古营丘包围在内，而后又进一步封闭为西南小城。汉代齐王宫亦建于此一带。”[16] 此说极有见地，较根据大小城墙叠压打破关系和出土物判定营造年代同样甚至更具说服力。临淄城内已探明的路网也大致呈方格网状。《考工记》被认为是齐地之书，齐临淄城、鲁故城考古勘探发掘结果对此是支持的。东周王城通常认为是西周初年周公营建的洛邑，其轮廓已基本探明，略呈方形，边长 3000 米左右，大约相当于“方九里”。城内中部为汉代的河南县城，它可能沿用了东周王城的宫城，这与汉齐王宫沿用齐临淄城的西南小城相似，是常见的现象（图 2）。若果真如此，则大致遵循“匠人营国”制度者又多一例。秦雍城是春秋中期至战国早期的秦都城，外城为不规则的方形，但根据马家庄一带发现的秦宗庙遗址，可知宫城也位于大城之中偏南，在大体上还是与“匠人营国”制度相符。楚纪南城是春秋早期至公元278年白起拔郢为止的楚国首都，外城为东北、西北二角斜抹的长方形城，内城位于中部偏东南，与秦雍城中宫城的位置相似，也在大体上符合“匠人营国”制度。魏安邑城是前385年至前340年的魏国都城，大城接近方形，唯西城墙曲折，大城中央有小城，“小城估计是魏侯的宫城，建造时间同大城。此大、小城的布局形式，与鲁都曲阜及《考工记》中所载周王城大致相仿。”[17] 薛城为始封于周初、灭于战国时期的薛国都城，平面接近长方形，城中部地势隆起，为宫殿区所在。荥阳娘娘寨城大城近长方形，长宽分别为1200米、800多米，内城平面为方形，面积约10万平方米。内城内有十字形街道通到四面城门，城中部有夯土台基，为宫殿区所在。[18] 从以上数例能够看出，虽然没有与“匠人营国”制度相同的城市，但方形大小城相套，且小城近于大城中部的例子较多，而且这种形制从西周初期就已经存在。还值得指出的是，秦、楚这些相对后进的国家，都城兴建的年代虽晚，但形态上与齐鲁这些老牌国家没有两样，这是大小城相套形态具有文化认同意义，且具有强大影响力的标志。

与方形大小城相套者相比，大小城相倚者更受学术界关注，但实例其实并不多，能够举出的比较典型的例证如前述齐临淄城外，笔者所知就只有郑韩故城、邯郸赵国都城了。郑韩故城由东西两城构成，西城与东城共用之中墙的长度为4300米，西城北墙长2400米，其规模大约相当于鲁故城（南北2500米、东西3500米左右）。宫城位于西城中部略北，呈长方形，东西500米，南北320米。西城与其中的宫城构成大小相套的形态。邯郸赵国都城由王城和大北城两部分组成。王城为宫城，较复杂，由东城、北城、西城三部分组成，西城是三城的中心，形状近正方形，周长5680米，近中部有被称为“龙台”的大型夯土台，东西264米、南北296米。西城与其中的龙台又构成方形大小城相套的形态。齐临淄城小城近长方形，南北2195米、东西1402米，城北部有桓公台、金銮殿等大型夯土台基构成的宫殿区。以上三城皆兴建于东周时期，之所以作大小城相倚，当与统治担忧自身安全、不愿被郭城包围有关，但在新建的小城中，仍采取将宫城包裹于内的方形大小城相套形态，“匠人营国”制度仍然得到贯彻。

一些不能归入上述两类模式的城市如侯马晋国都城也体现出“匠人营国”制度。侯马晋国都城新田没有发现大型城址，但却发现距离甚近的小城8座，其中有四城紧靠在一起，四城之一的牛村古城年代大约为前6世纪半到前5世纪半，平望古城的年代为春秋中期到春秋战国之交，两城的城墙长度都在千米以上。牛村古城的中部略北，平望古城的中部都有大型夯土台基，当为宫殿区或宫城所在，也构成方向大小城相套的例证。

方形大小城相倚的实例虽然不多，但代表了历史发展的方向。甚至汉长安城也可以从这个角度加以认识。未央宫位于长安城之一角，可以将整个长安城看作大城，将未央宫看作小城，将未央宫前殿看作宫城的核心区。汉长安城是按照王城系统进行规划的，但在发展过程中不断发展调整以适应帝都的需要。按照这种理解，既不必要将长安城与“匠人营国”制度做僵硬的比附，也不必对《考工记》的年代和流传过程曲为之解。[19] 至于将长安城北的曲折说城象征北斗之形，还存在着超长中轴线，更有强行提升设计者思想境界的嫌疑。还是贺业矩的意见中肯实在："西汉建都长安，开始也并无什么宏伟规划，不过在秦代离宫基础上稍事修缮因陋就简而已。当时正值'天下汹汹'，所以萧何营建未央宫，刘邦还批评他：'何治宫室过度也'。直到惠帝时，长安才正式筑城。武帝时社会生产蒸蒸日上，经济力量日益雄厚。这时长安营建了很多宫廷建筑，如桂宫、建章宫、明光宫等。虽然大兴土木，却没有提及改造长安城的计划，而是就原有基础加以扩建。所以从长安城建设过程看，可以说还缺乏较为全面的规划。因此，城的总体布局不免失之松散。"[20]

根据以上分析可知，不论是城市的营建时间，还是城市的平面类型，也不论是中原还是秦楚，在这些代表或深受周文化影响的国度，在方形的宫城外再套上一个不一定呈方形的外城几乎是当时的通制。虽然考古工作有限，还受到地形等因素的影响，但以方形宫城为中心延伸出去的路网只能是方格网状的，如鲁故城和齐临淄城，这种形态已经符合"匠人营国"制度的基本精神。

图 3　安阳洹北商城

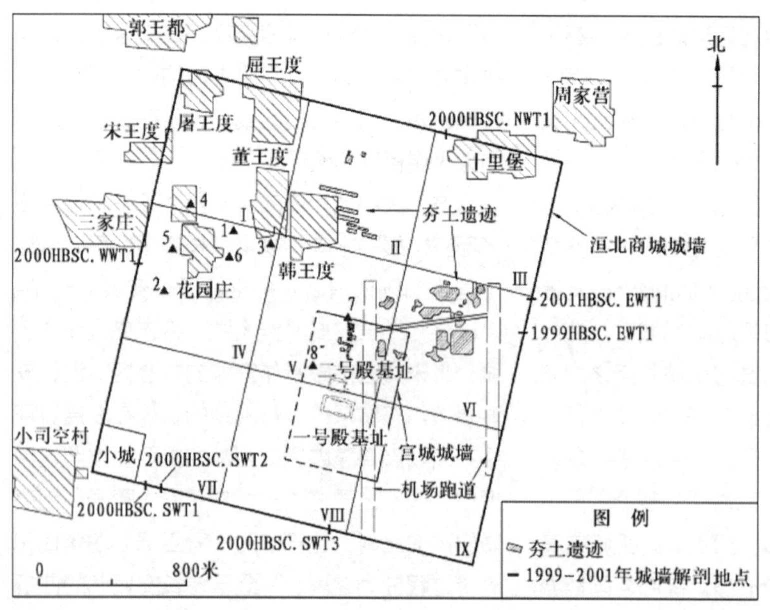

如果将秦雍城马家庄宗庙遗址，以及雍城北部和洛阳东周王城可能存在的市考虑进来，"左祖右社，前朝后市"的可能性不能说完全子虚乌有。至于"方九里"却不必过于认真，所谓"大都，不过叁国之一；中，五之一；小，九之一"[21]，"大县城，方王城三之一。小县立城，方王城九之一。都鄙不过百室，以便野事"[22]是史有明文的。总之，考古和文献资料证明"匠人营国"制度大致存在于周代。

二、舍圆用方

"匠人营国"制度的基本精神在西周初期创建的齐临淄城、鲁故城等城市中已经得到体现，那么，这是西周创立的新制度，还是对历史传统的继承，我们有必要加以探寻。

探寻的情况令人诧异，方形大小城相套和相倚的城市在商代都已存在，其中可以列举出的大小城相套者有洹北商城、垣曲商城、焦作府城，大小城相倚者以偃师商城为典型。

洹北商城近正方形，边长 2100~2200 米，宫城位于中部偏东，平面长方形，长 795 米、宽度超过 515 米（图 3）。宫城中发现大范围的夯土台基，排列紧密有序。有的台基规模很大，如一号基址面积达 1.6 万平方米，当是宗庙宫殿类遗存。比较奇特的是，在外城西南角有一小城，长 255 米、宽 240 米。焦作府城和垣曲商城都不是都城，而是一个区域中心城市。焦作府城近正方形，城墙长约300米，城内中部靠北发现类似宫殿区的夯土台基。垣曲商城城墙的长度只有350~400米，在城中心发现成片的夯土台基。两座城址的规模相当于《左传》中的“小都”或《逸周书》中的“小县”,它们的布局形态说明“匠人营国”制度是个通则。

偃师商城的小城位于大城的南半部，近长方形，长宽分别为1100米、740米。小城内中部靠南有宫城（图4）。在小城和大城内都发现纵横交叉的道路，它们将偃师商城分隔成块状。郑州商城也可能属于大小城相倚制，其宫殿区位于商城的东北部，东西大约750米、南北500米。在宫殿区的西北部曾发现东西向的大壕沟，安金槐推测这条大壕沟是宫殿区北部的防护沟，并认为占据商城南半部的汉城北墙的护城河可能利用了商代宫殿区南边的防护沟，还推测宫殿区除东部紧靠东城墙外，其他三面都应有夯土城墙和防护沟。[23] 按此说，郑州商城的宫殿区构成小城。不过，由于小城范围内存在大量现代建筑，无法进行大规模钻探和发掘，对小城内的布局情况了解有限，尚不能确定小城的核心地带是否为一封闭规整的宫城。

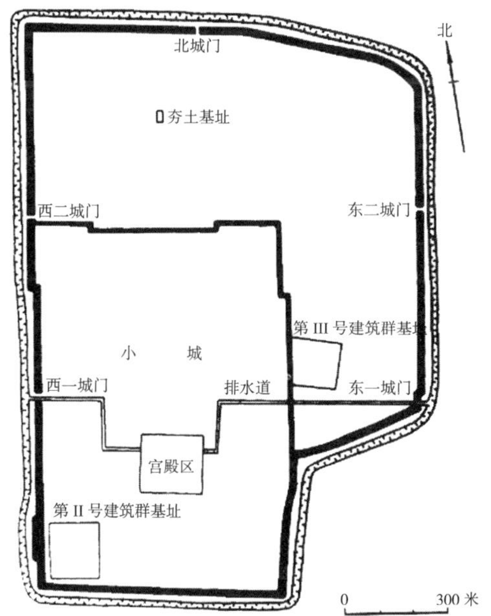

图4 偃师商城

商代城市发现的并不多，其中有些城的性质比较特殊，如盘龙城可能是军事性的，似不便纳入“匠人营国”制度下加以讨论。文中列举的数例城市皆位于中原地区，已具有相当的代表性，它们的宫城基本位于小城中部，大概能够说明“匠人营国”制度不是周代的发明，而是渊源有自。

不过，再往前追溯至中国城市出现的新石器时代晚期，特别是龙山时代，方形大小城相套的例子就不见了，只能见到一些方形城址，而且可以举出的例子也不是很多，但分布范围不限于中原地区。中原地区有登封王城岗、淮阳平粮台、新密古城寨、辉县孟庄等古城，其他地区的发现集中在四川和山东地区，这显然与考古工作的广泛和深入程度有关。四川成都附近有新津宝墩城、郫县古城、都江堰芒城，山东有寿光边线王城等。

能够更多地列举出的是形态不呈方形的城市，它们的情况又可以分为两类，一类不甚规则，一类接近圆形。不甚规则者如郑州西山、天门石家河、石首走马岭、章丘城子崖、邹平丁公、阳谷景阳冈、良渚、陶寺、夏县东下冯、温江鱼凫城等古城，这些城市形态主要受到自然地形的强烈影响，经常是将一些高地连接成城墙，只在局部地区体现一定的人为干预。出现这类城市的地方往往并不缺乏用以建设方形城所需的较平坦的地块，但省工省时以及对形态的忽视似乎更反映城市营造者的初衷。

近圆形城是这里讨论的重点。典型者为澧县城头山古城（图 5），江陵阴湘城大概也可以归入此类。这类城的数量虽然不多，但很容易让人们将之与更早的仰韶时代的姜寨环绕形聚落（图 6）以及半坡聚落、尉迟寺遗址（图 7），较晚的西周时期的宁乡炭河里古城以及霍丘堰台聚落联系起来。氏族内的房屋如果以长老所居或公共议事厅为中心分布，就可能形成圆形聚落，因此这可以说是一种自然形成的聚落形态，是与氏族血缘关系和组织结构相匹配的聚落形态。姜寨是目前发掘出来的典型的圆形聚落，很多聚落揭露得不完整，但原来的形态很可能接近圆形。圆形城市可能是借鉴了圆形聚落的外部形态扩展而成，但两者形成的动因和过程是不相同的。圆形城市不可能自然形成，必须经过人为的严密规划。城头山城的直径约 325 米，炭河里城的复原直径近 700 米，两者都不可能是自然发展的产物。圆形城市与方形城一样，都不是自然而是人为规划和营建的产物，都体现了人类对自然的强烈干预。因为与圆形聚落的亲缘关系，圆形城似乎更容易得到沿用。但是，数十年的中国城市考古成果清晰地显示，与方形城相比，圆形城的数量不仅很少，而且在西周之后就再未闻有所发现，这不是能用考古发现的偶然性解释得通的。合理的认识应该是，在中国城市发展的早期阶段，先民们有意识地放弃了圆形城市形态，而采用了方形城市形态，可以概括为舍“圆”用“方”。这种选择经历了相当长的历史过程，并且形成丰富的内涵，“匠人营国”制度是对其内涵明晰而宏观的表述。还需要指出的是，目前发现的两座圆形城都位于中国南方的湖南省境内，不排除以后在中原地区发现圆形城市的可能性，但即使有所发现，其数量也将不足以与已经发现的方形和不规则形城抗衡。虽然中原地区并不缺少环形聚落，中国南北方的文化交流也始终不断，但可以说，舍“圆”用“方”以及“匠人营国”

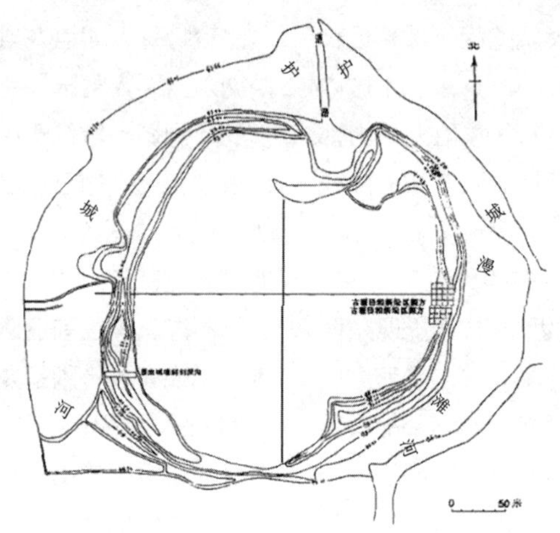

图 5 澧县城头山城址

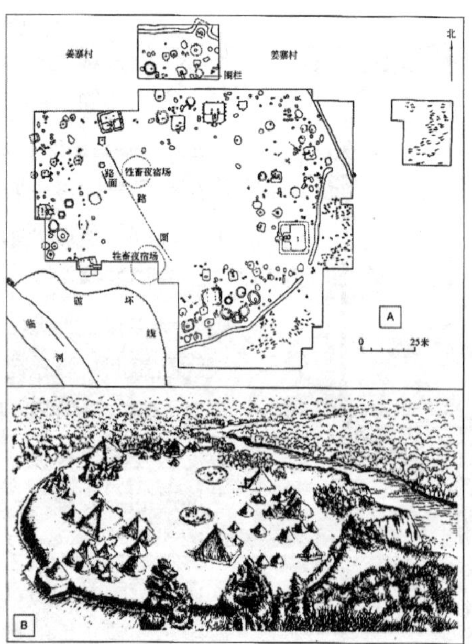

图 6 姜寨遗址平面图和复原示意图

制度的形成主要是在中原地区实现的。

方形城在后来的中国历史上占据绝对的主流，乃至于让人觉得此乃天经地义的城市形态。西方古代有较多的圆形城，特别是中世纪以后兴起大量的圆形城并一直延续至今，与中国古代城市形态形成鲜明的对比。由上面的考察可知，中国并非没有圆形城，只是在发展过程中被淘汰了。为什么随着时代的变化，圆形城被淘汰，方形城一统天下？这是值得深思的问题。

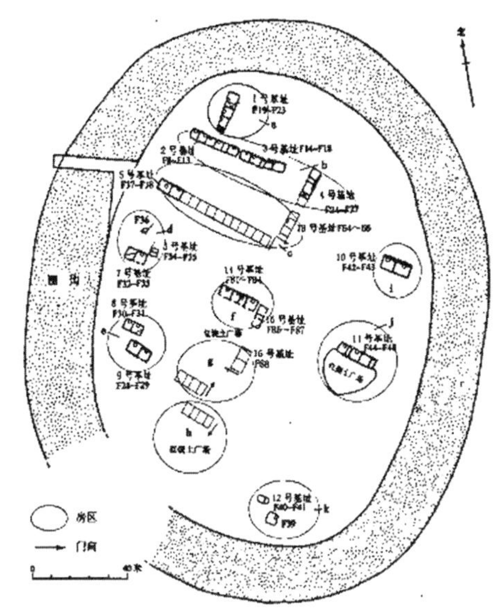

图 7　尉迟寺环壕聚落

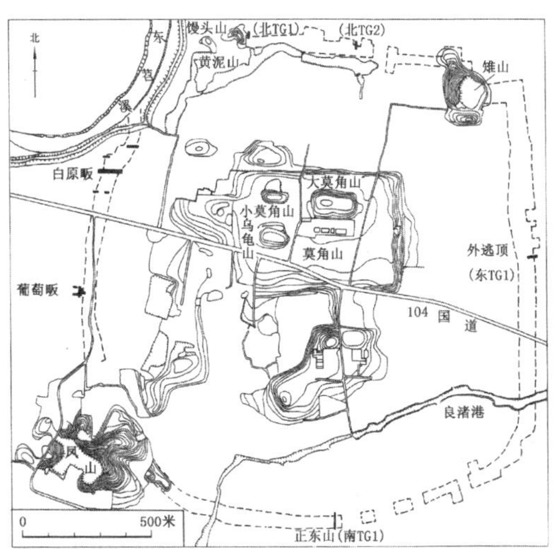

图 8　良渚古城平面图

三、哲学基础

没有文字材料能对舍圆用方问题给予直接的回答，但仍有不少材料能够帮助我们对这种现象进行理解。

良渚古城是发掘得相对充分的史前城，一些迹象有助于我们对问题的探讨。古城略呈圆角方形，东西 1500~1700 米、南北 1800~1900 米，城址中心是东西 670 米、南北 450 米的长方形大土台，大土台上又有大莫角山、小莫角山、乌龟山三座土台，上有大型夯土基址。大土台东南部有“燎祭”遗迹，还有一座良渚中期墓葬（图 8）。大土台西北部是著名的反山遗址，系长 90 米、宽 30 米的人工土墩，在上面清理出 11 座良渚墓，发现棺床和朱漆木棺遗迹，出土玉器 1100 件套。良渚古城被认为是良渚古国的“王都”，巨大的莫角山人工土台和“燎祭”遗迹，以及埋葬高等级墓葬的反山给人以这座城主要不是为人而是为神修建之感，代表神的就是反山墓主。[24] 在城内核心部位发现高等级墓葬的情况并不少见，著名的还有二里头遗址的二号宫殿址后部。这些现象昭示了这类城市的基本性质。“匠人营国”制度中的“左祖右社，前朝后市”所表述的也可以理解为以神而非人为中心。明白这一点，对理解方形城市占据中国城市的主流有直接的帮助。如果将莫角山大土台看作一个内城，那么良渚古城与后来的方形大小城相套的形态是非常接近的。大土台和小城都作为代表神的君主的居所，二者都被处理成方形而不是其他形状，不禁让人想到中国古代宇宙思想中最重要的天圆地方说[25]，这恰好在良渚古城的时代已有不少物证。

可以列举的最具代表性的物证有良渚等遗址中发现的玉琮和凌家滩遗址中发现的玉片。玉琮呈外方内圆的柱状，中间有穿孔，表面多装饰几何化的兽面纹。礼书中有以琮礼地、敛尸的记载。考古发现的玉琮有经过火烧并打碎等祭祀仪式后作为敛尸用品的墓例，如常州寺墩 M3。学术界普遍认为："玉璧、玉琮是祭天地的礼器，占有这些礼器的人，应掌握有特殊的权力。"[26]张光直说："结合上述有关玉琮本身性质诸特征来看，我们很清楚地看到在良渚文化社会中有权力有财富的人物，使用有兽面纹、内圆外方的玉琮，亦即使用贯通天地的法器，作为他们具有权力的象征。"[27]玉琮的方形轮廓代表大地，掌握玉琮者实质上代表和掌握着大地，那么，将使用玉琮为祭器的祭坛，将掌握玉琮者的居所建成象征大地的方形是顺理成章的。良渚文化之外，玉琮在石家河遗址、薛家岗遗址、陶寺遗址、广东曲江石峡以及后来的殷墟遗址中都有所发现，张光直说："琮被发现于沿海地区的良渚文化和内陆地区的陶寺类型，这并非偶然，它无疑代表了一种跨地区传播的宇宙观或者甚至是一种使该宇宙观发挥重要作用的广泛基础。若我们把玉璧包括在宇宙观的范畴内，齐家文化亦被包括在内了。"[28]方形城成为历史发展的趋势与玉琮及其所代表的宇宙思想的扩散同步。

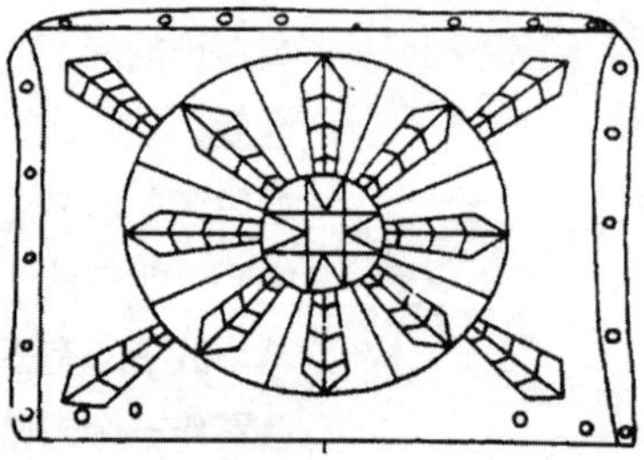

凌家滩玉片比玉琮更直接地表达了宇宙思想，其正面为指向四方和八方的、外圆内方的神秘图案，出土时位于墓底正中央，"估计原来是放置在墓主胸部"（图 9）。玉片之外，凌家滩遗址也发现祭坛，祭坛上和周围也发现数十座墓。冯时认为：玉版侧视呈弧形和图案中的两重圆圈象征天，其方形的外轮廓象征地，圆圈外的四只箭标形图案象征维系天地的四维，是当时天圆地方宇宙观念的图解。[29]很多学者认为，凌家滩玉片图案与后世的式盘、铜镜上的规矩纹相似，都包含了古代的空间和时间思想，表现的是宇宙天地模式。葛兆光说："中国古代思想世界一开始就与'天'相关，在对天体地形的观察体验与认识中，包含了宇宙天地有中心与边缘的思想，而且潜含了中国古代人们自认为是居于天地中心的想法，这于中国这一名称的内涵有一定的关系，对天地的感觉与想象也与此后中国人的各种抽象观念有极深的关系。"[30]将祭坛建在城市中央，将祭祀先祖社稷的宗庙明堂建在城市中央，将代天地行使管理人间职权的君主朝寝建在城市中央，并将它们建成与大地同形的方形，达到所谓"允执厥中""定之方中""宅兹中国"的境界，这从观念到形态上都是合适的。这大概就是我们所看到的，尽管外面大城的轮廓可能不甚规整，但宫城都呈方形的缘故。

图 9 安徽凌家滩玉器

学者们还举出了更多的证据说明中国天圆地方观念的古老。如甲骨文中的四方观就是大地呈四方形的直接表白。再如甲骨文中的“巫”字的含义，张光直说：“甲骨文中的巫字作，即两个I字相交叉。《说文》：‘工、巧饰也，像人有规矩也，与巫同意。’金恒祥《续甲骨文编》把甲骨文的巫字排在‘巨’字下，引《说文》：‘规巨也，从工象手持之。’这都明确指出巫与巨的关系，也就说明了甲骨文中巫字的来源，即巫是使矩的专家，能画圆方，掌握天地。”[31]包括商王在内的早期中国统治者就是集君主、军事首领于一身的大巫。再如殷墟的“亞”字形大墓，高去寻先生认为“不容怀疑的它应该是当时丧礼的一种建筑制度。这种丧礼制度的建筑可能是象征着当时贵族社会的一种礼制建筑，……我们现在称它为古代的宗庙明堂建筑。”[32]张光直受墨西哥奥尔美克文化地神形象的启示，进一步推测到：“照这样看来，要说明亚形的意义与起源，我们必须解释为什么方形的宗庙明堂的四个角都凹入以致形成‘亞’形。……这个‘亞’形的口便是奥尔美克人的一张宇宙图，张开的大口是天地的分界，而四角的树木是协助奥尔美克人登天入地的四株‘宇宙之树’。这幅宇宙图给我们的启示，是说大地本是方形的，但四角上各植一树，造成凹入的角隅，造成‘亞’形的形成。从这里我们再回头看‘亞’形，便引起这样的一个问题，就是殷代的‘亞’形会不会也是这样形成的？作为天地沟通的场所的宗庙明堂是不是在四隅都植有（实有的或象征性的）‘若木’、‘建木’，或‘扶桑’这一类沟通天地的神木，而为了四木而造成四角的凹入？换言之，殷代宗庙明堂是否因为四角有四木而造成‘亞’形的。”[33]洹北商城的形状几乎为正方形，在西南角有一方形小城，是不是本来也构成一个“亞”字形，从而更完美地体现了天圆地方的宇宙观点？

我们不拟再列举其他资料说明天圆地方观念的古老性及其对中国城市、宗庙明堂、祭坛、祭器形态的影响。以农为本的华夏民族对天地具有独特而深刻的认识，法天则地、与天地同形同构成为华夏民族的基本思想。“国之大事，在祀与戎”，祭祀神与祖先成为国君的第一要务和自身合法性的证明，将宗庙明堂建成方形，将宗庙明堂所在的宫城建成方形，将宫城所在的大城建成方形，也是在确凿无疑地宣示着国君具有沟通天地的能力和神性，这是一种带有宗教性的思想，而且是至关重要的。在这种思维方式和宗教式理念的支配下，圆形城的淘汰是注定的，是历史的必然选择。

总之，中国古代城市的基本原则是法天象地，《考工记》将这个思想用最清晰的文字表达了出来，因此，“匠人营国”制度不应只作为一时一地意义上的文字加以理解，而应该将这段文字作为理解中国古代城市，特别是历代都城发展演化史的主脉。

注释：

① 王仲殊．关于日本古代都城制度的源流 [J]. 考古，1983（4）.

② 张光直．关于中国初期“城市”这个概念 [M]. 载氏著《中国青铜时代》二集，6 页，三联书店，1990.

③ 贺业矩认为这种路网与井田制有关，参见氏著《考工记营国制度研究》之第二章“王城规划”、第六章“道路规划”，北京：中国建筑工业出版社，1985.

④ 这在很大程度上依赖于考古工作，但目前的中国城市考古深入到宫城内部具体布局状况的还很少，而且不少遗址的保存状况欠佳，以至于不可能反映当时的布局状况。

⑤ 许宏．先秦城市考古学研究 [M]. 北京：北京燕山出版社，2000.
⑥ 同注释⑤。
⑦ 同注释⑤。
⑧ 曲英杰．古代城市 [M]. 北京：文物出版社，2003.
⑨ 杨宽．中国古代都城制度史研究 [M]. 上海：上海古籍出版社，1993.
⑩ 徐苹芳：《中国古代城市考古与古史研究》，氏著《中国历史考古学论丛》，90 页，允晨文化公司（台北），1995 年。
⑪ 同注释⑤。
⑫ 同注释⑧。
⑬ 刘庆柱对大小城有专门的讨论，值得参看，见刘庆柱．中国古代都城考古学研究的几个问题 [J]. 考古，2000（7）.
⑭ 贺业矩也强调小城的重要性。在回答"也许有人要问，为什么《匠人》'营国'只说到城，却没有涉及外廓（郛）？"时，他说："由于奴隶社会的城，本为大小奴隶主的政治军事堡垒，而廓实际上不过是城的外围防护设施，仅居民而已。一切宫室、宗庙、社稷等都在城内，故当时城邑的规划重点自必在城，而不在廓。因此，《匠人》王城规划制度当着重在城的规划。"贺业矩对城、郭性质差异的认识是恰当的，但他并没有直截了当地说出小城才是"匠人营国"制度直接的对象。在小城与其中宫城的关系上，贺业矩也说到了"择中"思想（源自《吕氏春秋·慎势篇》"择天下之中而立国，择国之中而立宫"，《荀子·大略篇》"王者必居天下之中，礼也"。），还介绍了"中商""土中"等概念，这也是合理的，但没有如本文这样从中国宇宙思想的角度并辅以出土文物进行论证。参见贺业矩．考工记营国制度研究 [M]. 北京：中国建筑工业出版社，1985.
⑮ 由于考古工作的有限性，以及不排除个别例外，并不是已经发现的周代都城遗址都能归入两类之中，如易下都在东城北部又有隔墙，有些大型夯土台在城外，这些迹象难于理解。
⑯ 同注释⑧。
⑰ 刘叙杰，主编．中国古代建筑史——原始社会、夏、商、周、秦、汉建筑（第一卷）[M]. 北京：中国建筑工业出版社，2003.
⑱ 张家强：《河南荥阳娘娘寨两周时期城址》，国家文物局，主编 .2009 中国重要考古发现 [M]. 北京：文物出版社，2010.
⑲ 王仲殊在《汉代考古学概说》中列举的汉长安城与"匠人营国"制度相合者有以下若干方面：长安城的平面不甚规整，但接近正方形；共十二个城门，每面四门；每个城门有三个门道，主要大街分为三股，即一路三涂；未央宫和长乐宫在南，东、西市在北。在《关于日本古代都城制度的源流》（《考古》1983 年 4 期）中，王仲殊说："也许是由于《考工记》的规制在西汉初年受到重视而在设计首都长安时被充分参照，相反，也可能是由于汉儒从长安城的实际情况出发，增改了《考工记》的'匠人营国'部分。"
⑳ 不过，贺业矩就此说："看来汉长安城规划与《考工记·匠人》营国制度不合，正是理所当然，也是势所必然。"这是因为贺业矩虽然考虑了长安的兴建过程，但有时还是不自觉地将长安城作为一个整体看待的缘故，这有别于本文将长安城置于中国城市，特别置于都城既有延续又有发展变化的历史过程中加以看待。
㉑《左传·隐公元年》。
㉒《逸周书·作雒解》。
㉓ 安金槐．试论郑州商城的地理位置和布局 [C]// 中国商文化国际学术讨论会论文集．中国大百科全书出版社，1998.
㉔ 余杭玉架山良渚文化环壕聚落也可参考，它接近方形，边长 134~155 米，北段中部略向外凸出。环壕内有大型堆筑土台、墓葬、居住址等遗迹，是不可多得的良渚文化小型完整聚落的例证。
㉕ 参见芮沃寿．中国城市的宇宙论 [M]// 施坚雅主编．中华帝国晚期的城市．中华书局，2000.
㉖ 南京博物院．江苏吴县草鞋山遗址 [J]. 文物资料丛刊．第 3 辑，文物出版社，1980.
㉗ 张光直．谈"琮"及其在中国古史上的意义 [M]// 氏著《中国青铜时代》二集．三联书店，1990：76.
㉘ 张光直．古代中国考古学 [M]. 沈阳：辽宁教育出版社，2002.
㉙ 冯时．中国天文考古学 [M]. 北京：社会科学文献出版社，2001.
㉚ 葛兆光．中国思想史（第一卷）[M]. 上海：复旦大学出版社，2001.
㉛ 张光直．谈"琮"及其在中国古史上的意义 [M]// 氏著《中国青铜时代》二集．三联书店，1990：72.
㉜ 高去寻．殷代大墓的木室及其涵义之推测 [J].“中央研究院”历史语言研究所集刊，1969，39：181-182. 转自张光直．说殷代的"亞"形 [M]// 氏著《中国青铜时代》二集．三联书店，1990：85.
㉝ 张光直．说殷代的"亞"形 [M]// 氏著《中国青铜时代》. 三联书店，1999：313.

建筑考古学：
从科学的田野工作到保护

Building Archaeology：
From Scientific Fieldwork to Conservation

Elke NAGEL，Manfred SCHULLER

摘要：对建筑考古目标和方法的简要介绍，表明了其科学领域的广度，及其记录技术在任何考古研究中的基础性作用。建筑考古学的主要范畴是以建筑为主要资源，探索建筑时代、结构、物质性及其历史发展的脉络。调查从精细观察和全面记录开始，从而得到准确的图纸。现场发现将通过佐证资料来加强，例如档案和文献，来完善一个对象的建筑历史图景。关于雷根斯堡大教堂的研究项目提供了丰富多样的发现，启发了对这一宏伟建筑历史研究的深入认识。从传统的手工记录到三维地面激光扫描，当下关于适当记录方法的讨论只能通过比较他们的结果和所需的成本来推进。报告简述了两种实验环境，每种比较两个竞争的技术手段：建筑历史、慕尼黑工业大学建筑考古和遗产保护专业主任已经对传统手工测量和全站仪记录进行测试；另一个样例包括三维扫描。最后，文章总结了记录工具、技术以及建筑考古对保护规划影响。

关键词：建筑考古；专业实践；德国

Abstract：A brief introduction about the aims and methods of building archaeology shows the broadness of the scientific field and the technological implementation of recording as the basis for any archaeological research. Main scope of building archaeology is to explore an edifice's age，construction，materiality as well as the chain of its historic development by using the building as main source. The investigation begins with close observation and thorough recording resulting in precise drawings. On-site findings will be enhanced with secondary sources，such as archive material and literature to complete the picture of an object's architectural history. The research project on Regensburg Cathedral offers insights in the great variety of findings enlightening the grand building's history. Ongoing discussions about adequate recording methods，ranging from traditional hand recording to 3D terrestrial laser scanning，can only be forwarded by comparing their results and required effort. The report sketches two experimental settings，each comparing two rivalling technologies：The Chair for Building History，Building Archaeology and Heritage Conservation（Technical University Munich）has put traditional hand measurement and total station recording to the test and a second example includes 3D scanning. The essay concludes with documentation tools and techniques and the influence of building archaeology in conservation planning.

Keywords：Building archaeology；Expert practice；Germany

作者简介：
Dr. Elke NAGEL，strebewerk，Architekten GmbH，Germany.
Dr. Manfred SCHULLER，Technical University of Munich，Department of architecture，Chair for Building History，Building Archaeology and Heritage Conservation

Building Archaeology (in German: *Bauforschung*) proves likewise to be a general scientific method and a universal research tool to investigate the wide array of all kinds of historical buildings and construction types that have been erected from the Antiquity to the recent past. In the mind of the general public Building Archaeology is associated with the great and famous monuments. In terms of scientific research, however, small and recent average buildings contain as much information about the history of building and construction. In respect to the individual object three main questions direct the building archaeologist who will investigate: 1) when a building was erected, 2) how it was constructed, 3) which alterations occurred in the course of history.

The main source always is the building itself. On-site investigation methods range from meticulous recording, accurate representation drawings, probing of evidence, as well as taking samples in order to identify and date the materials with scientific laboratory techniques. The material investigations are complemented with research in literature, archives and all available sources that enlighten the chain of history and supplement in-situ evidence by historical, social and sometimes socio-economic information. Finally, a comprehensive synopsis of all the data leads to understand the building in its materiality, construction and historical development. Each project starts with a specific question; every structure has to be understood individually. At the same time, every perception adds a piece to the puzzle of building historical knowledge. Therefore, instead of aiming at exploring individual cases, the research field expands to the levels of conceptualisation and theory formation. Building Archaeology transfers the story telling from the history of a building to building history.

In the following lines, a selection of research cases will explain the general principles of Building Archaeology as published, for example, by ICOMOS in the *Monuments and Sites series*.[1] In the recent years, the Chair for Building History, Building Archaeology and Heritage Conservation (*Lehrstuhl für Baugeschichte, Historische Bauforschung und Denkmalpflege*) at the Faculty of Architecture, Technical University Munich, has analysed a wide range of buildings from antique Greek architecture, Roman villas, medieval monasteries, roof struc-tures, houses, Renaissance and Baroque architecture, and has explored construction techniques ranging from Christian and Islamic traditional ones to modern steel structures.[2]

Scientific Building Archaeology

The research on Regensburg Cathedral is one of our most representative projects.

Since it is impossible to show all the facets of such a project, a few highlights will introduce the accuracy of the recording, the extraordinary depth of evidence analysis and the translation of historic information into stories for a wide audience. Members of the scientific team, gathered around Manfred Schuller, have spent several decades recording and collecting information on construction, design, material, craftsmanship and building periods. Drawings of all the elevations, several vertical sections, multiple horizontal sections and details literally piled toweringly. Thanks to the long-term working period, the project on Regensburg Cathedral has tremendously improved the recording techniques from traditional hand measurement to 3D terrestrial laser scanning. All these techniques have been applied to parts of the cathedral, but their aim always was the same. Indeed, in order to explore the history and construction of historic buildings, creating reliable and precise recording drawings is the most important and first step. The richness of details can be understood regarding the complexity of the large drawings, of course, but the value of the research is shown in detail drawings that illustrate the technical or structural evidence. Another example of the story telling construction would be the finding of a hidden inscription of the year 1496 on one of the stone blocks, which helps to identify a datation of the building sequence [Fig. 1]. In combination with such exceptional findings, close focus on traces of tools sheds light on the building process and the techniques employed.

Fig.1 Regensburg Cathedral: detailed recording drawing of a stone block with several hints to the construction history and the dating inscription of 1496 [© Manfred Schuller, Chair for Building History, Building Archaeology and Heritage Conservation, TUM].

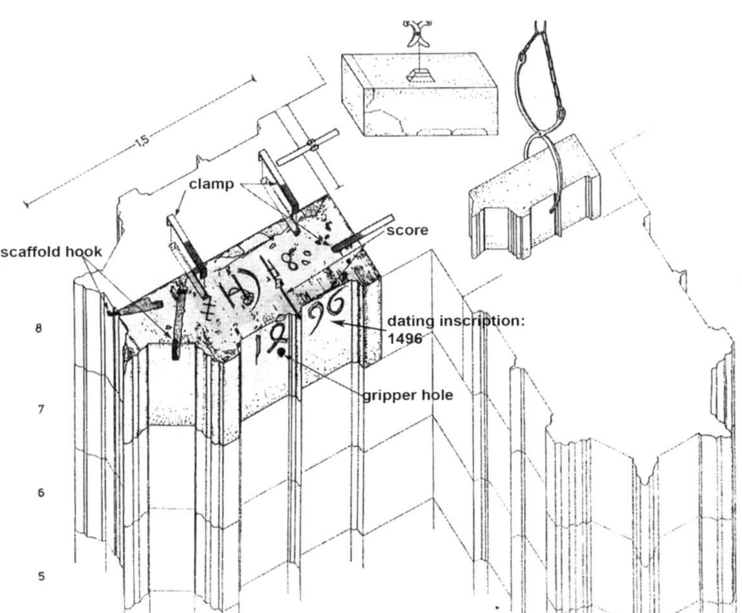

The team aimed to represent accurately how the magnificent cathedral looks like in its current state, as well as to understand its original design and how its fine structure was constructed in historic times [Fig. 2]. Therefore, apart from the general historical and building archaeological research on the medieval cathedral, a major part of the project concentrated on construction history. In order to read the traces and interpret the findings correctly, many more steps had

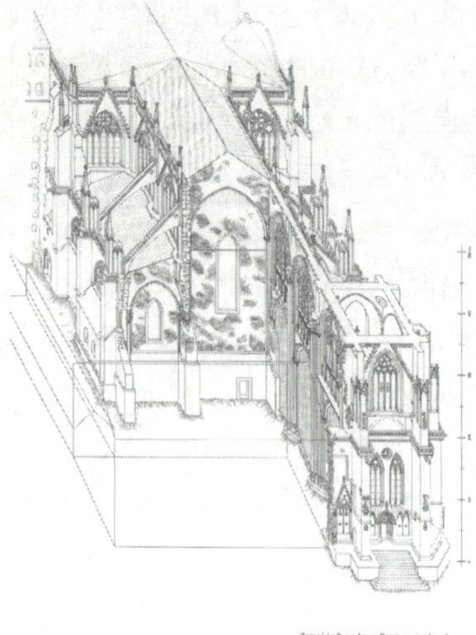

Fig.2 Regensburg Cathedral：Reconstruction drawing of the construction genesis of Regensburg Cathedral showing the building states of 1370 and 1500 [© Manfred Schuller，Katharina Papajanni，Chair for Building History，Building Archaeology and Heritage Conservation，TUM].

to be undertaken：archival and literature research，art historical research，stone and mortar expertise，investigations with x-ray and electric current for detecting metal parts — to name a selection. The data were collected in several volumes of research reports，enriched with photographs and drawings. Yet，most important for the visualisation of the acquired knowledge，this wealth of information resulted in a series of reconstruction drawings of the building process，arranged for the observer in a most intelligible way.[3]

Building Recording：from traditional hand drawing to 3D terrestrial laser scanning

How can evidence be observed and represented the best possible? How can the building be understood in the most comprehensive way? The choice of the most appropriate recording technique，therefore，is crucial and not always obvious. In the past，the surveyors carried out traditional recording campaigns with hand drawings as outcome. Today，though largely dependent on prevailed conditions，a number of different methods are available. The choice of expedient methods，therefore，constitutes the strategic starting point of any project — not only，but mostly，since the market has been flooded by measuring devices.

A few years back，the staff of the institute tested two methods by recording the same building in different ways in a competitive set up to explore each method's power and limitations. The object was a winegrower's seasonal dwelling in the vineyards in South Tyrol，Italy [Fig. 3]. The two and a half storied house with two almost identical floors，consisting of four rooms and a stately hallway each，offered perfect exper-

Fig.3 Winegrower's summer dwelling "Yngram Hof" in South Tyrol，overall photograph [© Isabel Mühlhaus for Chair for Building History，Building Archaeology and Heritage Conservation，TUM].

imental conditions.[4] Several structural and decorative features enabled a reconstruction of the five major building phases from *ca*. 1500 to present, showing the gradual enlargement of the building to its current shape. Simultaneously, we used traditional hand recording and a total station to show the advantages and shortcomings of each method. A ground plan and a section drawing were produced by each method and could be compared properly.

- The traditional hand drawing technique proved to be precise and rich in evidence, but was considerably more time-consuming on site. Apart from the time, the outcome were wonderful hand drawings, showing a world of information by the rendering of textures and the inclusion of archaeological evidence. Setting up a proper measurement system took some time and fixing the reference lines in the space and on the walls is always problematic. Such problems, however, should not exclude traditional recording from the list of improved methods. Considering that most of the drawings produced are not meant for mere documentation but as part of the wider spanning restoration process, hand drawings proved to be less flexible because they had to be redrawn in a CAD-programme for further use. Nonetheless, the hand recording team produced a complete set of documentation on site, including all evidence.

- Recording with a total station that feeds all data into the CAD-programme enabled obviously quickened workflow on site, less effort for setting up the reference system and, not the least, enabled working on higher levels without scaffolding or ladder. Comparing, in the first step, total station measuring with hand measuring always are at the expense of the abundance of details. Indeed, details such as windows or pieces of evidence have to be recorded separately and added to the CAD drawing later on. Despite completing fieldwork more quickly, the total station team took almost as long to complete the drawings to a competitive standard. A most obvious advantage is that the digital drawing can easily be shared with other people involved in the project.

Finally, the two sets of drawings were indistinguishable and offered the same density of detail, value of information and options in further use [Fig. 4]. As a conclusion, both methods proved feasible for a building of a limited size and complexity, the manageable number of required drawings and the aim of a basic documentation.

For the measuring the elevations of the building, photogrammetry was tested against the total station. Stereo-photogrammetry has been a potential recording technique for a long time. Due to the expensive expert equipment needed, the technique did not qualify for widespread use, let alone for teaching at a school of architecture. Recently developed IT-based techniques promised to reach competitive results with conventional camera equipment. The method comprises photographs from different angles — yet as orthogonal as possible — and a set of minimum five measured fix point coordinates per sectional picture. A CAD-based computer programme produces geometrically rectified single-picture photogrammetric images that can be patched to a complete elevation image. As intermediate step, they serve as basis for drawings. Moreover, these picture-plans may be regarded as results in their own right, being sufficiently significant for mapping damages or restoration project planning. Both techniques, however, revealed shortcomings in respect of the decorative details. The photogrammetry is restricted to a single geometrical plain, which means that pro- or rejecting objects have to be dealt with separately. Tachymetric measurements also have to be supplemented by closer observation and, not seldom, by detail hand measurements. In consequence of this project, the institute published a textbook on building recording, explaining and evaluating the different measurement and drawing techniques.[5]

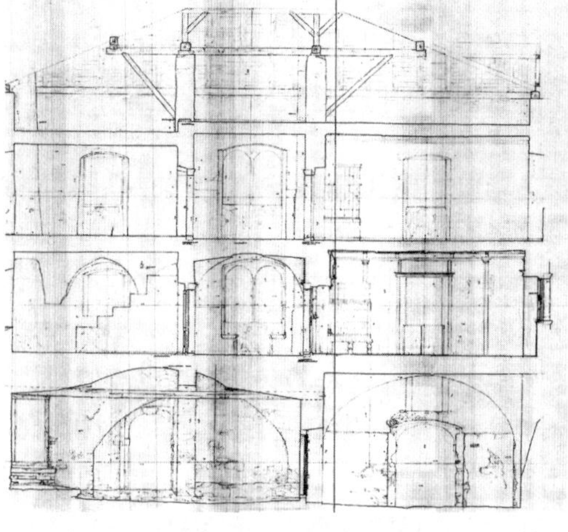

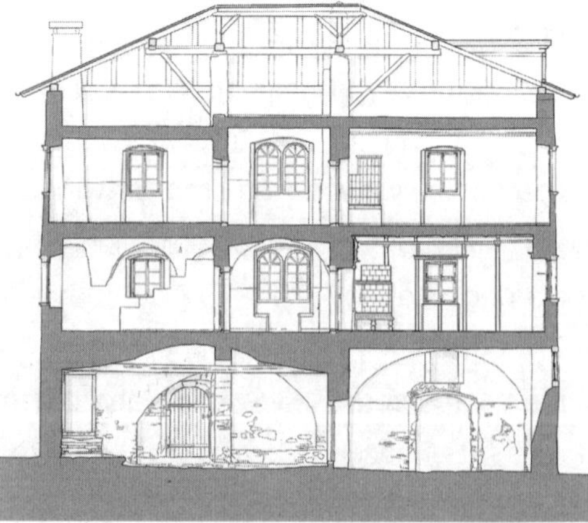

Fig.4 Winegrower's summer dwelling "Yngram Hof" in South Tyrol, recording drawings of the longitudinal section: traditional hand drawing and the respective CAD-re-drawing [© Chair for Building History, Building Archaeology and Heritage Conservation, TUM].

A general statement is that the scope of the project determines the method. Another example shows the outstanding value of terrestrial 3D scanning, even for small buildings, when both the task and the research object's state of repair require distant yet precise recording. The bell tower of a village church revealed major structural and static problems by bending over to one side quite rapidly.[6] The structural problems became obvious in severe cracks in the brickwork of the walls but their source could not be revealed without further investigation into the construction geometry. Subsequently, the first task was to find out why the tower began to lean. This required to understand how the belated added tower had been included into the main structure of the medieval church. Finally, we had to suggest ways to safeguard the historic fabric. As time on site and approach inside the tower were significantly restricted, we decided to combine two methods: scanning the interior and recording the exterior by total station. Using the total station inside the tower would have been very laborious. Terrestrial 3D scanning produced a point cloud to the so called ¼-resolution (pattern 6 mm × 6 mm with 10 m distance) of the entire interior of the building, including all the levels of the tower, required three full workdays on site. The scanned picture served as basis for the longitudinal and cross section drawings as well as the ground plans. The three-dimensional point cloud benefited the analysis because it allowed to produce a large number of horizontal and vertical section drawings at any required position. Back to the office, the laser scanning data had to be processed and transformed into drawings. The positions of the eight horizontal and four vertical section drawings was fixed in coordination with the structural engineers. The features of the building were deducted from the point cloud and the archaeological and structural evidence sketched on site had to be included. In comparison with the relatively short time on site, the worktime in the office was considerable: completing all the drawings of the interior took about hundred hours. After having exploited the scan data as thoroughly as possible, going back to the building for a close check was indispensable because of the technical limitations of scanning and inevitable shadings of some parts of the structure. Furthermore, a number of details had to be drawn more precisely, for example some structural details of the roofing and the weariness materials. These details had to be included additionally. Last but not least, the exterior of the building had to be recorded using a total station. In this case, the effort of scanning was justified by the complexity of the task and the large number of drawings that had to be geometrically referenced to one another in order to fully understand the construction of the bell tower and its stability problems.

Enhanced Plan Drawings

Recording drawings is confined to represent accurately the current state of a building, without interpretation or in-

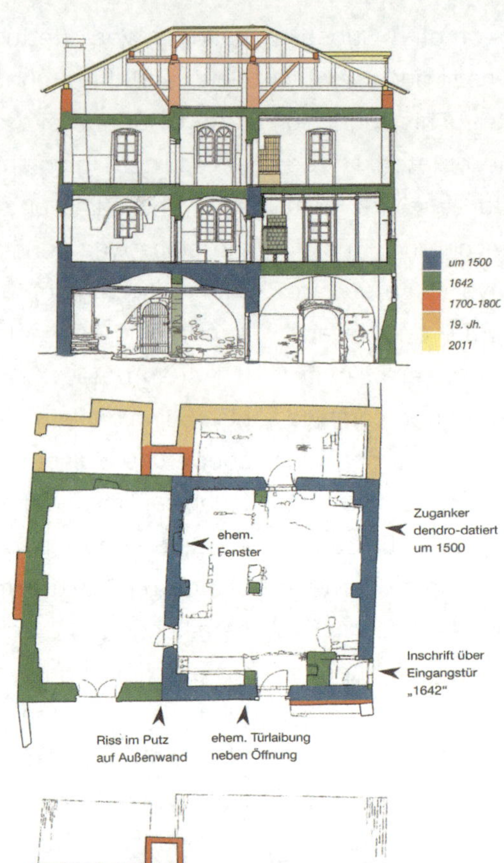

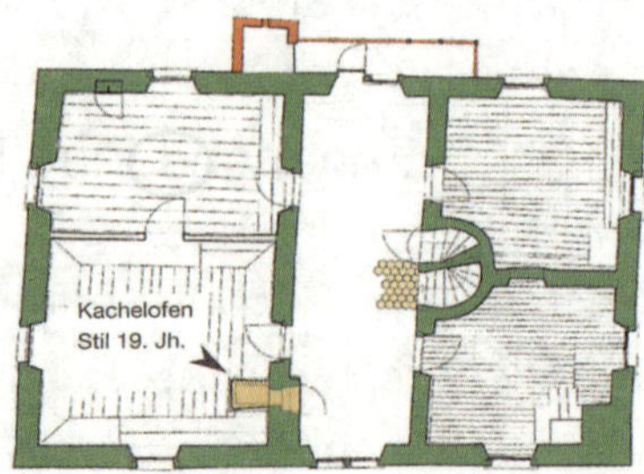

Fig.5 Phase hatching representing the construction sequence of the Yngram-Hof [© Chair for Building History, Building Archaeology and Heritage Conservation, TUM].

put of external knowledge. In a second step, the plain drawings can be enriched with insights on the historical structure, such as comments on evidence, material analyses or markings for construction phases. Furthermore, information can be added with the aim of orienting future activities, such as mapping of conservation measures or highlighting of especially valuable and therefore intangible parts of the edifice when planning new uses [Fig. 5].

Documentation Methods: catalogues of findings, written report and room book

Full extent building archaeological documentation encompasses more formats than plan drawings and must include a reporting essay, a systematic catalogue of the found evidence or room-by-room capture to envisage the spatial conditions of architectural features. The main difference is the approach from either the analytic historical or the architectural design point of view. Here again, the purpose and the future processing of the results are determining factors.

Findings and evidence need to be recorded in a scientific catalogue. Although there are manifold ways to structure the matter, every catalogue should share the scope of representing phenomena as precise as possible: layers of paint or coating, traces of refurbishment, changes of plan during a construction phase, marks as sole remains of lost building elements, etc. Due to its format, a catalogue lists all evidence and allows to interpret the very finding, but fails in placing the evidence in a larger context. Therefore, the written report provides an opportunity to summarize, interpret and evaluate the findings in-situ as well as other complementary sources. By organizing all information to a gapless tale, the building archaeologist brings the history of the place back to life.

When building archaeological research is the first step towards the restoration of an entire building, the 'room book' provides a solid base. Each room, identified with an alphanumerical code, is represented by a systematic set of data: 1. geometric information (distances, area, height), 2. architectural information about walls, floor and ceiling (construction and surfaces including colours and decoration, windows, doors, etc.), 3. cross-disciplinary information (evidence from investigations, results of material expertise, etc.). In the further steps of a conservation project, the aims of the architects and/or restorers, the requirements of conservation authorities and the measures of expert planners can be added. After completion of the project, the 'room book' becomes a highly valuable documentary record.

From Research to Conservation

Building Archaeology makes use of construction theories and practices derived from the known building processes and examinable objects in order to explain strategies of the past with the aim to improve the future of the building. Scientific research concentrates both on history of knowledge and theory development based on in-situ evidence as framework for architectural practice. In C20, for quite a while, the artificial value seemed to have displaced the construction, but Building Archaeology returned to its original focus of analysing the construction, including all traces of production and transport. Understanding how a building arose from its foundations and telling the story of the development of an artefact results in an equal safeguarding of knowledge and fabric.[7] Building Archaeology, therefore, is not only a looking-back research discipline, a pure *art pour l'art,* nice to know but meritless. On the contrary, Building Archaeology provides conservators and architects with indispensable knowledge about the building stock and about the historic construction techniques. Building archaeologists investigate deeply into the structural conditions, the state of repair, origins of damages and decay. Practical advice on future repairs can only be derived from this profound knowledge about materials and assembling. Supplying the knowledge often correlates with involvement in the planning of restoration measures.

Furthermore, the theoretical approaches of architectural research as well as the development of strategies for heritage value assessments and value-orientated preservation of the building stock are most important aspects. Visionary theory entities can solely develop on the cognition of the past. After having learned from the material evidence, the building archaeologist leaves the level of observation and shifts to the level of the scientific discourse. Adequate architectural concepts within existing building stock rest on awareness of historical impressions and the interpretation thereof. Appropriate refurbishment and careful use are the best ways to maintain the built heritage. Reading the traces and communicating the findings to other specialists involved belong to the noblest tasks of the building archaeologist: give the past a future.

notes

① Schuller, Manfred, *Building Archaeology*, Series Monuments and Sites, 7, Paris-Munich: ICOMOS, 2002.

② For more information see the institute's website: www.baufo.ar.tum.de.

③ Schuller, Manfred; Hubel, Achim (eds), *Der Dom zu Regensburg 2010-2016*, Regensburg: Friedrich Pustet Verlag, 2016.

④ In terms of technical complexity, the chosen object for this exercise has been a very simple example for the employment of total station recording. Yet, scope of the experiment was the comparison of results and time management between two different measuring techniques in a sensible setting, not testing the technological capacity. Both techniques, of course, can be employed at much more complex projects, especially since the reflectorless and contactless measurement technique with a total station allows for decisively larger distances and heights.

⑤ Busen, Tobias; Knechtel, Miriam; Knobling, Clemens; Nagel, Elke; Schuller, Manfred; Todt, Birte, *Bauaufnahme*, 2nd ed., Munich: TUM University Press, 2017.

⑥ Project carried out by the author on behalf of strebewerk. Architekten GmbH Stuttgart and Wüsteney Vermessung, Esslingen.

⑦ Hassler, Uta (ed), *Bauforschung: Zur Rekonstruktion des Wissens*, Zurich: vdf Hochschulverlag AG an der ETH Zürich, 2010, p. 81.

几何学、宇宙论以及中国早期佛教建筑的设计：从嵩岳寺塔的平面谈起

Geometry，Cosmology，and the Design of Early Buddhist Architecture in China：The Plan of the Songyuesi Pagoda

梅晨曦 | Tracy MILLER
左拉拉　译 | Translated by ZUO Lala

摘要：本文试图论证嵩岳寺塔的平面反映了一种在南亚早已被广泛使用的建筑设计手段——利用几何图形对寺庙建筑进行加密以取得“生”的力量。笔者在义慈惠石柱小石殿底座的关键位置发现了一些由圆构成的图形，而这些图形显示了如何用圆来构成一朵象征永生的莲花。同样的设计也被用在决定义慈惠石柱小石殿的柱网布局以及嵩岳寺塔平面的内外部比例。在南亚，这样的设计亦用来展现“梵天实在曼荼罗”——一种用来构建印度教或佛教寺庙平面的图形。这种图形早在公元后就在南亚发展起来了。在敦煌的占卜文献中也发现了具有同样外观的图形，这意味着在中国早期的历史中，人们就试图用图形设计来控制时间以及未来。这项设计手段的使用赋予建筑以生命并提高了佛教建筑的宗教功效。这可能也帮助了佛教“真谛”在东亚的传播与接受。

关键词：嵩岳寺；义慈惠石柱；塔；梵天实在曼荼罗；占卜图；佛教建筑与仪式

Abstract：This article argues that the plan of the Songyuesi Pagoda reflects design strategies popularized in South Asia to encode temple architecture with generative power. Using a diagram found in key locations of the abacus and miniature hall supported by the Yicihui Pillar，the author demonstrates how the circle could be used to produce an infinitely regenerating lotus blossom. The same design scheme was employed both to determine the columniation of the Yicihui Pillar miniature hall，but also the interior and exterior proportions of the Songyuesi Pagoda plan. It was also used to layout the Vāstupuruṣa maṇḍala，the building diagram used as a ground plan for Indic temples（Hindu as well as Buddhist）developing during the early centuries CE. Its appearance in later divinatory diagrams preserved at Dunhuang suggests an association with attempts to control time and the future in early imperial China. The use of this design technique to enliven the structure and enhance the efficacy of Buddhist architecture may have helped prove the truthfulness of Buddhist teachings in East Asia.

Keywords：Songyuesi；Yicihui Pillar；pagoda；Vāstupuruṣa maṇḍala；Divinatory diagrams；Buddhist architecture and ritual

作者简介：
梅晨曦，美国范德堡大学（Vanderbilt University）。
译者简介：
左拉拉，美国海军学院（United States Naval Acadeny）

笔者近年致力于探究在中国中世纪礼制建筑的设计过程中，完美的几何图形（例如圆以及正多边形，译者注）是否被运用在提高礼制建筑的功效上。笔者已在其他文章中论及，河北义慈惠石柱的浮雕显示了早在公元六世纪东亚的佛教建筑就已采用了在南亚建筑中常见的利用曼荼罗图形设计的方法。[①]作为这一课题的一部分，本文将通过对河南嵩山嵩岳寺塔（北魏，523年，图1）平面的分析，来继续考察这一设计方法的意义。[②]

虽然义慈惠石柱（图2）与嵩岳寺塔在外观形式上不尽相同，但两者皆为建造于公元六世纪的佛教建筑或纪念物。并且，两者在设计上都融合了8与12这两个数字的概念，以表达时间与空间的区分。例如，笔者在义慈惠石柱上发现了刻有象征宇宙生成的莲花与圆的图案。而将这些图案等比例地镌刻在佛教建筑或纪念物中，则类似于对佛教建筑或纪念物加入一种特殊的密码。笔者认为，这种通过图像或几何图形对佛教建筑或纪念物进行“加密”的体系，是通过佛教由南亚传至东亚的。南亚寺庙的实例更反映了在南亚无论是印度教建筑还是佛教建筑，都可能利用了这一图像体系将宗教的力量赋予高层寺庙建筑，同时亦起到了保护建筑内部的作用。

早在汉代，中国人就采用了同样的几何图形来描绘宇宙——汉代的铜镜与占卜文献中都能找到相似的几何图案，用来表达与塑造天、地、人之间的关系。因此，本文将试图论证这些原本就存在于中国的图案与由南亚传入的佛教建筑中的几何设计方法的相似性，可能大大提升了佛教在东亚的关注度与接受度。中国传统占卜中所使用的这些神奇的几何图案与佛教建筑中的莲花造型平面之间的相似性可能更容易使人相信这一类事物具有诞生与转换生命的力量。

图1 河南嵩山嵩岳寺塔（北魏，523年，高39.5米）正立面（图片来源：作者）（左）

图2 河北定兴义慈惠石柱（石灰石，高7米，公元567-570年）（图片来源：作者）（右）

一、义慈惠石柱与具有生成功能的圆

义慈惠石柱的建造日期略晚于嵩岳寺塔，它是中国佛教建筑保留印度建筑设计方法的重要证据。义慈惠石柱高7米，自下而上分别由五个部分组成：

（1）刻有十二瓣覆盆莲花的柱础；

（2）自下而上略有收分的八边形柱；

（3）水平放置于柱顶的长方形石盘；

（4）立于石盘之上面阔三间进深两间的微型石殿；

（5）由另一块独立石料构成的石殿屋顶。[③]

义慈惠石柱的表面刻有一篇3400余字的碑文，记载了石柱的建造历史，并提供了超过200名佛教结社成员的姓名。[④]石柱的前身原为木柱，约在公元 567—570 年间改为石柱。

从外观上看，义慈惠石柱上的微型石殿采用了源自黄河流域的典型中国宫殿建筑的形制，而非南亚建筑。然而，石殿的柱网设计却显示了来自南亚的佛教宇宙观念（图 3）。⑤

这座长方形石殿面南背北，正面四柱，侧面三柱，形成了三间乘以两间的格局。南立面与北立面的当心间均有一尊坐佛，次间则刻有窗户。在东西两侧的山墙上，每一间的正中均刻有一个七环相套的图案。同样的图案也被刻在了石殿基座的底部，并与四方角石的位置一一对应（图 4）。在每两块角石之间，又共有六幅八瓣莲花图，其中南北长边上各两幅，东西短边上各一幅。这些八瓣莲花的外接圆与位于角石位置的七环相套图的外接圆的直径相同。刻在石盘底部四个七环相套图与六个八瓣莲花图在数量上（以及位置上，译者注）恰恰对应了石殿的十根柱子。此外，另一种莲花图案，分别两两位于石盘的东西两边，共四幅。另外，还有一些圆环与圆盘的图案嵌在八瓣莲花图的中间。在整个石盘底部，既刻有自然形态的莲花，又刻有几何（抽象，译者注）形态的莲花。

图 3　义慈惠石柱中的微型石殿及石刻细节（图片来源：作者）

图 4　义慈惠石柱中的石盘及浮雕细节（图片来源：作者）

二、义慈惠石柱莲花图案的衍生

进一步分析这些八瓣莲花图的形成过程，或许会发现一些神奇的特点（图 5）。首先，七环相套图是通过用圆规来分割圆而形成的。从几何学的基础知识可知，圆周可以由它的半径等分成六份。因此，用任意半径画一个圆，以圆周上任意位置为圆心，再画出另一个同等半径的圆，令其圆周与原来的圆心相交。将两个圆周上的交点分别与两个圆心相连，便可获得一个 60 度的锐角。依此重复操作，则可将处于中心的圆等分，并形成一个花朵的形状。将外侧圆周相交的点与中间的圆心继续相连，则又可获得一个 60 度的锐角，这样可以将圆继续等分成 12 份，并且能很快获得一个直角。继续在这些位置画圆，则可将圆等分成 24 份。此时，最中心的圆内形成了一个放射状的（十二瓣，译者注）莲花图形。

如果在一座建筑基址上放置一根垂直木桩，并且以这跟木桩的位置为圆心画一段弧，在弧上分别记录下日出和日落时的阴影位置，再作一根弦连接记录点，便可以找到东西方向。通过圆规再作两段等半径的相交弧，则可以找到正北方向。最后以木桩为圆心画一个完整的圆，则可以得到一个被等分成四份的圆。将这个被四等分的圆再进行八等分，则可以用来构建一个完美的正方形，同时也确定了东西南北的方向。此时正中的花朵图案直径略小于之前的七环相套图，这就是在八瓣莲花图中莲心的位置。事实上（在义慈惠石柱的石刻上，译者注），工匠花了很大力气来展现这两种图案（七环相套图与八瓣莲花图，译者注）之间的联系。八瓣莲花图的使用显示了当时的工匠已经熟练掌握了这套方法，但仍在试图融入对南北方向的定位（图 6）。义慈惠石柱上的七环相套图尚且无法做到南北定向——严格来说它仍然只是“圆”而不是“方”。

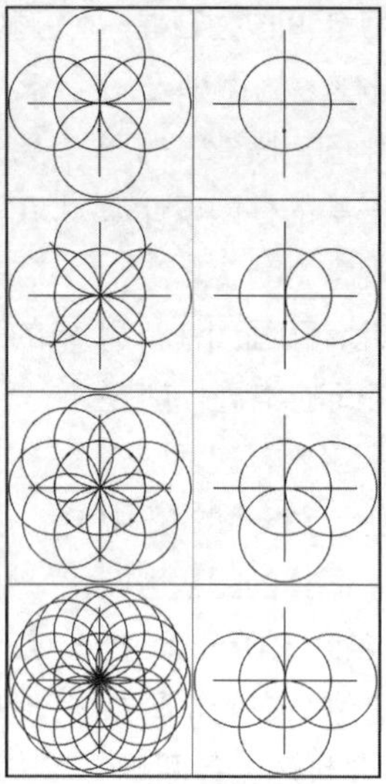

图 5　图示一个圆被 6 个或者 12 个同直径的圆等分（图片来源：作者）（左）

图 6　图示一个圆被 8 个或者 16 个同直径的圆等分（图片来源：作者）（右）

这一几何体系不但被用来制作这两种石刻图案，而且还被用来确定佛殿的平面。对以木结构为主的中国建筑来说，确定柱网的位置及其与结构的对应关系是一项最重要的工作。[⑥]通过对石盘上这些图案的观察，可以发现这些图案与石殿平面之间的联系。石盘底部四个角石的位置上分别刻有七环相套图（图 7）；而八瓣莲花图，又被两两置于石殿的南北两侧。同样，东西两侧也各有一朵八瓣莲花图。如前文所述，这十个图案恰好对应了石殿的十根柱子。[⑦]

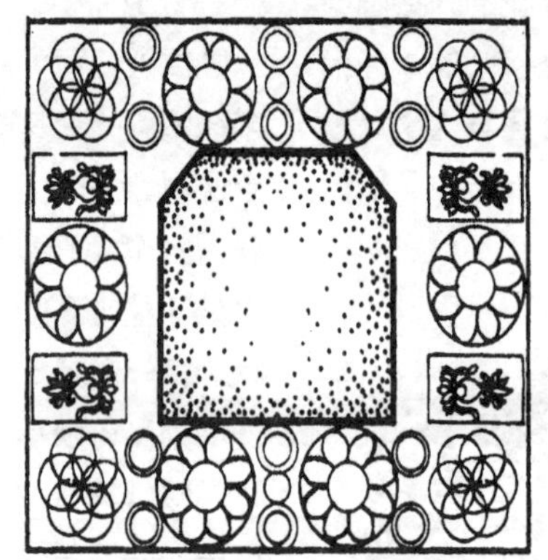

图 7　义慈惠石柱石盘底部浮雕（图片来源：《刘敦桢全集》，第二卷，171 页）

如以石殿面阔作为圆的直径，绘制一个放大的七环相套图并与石殿的矩形平面叠加，则可发现：矩形平面的长边恰恰穿过圆弧交点，并被圆周分成了三间；矩形的短边被则被分成两间（图 8）。据此可以找到角柱的位置，并确定角柱与其他柱子之间的距离。（也就是说，石殿平面柱网布局可由这个七环相套图决定。译者注。）

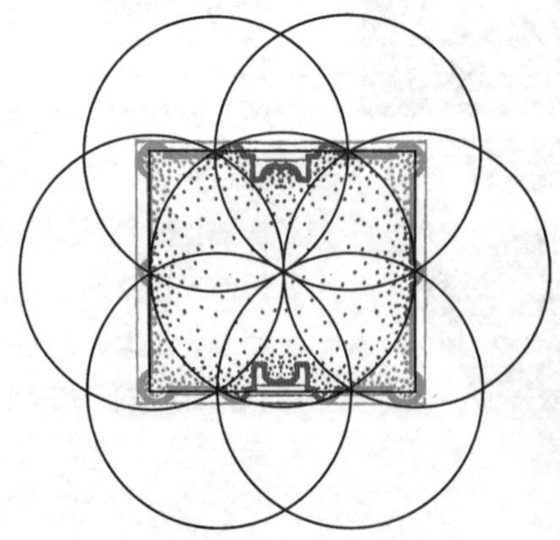

图 8　图示以石殿宽度为直径的圆被 6 个穿过石殿中心的同直径的圆等分（图片来源：作者根据《刘敦桢全集》，第二卷，171 页重绘）

此外，七环相套图与八瓣莲花图（图 9）以及柱础上的十二瓣覆盆莲花也有生成关系（图 10）。这样就得到了两个相互联系的元素：一个是圆规可对圆进行无限分割的可能；另一

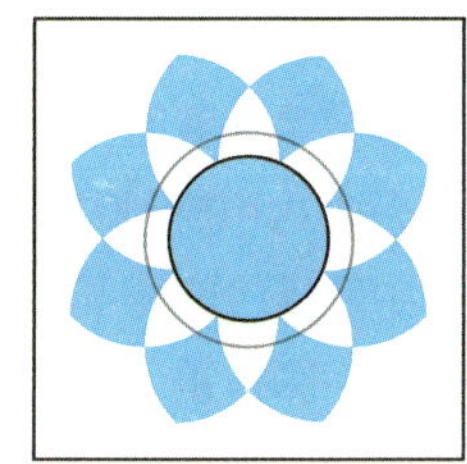

图 9 图示一个圆被 8 个而不是 6 个同直径的圆等分，其中心可产生一朵直径略小的花萼。因此八瓣莲花的图案可以用同样的方法获得（图片来源：作者）

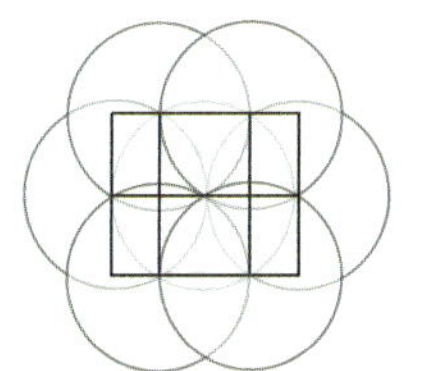

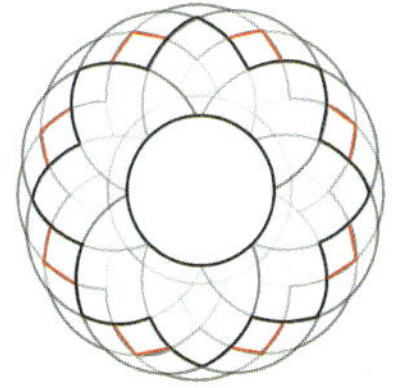

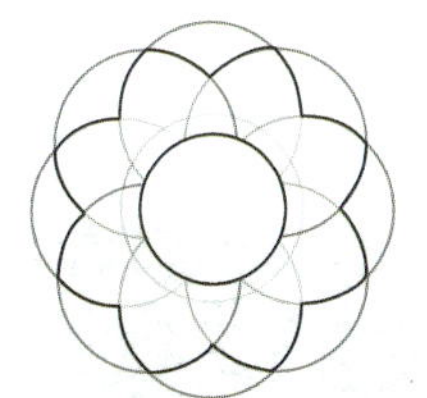

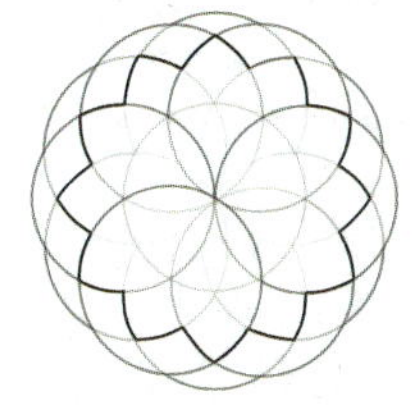

图 10 义慈惠石柱莲花图案设计的渐进思路（图片来源：作者）

个是莲花作为一种自然生物有传送能量并赋予重生力量的潜能。这两种元素都在南亚早期的宗教建筑中存在。

三、时间、空间及宇宙再生对印度寺庙建筑的加密

佛教建筑 / 纪念物的设计反映了南亚寺庙建筑的象征意义。南亚的许多文献已经证明，形式上精确的建筑图形，特别是“梵天实在曼荼罗”（Vāstupuruṣa maṇḍala），常被用来赋予寺庙建筑诞生与重生的力量。虽然伐罗诃密希罗在公元六世纪编写的天文著作《广集》（*Bṛihat Saṃhitā*）为我们提供了“梵天实在曼荼罗”的图像，然而实际技术的运用早已存在了很长一段时间。佛教建筑 / 纪念物中所体现出的建筑文化事实上是广义的南亚宗教景观的一部分。在印度，即使看似印度教的建筑，实际上也有可能是佛教寺庙。[⑧]“梵天实在曼荼罗”极有可能也曾被运用于佛教高层寺庙的平面规划中。佛教建筑的建造者希望通过同样的手段来对佛教寺庙进行“加密”，以期能够掌控时间和空间。[⑨]

让我们来看一下这种“加密”是怎么做到的。在南亚祭祀建筑中，最重要的两个部分就是坛与柱。早在公元六世纪到七世纪，大部分印度教寺庙就依靠“梵天实在曼荼罗”的方形网格来规划平面，具体地再现了神坛作为第一道献祭，以防恶魔阻止天地分离、季节时间的轮回（图 11）。[⑩]

这些静止的几何平面（象征坛，译者注）则以曼荼罗中心象征性的柱为轴进行旋转。静止的几何平面通过旋转便被赋予了仪式的力

量。美国印度艺术史学家 Kramrisch 在她的著作《印度教寺庙》中解释道，曼荼罗衍生出来的坛也被理解为是一种用来表达和控制时间的工具——这与《考工记》中所描绘的情况类似：人们利用日出与日落时的阴影位置可将一块选定的建筑基址分成东西两块，然后再分南北，最后可以被进一步地分割，“因此利用这种几何的推进，原先的 2 点变成了 4，然后是 8，然后再是 16 与 32。”[11]

组成坛的方形砖的位置由曼荼罗所决定，共同形成了对年、季、时间的象征。因此，曼荼罗通过月亮的盈亏以及太阳运动所产生的日与年显示了生与重生，创造与再创造的力量。

根据网格的布局，曼荼罗的中间可以是一个点，也可以是一个方格（常见为 8×8 或者 9×9 的方格）。这里是婆罗门的空间，象征生的力量。在更早的年代，这种力量则位于印度教寺庙的“藏住舍”（garbha gṛha）的位置，通常用一朵莲花的图案来显示它的重要性。象征着每年春天花胚从黑暗的“生”的中心升起，孕育出神圣的花朵。在印度迪欧加一座六世纪的寺庙中，也有图像描绘了同样的场景（图 12）。至于更晚近的建筑平面中莲花的位置也一模一样。

另一位南亚艺术史学者 Michael Meister 表示，圆形被用来决定曼荼罗方位的一部分原因可能是因为曼荼罗的几何力量（图 13）。方形曼荼罗的四个角通常被认为是弱点，最易受到恶魔的入侵。既然高层印度教寺庙变得越来越复杂，那么用一个圆形来衍生出方形曼荼罗，甚至旋转原来的网格平面，或许可以保护建筑的四个角。Meister 表示，将这座在七世纪以前建造的八边形的湿婆庙旋转 45 度会比简单的方形更好地帮助这座建筑抗击负面的力量，但与此同时方形的吠陀坛还是被保留了下来（图 14、图 15）。

除了避邪作用以外，Meister 认为使用圆形来生成方形的技术也保留了结合其他宇宙时间观的可能，例如被旋转的星球以及十二宫等概念。这些都是公元初从西亚传入南亚的。如

32 units around the perimeter
(regents of the 4 planets
and 28 Nakshatras)
center contains
generative principal
PĀPARĀKṢASĪ
PILIPIÑJĀ
CARAKĪ
JAMBHAKA
ŚARVA-SKANDA
PŪTANĀ
ARYAMAN
VIDĀRĪ

ROGA	AHI	MUKHYA	BHALLĀṬA	SOMA	BHUJAGA	ADITI	DITI	AGNI
PĀPA-YAKṢMAN	RUDRA						ĀPA	PARJANYA
ŚOṢA		RĀJA YAKṢMAN	PṚTHIVĪDHARA			ĀPA VATSA		JAYANTA
ASURA		MITRA	brahman			ARYAMAN		INDRA
VARUṆA								SŪRYA
KUSUMA-DANTA								SATYA
SUGRĪVA		INDRA	VIVASVĀN			SAVITṚ		BHṚŚA
DAU-VĀRIKA	JAYĀ						SĀVITRA	ANTAR-IKṢA
PITARAḤ	MṚGA	BHṚṄGA-RĀJA	GAN-DHARVA	YAMA	BṚHAT-KṢATA	VITATHA	PŪṢAN	ANIḶA

图 11　根据伐罗诃密希罗所著的《广集》而重绘的“梵天实在曼荼罗”的 9x9 网格（图片来源：Stella Kramrisch，*The Hindu Temple*，卷一，32 页）

图 12　位于印度迪欧高的毗湿奴庙，建造于笈多王朝时期（公元 525 年）。神庙南面的雕刻刻画了毗湿奴诞生时莲花上的梵天从他的肚脐中缓缓升起的形象（图片来源：密西根大学艺术史系图像资料库）

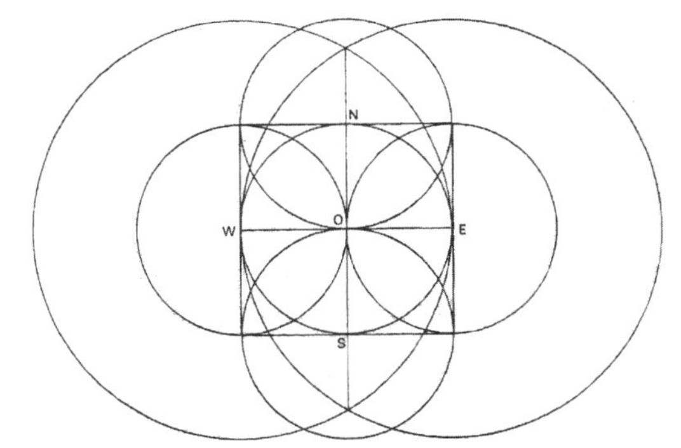

图 13 《绳法经》中所记载的由圆衍生出方形的方法（图片来源：Michael Meister）

果寺庙的建造者通过曼荼罗来取得神圣的力量、驾驭时间的轮回，那么在建造过程中结合一种新的宇宙观可能会增加它的力量和潜力。事实上，《广集》的作者伐罗诃密希罗是一位星相学家、天文学家以及数学家。因此，将这样的技术用在预言未来以及中国黄河流域的高层佛教建筑中时，并不应该令人惊奇。

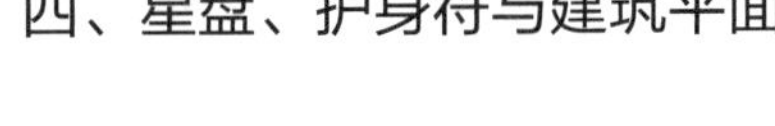

四、星盘、护身符与建筑平面

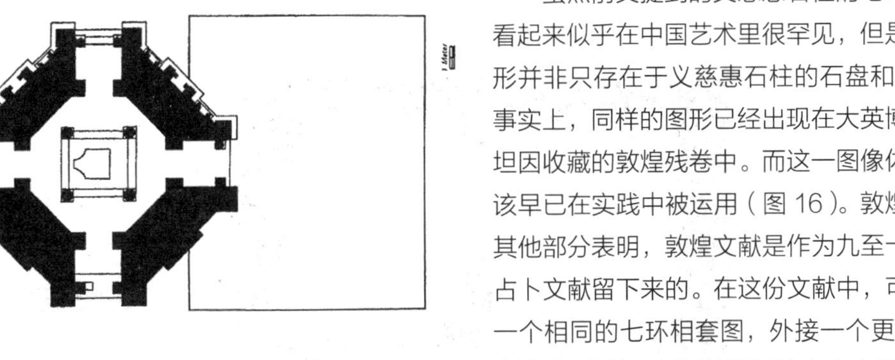

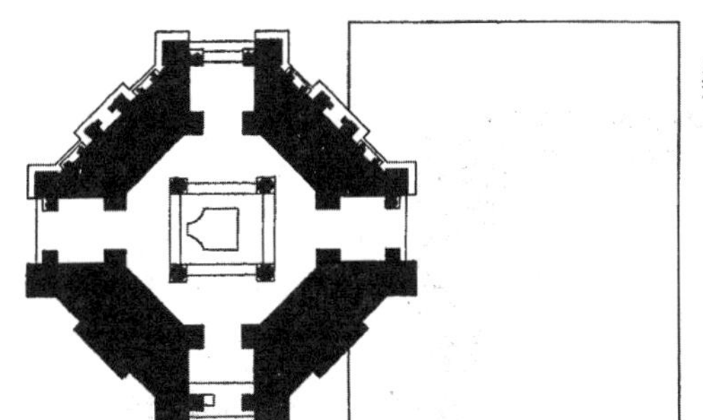

图 14　位于印度比哈尔邦 Muṇḍeśvrī 的湿婆庙平面（公元 636 年）（图片来源：Michael Meister）

虽然前文提到的义慈惠石柱的七环相套图看起来似乎在中国艺术里很罕见，但是这个图形并非只存在于义慈惠石柱的石盘和石殿上。事实上，同样的图形已经出现在大英博物馆斯坦因收藏的敦煌残卷中。而这一图像体系，应该早已在实践中被运用（图 16）。敦煌文献的其他部分表明，敦煌文献是作为九至十世纪的占卜文献留下来的。在这份文献中，可以看到一个相同的七环相套图，外接一个更大的圆。在这里，它被二项制的天干地支六十甲子包围，最外围则是五行。

通过对天干地支六十循环记日法的研究，Kalinowiski 认为圆形的构图可以帮助人们找到一个合适的二项式来确定他们的生年。她观察到，八卦卦相的分布是用正方形的角或边来表示八个方向。因此，圆形的布局与八卦是相连的，时间的循环亦与八个方向相关。至此，时间与空间相连，这恰恰与南亚的曼荼罗异曲同工。[12]

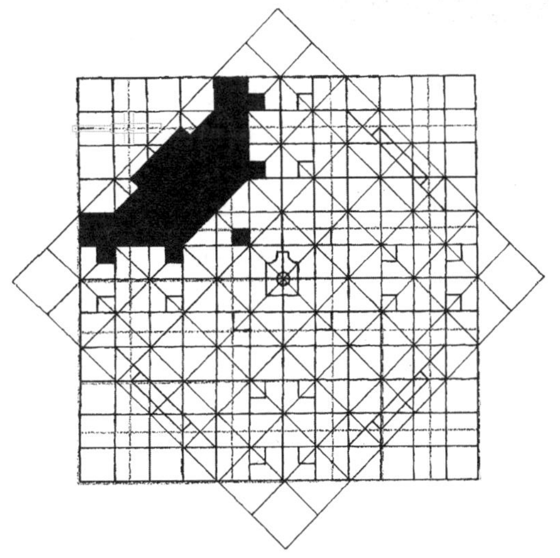

图 15　位于印度比哈尔邦 Muṇḍeśvrī 的湿婆庙平面；此图显示被旋转的方形网格可作为设计辅助工具（图片来源：Michael Meister）

这样的图形在更早的东周、两汉以及六朝时期的占卜文献中均有涉及。它与在汉代同时出现的规矩镜之间的相似性更引人注意。虽然 Kalinoswiski 没有讨论到规矩镜，但是规矩镜图像中表现的用半径将圆进行完美的六分，则一定与对宇宙的理解有关，与六十甲子也有数字上的对应。规矩镜的设计也显示出用圆规来切分圆早已被汉代工匠知晓（图 17）。

当然，占卜并不只是算命。丰富的文献已显示占卜术与对宇宙的理解之间的关系。例如在《淮南子》中，作者试图发现年、季、日循环的规律，以此来改善健康、在战争中获胜以及延年益寿，最理想的目标则是逃脱死亡。曾蓝莹，Marc Kalinowski，John Major 以及其他一些学者都谈论过铜镜的形式或多或少展现了当时的人们对这个世界的认知。在这个前提下，所有的图案都是“天体图”或者“星图”，圆形被视作宇宙的中心。用来设计镜子的数学魔法似乎成了汉代及后世流行的护身符。[13]

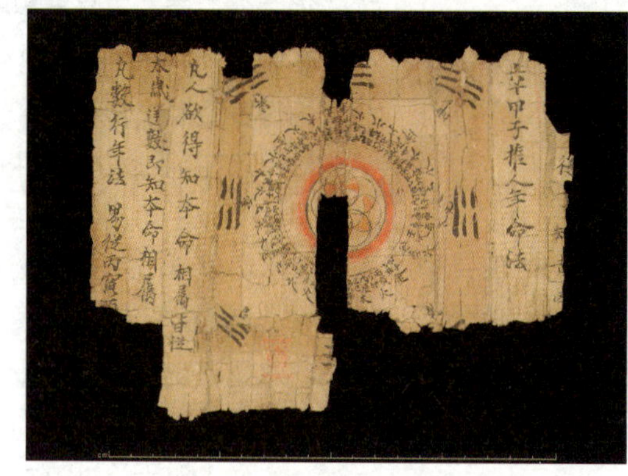

图 16 莫高窟文献中的占卜图形（公元 9 世纪到 10 世纪，纸墨，宽 4.2 厘米）（图片来源：大不列颠图书馆；大不列颠博物馆）

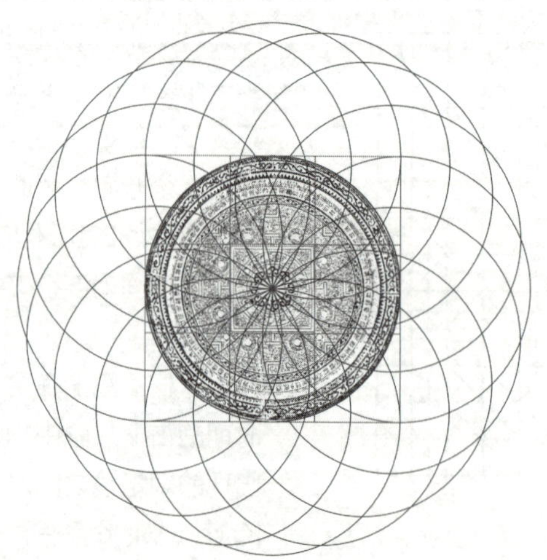

图 17 江苏尹湾汉墓四号墓出土的青铜规矩镜（直径 27.5 厘米，公元 1 世纪早期）。16 个与铜镜等直径的圆形穿过铜镜的圆心，形成了位于铜镜中心正方形内的“花朵”图案（图片来源：根据曾蓝莹，“Representation and Appropriation”，图五绘制）

五、嵩岳寺塔是用来占卜的建筑吗？

嵩岳寺最初为永平年间北魏皇帝的行宫，在公元 520 年时变成了寺庙，并命名为嵩高闲居寺，之后塔开始兴建直到 523 年完成。[14] 现在嵩岳寺塔 15 层的密檐结构高 39.5 米，矗立在一米高的台基上。塔基外圆直径为 10.6 米，内圆直径为 5 米。砖墙包括的地方有 2.5 米厚。从二层开始，平面的外延是十二边形，内沿则是八边形（图 18）。在主层（二层），十二边形的每边都有一个类似神殿的单层小龛，龛顶作窣堵坡形，龛与龛之间被一根柱子分开（图 19）。再往上的每一层，每一面都有一个拱门和两扇窗，与义慈惠石柱上的石殿类似。

十二边形的平面在中国非常罕见，因此人们对嵩岳寺塔的起源及其设计素材一直有很多疑问。塔身的曲线在很长一段时间内都被认为与印度教寺庙有关。但是如果对它的平面进行旋转，则可以发现塔的设计意图是试图用这些具有占卜作用的图形来控制时间与空间。塔的内部为八边形，暗示着想要与空间契合并使建筑面向东南西北四个方位。这与印度教寺庙的设计以及占卜图中的做法一样。此外，如同在印度 Muṇḍeśvrī 的寺庙中看到的，一个 12 × 12 的网格被旋转了 45 度，正好可以找到每一个小龛的尺寸（图 20）。

莲花的图案同样在这里存在。同义慈惠石

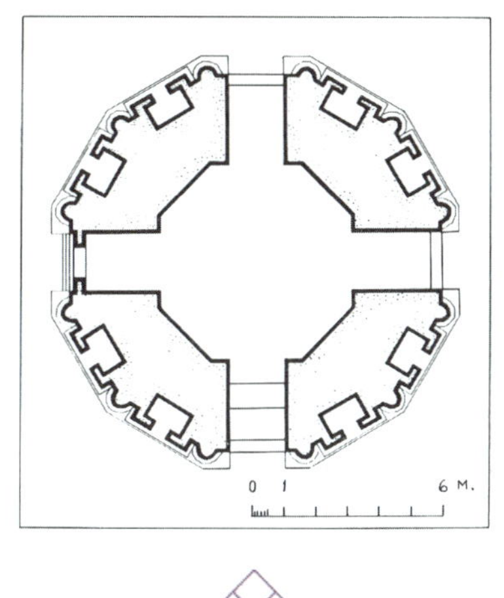

图 18　嵩岳寺二层平面；此图显示其十二边形的外轮廓及八边形的内轮廓（图片来源：范德堡大学视觉资料库）（左）

图 19　嵩岳寺塔壁龛细节（图片来源：作者）（右）

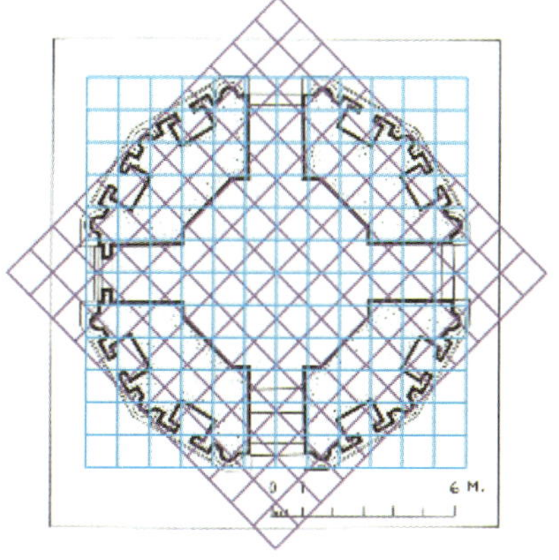

图 20　嵩岳寺塔二层平面。此图显示了一个 12×12 的网格在旋转了 45° 之后决定了塔内墙面与门廊的位置（左）

图 21　嵩岳寺塔二层平面。此图显示了 12 个穿过同一中心点的圆在塔身内部形成了一朵与塔心同直径的花朵（右）

柱一样，设计者在规划设计的时候，似乎已在头脑中用圆规生成了莲花。先从一个圆开始，然后根据嵩岳寺塔二层柱子的位置画出 12 个圆，连接莲瓣与圆弧相交的点，便可以获得一个十二边形。塔身内延的八边形的半径恰好由中心小莲花的外接圆半径确定（图 21）。

六、嵩岳寺塔平面的莲花与重生

通过将净化的概念加入具有护身符意义的早期宇宙图形中，对“莲花可以无限重生”这一概念的诠释可能改变了佛塔的形制。在古代中国除了想要延年益寿或长生不老外，早在公元前三、四世纪，对于净化与污化的担忧就很常见。[15] 因此，通过莲花来比喻纯净或者神圣的重生使得描绘“莲花藏世界”的《华严经》更为流行。在经文中，佛教宇宙被描述为由不计其数的风轮构成。在同时期的梵网经中，这种莲花是佛的宝座，在那里信仰者和菩萨都可以觐见佛，并获得保佑（图 22）。[16]“轮”这个词汇也表现了与旋转相结合的概念。用被半径完美分割的圆生成的莲花图案来设计佛教建筑平面，可能会帮助提高佛教礼拜的效用，以增强视觉化效果以及其他礼拜的实践。

七、掌控时空来创造神圣的重生

每一个风轮都有代表一整个宇宙的潜力，它即植根于本土的占卜技术，又融汇了外来的思想。然而当建造完成时，最初的设计痕迹的图案也就消失了。John Major 在 1984 年发表了讨论《淮南子》中有关图解宇宙结构的文章。[⑰] 文中说，阴阳家们比如东周的邹衍就曾经想要找到宇宙理论的共同线索。这便是中国可能接受从南亚或西亚而来的外来理论的基础。

图 22 梵网经中的莲花座（中国民间经卷，公元 5 世纪早期）（图片来源：根 据 Akira Sadakata 的 Buddhist Cosmology: Philosophy and Origins 的图 29 重绘）

图 23 嵩岳寺塔地宫中的唐代地砖（8 世纪前半叶）显示莲花由内圈的六瓣或八瓣莲心、外圈的十六瓣花瓣组成，并被 32 个圆珠环绕（图片来源：《文物》1992 年第一期 103 页图版四图五）

因此，有理由相信，各种互有关联的起源学说、宇宙的扩散以及“被净化的重生”这样的概念，通过这些几何图案来到中国，并使得南北朝时期的皇帝或普通人愿意接受。虽然这些用于建筑设计的圆并没有被发现，但是这很容易理解——占卜的技艺在实际中往往就是被刻意隐藏的。在嵩岳寺塔中，通往地宫的地砖表现了同样的主题：一个由“六”和“八”的概念建构的莲花。这一主题在义慈惠石柱中也同样得到表达（图 23）。因此，嵩岳寺塔的地基与义慈惠石柱的石盘都可以被看作是一座莲花池——如果想要逃离死亡，这便是能带来纯净的净土池。这项在南北朝时期由南亚新进引入的古老技术，正试着向它们在中国的受众证明佛教的“真谛”（Satya）。

注释：

① 有关义慈惠石柱的文章，详见“Naturalizing Buddhist Cosmology in the Temple Architecture of China: The Case of the Yicihui Pillar,” in Heaven on Earth: Temples, Ritual, and Cosmic Symbolism in the Ancient World（The University of Chicago Oriental Institute Seminars, No. 9）, ed. Deena Ragavan（Chicago: University of Chicago Press, 2013）, 17-39; “Of Palaces and Pagodas: Palatial Symbolism in the Buddhist Architecture of Early Medieval China,” Frontiers of History in China 10.2（2015）: 222-263, and “Perfecting the Mountain: On the Morphology of Towering Temples in East Asia,” Journal of Chinese Architecture History 2014（10）: 419-449.

② 义慈惠石柱位于河北省保定市定兴县石柱村，约建于北齐天统年间，公元 567 至 570 年。嵩岳寺塔位于河南省登封市嵩山南麓，为中国现存最古老的密檐塔，约建成于公元 523 年，北魏正光年间。译者注。

③ 参见傅熹年编 . 中国古代建筑史第二版 [M]. 北京：中国建筑工业出版社，2009. 以及刘敦桢 . “定兴县北齐石柱，” 刘敦桢全集，第二卷 [M]. 北京：中国建筑工业

出版社，2007. 将笔者的图片与刘敦桢团队在 20 世纪 30 年代考察的资料作对比，笔者并不确定付熹年文中使用的是旧的尺寸还是新的尺寸。此外，为了便于保护，石柱现已完全被一座亭子所遮盖。

④ 刘淑芬 . 北齐标异乡义慈惠石柱——中古佛教社会救济的个案研究新史学 4.5（1995），p. 41.

⑤ 关于中国早期宫殿与宗教建筑的木结构传统，参见刘叙杰 . 中国古代建筑史，第一卷，原始社会，夏商周秦汉建筑，第二版 [M]. 北京：中国建筑工业出版社，2009. 关于汉代及汉代以前几何图形在明堂礼制建筑中的运用，参见 Lillian Lan-ying Tseng.Picturing Heaven in Early China[M]. Cambridge，Mass.：Harvard University Asian Center，2011：37-88.

⑥ 证据显示外国访客早已认识到中国宫殿建筑中柱间距的重要性，并将其复制在他们自己的宫殿中。参见 William H. Coaldrake，Architecture and Authority in Japan[M]. London and New York：Routledge，1996：62.

⑦ 再次感谢 Jinah Kim 在这个问题上的观察。

⑧ 佛教徒结合了许多运用在高层寺庙建筑中象征印度教神祇的手段。如 Debala Mitra，Pramod Chandra，以及其他一些印度学者所讨论的，南亚的各种建筑类型包括萃堵波佛塔、石窟寺以及高层寺庙，不仅用作佛教用途，也被其他宗教团体的信众所采用。尽管有些神庙看起来似为佛教所建，同一批工匠也可能参与了其他任意教派的建筑的建设。详见 Debala Mitra.Buddhist Monuments[M].Calcutta：Sahitya Samsad，1971：21-56，especially 52；Pramod Chandra.On the Study of Indian Art[M]. Cambridge：Harvard University Press 1983：22.

⑨ 针对高层印度教寺庙、梵天实在曼荼罗与佛塔的关系已经有许多讨论。见张弓 . 汉唐佛寺文化史 [M]. 北京：中国社会科学出版社，1997；吴庆洲 . 建筑哲理意匠与文化 [M]. 北京：中国建筑工业出版社，2005. 感谢吴庆洲教授对这一课题研究提出的宝贵意见。

⑩ 这里对印度教寺庙建筑宇宙观的解释来自 Stella Kramrisch. The Hindu Temple. 2 Volumes[M]. Delhi：Shri Jainendra Press reprint ed.，1980，especially Vol. 1，pp. 21-97. Kramrisch 对《广集》中的一段引用注解道：“梵天实在曼荼罗的形状是方形的……它可以转变为三角形、六边形、八边形以及等面积的圆并保持同样的象征意义” Kramrisch 1980，Vol. 1，21.

⑪ Kramrisch 1980，Vol. 1，30.

⑫ Marc Kalinowski，“Time，Space And Orientation：Figurative Representation of the Sexagenary Cycle in Ancient and Medieval China，” in Graphics and Text in the Production of Technical Knowledge in China：The Warp and the Weft，ed. Georges Meiailie.Vira Dorofeeva-Lichtmann，and Francesca Bray[M]. Leiden：Brill，2007：140.

⑬ “It finally relates visual production to personal welfare，pledging everlasting prosperity，glory and happiness. 它最终将视觉表现与个人福祉、永续繁衍的誓言、荣耀与幸福联系在一起。” 见 Lillian Tseng.Representation and Appropriation：the TLV Mirror in Han China[J]. Early China，2004，29：206.

⑭ 另外一个原因可能与宋云（约六世纪）以及他的团队在公元 522 年从印度回到北魏首都有关。参见 Édouard Chavannes.Voyage de Song Yun dans l'Udyāna et le Gandhāra[J]. Bulletin de l'Ecole française d'Extrême-Orient Volume 3，Numéro 1（1903）.

⑮ Lillian Tseng，“Representation and Appropriation，” 206.

⑯ Exposition of the Sūtra of the Brahma's Net，translated by A. Charles Muller，205-206.

⑰ John S. Major，“The Five Phases，Magic Squares，and Schematic Cosmography，” in Explorations in Early Chinese Cosmology，ed. Henry Rosemont，Jr.，133-166；esp. pp. 149-150. Chico，Calif.：Scholars Press，1984.

遗址与建筑

Archaeological Site and Building

辽上京皇城西山坡一号基址的建筑构造探讨

The Architectural Structure of Foundation No.1 at Xishanpo in the North City of Liaoshangjing

汪盈 | WANG Ying

摘要：辽上京皇城西山坡一号基址经过考古发掘，确认为一座六角形木回廊砖构楼阁塔基址。一号塔基遗址保存较为完好，遗迹遗物现象丰富，建筑构造具有特色，是研究辽金时期建筑的珍贵考古资料。本文就现已发表的考古发掘资料，对西山坡一号塔基的建筑构造进行分析和探讨。

关键词：辽上京；塔基；建筑考古

Abstract：The archaeological excavation confirmed that Foundation No.1 at Xishanpo in the North City of Liaoshangjing is a brick-and-wood-structured hexagonal pagoda-foundation surrounded with a winding corridor. Foundation No.1 is well preserved，rich in relics and architectural features. It provides valuable archaeological evidence for studying the buildings in Liao and Jin Dynasties. Based on the published archaeological excavation data，this chapter analyses and discuss the architectural structure of Foundation No.1.

Keywords：Liaoshangjing；Pagoda-Foundation；Architectural Archaeology

作者简介：
汪盈，中国社会科学院考古研究所，助理研究员。

辽上京皇城西山坡遗址是辽上京城内一处位置重要、规模宏大的佛教寺院遗址。其中的一号基址经过考古全面发掘，遗址保存较为完好，遗迹遗物现象丰富，建筑构造具有特色，是研究辽金时期建筑的珍贵考古资料。

一、考古发掘概况

辽上京始建于辽神册三年（918 年），初名“皇都”。至辽会同元年（938 年）基本建成，更名“上京”，并设立临潢府。直到辽天庆十年（即金天辅四年，1120 年）被金兵攻占，上京城作为都城存在了近二百年之久。辽上京是辽代营建最早、使用时间最长的首都，也是中国游牧民族在北方草原地区建立的第一座都城，在中国古代都城发展史上具有重要的地位。

辽上京城址位于今内蒙古自治区赤峰市巴林左旗林东镇东南，1961 年被列为第一批全国重点文物保护单位。城址总平面略呈“日”字形，分为南北二城，两城并列，总面积约 5 平方千米。根据《辽史 · 地理志》记载，北城谓之皇城，南城谓之汉城。皇城是契丹皇帝宫殿区、贵族生活区和中央官署之所在。汉城是汉人及渤海、回鹘等族工商业者和外国使者的集居之所。其中，北部的皇城城墙保存较好，整体格局基本完整，皇城平面呈不规则方形。宫城位于皇城中部偏东，平面呈近方形。

图 1　辽上京皇城西山坡一号、二号、三号基址考古发掘全景[①]

西山坡是辽上京皇城西南的一处自然高地，也是全城的制高点。西山坡上尚存多组东向院落的地面遗迹。其中，核心建筑为南、北并排的两组东向院落。北院西部有三座南北并排分布的建筑基址，地面保存较高，曾屡遭盗掘破坏。中间的基址位于该组中轴线上，规模最大，地表直径约 50 米，高度超过 2 米。南、北两座基址规模略小，左右基本对称分布，直径约 10 米。

在以往的调查研究中，关于西山坡建筑遗址的性质，学者们提出了寺院或皇帝宴寝之所等不同的假设。基于西山坡遗址在皇城中所处位置的重要性和基址的庞大规模，其建筑年代和建筑性质对研究辽上京城址的布局和沿革具有十分重要的意义。因此，中国社会科学院考古研究所内蒙古第二工作队和内蒙古文物考古研究所联合组成辽上京考古队，于 2012 年对西山坡遗址进行了考古踏查、试掘和发掘。

经过考古清理，发现了塔基、殿址、院墙址等建筑院落遗迹。其中，对西山坡北组院落西部的三座基址进行了全面揭露，发现三座大型六角形建筑基址（图 1）。这三座六角形基址中，中央规模最大者编号为一号基址，南、北两侧分别编号为二号、三号基址。综合考古发掘的遗迹现象和出土遗物情况，可以判断这三座建筑基址是三座六角形砖塔塔基。三座塔基于辽代始建，至少进行过两次大规模修筑，金代以后才逐渐废弃[②]。本文主要就现已发表的考古发掘资料，对西山坡一号塔基的建筑构造进行分析和探讨。

图 2 一号塔基考古发掘后全景

图 3 一号塔基西侧慢道南壁砖砌象眼

图 4 一号塔基台明铺砖及砖痕

二、一号塔基的建筑构造

一号塔基是一座六角形木回廊砖构楼阁塔基址，坐西朝东。塔基由夯土台基和残存塔身两部分组成（图 2）。夯土台基规模宏大，平面呈六角形，由夯土、包砖、砖砌散水、东侧月台和西侧踏道组成。残存塔身包括柱础、墙体、白灰墙皮、石条、地面铺砖及砖痕等遗迹，可由此确认塔身残存的结构由双套筒砖构、双向楼梯、塔心室、木构副阶构成。一号塔基的建筑构造特点主要包括以下几点。

（一）六角形包砖夯土台基

一号塔基建有一座宽大的六角形台基。台基边长约 20 米，对角直径约 40 米，总高约 2 米。台基由夯土夯筑而成。台基外壁砌单层包边砖，采用磨砖对缝做法，以白灰粘合。夯土与包边砖之间，采取夯土层间加砌平铺断砖的做法。

夯土台基的东西两面有登临设施。台基东面遗迹残损严重，仅存夯土和局部包砖及散水。根据遗迹现象，推测台基东面原有包砖夯土月台，由月台南北两侧踏道或慢道登临[③]。月台夯土下叠压有残损的砖砌涵洞、象眼和早期夯土，可知是较早修筑的斜坡慢道遗存。早期慢道形制残损严重，已无法复原。台基西面为包砖夯土斜坡慢道，慢道南壁包砖保存较好，尚存砖砌象眼。象眼为三角形，砌砖层叠内收递减，如《营造法式》所载[④]（图 3）。

除台基及月台、慢道的包砖外，均做单行砖散水。散水外砌侧立砖两周，即《营造法式》所载“线道”[⑤]。

六角形夯土台基之上共有柱网三周，六面每面三间。这三圈柱网及墙体，由外向内将建筑底层平面分为砖铺台明、木构副阶和砖构塔身三部分。台明部分地面铺砖。在铺砖残缺处，考古发掘也清理出砌砖泥缝的清晰痕迹（图 4）。现基台边缘铺砖及夯土均已损毁，复原宽约 5 米。木构副阶的铺砖地面上出土大量泥塑像。塔身的残存遗迹现象可以复原塔身的建筑结构为双套筒结构，内置双向楼梯，塔身中央设有六角形塔心室。

（二）双套筒塔身结构

塔身即内圈柱网结构，为六角形砖构建筑。塔身边长约 8.6 米，对角直径约 17.2 米。从残存塔砖在不同位置的不同铺砌方式可知，塔身结构为双套筒结构，由外套筒、楼梯通道、内套筒、塔心室四部分组成。

外套筒由塔砖实心砌筑。其中芯均为侧立砖砌筑而成，以白灰粘合；外壁和内壁各砌一道顺砖，外壁涂有白灰皮（图 5）。内套筒亦呈六角形，砌筑方式与外套筒相同。

外套砖筒内原立有石柱，每面面阔三间（图 6）。当心间柱心距为 5 米，两梢间柱心距均为 1.6 米。现石柱多已断裂倒塌，散落于塔身内外的倒塌堆积中。幸运的是，尚有一根石柱保存在原位，还有部分石柱保存了原始的倒塌位置，断裂茬口可以拼合。从保留原位的石柱可见，石柱打磨并不规则，完全被包砌在砖体结构之内，以白灰粘合。这些遗迹现象可以确认外套砖筒内立有石柱的建筑结构和形制做法，其作用是加强砖构建筑底部、角部的承重和拉结。这些石柱均立于平石柱础之上，两者连接处以白灰找平、粘合。柱础嵌于夯土台基内，保存完好，共 18 个，形状均为不规则方形。在考古清理中，在大部分平石柱础的础面上发现了清晰的十字墨线，这是在营造过程中取正定平时的放线痕迹。经过测量发现，虽然柱础形状及其安置位置不是很规则，但是础面上的墨线中心彼此准确相对。一号塔基所发现的营造墨线遗迹是我们研究辽金建筑营造次第和建筑技术的重要考古资料。

图 5 一号塔基外套砖筒侧立砌砖及砖痕

图 6 一号塔基外套砖筒内柱

（三）双向“壁内折上式”楼梯结构

塔身前、后设门，可进入塔身，通往位于内、外套筒之间的楼梯通道。其中西面的后门保存较好。后门门洞内铺砖，尚存石门限和石门砧，石质坚硬，雕工精致。门内铺砖地面中央存有一石经幢残件，则塔身内原来可能供奉经幢。经幢残件为八角形，四正面雕有卷云纹，四隅面雕有兽首，其上为宝妆莲座（图 7）。

从尚存的地面铺砖和砖痕可以发现，后门内右手方向由顺砌砖封闭，而左手方向地面仍为通道的地面铺砖。以此为线索，前门内右手方向砖痕均毁，而左手方向也仍为通道的地面铺砖砖痕，即前门与后门的通道呈

图 7 一号塔基内出土经幢残件

180° 旋转对称。因此，塔身内、外套筒之间的六角形通道即为旋转而上的梯道，向上的阶梯已全部无存。前、后门各设一组楼梯，且均设在进门的左手方向，符合佛教礼拜“右绕”的习俗。这种两组梯道可同时攀登的结构，即为双向楼梯结构。

在同时期的双套筒砖构楼阁塔中，常见有“穿心式”和“壁内折上式”两种楼梯结构。涿州智度寺塔和呼和浩特万部华严经塔是两座地面建筑保存完好的辽代大型楼阁塔实例，平面均为八角形，塔身均为双套筒结构。这两座塔分别采用了上述两种楼梯结构。智度寺塔塔身内筒砖构在一层设有六角形塔心室，塔心室高于底层楼梯回廊半层。楼梯从两个相对方向攀登，穿过塔心室转折，再向两个相对方向上行，即为双向“穿心式”楼梯⑥。万部华严经塔塔身内筒砖构为八角形，一层内筒外壁各面封死，无法进入，内筒内部结构不明。内筒外壁的四正面设有龛室，龛内供奉佛像、经卷等。双向楼梯均沿内筒外壁及外筒内壁之间的通道曲折向上攀登，并不通过内筒塔心，即为双向“壁内折上式”楼梯⑦。根据仅存的地面铺砖和砖痕铺砌方式，可知一号塔基的塔心室地面高程与楼梯通道相平，推测塔心室也不与楼梯通道相通，因此一号塔基的楼梯应为双向“壁内折上式”结构。

图 8 一号塔基底部结构中的平铺石条

另外，在夯土台面上局部有成排平铺的石条，北侧一排，南侧两排，并不平行（图 8）。石条打磨不规则，四周抹白灰砌侧立砖，被砌在塔身底部，完全不露明。这些石条的安置方向不是很有规律，与六角形塔身边长方向不完全平行，也不与塔身内、外套筒或楼梯通道相对。因此不能确定其是否与砖构塔身的底部承重结构相关。这些平铺石条长度不完全相等，与外套筒内的石柱相较，长度略短，截面尺寸相仿，打磨方式与程度也相似，或可考虑是否与一号塔基的早期建筑结构和用材相关。

（四）六角形塔心室

在内套筒中央，设置六角形塔心室，局部地面还存有平铺砖。从保存较好的内套筒后壁看，其以一排顺砌砖封堵塔心室，即从塔身后门无法进入塔心室。另外三面也均有顺砌砖或砖痕，可确认没有进出通道。内套筒前壁和左前壁处破坏严重，砌砖痕迹全部无存。参考塔心室铺砖地面的高程与楼梯通道相平，可认为塔心室没有与楼梯相通。在内套筒残存砌砖之上的倒塌堆积中，发现一尊石雕残佛像，有可能是原塔心室之内的供奉。塔心室中前部近一半面积被巨大盗坑所破坏，未发现可以确认塔心室下方是否设置过地宫的迹象。盗坑底部深度基本和塔基的始建面相平（图 9）。

从现存辽代砖塔遗存看，双套筒结构的楼阁砖塔尚未有发现地宫的实例。经考古清理发现地宫的辽代砖塔主要结构有两类：一类是实

图 9 一号塔基六角形塔心室及破坏坑

心砖砌结构，在塔体内不同高度设有小型地宫、中宫、天宫等以瘗埋舍利、经幢等；另一类是单砖筒结构，单层砖构塔壁内设有塔心室，有的塔心室一直向上延伸形成中空塔腹，这类砖塔通常在塔心室上下设置天宫和地宫[8]。北京房山北郑塔是一座辽代重建的八角形密檐实心砖塔，其地宫建于夯土台基的铺砖地面之上，完全被砖塔基座包砌。地宫内安置石函。地宫盖板上方安置石经幢，直接包砌于实心砖体内[9]。辽宁朝阳北塔是一座在辽代经过大规模重建的方形密檐砖塔，其塔心室、地宫均重砌于辽代重熙年间。塔身正面开券门，可进入塔心室，其内供奉佛像。地宫位于塔心室下方，其内瘗埋石经幢和石函。从建筑结构上看，朝阳北塔建有较高的基座，其上为塔身。因此，塔心室下方的地宫位于基座之内，地宫底部并未低于建筑的始建面[10]。由此，结合一号塔基被盗坑破坏的现状，考虑石佛像、石经幢残件的出土，一号塔基仍有在塔心室下方建有地宫的可能性。

图 10 一号塔基副阶外圈柱础及墙体（左）
图 11 一号塔基中圈柱础及砖砌像座（右）

（五）木构副阶及泥塑像

副阶即外圈和中圈柱础之间形成的木构回廊，地面铺砖，进深 5.3 米。副阶亦为六角形，每边面阔三间。外圈柱础间残存墙体结构遗迹，为单层土坯墙外砌单层砖墙。两圈柱础当心间对缝，面阔 5 米；外圈梢间面阔 5 米，中圈梢间面阔 2 米。外、中两圈柱础形制均为覆盆柱础，有素面、莲瓣纹饰和动物纹饰三类。柱础保存状况较差，风化和磨蚀现象严重，显然经过长期露明使用。位于西面的外圈明间柱础保存较好，其上开有安置门槛的榫口，但榫口打破了柱础原有的雕花纹饰。另外，现存的单层土坯墙直接叠压在榫口之上，而未见门槛遗迹。说明副阶的建筑结构曾经有过重修，有可能经过了从开敞到设置木门槛再到以土坯墙封堵的过程。柱础上原均立木柱，从残存的木炭痕迹来看，柱径约 45 厘米（图 10）。

中圈柱础是在塔身外套筒之外单独设置的一圈柱础。中圈柱础间残存单层顺砖砌筑的墙体遗迹，中圈墙体与塔身外壁之间以碎砖填砌。紧贴中圈墙体，发现几处砖砌抹泥的像座（图 11）。也就是说，副阶回廊把塔身外壁底部有白灰墙皮的部分完全包砌起来。这个现象提示我们，木构副阶与砖构塔身是否是同时兴建的遗迹。目前暂未发现可进一步证实的线索。

在副阶东面前门的位置，门道一侧原址保留了一处泥塑立像，残存仰莲座及泥塑跣足，彩绘贴金。在副阶的铺砖地面上，出土了大量的倒塌泥塑造像残块。其中有六尊泥塑罗汉像保存较为完好，尚可大体复原，其规模和原址保存的立像相仿，约半人大小。还有一些头像、身体、服饰残块，现仍在进行室内修复工作。除此之外，还出土了大量稍小的泥塑人像、动物像、建筑影塑等残块，出土遗物还包括大量铜钱和部分陶瓷器残片等（图 12）。由此说明，在副阶回廊之内，原安置供奉了大量泥塑造像，很可能还有围绕塔身外壁底部而建的影塑，并且副阶内曾有信徒进行供养活动。

图 12　一号塔基副阶出土泥塑像

在现存辽塔地面建筑和塔基中，几乎未见建有副阶的砖构楼阁塔，仅有应县木塔一例尚存副阶。在同时期南方的五代、宋塔中，多有在砖塔外建木构副阶的形制做法。如吴越时期的杭州雷峰塔，塔基平面结构和西山坡一号塔基相似[11]。但是在这些建有副阶的同时期佛塔中，副阶结构在塔身外多仅作外圈一圈柱础，且未见在副阶回廊内供奉尊像的设置。在北朝时期的方形佛塔中，多有在底层回廊内、中心塔体外壁奉安泥塑造像的传统[12]。如洛阳的北魏永宁寺塔基，平面为方形，共有柱网五圈，内部四圈为土坯木柱混砌的塔心实体，第四圈和第五圈之间为回廊。在第四圈木柱土坯实体的外壁上，有内凹的壁龛遗迹。结合回廊中出土大量泥塑残件，可知土坯塔身外壁原有彩绘并贴附影塑[13]。到隋唐时期，将佛塔副阶回廊作为供奉尊像的建筑空间安排似已不多见。综上所述，一号塔基的副阶形制及功能是辽金时期一处特殊的佛塔实例。

三、一号塔基与二号、三号塔基的比较

在一号塔基左右两侧的两座六角形建筑基址，分别是二号、三号塔基。两座塔基均坐西朝东，体量小于一号塔基，建筑构造也有所不同。

二号塔基破坏严重，从考古发现的遗迹来看，地面以上仅存台基和散水，地面以下存有地宫（图 13）。二号塔基的台基是一座六角形的包砖夯土台基，边长为 5.9 米，对角直径为 11.8 米。夯土台基被一个大盗坑完全破坏，

直至地宫底部。塔身已荡然无存，台基原始高度也无法复原。二号塔基西侧台基包砖保存完好，可确认没有踏道；东侧台基包砖被破坏，未见踏道夯土或踏道散水的迹象。因此，二号塔基可能是一座不可登临的六角形砖塔。地下部分的主要遗迹由斜坡通道、砖砌甬道、砖砌地宫三部分组成。在夯土台基下方的基岩中开挖出平面为“甲”字形的土圹，由斜坡通道通往底部，底部中央用砖砌筑甬道和地宫。地宫和甬道顶部全部无存，四壁仅存底部局部砌砖。根据白灰墙皮和砌砖的叠压关系可知，二号塔基的地宫至少有三次修筑。地宫内遗物也被盗掘一空。

三号塔基破坏更加严重，除具体尺寸外，其建筑构造与二号塔基相同（图 14）。夯土台基边长 5.7 米，对角直径 11.4 米。地宫不仅遗物被盗，而且砌砖几乎被取走，仅存部分砖痕，可得知其营造情况。幸运的是，在三号基址的盗坑扰土中，发现彩绘舍利石棺残块（图 15）。由此可确认塔基内确曾瘗埋供奉舍利。

图 13 二号塔基考古发掘后全景

图 14 三号塔基考古发掘后全景

从建筑规模上看，二号、三号塔基的台基边长比一号塔基小很多，是其尺寸的四分之一略多。由此亦可推测，一号塔基的塔高也应是二号、三号塔基的数倍。三座塔基均坐西朝东，一字排开。这种一大两小、三塔并列的佛塔布局在辽金塔中也是特殊的实例。

从建筑构造上看，根据边长推测二号、三号的塔身结构应为实心砖塔或仅有较小中空塔腹的单筒结构，不会像一号塔基一样是设有楼梯的双套筒楼阁塔。二号、三号塔基的地宫构造也与一号不相同，因此瘗藏供奉舍利的方式也有所不同。二号、三号塔基虽很可能不可登临，但设置了可进出的具有斜坡通道、甬道的地宫。按二号塔基地宫曾有多次修筑的线索，这两座塔基的地宫很有可能曾被多次开启并进行供奉活动。在辽金塔基中，这种设有斜坡通道、类似墓葬结构的地宫并不多见。赤峰宁城的辽中京半截塔地宫构造与此较为相似，是一处保存较好的辽代实例。辽中京半截塔的地宫也由地宫宫室、甬道和台阶通道组成，只是台阶通道的平面略有不同[14]。这种地宫形式与绝大部分辽塔在塔身砖构内设置的地宫等仅供安置舍利的宫室形式不尽相同。

从营造做法上看，三座塔基夯土台基的包砖做法均是在夯土台基外先用碎砖和土找齐，最外再做单层包砖，采用磨砖对缝做法，以白灰粘合。散水也均是用单排砖，其外均用两排

图 15 三号塔基出土舍利石棺残件

侧立砖作线道。用砖的质地和规格也完全一致。可以说明三座塔基至少曾在同一时期经过同时修建和使用。

四、小结

通过对辽上京皇城西山坡一号塔基的分析及其与二号、三号塔基的比较，对一号塔基作为一座六角形木回廊砖构楼阁塔基的建筑构造特点认识更为明确。一号塔基建有宽大的六角形包砖夯土台基；塔身为双套砖筒结构，双筒之间设有双向壁内上折式梯道，塔身内设有六角形塔心室；塔身外建有木构副阶，副阶回廊内供奉大量泥塑尊像。一号塔基的考古遗迹现象复杂，建筑性质和功能明确，建筑形制结构和布局方式特殊，为研究辽金时期的佛塔建筑提供了宝贵的考古资料。通过对一号塔基建筑构造的探讨，一方面，使我们对辽上京皇城西山坡佛寺遗址的认识更为深入，是我们进一步研究辽代都城规划布局、辽代都城建筑形制和营造特点的基础工作；另一方面，也为我们探讨辽金时期佛教的源流和传播、不同地区之间的影响关系提供了新的线索。

（本文得到辽上京西山坡遗址考古发掘项目领队董新林研究员的支持，谨致谢忱。）

注释：

① 中国社会科学院考古研究所内蒙古第二工作队，内蒙古文物考古研究所. 内蒙古巴林左旗辽上京皇城西山坡佛寺遗址考古获重大发现 [J]. 考古，2013（1）：3-6.

② 图 1~ 图 15 图片来源：中国社会科学院考古研究所内蒙古第二工作队，内蒙古文物考古研究所. 内蒙古巴林左旗辽上京皇城西山坡佛寺遗址考古获重大发现 [J]. 考古，2013（1）：3-6. 汪盈，董新林，等. 辽上京皇城西山坡佛寺遗址考古发掘 // 国家文物局. 2012 中国重要考古发现 [M]. 北京：文物出版社，2013：140-144.

③ 可参考应县木塔南侧月台及踏道形制，见陈明达，应县木塔 [M]. 北京：文物出版社，1966：实测图 4~5.

④（宋）李诫，营造法式 [Z]. 见梁思成，梁思成全集（第七卷）[M]. 北京：中国建筑工业出版社，2001：275.

⑤（宋）李诫，营造法式 [Z]. 见梁思成，梁思成全集（第七卷）[M]. 北京：中国建筑工业出版社，2001：274.

⑥ 田林，杨昌鸣. 涿州智度寺塔初探 [J]. 文物，2004(5)：89-96.

⑦ 张汉君，辽万部华严经塔建筑构造及结构规制初探 [J]. 内蒙古文物考古，1994（10）：69-74.

⑧ 汪盈. 辽塔分布及形制初探 [D]. 北京：北京大学，2009：38.

⑨ 齐心，刘精义. 北京市房山县北郑村辽塔清理记 [J]. 考古，1980（2）：147-158.

⑩ 辽宁省文物考古研究所，朝阳市北塔博物馆. 朝阳北塔：考古发掘与维修工程报告 [M]. 北京：文物出版社，2007：154-155.

⑪ 浙江省文物考古研究所. 杭州雷峰塔五代地宫发掘简报 [J]. 文物，2002（5）：4-32.

⑫ 梁银锦. 朝阳北塔出土泥塑像的渊源及奉安场所探讨 [J]. 边疆考古研究（第 7 辑）：259-282.

⑬ 中国社会科学院考古研究所. 北魏洛阳永宁寺 [M]. 北京：中国大百科全书出版社，1996：13-19.

⑭ 内蒙古文物考古研究所，赤峰市博物馆，宁城县博物馆. 辽中京半截塔台基覆土及地宫发掘简报 [J]. 内蒙古文物考古，2005（2）：13-26.

建造纪念碑：
考古学、树轮年代学和遗产研究

Building a Monument:
Archaeology，Dendrochronology and Heritage Research

Vincent DEBONNE

摘要：建筑遗产的考古学研究本身并非最终目标，而是一种更好的理解遗产的方法，这为建成遗产的合法性保护赋予了坚实基础。精确的年代测定在建筑的考古分析中至关重要。和以往相比，遗产研究在今天拥有更多不同的科学处理方法，使得历史建筑时间和空间的可靠判断成为可能。在比利时，树轮年代学因其目前相对最高的测年精度，成为所有科学测年技术中使用最多且最适用的。就像其他所有方法一样，树轮测年不能单独应用，而是必须和初步的建筑现场考古分析相配合，包括建立相对年表。树轮分析不仅提供了建筑的建造年代，同时促进了区域性建筑材料和建筑技术年表的建立。通过该区域的形制年代学研究，可以推测无可测年木构件的建筑年代。最后，树轮年代学可以对历史建筑建造时的自然环境提供新的见解。在这里，建筑史、考古学和历史生态学等学科之间的分野消失了，为遗产提供了整合的和全局性的研究途径。

关键词：木材和砖的断代方法；树轮年代学；建筑考古；中世纪；比利时

Abstract: Archaeological research of architectural heritage is not an end in itself，but a means to better understanding the heritage at issue. This enables a well-founded motivation of the legally anchored conservation of built heritage. Precise dating is of crucial importance in the archaeological analysis of buildings. Now more than ever，heritage research has at its disposal various scientific methods which allow a sound definition in time and space of historic buildings. In Belgium，dendrochronology is the most used and most suitable of all scientific dating techniques，because of its as yet unsurpassed precision in dating. As is the case though for all methods，tree ring dating cannot be applied in an isolated manner，but necessarily follows a preliminary archaeological analysis of the building at hand，including the establishment of a relative chronology. Tree ring analysis offers more than construction dates of buildings，it also facilitates the development of regional chronologies of building materials and building techniques. By use of such local chrono-ty-

作者简介：
Dr. Vincent DEBONNE，Flanders Heritage Agency，researcher；University of Leuven，associated researcher.

pologies, dates can then be proposed for buildings without datable wood. Finally, dendrochronology can offer new insights in the natural environment in which historic buildings came to be. Here, the divides between disciplines such as architectural history, archaeology and historical ecology disappear to make way for an integrated and holistic approach to heritage.

Keywords: Dating methods of timber and bricks; Dendrochronology; Building archaeology; Middle Ages; Belgium

Mere venerable age and aesthetic qualities are insufficient to fully motivate the recognition and preservation of historical buildings. It also requires an accurate and well-founded definition in time and space of the building at issue. Therefore building archaeology is an integral part of the conservation of built heritage: through the identification and dating of construction phases it is possible to gain a better understanding of the historical context in which a building was erected and further evolved. This way one can trace the particular historical value which elevates a merely old building into a monument.

In Belgium, building archaeology, a discipline on a steady rise since the 1970s, has allowed a better understanding of built heritage. Such is the case especially for heritage of the Middle Ages with many buildings having legal protection as state-listed monuments. Of these a select number are also inscribed on the World Heritage List.[1] Until fairly recently, the construction date of several major medieval buildings remained uncertain. Proposed dates of construction were broad estimations, based on stylistic features or written mentions of an often brief and anecdotal nature. However, building archaeology and most notably scientific dating have produced accurate and well-founded construction dates which in many cases have forced to review accepted construction histories. Nonetheless, an adjusted dating does not undercut the heritage value of a building, on the contrary: the deepening of the historical dimension strengthens the motivation behind the legally anchored conservation of architectural heritage.

Scientific Dating

As a result of the geology of Belgium (See p.202, Fig.1), a considerable part of the medieval heritage is built in brick. The northwestern part of the country near the North Sea coast is poor in natural building stone but rich in clay, which from the early 13th century onwards was used in massive quantities for brick production. Objects of fired clay, which apart from bricks also includes tiles and pottery, can be dated by use of scientific methods.[2]

Archaeomagnetism can provide reliable dates of architectural ceramics, on the condition of them being preserved at the location of their actual firing, usually the kiln in which they have been fired.[3] However, archaeomagnetic analysis of ceramics which have been displaced after firing, for example bricks in walls, does not produce credible dates. This was experienced in the church of Belsele near Antwerp. Archaeomagnetic analysis of a brick wall yielded two dates, in the 11th to 12th centuries (1066[-75, +119]A.D.) and in the late 15th to early 16th centuries (1504[-44, +43]A.D.), both dates being in disagreement with the actual construction of said wall around 1270.[4] Adding to the impropriety of archaeomagnetism for dating displaced architectural ceramics is the destructive nature of the method, which requires drilling multiple samples in brick masonry.[5] At the moment, the contribution of archaeomagnetic analysis of displaced ceramics lies not in dating, but rather in understanding the techniques of production. Since the method identifies the orientation of ferromagnetic minerals within the fired clay object to the earth's magnetic field, archaeomagnetism can be used to detect the position of architectural ceramics during their firing and, consequently, the construction of the kiln.[6]

In contrast to archaeomagnetism, luminescence dating of bricks, either thermoluminescence (TL) or optically stimulated luminescence (OSL), produces credible and fairly narrow dates, as evidenced by research in England and France.[7] Tentative applications of OSL have confirmed the feasibility of this technique in Belgium, although results are dependent of the mineral properties of the clay fabric. Successful dating requires for the quartz grains of the ceramic object to be sufficiently luminescent. The luminescence of bricks in the church of Belsele proved too weak to allow luminescence dating.[8] Inversely, bricks in the church of Our Lady in Bruges appeared suitable for dating. Indeed, the clays used for the bricks in Belsele and Bruges are different: clay of tertiary origin in Belsele, whereas in Bruges clay was extracted from marine deposits of the quaternary period.

Rehydroxylation is the most recently developed of brick dating techniques.[9] The method dates ceramics by measuring the residual moisture content compared to the average temperature during the lifetime of the ceramic object. Dating by use of rehydroxylation has produced credible results in England. The technique, which is still in an experimental phase, has not yet been applied in Belgium.

For now, tree ring dating or dendrochronology of wooden constructions, such as floors and roofs, is the most used of scientific dating techniques in Belgium. In ideal circumstances, dendrochronology produces extremely narrow dates, more so than the methods already mentioned.[10] The precision of tree ring dating is dependent on the amount of tree rings within the sampled piece of wood. With bark still attached, the felling of the tree that produced the sampled piece of wood can be dated up to a single year. When bark is no longer in place but sapwood is preserved, an interval dating can be obtained, giving a range between the earliest and the latest possible year of felling. Heartwood, without bark nor sapwood, only allows *terminus post quem* dating, the earliest possible year of felling. Successful and reliable tree ring dating demands a statistically sufficient number of tree rings. When this demand is not met, as is the case for wood of rapid growth containing a limited amount of broad tree rings, no felling date can be obtained. Large beams are not necessarily more suitable for dating than smaller pieces. Thinner beams are often quartered sections of the trunk and so contain the same amount of tree rings as large beams. Additionally, large beams are often observed to have been made of rapidly grown wood, containing less tree rings than thinner beams. In Belgium, wood in medieval constructions is almost exclusively oak, whereas in the Netherlands pine came into use as early as the 13th century.[11]

A question often raised regarding dendrochronology is whether the felling date is contemporary with the construction date. In pre-industrial Northwestern Europe this is generally the case: wood for constructive purposes was worked and assembled at most two years after felling the needed tree (s).[12] Assembling freshly cut, wet wood has multiple advantages. Since the wood can be smoothly worked, joints are easy to cut. As the wood dries and hardens, the joints lock together and become more firm, strengthening the entirety of the wooden construction. The confrontation of tree ring dates and datings taken from other sources, for example building contracts, indeed confirms the rapid processing of wood into constructions, as showcased by the following examples.

After a devastating fire in 1677, the roof of the main church of Tongeren, in the east of Belgium, was rebuilt.[13] The preserved building accounts and the contract with the carpenter offer a detailed chronicle of the reconstruction of the roof from 1678 until 1680. The tree ring dates of beams in the roof coincide with dates in the abovementioned texts, confirming the use of freshly cut, wet wood. The preservation of waney edge (the transition between wood and bark) in 27 samples allowed to recognize five distinct felling campaigns, evidencing a seasonal course of the building site. Here, tree ring dating has not only confirmed but even refined the written sources.

The barrel shaped roof of the already mentioned church of Belsele was tree ring dated to 1266-71d[14] [Fig. 1]. The simultaneity of the roof and the brick built wall underneath was confirmed by radiocarbon analysis of lime mortar from the brick masonry, yielding the date 1263-95 A.D. (95.4% probability).[15] The radiocarbon dating was not performed on organic inclusions within the mortar, such as charcoal, but on the carbonate formed during the hardening of lime putty $Ca(OH)^2$ into solid lime mortar $CaCO^3$.[16]

A final example of the roof being contemporary with its supporting construction is the southern sick ward of the former Saint John's Hospital in Bruges [Fig. 2]. The western part of the roof was tree ring dated to 1283-85d, which coincides with written sources.[17] The accounts of the hospital for the year 1291 list several expenses which undeniably point to the completion of the roof of the southern sick ward: payments to sawyers, carpenters, tilers and the wood supplier from the Dutch city of Dordrecht, then a major marketplace for construc-

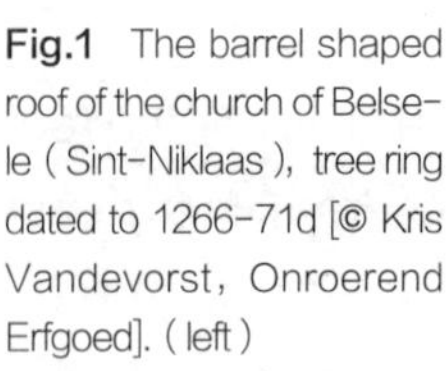

Fig.1 The barrel shaped roof of the church of Belsele (Sint-Niklaas), tree ring dated to 1266-71d [© Kris Vandevorst, Onroerend Erfgoed]. (left)

Fig.2 Bruges, Saint John's Hospital. Western façade of the southern sick ward [© Vincent Debonne]. (right)

tion wood, and purchases of corbels, laths, stakes and different kinds of roof tiles.[18]

Preliminary Archaeological Analysis

To arrive at a correct interpretation of dates obtained by dendrochronology, the sample taking must be preceded by preliminary archaeological analysis to establish a relative chronology of the wooden construction under investigation and to evaluate its relation to the building it is part of. The roofs of the church of Our Lady in Damme are a striking example of the importance of preliminary archaeological analysis.[19] Today a picturesque village, from the 12th to the 15th centuries Damme was a prosperous trading town, serving as the outport of the city of Bruges, 10 km away. The medieval parish church of the town is of the so-called hall church type, having three naves of equal height, each with its own saddleback roof. The roof constructions of the three naves are still the original ones. In the western half of the central nave, sample taking for tree ring dating was determined by archaeological analysis of the roof. The roof has an alternation of plain rafters and rafters with open joints. There is also a noticeable difference in dimension: the rafters with open joints have square sections (16 × 16 cm) whereas the plain rafters have rectangular sections (10 × 18 cm). Samples for tree ring dating were taken in both the square and rectangular rafters, confirming the reuse of older beams: the square rafters with open joints are cut from trees felled in the winter of 1241-1242d, the rectangular rafters are over half a century younger, dated to 1312-15d [Fig. 3]. The square rafters were part of the roof covering the first choir of the church, built in limestone. They were then reused in the early 14th century, as the original choir was extended and heightened, using brick. In the case of Damme, preliminary archaeological analysis of the roof construction was crucial in establishing a sound construction history of the church. If only the square rafters would have been sampled, assuming these contained more tree rings than the rectangular ones, then tree ring

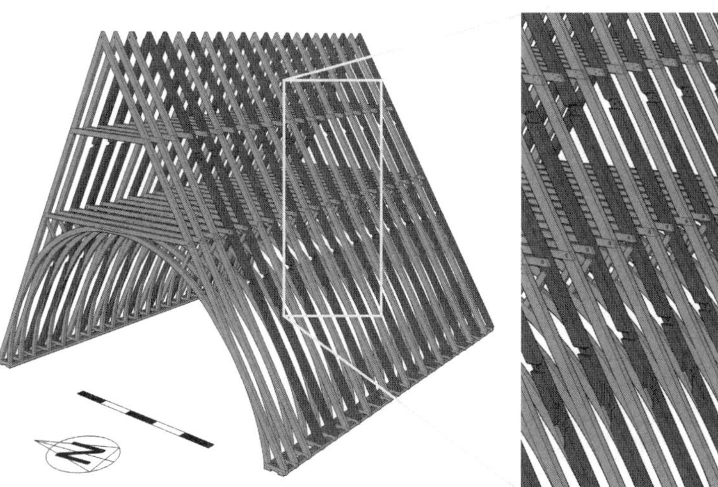

Fig.3 3D-model of the roof above the two westernmost bays of the central choir of Our Lady's church in Damme. Brown: reused rafters dated to 1241-42d; red: rafters dated to 1312-15d [©Vincent Debonne].

dating would only have yielded the one date of 1241-42d, leading to an erroneous construction history of the church.

Another example showcasing the importance of preliminary archaeological research is the bell tower of the church of Our Lady in Bruges.[20] Measuring 115 m, the tower is among the tallest brick buildings of Europe. The buttressed trunk of the tower, reaching a height of 80 m, was built in ca. 1280-1340. The original spire was dismantled and rebuilt in 1519; the current spire dates from 1855-58. Inside, the trunk contains seven storeys divided by floors consisting of bridging joists on cross beams supported by corbels. Samples for tree ring dating were taken from both the corbels and the cross beams, these having massive sections up to 0.5 x 0.5 m, as well as the smaller bridging joists, which contained as much tree rings as the bigger cross beams. The tree ring date obtained for the floor (1343-68d) however is not the construction date of the trunk of the bell tower. The walls of the second storey contain traces of large openings with pointed arches, perhaps intended as belfry windows. Soon these were filled in with brick masonry to counter the alarming deformations of the tower, caused by the initially far too slender skeletal design. The corbels of the cross beams are part of the brick masonry filling up the openings. As a result, the tree ring date of the floor dates the filling of the openings, this being a secondary intervention in the tower.

Fig.4 Roof of the northern side-aisle of Saint James' church in Bruges, tree ring dated to 1482-92d [© Vincent Debonne].

Building Local Chrono-typologies

Since dendrochronology offers precise and absolute dating of buildings and their construction phases, it is possible to develop chronologies of building materials, construction techniques and architectural forms. These chrono-typologies can in turn be used to date buildings where scientific dating is not possible.

Until recently the northern aisle of Saint James' church in Bruges was dated to the 13th century, mainly based on the typology of the roof construction: a common rafter roof of identical trusses set up next to one another, without longitudinal bracing[21] [Fig. 4]. The absence of bracing between the trusses led architectural historians to date the roof to the 13th century. This dating however was doubtful: the roof follows the curve of the outer wall of the nave, which links to the western front of the church, built in the 15th century. Tree ring analysis of samples taken from original beams removed during the restoration of the roof gave a felling date between 1482d and 1492d. At that time, far more intricate types of roofs were already in use in Bruges, in churches but also in secular buildings such as private houses, cloth halls and sick wards of hospitals. The late 15th-century dating shows the longevity in Bruges of common rafter roofs which apparently are not typical of the 13th century. Instead of a sharp chronological divide there is a coexistence of different construction techniques and architectural forms, which underlines the often decisive contribution of tree ring dating.

In Belgium and the Netherlands, dating by use of brick sizes and, to a lesser degree, masonry bonds is a common practice in building archaeology. Considering the size of bricks has decreased over time, a chronological value can be attached to brick dimensions. The main flaw though of dating by use of brick sizes has been the uncertainty of the construction dates of buildings used for referential brick dimensions. Recently however, a local chronology of medieval brick sizes and masonry bonds has been made for the city of Bruges, where the accurate tree ring dates of several brick buildings enable the development of a well-founded chronological framework.[22] Four phases in the evolution of brick sizes could be distinguished in Bruges during the 13th and 14th centuries. The first phase, dated to 1200-60, is marked by the use of two modules: one brick size measuring around 27 cm in length and another, much bigger size of 30 to 33 cm in length, characterized by rather large variations in length, width and height. In the period 1260-1300, the small module is no longer in use, in favor of the large but more uniformly dimensioned brick size. From 1300 onwards there is a steady decrease in size with a strikingly sharp drop around 1340, most likely due to the fixation of a standard brick size by the Bruges municipality, as previously suspected independently on the basis of written sources.[23] As for masonry bonds, 'Flemish' or 'Gothic' bond was in use throughout the 13th century until the first quarter of the 14th century, coexisting since ca. 1270 with English bond which remained in use into the 16th century.

The chronology of brick sizes and masonry bonds in 13th- and 14th-century Bruges was put to the test in the house located Kraanplein number 4.[24] Previously dated to the 16th to 17th centuries on the basis of the general outlook of the plastered exterior,[25] closer inspection of the interior and its visible constructive features quickly revealed the medieval origin of the house. The local chronology of brick sizes and masonry bonds pointed towards a construction in the years 1270-1300. The suspected construction date was confirmed by tree ring analysis of the floors and roof construction, yielding the date 1276-1279d. The measurements of bricks from the accurately dated house can now be added to the dataset of dated brick sizes, thereby statistically strengthening the local chronology of brick dimensions.

Revealing the Historic Context

Not only does scientific dating provide absolute and, in the case of dendrochronology, very precise construction dates, in doing so it also allows to comprehend the particular historical environment in which a building came to be.

The 13th-century construction phases of the abovementioned church of Damme — the first choir (1241-42d) and the western half of the southern nave (1283-91d) — coincide with the boom of Damme as a seaport town.[26] The construction phases of the church are remarkably simultaneous with other building sites in the town, namely the merchants' hall at the market square (mentioned in 1241) and the sick ward of Saint John's hospital (1270-85d). On the other hand, the completion of the church in 1312-15d contradicts the common image of Damme being in decline from 1300 onwards. The tree ring dating based construction history of the church raises new questions: was Damme really as much in decline as historiography states, or should the church be viewed as an oversized negation of the economic downfall of the town? In the case of the house Kraanplein number 4 in Bruges, the archaeological research and the dates obtained by dendrochronology compliment well known iconographic sources[27] [Fig. 5, Fig. 6]. The house is pictured on street views in paintings by the Bruges masters Hans Memling (1430-94), Simon Bening (1483-1561) and Pieter Pourbus (1523-84), showing the then renowned

Fig.5 The house at Kraanplein 4 in Bruges [© Vincent Debonne]. (left)

Fig.6 The house at Kraanplein 4 in Bruges, as depicted on the portrait of Jan Eyewerve (1551) by Pieter Pourbus [© Bruges, Groeningemuseum]. (right)

treadwheel crane on the Kraanrei canal. Because of the revised dating of the house in the years 1270, it can be concluded that the street view depicted by Memling, Bening and Pourbus shows a built reality which at the time of painting already existed for over two centuries.

Dendrochronology not only provides dates, it also gives an insight into the origin of wood used for construction, thus linking built heritage to the history of trade and historical ecology. Until recently, tree ring dating in Northwestern Belgium solely made use of non-local reference chronologies of oak in foreign regions such as Southern Belgium and neighboring areas of Western Germany and Northern France. Since it could not be matched to foreign reference chronologies, indigenous oak was considered unsuitable for dating. Nevertheless, a reference chronology of oak spanning the period 808 A.D.-1530 A.D. has recently been developed, based on a multitude of measured tree rings of oak retrieved from archaeological excavations. Among these were the wooden remains of the borough of Saint Michael's, a disappeared medieval suburb of Ypres in Western Belgium, a town levelled in the First World War but retaining a largely undisturbed archaeological substrate[28] [Fig. 7]. A reference chronology of local oak now at disposal, tree ring analyses of medieval roofs not only point to southern Belgium as a possible provenance of wood but also suggest a local origin. The likely use of locally grown oak is in agreement with landscape history, as is the case in the 13th-century roof of Belsele church. The local origin of the wood as shown by dendrochronology fits medieval texts which confirm the nearby presence of stretches of natural forest in the 13th century.[29] Near Ypres, Saint John's church in Poperinge is a similar case [Fig. 8]. Tree ring analysis dated the roof to the middle of the 14th century, a significant adjustment of the previously accepted dating, as well as indicating a possible use of local oak.[30] Again, a local origin is corroborated by historical data. During the building of Saint John's church around 1350, Poperinge did not have access to navigable waterways which could have enabled the import of foreign oak

Fig.7 Ypres, excavation site of Saint Michael's borough [© Onroerend Erfgoed].

from Southern Belgium, as was the case in coastal cities like Bruges and Damme. The near-impossibility of transport over water seems to have directed the builders towards the remaining local wood reserves. Also in Poperinge, the 14th-century church of Our Lady preserves a roof undoubtedly made of local wood. Whether dating back to the 14th century or of a later date could not be established, but even without decisive tree ring dating the roof was not without a surprise. The entirety of the roof was not made of oak but elm (*Ulmus*), a finding once more in agreement with historical data. During the early modern period, the area to the west of Ypres and up to the North Sea coast was renowned for the cultivation of elm, also known as the poor man's oak.[31] Thus the roof of Our Lady's church is a remarkable material testimony of a once thriving regional botanical industry.

Fig.8 The roof of the nave of Saint John's church in Poperinge, tree ring dated to 1347-56d [© Vincent Debonne].

Conclusion

Over the past decades, dendrochronology has undeniably proven its value for heritage research and conservation in Belgium. Construction dates based on style and general architectural history have been adjusted considerably, often forcing to rejuvenate commonly accepted chronologies and, more importantly, revealing the unique historical value of buildings. Thus building archaeology is intimately tied to conservation of architectural heritage. The house Kraanplein number 4 in Bruges is a case in point. Archaeological analysis and tree ring dating showed the hitherto unknown medieval origin of the house, still preserved from the cellar up to the roof. Based on the findings of the archaeological research, the municipal heritage service has supervised the restoration of the house, in this way conserving an unsuspected example of medieval architecture. However the contribution of dendrochronology is not limited to dating. By identifying the provenance of wood used in monuments, building archaeology touches upon landscape history and historical ecology, adding a holistic dimension to the research and conservation of architectural heritage.

notes

① The city hall of Brussels (1998), the Flemish beguinages (1998), the belfries of Belgium and North France (1999), the medieval city centre of Bruges (2000), and the cathedral of Tournai (2000).

② Debonne, Vincent; Bailiff, Ian; Blain, Sophie; Ech-Chakrouni, Souad; Hus, Jozef; Van Strydonck, Mark; Haneca, Kristof, 'Wase baksteen gedateerd. Natuurwetenschappelijk dateringsonderzoek in de Sint-Andreas- en Sint-Gislenuskerk in Belsele (Sint-Niklaas)', *Relicta. Archeologie, Monumenten- en Landschapsonderzoek in Vlaanderen*, 12, 2015, p. 181-218.

③ Hus, Jozef; Ech-Chakrouni, Souad; Jordanova, D.; Geeraerts, R., 'Archaeomagnetic investigation of two Mediaeval brick constructions in North Belgium and the magnetic anisotropy of bricks', *Geoarcheology: An International Journal* 18.2, 2003, p. 225-253. On the method of archaeomagnetic dating: Hodsdon, Joan (ed.), *Archaeomagnetic Dating. Guidelines on producing and interpreting archaeomagnetic dates*, London: English Heritage, 2006, p. 3-13.

④ Debonne *et al.*, 'Wase baksteen gedateerd...', as in note 2, p. 198-206.

⑤ In Belsele twelve bricks were drilled, yielding sixteen samples. An additional nineteen samples were taken from ten loose bricks which undoubtedly were part of the brick masonry.

⑥ Sapin, Christian; Baylé, Maylis; Büttner, S.; Guibert, Pierre; Blain, Sophie; Lanos, P.; Chauvin, A.; Dufresne, P.; Oberlin, C., 'Archéologie du bâti et archéométrie au Mont-Saint-Michel, nouvelles approches de Notre-Dame-sous-Terre', *Archéologie Médiévale*, 38, 2008, p. 71-122 (esp. 102-108).

⑦ Bailiff, Ian K., 'Methodological developments in the dating of brick from late-medieval and post-medieval English buildings', *Archaeometry*, 49, 2007, p. 827-851; Blain, Sophie; Bailiff, Ian K.; Guibert, Pierre; Bouvier, Armel; Baylé, Maylis, 'An intercomparison study of luminescence dating protocols and techniques applied to medieval brick samples from Normandy (France)', *Quaternary Geochronology*, 5, 2010, p. 311-316.

⑧ Debonne *et al.*, 'Wase baksteen gedateerd...', as in note 2, p. 206-208.

⑨ Wilson, Moira A.; Carter, Margaret A.; Hall, Christopher; Hoff, William D.; Ince, Ceren; Savage, Shaun D.; McKay, Bernard; Betts, Ian M., 'Dating Fired-Clay Ceramics Using Long Term Power Law Rehydroxylation Kinetics', *Proceedings of the Royal Society A: Mathematical, Physical & Engineering Sciences*, 2009, 465.2108, p. 2407-2415.

⑩ Baillie, M.G.L., *A Slice Through Time. Dendrochronology and Precision Dating*, Abingdon: Routledge, 1995.

⑪ Stenvert, Ronald; van Tussenbroek, Gabri (eds), *Inleiding in de bouwhistorie. Opmeten en onderzoeken van oude gebouwen*, Utrecht: Matrijs, 2007, p. 74.

⑫ Miles, Dan, 'Refinements in the Interpretation of Tree-Ring Dates for Oak Building Timbers in England and Wales', *Vernacular Architecture*, 37, 2006, p. 84-96; Hoffsummer, Patrick, 'The Evolution of Roofing in Northern France and Belgium from the 11th to the 18th Century as Revealed by Dendrochronology", in: Haneca, Kristof; Verheyden, A.; Beeckman, H.; Gärtner, H.; Helle, G.; Schleser, G.H. (eds), *TRACE - Tree Rings in Archaeology, Climatology and Ecology, Volume 5. Proceedings of the Dendrosymposium 2006, April 20th-22nd, Tervuren, Belgium*, Schriften des Forschunszentrum Jülich, Reihe Umwelt, 74, Jülich, p. 21-27.

⑬ Haneca, Kristof; van Daalen, Sjoerd, 'The Roof is on Fire! A dendrochronological reconstruction of the restoration of the Basilica of Our

Lady in Tongeren (Belgium)', *Dendrochronologia*, 44, 2017, p. 153-163.

⑭ 'd' refers to a date obtained by dendrochronology.

⑮ Debonne *et al.*, 'Wase baksteen gedateerd...', as in note 2, 194-198.

⑯ Heinemeier, J.; Ringbom, Å.; Lindroos, A.; Sveinbjörnsdóttir, Á.E., 'Successful AMS ^{14}C dating of non-hydraulic lime mortars from the medieval churches of the Åland islands, Finland', *Radiocarbon*, 52.1, 2010, p. 171-204; Ringbom, Åsa; Lindroos, Alf; Heinemeier, Jan; Sonck-Koota, Pia, '19 years of mortar dating: learning from experience', *Radiocarbon*, 56.2, 2014, p. 619-635; van Strydonck, Mark, 'Radiocarbon dating of lime mortars: a historic overview', in: Papayianni, Ioanna; Stefanidou, Maria; Pachta, Vasiliki (eds.), *Proceedings of the 4th Historic Mortars Conference HMC2016, 10th-12th October 2016, Santorini, Greece*, Thessaloniki, 2016, p. 648-655.

⑰ Debonne, Vincent, *Uit de klei, in verband. Bouwen met baksteen in het graafschap Vlaanderen, 1200-1400. Out of Clay, Laid in Bond. Building with Brick in the County of Flanders, 1200-1400*, unpublished PhD dissertation, Leuven: University of Leuven, 2015, vol. 2, p. 26.

⑱ Gysseling, Maurits (ed.), *Corpus van Middelnederlandse teksten (tot en met het jaar 1300). Reeks I: Ambtelijke bescheiden*, 15 vols, The Hague, 1977, I-3, p. 1567-1574.

⑲ Debonne, Vincent; Haneca, Kristof, 'Damme (Flandre occidentale). Analyse dendrochronologique du chœur-halle de l'église Notre-Dame', *Bulletin Monumental*, 170/1, 2012, p. 60-62; Haneca, Kristof; Debonne, Vincent, 'Precise Tree-Ring Dating of Building Activities despite the Absence of Bark: A case-study on medieval church roofs in Damme, Belgium', *Dendrochronologia*, 30/1, 2012, p. 23-34.

⑳ Debonne, *Uit de klei...*, as in note 17, vol. 2, p. 13-22.

㉑ Janse, Herman; Devliegher, Luc, 'Middeleeuwse bekappingen in het vroegere graafschap Vlaanderen', *Bulletin van de Koninklijke Commissie voor Monumenten en Landschappen*, 13, 1962, p. 299-380 (esp. 326-327).

㉒ Debonne, *Uit de klei...*, as in note 17, vol. 1, p. 223-227.

㉓ Sosson, Jean-Pierre, *Les travaux publics de la ville de Bruges, XIVe-XVe siècles: les matériaux, les hommes*, Brussels: Crédit Communal de Belgique, 1977, p. 78-79.

㉔ Debonne, Vincent, 'Bruges. Étude archéologique du bâti d'une maison du XIIIe siècle au 4, place de la Grue (Kraanplein)', *Bulletin Monumental*, 175/4, 2017, p. 410-414.

㉕ As mentioned in the inventory of architectural heritage in Flanders, https://inventaris.onroerenderfgoed.be/erfgoedobjecten/29422.

㉖ Debonne and Haneca, 'Damme...', as in note 19.

㉗ Debonne, 'Bruges...', as in note 24.

㉘ Haneca, Kristof; Dewilde, Marc; Ervynck, Anton; Boeren, Ilse; Beeckman, Hans; Goetghebeur, Paul; Wyffels, Franky, 'De 'houten eeuw' van een Vlaamse stad. Archeologisch en dendrochronologisch onderzoek in Ieper (prov. West-Vlaanderen)', *Relicta. Archeologie, Monumenten- en Landschapsonderzoek in Vlaanderen*, 4, 2009, p. 99-134.

㉙ Debonne *et al.*, 'Wase baksteen gedateerd...', as in note 2, p. 190-191.

㉚ Debonne, *Uit de klei...*, as in note 17, vol. 2, p. 60-62.

㉛ Haneca, Kristof, 'Historisch bouwhout uit Vlaanderen: import uit noodzaak? Dendrochronologisch onderzoek als bron voor houthandel en-gebruik', *Bulletin KNOB*, 114/3, 2015, p. 58-169 (esp. 167).

宋金时期晋东南墓葬仿木构建筑史料研究

A Study on the Wood-Imitating Architecture in Tombs of the *Song* and *Jin* Dynasties in Southeast Shanxi Province

俞莉娜　徐怡涛 | YU Lina，XU Yitao

摘要：晋东南长治、晋城地区近年发现了丰富的宋金时期仿木构砖室墓遗存，其仿木营造复杂、对地面木构信息的模仿表达细致。本文以现有已公开发表的墓葬材料为基础，结合作者实地调研成果，对这批墓葬中仿木构建筑史料所反映的时代特点、与地面木构建筑的模拟转换关系进行讨论。

本文首先立足于考古类型学的基本方法，关注了北宋至金代晋东南墓葬仿木构建筑史料所体现的大木作、小木作及构造做法等形制，将本地区宋金时期墓葬仿木构建筑史料分为三期。在分期结论的基础上，结合晋东南地区丰富的宋金木构建筑遗存，就地下墓葬仿木构与地面木构在不同时期内的形制“转译”关系进行探讨。在墓葬仿木构建筑史料对于木构建筑形制的模仿关系方面，可以分为北宋哲宗以前、北宋哲宗和徽宗时期、金初至金中晚期三个阶段。

本文还将结合周边地区的宋金仿木构墓葬实例，简要讨论墓葬仿木构建筑史料的地区差异和传播问题。同时，通过梳理墓葬仿木构针对模拟木构形象所发展出的构造细节，探讨古代砌墓匠人以模拟地面木构形象为目的所发展出的建材转换的特殊工艺技法，从而探究此地区宋金时期的营墓思想和观念的发展变化。

关键词：晋东南；宋金墓葬；仿木构建筑史料；分期研究

Abstract: Large numbers of tombs with sophisticated wood-imitating structures of Song and Jin dynasties have been excavated in southeast district of Shanxi province. The paper is mainly based on the information of published archaeological reports of tombs，aiming to figure out the era changes of wood-imitating architectures in tombs of the area. Furthermore, the thesis also discusses about the relationship between the wood-imitating architecture and the wooden architecture on the ground.

作者简介：
俞莉娜，早稻田大学理工学术院博士后，日本学术振兴会特别研究员（PD）。
徐怡涛，北京大学考古文博学院，教授。

First, the paper discusses the stage dividing of timber structure, joinery works, and the brick-building technics of wood-imitating architecture of Song and Jin dynasties, using the theory of archaeological typology. Based on these models, the author outlined 3 stages spanning over Song and Jin dynasties.

Besides, by comparing the imitating wooden architecture with the wooden structures on the ground, the thesis talks about the transformational relation between the two kinds of historical materials.

Moreover, as an independent form of architecture, the thesis also discusses the design and construction methods of brick-building technology.

In addition, since there are also large numbers of tombs excavated in the surrounding region of southeast Shanxi, the thesis also takes a brief look at the regional differences and communication between different districts.

Keywords: Southeast Shanxi; Tombs of Song and Jin Dynasties; Wood-Imitating Architecture; Stage Dividing

一、晋东南地区宋金墓葬仿木构发现与研究概述

中国墓葬中进行仿木营建的行为自西汉起即已出现，此后历代墓葬中，均不同程度地体现出对地面木构建筑营建方式的模仿。从整体情况来看，汉代墓葬以仿木构随葬品和墓室石质仿木构装饰为主；魏晋南北朝及隋唐时期，墓葬中以仿木构壁画装饰为主流，少见有砖石制仿木构装饰；晚唐五代，中原北方地区砖制墓葬中开始出现流行使用仿木构筑物的现象。发展至宋金时期，仿木营造的现象更为广泛地见于中原北方地区的平民墓葬中，且较唐末五代时期墓葬中的仿木营造更为复杂、对地面木构的模仿表达更为细致。

晋东南、宋金时期仿木构砖室墓多为新中国成立后进行基础设施建设时偶然发现的，自1964年在长治李沟村发现金代仿木构砖（石）室墓以来，截至2016年5月该地区已发现宋金时期仿木构砖室墓50余座，其中纪年宋墓9座，纪年金墓11座，年代跨度在1079（北宋元丰元年）—1208（金泰和八年）年之间。出土地点分布于长治、屯留、壶关、潞城、沁县、沁源、高平、陵川等市县（图1）。

王进先《长治宋金元墓室建筑艺术研究》一书以长治地区发掘出土的宋金元时期仿木构墓葬为研究对象，从墓室结构、各部做法、建筑彩画及墓室装饰等角度进行了综合考察[①]。此外，在针对区域性宋金墓葬的考古学研究中，对此地区材料有所涉及，如秦大树《宋元明考

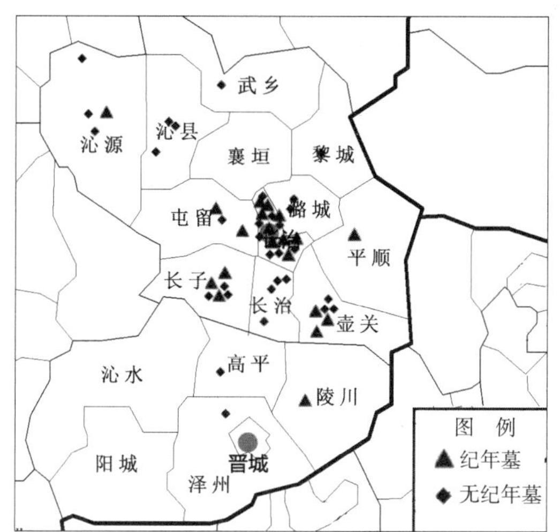

图1 晋东南地区宋金仿木构墓葬分布图（截至2016年5月）

古》一书中对北方宋金仿木构砖室墓的研究中将晋南、关中分为一区，并将北宋与金代仿木构砖室墓各分为三期[②]。许若茜在《山西金墓分期分区研究》中将晋东南金墓分为一区，并认为此区金代墓葬早晚延续性较强[③]。刘耀辉《晋南地区宋金墓葬研究》[④]、任林平《晋中南地区宋金墓葬研究》[⑤]等文中进行墓葬考古学分期分区研究时，均涉及晋东南地区的材料。此外，这批墓葬材料也运用至有关宋金墓葬装饰及葬俗文化的美术史研究中。

纵观既往研究，晋东南地区墓葬中的仿木构作为一种特殊的营造物，并未得到充分的关注和重视。而晋东南地区宋金时期的仿木构砖室墓葬，在墓葬考古的分区上存在其独有的地区特点，加上该地区在此时期存在丰富的地面木结构建筑遗存，因此为探讨该地区此时期砖制仿木构同地面木构的关系创造了极为有利的条件。

本文的研究即是利用上述之有利条件，在考古类型学方法的引导下就探讨仿木构材料同地面木构建筑之关系进行尝试，从中探索对仿木构材料研究之一般方法，从而为进行更广区域和更宽范围的仿木构材料研究提供范例。

二、晋东南宋金时期墓葬仿木构建筑史料形制分期

本文选择纪年明确、保存状况良好、信息记录完整的16座宋金时期墓葬为标尺实例，在仿木构大木作、仿木构小木作、仿木构屋檐以及仿木构构造做法四个方面进行形制排比，根据形制的演变状况形成分期结论。（详见文后附表）

（一）仿木构大木作形制分期

1. 总铺作次序

北宋哲宗元祐以前，该地区以五铺作双出杪斗栱（第二跳上不出令栱）以及四铺作单杪为典型斗栱形制，后者则一直延续至金代中后期。北宋元祐年起，开始流行五铺作单杪单下昂的斗栱形式，并一直延续至金章宗年间，偶见斗口跳等简单斗栱形制。金中期起还同时流行有四铺作单昂的斗栱形制。

2. 铺作对称性

就铺作对称性而言，该地区在北宋徽宗宣和以前，墓室各壁铺作对称。自宣和年间起出现墓室各壁铺作不对称的情况，通常为正壁铺作最为复杂（如出跳数量多、铺作用昂等），其次为墓门所在壁面，侧壁铺作最为简单。铺作不对称的情况一直延续至金章宗明昌年间，此间仍然并存有墓室各壁铺作对称的现象。

3. 补间铺作

该地区在金世宗大定以前，以做出一朵补间斗栱为主流形制。此时期内仅长治西白兔

村宋墓和长治魏村金墓，于每壁壁面出斗栱两朵[⑥]，而平顺县郊宋墓出补间斗栱三朵，为该地区唯一纪年实例。金大定末至明昌初年，普遍流行壁面出两朵补间斗栱的做法。

4. 跳头横栱

在该地区五铺作斗栱中，自北宋元丰元年（1078 年）长治故县 M2 至金明昌六年（1195 年）长治安昌金墓，均以计心单栱为主流形制。仅上限为元祐二年（1087 年）的壶关南村宋墓和宣和五年（1123 年）壶关下好牢宋墓两例见有计心重栱的做法，由此推测计心重栱做法在北宋晚期短暂存在于晋东南部分地区。仅天德三年（1151 年）魏村金墓一例见有五铺作偷心的做法。

5. 扶壁栱

北宋宣和以前，该地区仿木构斗栱为扶壁做泥道单栱的形式。北宋宣和年间至金天德三年（1151 年）流行扶壁栱做泥道单栱承枋并隐刻慢栱的形式，偶见泥道重栱和泥道单栱的做法。金天德三年（1151 年）后至金明昌年间，重新流行扶壁泥道单栱的形式。

6. 令栱、泥道栱长度比

在北宋徽宗宣和年间以前，该地区以令栱短于或等于泥道栱长为主流形制。北宋宣和年间至金章宗明昌年间，该地区以令栱长于泥道栱为主流形制，仅长子特高压宋墓及长子小关村金墓见有令栱短于泥道栱的现象。同时，如平顺县郊宋墓及沁源正中村金墓，见有令栱位出实拍栱和翼型栱的形制。

7. 栱臂做法

该地区宋金墓葬以栱臂平直为主流形制，纪年墓中仅壶关南村宋墓见有跳头横栱看面抹斜的做法，推测抹斜形制在北宋晚期短暂存在于晋东南地区墓葬中。

8. 昂

该地区纪年墓中用昂的实例不多。元祐七年（1092 年）平顺张家洼宋墓中同时见有批竹起棱和琴面起棱两类昂型，应是新旧形制并存的体现。除宣和五年（1123 年）壶关下好牢宋墓采用《营造法式》型琴面昂之外，其他墓例均用琴面起棱式昂的形制。

9. 耍头

该地区仿木构斗栱见有使用昂型耍头的传统，北宋中晚期流行使用批竹或批竹起棱的形式，金初至金大定前期流行使用琴面起棱型耍头的形式。蚂蚱头型耍头最早见于北宋元祐七年（1092 年）平顺张家洼宋墓，此后一直延续至金明昌年间，值得注意的是，北宋所见蚂蚱头实例均不做鹊台，而金代蚂蚱头实例均表现出鹊台的形制。

10. 斗欹做法

该地区标尺实例中，金天德年间以前流行仿木构斗栱做出内䫜斗欹的现象，北宋晚期几例纪年实例还见有斗欹深内䫜并略有下撇出峰的情况。自金天德年间起，开始在纪年墓葬实例中见有斗欹做出直线不内幽页的现象，此时期斗欹内䫜的实例，也不再见有北宋晚期下撇出峰的现象。

11. 仿木构大木作形制分期结论

第一期：北宋哲宗元祐年间以前（1086 年以前）

该期典型形制为，墓室各壁铺作对称，斗栱见有四铺作单栱和五铺作双出杪两种形式，补间铺作每间一朵，扶壁为泥道单栱的形式，不做令栱或令栱与泥道栱等长。栱臂平直不抹斜。耍头见有批竹起棱型。斗欹内䫜明显。墓室柱头均出有普拍枋。

第二期：北宋哲宗元祐至北宋徽宗宣和五年以前（1086—1123 年）

该期典型形制为，墓室各壁铺作对称，见有四铺作单杪、五铺作双杪及五铺作单杪单昂的形式，补间铺作并存每间一朵和两朵，跳头出现出重栱的做法，扶壁并存泥道单栱和泥道单栱承枋隐刻慢栱两种形式，令栱并存有较泥道栱为短和为长两种形式。栱臂出现跳头横栱抹斜的现象。昂型并存见有批竹起棱和琴面起棱平出昂，耍头并存见有批竹式和批竹起棱式，并出现蚂蚱头耍头。斗欹内顱明显，部分墓葬见有下撇出峰的现象。墓室柱头均出有普拍枋。

第三期：北宋徽宗宣和五年至金章宗明昌年间[⑦]（1123—1195 年），分为前后两段

前段为北宋徽宗宣和五年至金世宗大定十四年（1123—1174 年）。典型形制为，墓室仍以铺作对称为主流形制，但北宋末期开始见有墓室铺作不对称、突出南北壁的现象。出现五铺作单杪单昂的做法，仍并存有四铺作单杪的形式，补间铺作仍以每间一朵为主流形制，跳头并存出重栱和偷心的形式，扶壁栱以泥道单栱承枋隐刻慢栱为主流形制，出现泥道重栱做法，令栱以长于泥道栱为主流形制，并存令栱短于泥道栱的做法。栱臂平直不抹斜。耍头并存见有蚂蚱头、批竹起棱式和琴面昂型。昂并存有《营造法式》型琴面昂和琴面起棱型平出昂式。斗欹做法仍以做出内顱为主流形制，金天德年间开始见有斗欹不做内顱的现象。墓室柱头均出有普拍枋。

后段为金世宗大定十四年以后至金明昌年间（1174—1195 年）。典型形制为，墓室并存有铺作对称和不对称的铺作布置形式。铺作见有四铺作单杪、四铺作单昂、五铺作单杪单昂三种形式。补间斗栱以出两朵为主流。跳头为计心单栱，扶壁栱以泥道单栱为主流形制，令栱长于泥道栱。栱臂平直不抹斜。耍头以蚂蚱头为主流形制，昂均为琴面起棱式平出昂。斗欹内顱退化，不见有上一期深内顱的做法。墓室柱头出现不用普拍枋做法，并见有使用月梁型阑额（图 2、表 1）。

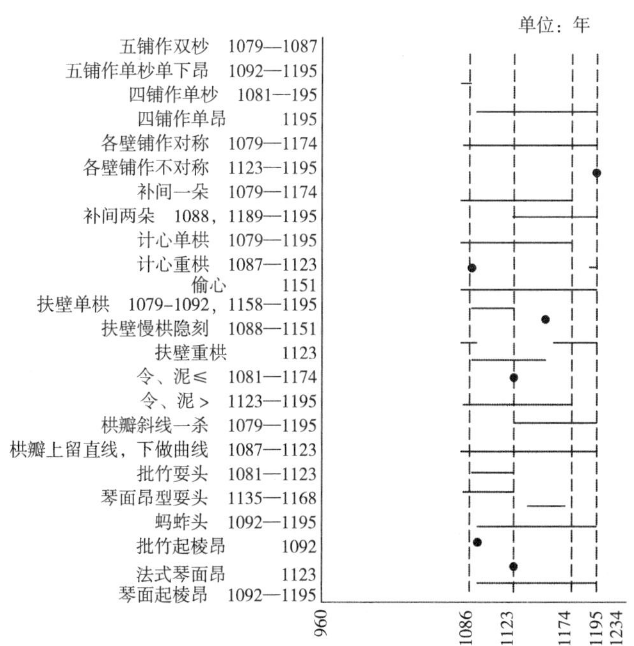

图 2　晋东南地区仿木构大木作形制分期图

（二）仿木构小木作形制分期

该地区仿木构小木作形制受到墓葬形制的限制，即晋东南地区宋金墓葬以方形带耳室墓为主流形制，由于壁面有连通耳室的需要，因此墓葬主室壁面以砌筑多处假门窗为主流装饰形制，其余装饰题材（如孝悌、劳作、庖厨、人物等图像题材）均附属于假门窗而布置。主室通向耳室的开口，多做成券门或仿木构版门

晋东南仿木构大木作史料分期表 表 1

分期	年代区间	典型实例
第一期	北宋哲宗元祐年间以前（1086 年以前）	长治故县 M2 墓室斗栱　长治五马村宋墓墓室斗栱
第二期	北宋哲宗元祐至北宋徽宗宣和五年以前（1086—1123 年）	壶关南村宋墓墓室斗栱
第三期	前段：北宋徽宗宣和五年至金大定十四年（1123—1174 年）	壶关下好牢宋墓北壁柱头斗栱　长治魏村金墓墓室斗栱
	后段：金大定十四年以后至金明昌年间（1174—1195 年）	长治故漳村金墓墓室北壁斗栱

的形制。如每面仅通耳室一个或不做耳室，则壁面流行一门二窗的布置，门洞左右多布置有较小的方形破子棂窗。

该地区仿木构小木作不见有明显的年代变化，仿木构假门形制仅在金大定年间出现有使用格子门门扇的情况，格眼为简单几何形，改变了此前仿木构假门均为版门形制的现象（图 3）。

（三） 仿木构屋檐形制分期

1. 屋檐做法

该地区在金世宗大定以前，墓葬主室以做出仿木构屋檐为主流形制，具体表现为在橑檐枋上置檐椽一层（部分墓葬见有使用飞椽的现象），其上覆瓦。金大定年间长子小关村墓及长治故漳村金墓不见有墓室出檐的现象。

2. 墓室檐高

该地区在北宋宣和年以前，墓室均为四壁檐高相等的形制。宣和五年（1123 年）壶关下好牢墓首见有墓室壁面檐高不等的现象，北壁及南壁高于侧壁，侧壁屋檐上部做出歇山顶，以示房屋山面。檐高不等的做法一直保留在金代仿木构墓葬中。

（a）

（b）

图 3 晋东南宋金时期仿木构门窗实例（a. 长治王村宋墓，1079 年；b. 长治故漳村金墓，1189 年。摄于长治市博物馆）

南北壁高于侧壁的形制同墓室铺作不对称的形制相对应，可见墓室仿木构设计中存在将正壁强调突出的意识。

3. 出檐数量

该地区宋金墓葬墓室以出单檐为主流形制。纪年墓中仅天会十三年（1147 年）屯留宋村墓见有出重檐的做法。其形成起因应是墓室孝行题材图像布置位置的变化。该地区北宋纪年墓中孝行题材图像多布置于门窗左右的壁面位置，无固定的分布。而自金初开始，孝行题材图像多布置于普拍枋之下，形成固定的装饰条带，该布置方式见于屯留宋村金墓、长治魏村金墓、长子石哲金墓和长子小关村金墓中。屯留宋村金墓四壁周圈布置孝行题材图像，为了保证这一装饰带的整体性，墓葬壁面以出重檐的方式将装饰带上下的墓葬装饰分隔开来。

4. 仿木构屋檐形制分期结论

第一期：金大定十四年以前（1074 年以前）

该期的典型形制为，仿木构墓葬均做出仿木构屋檐。墓室各壁以檐高相等为主流形制，纪年墓中仅北宋宣和五年（1123 年）壶关下好牢墓见有墓室各壁檐高不同的现象。墓室以出单檐为主，金代初期见有墓室出重檐的现象。

第二期：金大定十四年至金明昌年间（1174—1195 年）

该期的典型形制为，仿木构墓葬出现了不做仿木构屋檐的现象，如长子小关村金墓斗栱上仅叠涩以表现屋檐，仍并存有做出屋檐的做法。墓室各壁檐高并存檐高相等和檐高不等的做法，此做法和墓室斗栱对称性相对应。墓室以单檐为主流形制（图 4、表 2）。

（四）仿木构构造做法形制分期

1. 斗类构件加工

北宋哲宗元祐以前，该地区仿木构斗类构件加工均为条砖叠砌的加工方式，上限为元祐二年（1087 年）的壶关南村宋墓首见墓室整体使用预制斗类构件的现象。预制构件的做法一直延续至金章宗明昌年间。而叠砌做法在金代仍有保留。

就各斗类构件的体量大小而言，金大定晚期以前，无论是叠砌构件还是预制构件，一朵斗栱中栌斗体量最大，其余斗类体量相当。金

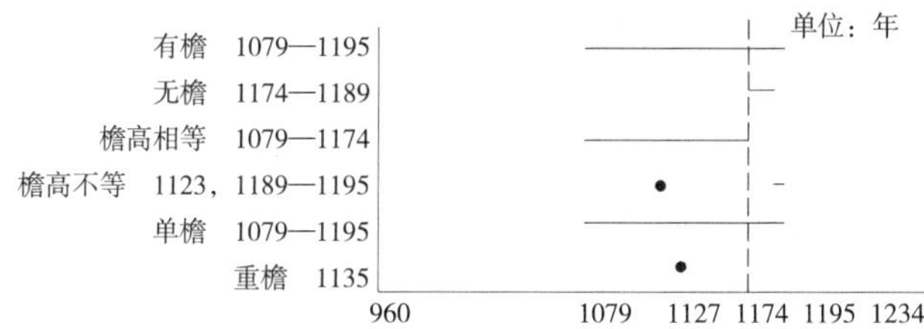

图 4　晋东南地区仿木构屋檐形制分期图

晋东南仿木构屋檐分期表　　**表 2**

分期	年代区间	典型实例	
第一期	金世宗大定十四年以前（1174 年以前）	长治故县王村 M1 仿木构屋檐	壶关下好牢宋墓仿木构屋檐
第二期	金大定十四年至金明昌年间（1174—1195 年）	长子小关村金墓屋檐	长治故漳村金墓仿木构屋檐

大定二十九年（1189 年）长治故漳金墓和金明昌六年（1195 年）长治安昌金墓，开始见有多种体量的斗类构件组合，即栌斗体量最大，其次为交互斗和齐心斗，散斗体量最小，且见有不同壁面同一斗类构件体量不同的现象。

2. 栱类构件加工

北宋元祐以前，该地区仿木构横栱构件加工，见有条砖立砌影作横栱和条砖平砌斫为横栱两种形式。年代上限为元祐二年（1087 年）的壶关南村宋墓首见有预制栱类构件的做法，此后北宋晚期至金章宗明昌年间，仿木构横栱构件加工并存见有条砖叠砌和预制构件两种加工形式。

3. 横栱布置

该地区自北宋神宗元丰年间起，即流行有将跳头横栱突出并置于出跳构件同一直线上的做法，如元丰元年（1078 年）长治故县 M1 及 M2，虽未做出形象化的跳头横栱，但将条砖立砌置于第一条华栱之上，已经反映出表现跳头横栱的意识。此后直至金世宗大定年间，墓室仿木构斗栱均做出突出或脱离壁面的形象，与跳头处于同一直线。值得注意的是，宣和五年（1123 年）长子特高压宋墓墓室令栱由薄砖块预制而成，栱身上部靠近壁面，下部位于跳头之上，可见该地区建造墓室仿木构斗栱时对表现跳头横栱的意识十分强烈。而金正隆年间至明昌年间，该地区墓室仿木构见有跳头横栱突出壁面但较跳头缩进于壁面，可见此时摒弃了脱离壁面、仅用交互斗承托预制横栱构件的不稳定结构，着重对仿木构斗栱进行正立面的表达。

4. 垂直壁面方向构件厚度

北宋宣和以前，该地区墓葬仿木构斗栱垂直壁面方向构件厚度相等。宣和五年 1123 年长子特高压宋墓首见华栱厚于耍头的现象，此后金大定十四年 1174 年长子小关村金墓和明昌六年 1195 年长治安昌金墓也见有华栱或昂厚于耍头的做法。垂直壁面构件厚度不等的做法鲜见于中原其他地区的宋金墓葬内，应是晋东南地区的特有做法。

5. 昂类构件加工

宋代晚期至金代，仿木构昂多以模制构件制成，仿木构昂以砖块做出底面平出的做法为主流形制，纪年墓葬中仅壶关下好牢宋墓用预制砖块做出斜向下昂的形制。

6. 仿木构构造做法分期结论

第一期：北宋哲宗元祐以前（1086 年以前）

该期的典型形制为，仿木构斗为条砖叠砌加工而成，各类斗体量相当，横栱为条砖加工而成，跳头横栱并存有突出壁面和浅浮雕的做法，垂直壁面方向构件厚度相同。

第二期：北宋哲宗元祐年间至金世宗大定十四年（1086—1174 年），分为前后两段。

前段为北宋哲宗元祐至北宋宣和五年（1086—1123 年）。典型形制为，仿木构斗栱出现使用模砖构件，部分地区发展出了高度模制化的做法，以壶关地区最为兴盛。同时并存有自上期延续下来的条砖叠砌加工的方式。各类斗体量相当。跳头横栱均突出或脱离壁面，以横栱与跳头处同一直线为主流形制。

后段为北宋宣和五年以后至金大定十四年（1123—1174 年）。典型形制为，宋末高度模制化的斗栱制作技术被摒弃，条砖为基础的构件加工形制得到发扬。部分斗栱构件仍见有使用模砖构件的做法。各类斗体量相当。跳头横

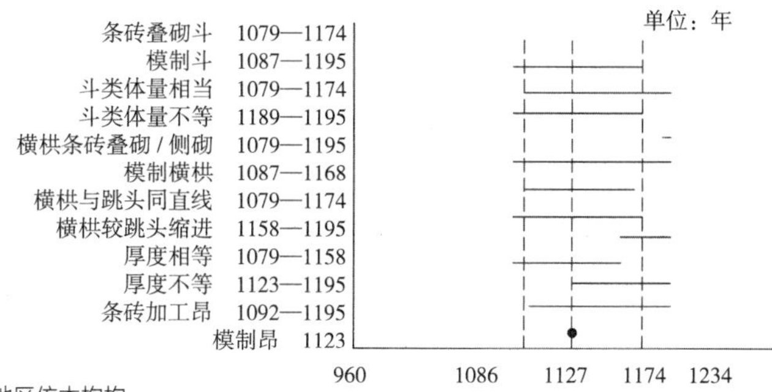

图 5 晋东南地区仿木构构造做法分期图

晋东南仿木构构造做法分期表　　表 3

分期	年代区间	典型实例
第一期	北宋哲宗元祐年间以前（1086 年以前）	长治五马村宋墓墓室斗栱
第二期	前段：北宋哲宗元祐年间至宣和五年（1086—1123 年）	长子特高压宋墓墓室斗栱　壶关下好牢宋墓墓室斗栱
	后段：北宋宣和五年至金大定十四年（1123—1174 年）	长治魏村金墓墓室斗栱　长子石哲金墓墓室斗栱
第三期	金世宗大定十四年以后至金章宗明昌年间（1174—1195 年）	长治故漳村金墓墓室斗栱

栱均突出或脱离壁面，以横栱与跳头处同一直线为主流形制。垂直壁面方向构件以厚度相同为主流，部分见有厚度不等的做法。

第三期：金世宗大定十四年以后至金章宗明昌年间（1174—1195 年）

该期的典型形制为，仿木构横栱以条砖叠砌做法为主流形制，但此阶段流行在彩画底层涂刷较厚的白灰以掩盖砖缝的痕迹。各类斗见有体量不等的现象，栌斗体量最大，其次为交互斗和齐心斗，散斗体量最小。扶壁位置层层叠涩使得跳头横栱突出壁面，但仍较跳头更为缩进。垂直壁面方向构件厚度不等，表现为耍头薄于华栱或昂（图 5、表 3）。

（五）总体分期结论

根据上文可知，晋东南地区墓葬仿木构建筑史料在大木作形制、屋檐形制、仿木构构造做法等方面存在时代变化上的一致性，大致可分为三期：

第一期：北宋哲宗元祐以前（1086 年以前）

该期仿木构斗栱仅见有四铺作单杪和五铺作双出杪两种较为简单的铺作形式。墓室各壁面铺作形式对称，补间每间一朵，墓室斗栱或出跳甚短、跳头横栱浮雕于壁面，或出跳较深远、跳头出贯通相邻斗栱的整条横枋并彩绘横栱。扶壁栱为泥道单栱的形式，令栱与泥道栱等长，栱臂平直不抹斜，耍头或不做，或做成批竹斜杀起棱的形式。墓室柱头均出普拍枋。墓室见有多处仿木构门窗布置，仿木构门为版门形制，仿木构窗多见有破子棂窗和直棂窗的形制。该期墓室均出有仿木构屋檐，各壁屋檐同高，不见有重檐的做法。该期仿木构斗栱以条砖为基础斫成各类构件，各斗类构件体量接近。同时，该期仿木构墓葬已存在将跳头横栱突出的意识，垂直壁面方向构件厚度均相等。

总体而言，该期的三座标尺墓葬中，故县M1、M2体现了华栱出跳深远、斗栱排列密集、不出跳头横栱、斗栱构件硕大的特点，五马村墓体现了华栱出跳较短、斗栱排列舒朗、表现跳头横栱、斗栱构件体量小等特点。可知该期并存了至少两种墓葬仿木构建筑的建造观念，是该地区仿木构墓葬发展的雏形期。

第二期：北宋哲宗元祐年间至金大定十四年（1086—1174年），分为前后两段

前段为北宋哲宗元祐年间至北宋宣和五年（1086—1123年），仿木构斗栱形制较上期复杂，出现了五铺作单杪单昂、五铺作双杪的铺作形制。墓室斗栱出现各壁不对称的情况。补间斗栱较上一期为多，跳头并存计心单栱及计心重栱的形式，扶壁以泥道单栱承枋隐刻（或壁绘）慢栱为主流形制。令栱和泥道栱长度比见有从短于向长于的变化过程。跳头横栱以栱臂平直为主流形制，但见有看面抹斜的做法。耍头见有从批竹式向蚂蚱头型的转变。斗栱出现用昂，昂型并存有批竹起棱式和琴面昂式两种，北宋末期还出现了与《营造法式》规定相符的琴面昂形式。偶见有出斜栱及令栱位出翼型栱的形制。此段延续了上期版门和破子棂窗组合的形制，同时见有主室开券门通耳室的做法，不做仿木构假门。仿木构墓葬均做出仿木构屋檐，墓室均出单檐，并存檐高相同和檐高不等的做法，檐高不等的实例均体现出突出正壁的设计思想。此段出现有砖制仿木构斗栱使用整体预制构件的做法，各斗类构件体量相近，跳头横栱出现构件脱离壁面、直接承于交互斗之上的做法，与跳头处同一直线。垂直壁面方向构件厚度相同。

后段为北宋宣和五年至金大定十四年以前（1123—1174年），此段仿木构斗栱形制延续了前段的形式，不见有新形式出现。补间以每间一朵为主流形制，跳头出现偷心做法，扶壁并存泥道单栱和泥道单栱承枋隐刻（壁绘）慢栱的形制。令栱并存见有短于及长于泥道栱的做法，仍见有令栱位出翼型栱的形制。耍头并存琴面昂型及蚂蚱头型。昂为琴面起棱平出式。仿木构门窗仍以版门和棂窗为主要组合形式，出现版门门框内不做门扇而改绘图像的做法。墓葬中均表现仿木构屋檐，仍见有檐高不等的做法，同前段不同的是，此段开始流行墓室斗栱下做出孝行图像装饰带的现象，因此部分墓葬见有出重檐的现象。就仿木构构造做法而言，该期斗栱构件并存有叠砌和预制两种加工方式，跳头横栱做法延续前段，垂直壁面构件厚度相等。

总体而言，晋东南墓葬仿木构至北宋晚期较上一期继续发展，表现为仿木构斗栱形制复杂、同类仿木构建筑史料出现数种并存形制、墓室不同壁面出现表现上的等级分异、仿木构构件加工方式更为精致等。进入金代之后，墓葬仿木构虽较北宋晚期略有简化，但整体反映出了对北宋晚期做法的延续。因此，可认为此期是该地区墓葬仿木构的发展变化期。

第三期：金大定十四年至金章宗明昌年间（1174—1195年）

该期墓室斗栱形式延续了上一期的特征。同时，此期流行的铺作不对称形制似是北宋末期做法的复兴。补间流行每壁两朵，五铺作斗栱均为计心单栱做法，扶壁均为泥道单栱形制，

令栱以长于泥道栱为主流形制。横栱均为栱臂平直。耍头均为蚂蚱头形式。昂头均为琴面起棱平出昂。墓室柱头出现不用普拍枋做法，并见有使用月梁型阑额。仿木构小木作方面，此期的主要变化是流行起格子门门扇的做法。该期出现墓室不使用仿木构屋檐的墓例，墓室檐高不等、南北壁檐高高于侧壁的做法仍然存在，上期后段所见重檐做法在此期消失。该期仿木构斗栱构造以条砖为基础的加工形式为主流，在部分构件上仍见有使用预制栱的做法，与此前不同的是，此阶段仿木构斗栱表面多涂刷较厚的白灰层，以掩盖砖缝的痕迹（如长治安昌金墓及故漳金墓）。仿木构斗类构件开始出现体量大小的明显差异。跳头横栱突出但不脱离壁面，流行跳头横栱较跳头构件更为缩进的做法。垂直壁面构件流行厚度不同的做法，表现为耍头较出跳构件为薄（图6）。

总体而言，该期在延续上一期后段的仿木构形制后出现了变化，表现为出现了北宋末期檐高不等和铺作不对称的墓室营建思想的复兴、斗类构件比例出现变化、栱臂回归生硬直线的处理等，可看出该期墓葬仿木构出现了程式化处理的现象，可认为该期是晋东南墓葬仿木构发展的形制固定期[⑧]。

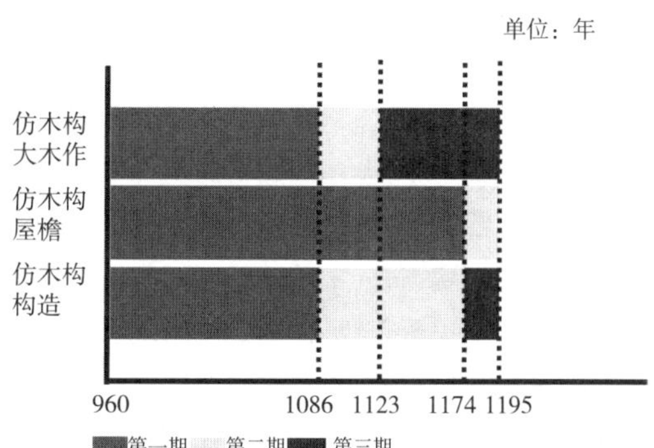

图6　晋东南地区墓葬仿木构建筑史料总体分期图

三、晋东南墓葬仿木构建筑史料与地面木构建筑的对比

徐怡涛《长治、晋城地区的五代、宋、金寺庙建筑》[⑨]一文中将晋东南五代、宋、金时期木构建筑斗栱构件组合分为三期，五代至北宋熙宁元年前后、北宋熙宁元年前后至北宋宣和元年前后、北宋宣和元年至金（其中又分为北宋宣和元年至金大定时期，金大定时期至金末两段），分期过程中考量了斗欹曲线、横栱、耍头、下昂等多种构件形制。本节将以此分期结论为参考对象，结合晋东南宋金时期木构建筑遗存，考量晋东南墓葬仿木构斗栱与地面木构斗栱的对比关系。

（一）总铺作次序

晋东南五代至金带木构建筑铺作形制有以四铺作和五铺作为主（图7、图8），仅高平崇明寺大殿柱头铺作采用七铺作形式。四铺作斗栱最早见于晚唐平顺天台庵大殿及五代平顺龙门寺西配殿，均采用不出令栱的斗口跳形式。北宋一代木构建筑以采用五铺作为主流，并存见有四铺作单杪的斗栱形式。至金大定年间，开始出现四铺作单假昂的形式，并一直延续至金末。五铺作斗栱最早见于五代后晋天福五年（946年）的平顺大云院弥陀殿，为五铺作双杪偷心形式，此后北宋初至北宋中期嘉祐年间，流行五铺作单杪单下昂偷心形式，北宋熙宁年间起直至金大定年间，均流行五铺作单杪单下昂计心重栱形式，少见有五铺作单杪单下昂计心单栱和五铺作双杪计心重栱形式，至金中期正隆年间起，由于柱头假昂的出现和流行，开始出现五铺作

图 7 晋东南宋金仿木构及木构四铺作斗栱示例（左）
（a）长治五马村宋墓墓室斗栱，1081 年；（b）长治上好牢 M1 侧壁斗栱，北宋晚期；（c）长子特高压宋墓墓室斗栱，1125 年；（d）长子小关村金墓墓室斗栱，1174 年；（e）长治故漳金墓侧壁斗栱，1189 年；（f）泽州北义城玉皇庙柱头斗栱，1110 年；（g）泽州高都天齐庙大殿柱头斗栱，1178 年；（h）陵川石掌玉皇庙大殿山面补间斗栱，1208 年（图片来源：a、b、d 图源自墓葬简报；c 图源自长子县文物局提供；其余为作者自摄）

图 8 晋东南宋金仿木构及木构五铺作斗栱示例（右）
（a）长治王村 M1 墓室斗栱，1079 年左右；（b）壶关南村宋墓墓室斗栱，上限 1087 年；（c）壶关下好牢宋墓正壁斗栱，1125 年；（d）长治魏村金墓墓室斗栱，1151 年；（e）长治故漳金墓正壁斗栱，1189 年；（f）平顺大云院补间斗栱，940 年；（g）陵川南吉祥寺柱头斗栱，1030 年；（h）高平开化寺中殿柱头斗栱，1073 年；（i）晋城崇寿寺中殿柱头斗栱，1119 年；（j）高平西李门二仙庙中殿柱头斗栱，1157 年（图片来源：b、c、d 图源自墓葬简报；其余为作者自摄）

双昂计心重栱形式，并一直延续至金末。

根据以上的考察可知，晋东南宋金仿木构铺作形制也以四铺作和五铺作为主，四铺作斗栱最早见于北宋元祐年间长治五马村宋墓，并一直延续至金中晚期。五铺作斗栱最早见于宋元丰年间的故县 M2，为双出杪形式，应是五代以来木构做法的延续，且故县 M2 所见双出杪不做令栱的斗栱形式，也是中原北方地区宋代砖塔仿木斗栱所采用的主流形制。自北宋元祐年间起，晋东南墓葬中开始流行五铺作单杪单昂形制，并一直延续至金明昌年间，这类斗栱形式也是地面木构所见主流形制，可见地下墓葬营造自哲宗时起开始注重对地面木构建筑斗栱形式的模仿。

值得注意的是，晋东南墓葬中自北宋晚期起便见有墓室各壁铺作布置不对称的现象，表现为正壁及墓门所在壁面使用五铺作、侧壁使用四铺作的情况，此形制一直流行至金代中晚期。结合正壁檐高高于侧壁的共存形制，推测此类型墓葬设计时将墓室视为一建筑组群院落，正壁为院落正房，而侧壁则表现为偏房形式。

（二）补间铺作

晋东南地面木构在金代以前，以不做补间或补间一朵为主流形制。自金天会年间陵川龙岩寺大殿出现当心补间两朵、次间补间一朵的形制后，这类补间斗栱的组合一直保留至金代中期。但金代仍并存有较多不做补间或者补间一朵的木构实例。

晋东南墓葬以方形为主流平面形式，补间斗栱的布置受墓葬平面形式的制约较小。金大定晚期以前，该地区墓室补间斗栱以不出补间或出一朵补间斗栱为主流形制，仅北宋元祐年间长治西白兔村宋墓及平顺张家洼宋墓出现补间两朵及以上的做法。金大定晚期至明昌年间，该地区出现了固定使用补间两朵的墓葬实例。

墓葬中所流行的无补间或一朵补间的做法，与地面宋金木构中所体现的流行做法一致。参考北宋晚期墓葬中壁面做出三开间的主流形制，元祐年间所出现的补间两朵及以上的做法，可能是壁面省去表现明间立柱所致，不能因此推断补间两朵的形制早在北宋哲宗年间即出现。墓葬中至金大定晚期才流行真正意义上的补间两朵形制，较地面木构中该形制的出现晚了半个世纪之多。

（三）跳头横栱

晋东南地面木构在北宋熙宁以前，流行跳头偷心做法，仅在高平崇明寺大殿柱头斗栱之上见有跳头出重栱的形式。自熙宁年间起该地区木构建筑流行使用计心重栱的形式，并一直延续至金代末年，期间偶见有计心单栱的做法。

墓葬中所见计心重栱的形制出现于北宋哲宗时期，并一直延续至北宋宣和年间，壶关南村宋墓、壶关上好牢 M1 及壶关下好牢宋墓为实例所见使用计心重栱的墓例。然而，金代墓葬仿木构实例均不见有使用计心重栱的做法，而以计心单栱为绝对的主流形制，与地面木构流行做法不符。由此可知，计心重栱的形制在墓葬中的出现较地面木构滞后十几年，且很有可能是北宋晚期仅限于壶关地区的流行做法。金代墓葬中摒弃计心重栱的做法可能是因为跳头横栱加工困难、计心单栱较重栱形制更易于表现所致。

（四）扶壁栱

晋东南地区五代至金末一直流行单栱承枋并隐刻慢栱的形制，偶见无隐刻慢栱的单栱承枋式扶壁栱，仅正隆二年（1157 年）的西李门二仙庙大殿和明昌年间的韩坊尧王庙大殿采用扶壁重栱的形制（图 9）。

宋金墓葬仿木构中扶壁以单栱承枋形制为主流，仅长子特高压宋墓见有完整的扶壁重栱形制，西白兔村宋墓、下好牢宋墓及魏村金墓则见有影作慢栱的现象，与地面宋金木构主流形制一致。就影作慢栱出现的时间而言，墓葬仿木构中影作慢栱出现时间晚于木构一百多年。而长子特高压宋墓则反映了扶壁重栱的形

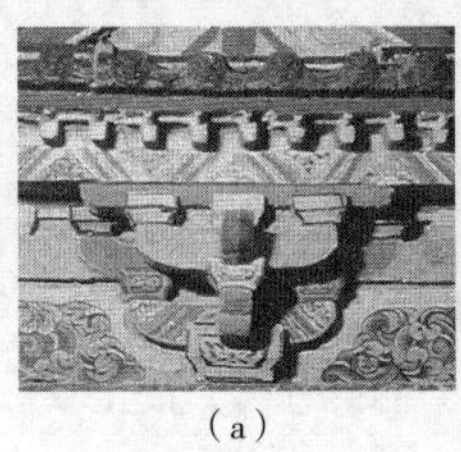
(a)

(b)

(c)

(d)
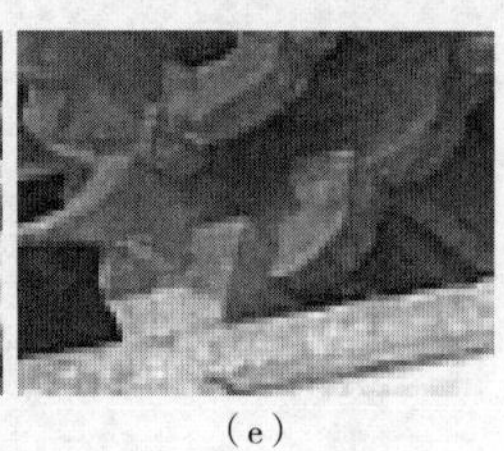
(e)

图 9 晋东南宋金仿木构及木构扶壁栱形制对比
(a)壶关下好牢宋墓侧壁斗栱，1125 年；(b)长子特高压宋墓墓室斗栱，1125 年；(c)沁源正中村金墓墓室斗栱，1168 年；(d)晋城青莲寺中殿柱头斗栱，1089 年；(e)高平西李门二仙庙中殿柱头斗栱，1157 年(图片来源：a、c 图源自墓葬简报；b 图源自长子文物局提供；其余为作者自摄)

制在北宋晚期可能已出现于地面木构之中。由于仿木斗栱中扶壁栱采取壁绘和浮雕两种表现方式，其本身即为一纯装饰构件，因此不表现慢栱可能是追求加工便利所致。

(五)令栱泥道栱长

实例所见五代至北宋元丰年间木构建筑斗栱令栱均短于或等于泥道栱长，而至元祐年间首见有令栱长于泥道栱的做法，并成为延续至金末的流行形制。

仿木构中最早出现完整令栱的五马村宋墓令栱与泥道栱等长，而自壶关南村宋墓起仿木构以令栱长于泥道栱为主流，仅长子小关村金墓令见有令栱短于泥道栱。由于壶关南村宋墓仅是出土有元祐二年(1087 年)题记的经幢，墓葬建造年代应晚于此纪年，推测令栱长于泥道栱的形制在哲宗中晚期流行至地下墓葬中，对比地面木构的变化过程，此形制在墓葬中的出现几乎与地面同期。

(六)昂型

晋东南地区最早的用昂实例见于五代大云院弥陀殿转角铺作，为批竹式昂型。北宋时期五铺作建筑均使用下昂，昂型以批竹起棱式为主，偶见从五代延续下来的批竹斜杀式昂型，北宋末期出现了琴面起棱式昂型和同《营造法式》规定相同的琴面昂型。金代延续了北宋晚期的做法，铺作用昂以琴面起棱式和《营造法式》昂型并存。

墓葬仿木构斗栱用昂实例最早见于北宋元祐年间的平顺县郊宋墓，较木构实例晚了约一个世纪。就昂型来看，平顺县郊宋墓中并存了批竹起棱及琴面起棱两种昂型，几乎同时期的原起寺青龙塔也见有琴面起棱昂型，可见琴面起棱昂型在哲宗初年已经流行于晋东南地区。宣和五年(1123 年)下好牢村宋墓则首见采用《营造法式》琴面昂型，仅比晋东南最早使用琴面昂的崇寿寺大殿晚了四年。进入金代以后，仿木斗栱以采用琴面起棱式昂型为主流，为地面木构建筑所流行的形制之一，《营造法式》型琴面昂仅在长治石槽金墓[⑩]及晋城南社金墓[⑪]中得见，推测是因此类昂型加工困难而遭到了摒弃。值得注意的是，晋城南社金墓中在同一斗栱中并存有《营造法式》型琴面昂及琴面起棱昂型，同晋城金代中晚期部分木构实例的做法一致(图 10)。

由此可以推测，仿木构斗栱中昂出现较晚的原因是砖制技术在很长一段时间内未能解决昂类构件的制作方法，这一难题在晋东南地区于北宋晚期得以解决。而在仿木构昂类构件出现以后，昂型的变化则迅速跟随木构斗栱昂型的变化而发生改变。

晋东南五代平顺大云院弥陀殿铺作用耍头形式为批竹斜杀式，北宋初至宋末大观以前，除高平崇明寺大殿采用蚂蚱头耍头外，均使用昂型耍头，即耍头形制同铺作出跳昂型相同。宋末大观年间起出现使用楮头型耍头的做法，宣和年间开始流行《营造法式》中所规定的蚂蚱头型耍头，蚂蚱头型耍头一直流行至金末，期间少见有延续使用昂型耍头和并存使用昂型耍头和蚂蚱头型耍头的做法。

宋金墓葬仿木构中于长治五马村宋墓中首先见有使用耍头的构造，耍头形制为批竹起棱型，并一直延续至北宋晚期，墓葬批竹及批竹起棱式耍头的消亡时间与地面木构几乎同时。元祐年间平顺县郊宋墓始见楮头耍头形制，较地面木构实例略早，由此推测晋东南地区耍头形制的变革应在北宋哲宗时期即已出现。宣和年间下好牢村墓首先出现使用蚂蚱型耍头的做法，与地面木构该形制的出现几乎同时。金代墓葬实例中，昂型及蚂蚱头型的耍头形制并存，直至金大定晚期，蚂蚱头形制才占据了主流地位。两类形制的并存现象同地面金代木构建筑实例所反映的面貌相符，由此可知昂型耍头作为具有地区特色的斗栱形制在金代中期以前，仍然在晋东南地区占有重要的地位（图 11）。

（七）栱端做法

从实例来看，晋东南五代至宋初木构建筑横栱端头平直，宋初大中祥符年间开始出现令栱端头抹斜的做法，此后至北宋晚期一直流行跳头横栱端头抹斜做法。至宋末宣和元年崇寿寺大殿上又出现令栱端头平直做法，并一直流行至金代中期。金大定时期起横栱端头抹斜的做法又重新复苏。

而在仿木构实例中，真正意义上的横栱做法于北宋晚期才开始存在，北宋元祐至宣和这段时间内，仿木构斗栱中横栱形态见有端头抹斜的做法，如壶关南村宋墓、壶关上好牢宋墓[⑫]、长治郭堡村宋墓[⑬]等。而至宋末宣和五年 1123 年的下好牢宋墓，横栱端头即变化为平直做法，此后该地区墓葬仿木构中横栱均为端头平直做法。宋末时期仿木构墓葬横栱端头抹斜的做法和此时期木构实例符合，仿木构

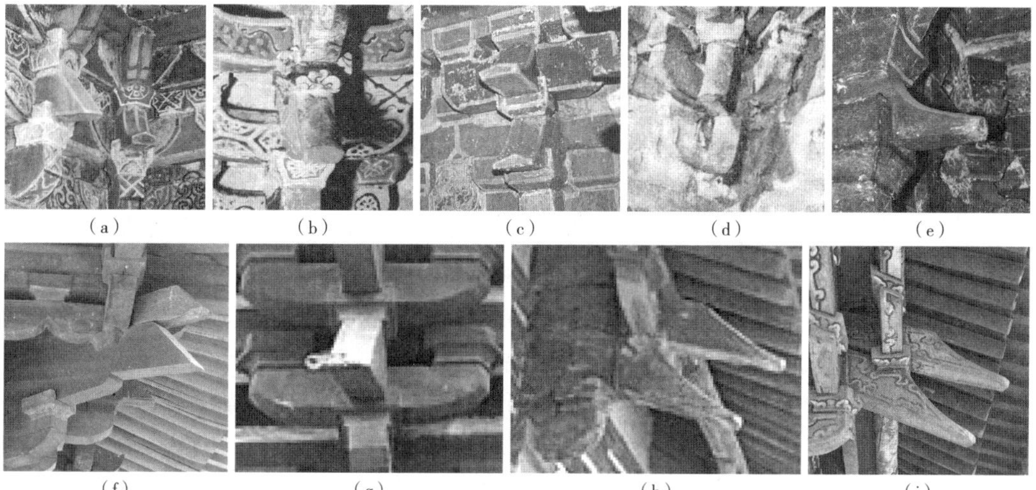

图 10 晋东南宋金仿木构及木构昂型对比
（a）平顺县郊宋墓墓室斗栱，1092 年；（b）壶关下好牢宋墓正壁斗栱，1125 年；（c）长治魏村金墓墓室斗栱，1151 年；（d）晋城南社金墓前室转角斗栱，金代中期；（e）长治故漳金墓正壁斗栱，1189 年；（f）平顺大云院大殿转角斗栱，940 年；（g）高平开化寺中殿柱头斗栱，1173 年；（h）泽州小南村二仙庙大殿柱头斗栱，1097-1107 年；（i）陵川西溪二仙庙大殿柱头斗栱，1142—1165 年（图片来源：a~d 图源自墓葬简报；其余为作者自摄）

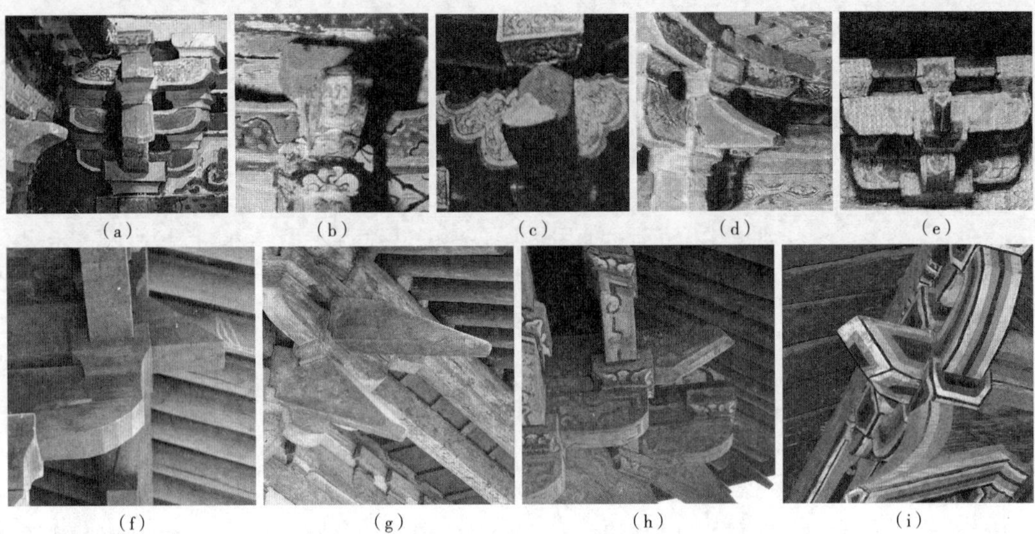

图 11　晋东南宋金仿木构及木构耍头形制对比
（a）壶关上好牢 M1 正壁斗栱，北宋晚期；（b）壶关下好牢宋墓正壁斗栱，1125 年；（c）沁源正中村金墓斗栱，1168 年；（d）沁县西林东庄金墓上檐斗栱，金代中期；（e）长治安昌金墓正壁斗栱，1195 年；（f）平顺大云院大殿柱头斗栱，940 年；（g）高平资圣寺中殿柱头斗栱，1082 年；（h）泽州小南村二仙庙大殿柱头斗栱，1097—1107 年；（i）晋城崇寿寺中殿斗栱，1119 年（图片来源：a~e 图源自墓葬简报；其余为作者自摄）

在宋末出现横栱端头平直的时间几乎与地面木构同时出现。而金代末出现横栱端头抹斜的复苏现象，推测应是因平直做法较抹斜做法简易，砖制仿木构件过程中对复杂做法摒弃的结果（图 12）。

（八）小结

通过以上对部分斗栱形制的分析，可以总结出河南中北部地区地下墓葬与地面木构斗栱形制的对比分期。

第一期为北宋哲宗以前（1086 年以前）。该期墓葬仿木构斗栱整体呈现朴素面貌，模仿程度较低。具体表现为，不做出成熟的跳头横栱、栱瓣曲线生硬、仿木构斗不做斗耳等现象，墓葬并存见有地面砖塔所见五铺作双出杪和扁平化的斗栱形象。但该期仿木构斗栱所反映部分细部形制见有对地面相应木构形制的模仿，如补间用铺作一朵、批竹起棱式耍头等。

第二期为北宋哲、徽宗时期（1086—1127 年）。该期墓室仿木构斗栱形制复杂化，在结构形式、组合配置、细部样式等多个方面体现出了对于木构斗栱的“仿真”意识。具体表现为，普遍使用五铺作斗栱、成熟的跳头横栱出现、斗栱出现用昂、栱瓣使用柔和曲线处理、普遍使用斗耳等现象。

该期地下墓葬仿木构斗栱中所反映的昂型耍头、跳头横栱抹斜、五边形交互斗、泥道单栱承枋隐刻慢栱、斗欹下撇出峰等形制，是晋东南地面木构斗栱自北宋初期发展而来的流行形制。此外，北宋晚期墓葬中所见蚂蚱头耍头的出现、批竹向琴面昂的变化、令栱增长、跳头出计心重栱等形制变化，与地面木构建筑同期所出现的形制变化过程时间差较短，几乎可以认为是同期变化。

第三期为金初至金中晚期（1127 年—12 世纪末）。根据前文的分析，金代墓葬仿木构斗栱形制基本延续了同地区北宋晚期的流行做法，金大定时期发展出了具有固定形态的斗栱

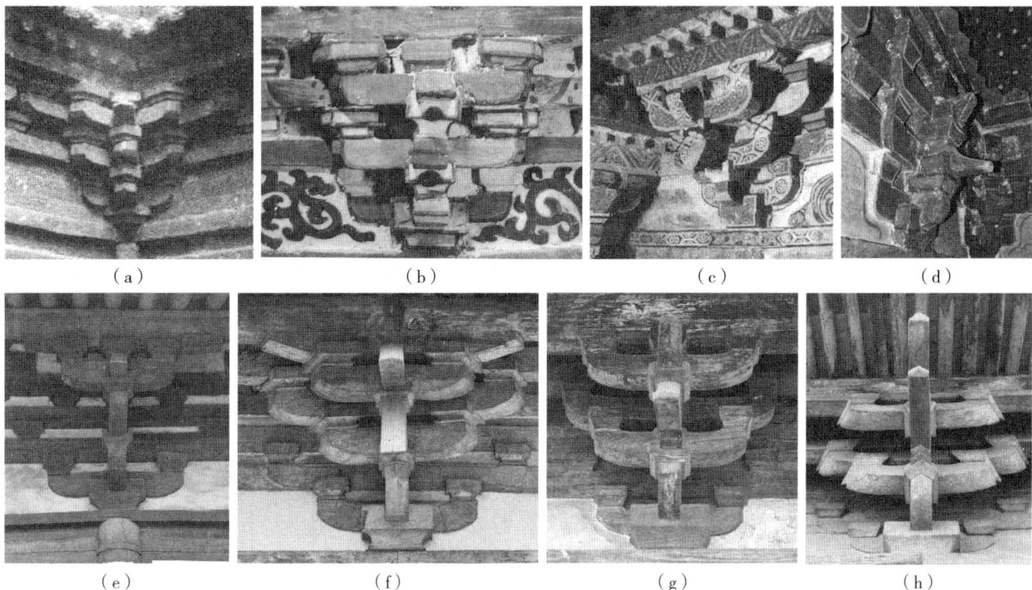

图 12 晋东南宋金仿木构及木构栱端形制对比
(a)壶关南村宋墓墓室斗栱，上限 1087 年;(b)壶关上好牢 M3 墓室斗栱，北宋晚期;(c)壶关下好牢宋墓正壁斗栱，1125 年;(d)长治故漳金墓正壁斗栱，1189 年;(e)平顺大云院大殿柱头斗栱，940 年;(f)高平资圣寺中殿柱头斗栱，1082 年;(g)陵川龙岩寺中殿补间斗栱，1131 年;(h)阳城开福寺中殿柱头斗栱，金大定年间(图片来源：a~c 图源自墓葬简报；其余为作者自摄)

形象。此阶段所体现出的令栱长于泥道栱、蚂蚱头与琴面昂型耍头并存、琴面起棱昂、补间两朵等形制，与地面木构建筑流行形制相符。但晋东南金代建筑中所流行的《营造法式》型琴面昂、泥道重栱，以及金大定时期又重新流行的栱端抹斜做法，在墓葬仿木构中没有表现，究其原因，一是横栱及昂类构件用砖材加工困难，墓葬中将此类装饰省略；二是金中期后墓葬仿木构体现程式化的面貌，此背后应包含着批量化加工生产的施工背景，使得墓葬仿木构斗栱表现形制统一化。

四、相关问题讨论

(一)晋东南宋金时期墓葬仿木构建筑史料分期所体现的时代背景

此处将结合相关文献史料简要阐述前文分期结论所体现的历史背景。首先从第一期至第二期的转变来看，北宋哲宗时期起所反映出的墓葬仿木构建筑的显著发展，同北宋晚期商品经济的繁荣和商人阶层的发展有关。前辈学者已经指出，北宋中期起仿木构砖室墓在平民中普及[⑭]，本文所用纪年墓葬材料，墓主身份也以乡绅、地主及商人为主流。在当时所流行的奢侈消费观的影响下[⑮]，这些拥有巨额资本的平民群体，力图通过营建装饰复杂的墓葬以达到对先人供奉、永葆家族兴盛的目的。墓葬装饰中所流行的墓主人像、戏曲、孝行等题材类型，与仿木构建筑史料同时呈现出复杂化的特征，也同时佐证了这一丧葬观念的存在。同时，在北宋晚期发展出的这种墓葬装饰需求，刺激了仿木构建筑史料营建技术的发展。

建炎元年(1127 年)，金兵南下，两河地区作为宋金交战前线，生产生活遭到了极大的破坏[⑯]。北宋灭亡后河南及山西南部人民不堪金人掠夺压迫，组织“红巾军”“八字军”

等起义军，活动于太行一带。宋金之交的社会动荡直接影响了这一时期的墓葬营造活动，金初至金海陵王以前，中原北方地区极少见有纪年仿木构墓葬遗存，作为北宋政治中心区的河南地区，金代初年不见有一座带有复杂仿木结构的墓葬实例。但值得注意的是，晋东南屯留县发现的金天会十三年仿木构砖雕壁画墓，为中原北方地区纪年最早的金代仿木构墓葬之一。此墓墓室见有多处题记，对我们理解宋金之交砌墓活动的情况提供了重要信息，东壁右侧载："乙卯岁｜当播人驱上皇少帝于｜领北外有康王走在江南｜幡家到江南回兵当年｜正月廿四大金皇帝崩也"，西壁左部载："砌造匠人李通家住沁州｜铜堤县底水村人是｜内为红巾盗贼惊移到此｜砌到葬一所系大金国｜女真军国领兵收劫赵皇家"，西壁中部题记："天会十三年岁次乙卯三月一日｜甲戌廿日甲午日癸时下枢宋村｜三命名荣在此，于□□□□□冢茔｜当年本村修盖佛殿□□□迁｜奉父母家兄大哥□□□□□□都｜归大夜命庵幽谷葬于此所后此五百｜年间必逢张强到此马四□□不良必｜须再葬"。由此可知，此墓则是墓主宋氏再葬之墓，而此墓砌匠李通原住沁州，因金初红巾起义军动乱移居至屯留。此外墓中题记还记录了宋金政权更替时康王南渡、金太宗去世等历史事件，可以窥之，宋金之朝代更替对于晋东南地区的影响轻于河南地区[17]，普通民众在金代初年对于新政权的认同感也较强，因此仿木构墓葬砌筑活动的恢复较快。继金熙宗"宋金议和"后，海陵王又主张实施汉化政策，中原北方地区逐渐实现了社会生产的稳定[18]，继承北宋晚期传统、为家族延续祈福为目的的营墓活动重新得到普及。

至金世宗时开始经济兴盛，农业及手工业高度繁荣，至章宗时达到了金代经济的鼎盛时期[19]，在这一历史背景下，晋东南地区仿木构墓葬再一次达到发展高峰期。与金代前期所体现的对于北宋晚期的继承情况不同，金世宗起该地区墓葬仿木构形制和技术都出现了新的面貌，特别是程式化表现形式的出现，表明这一时期墓葬营建出现了标准化批量生产的情况。

（二）晋东南宋金时期墓葬仿木构建筑史料所反映《营造法式》的影响与传播

探讨墓葬仿木构大木作史料所见《营造法式》的传播影响问题，需要着眼于在《营造法式》颁行前后墓葬仿木构的形制变化。

晋东南北宋宣和年间壶关下好牢宋墓，其仿木构斗栱所见琴面下昂、蚂蚱头耍头、栱端平直等形制，与同地区年代较早的南村宋墓、上好牢宋墓所见批竹起棱昂、昂型耍头及栱端抹斜的做法迥异，而这些形制恰恰是北宋晚期以前地面木构斗栱中所体现的地区流行做法。下好牢宋墓与地面同时期的晋城崇寿寺大殿所体现的形制变革一样，为接受了《营造法式》传播影响的产物[20]。由此也可以猜想在北宋末年，晋东南部分地区出现了模仿由《营造法式》传播而来的外来形制的热潮。

金代中前期墓葬流行的令栱长于泥道栱、琴面起棱昂等形制与《营造法式》制度相符，但仍存在昂型耍头与蚂蚱型耍头的并存，同时期地面木构也留存了较多使用昂型耍头的实例，可知虽经历了宋末效仿《营造法式》的热潮，部分斗栱形制为《营造法式》规定形制所取代、规范。晋东南的一些原有的地方特色形制并未因此在墓葬中消亡，在金代仍具有重要的地位。然而金世宗以后，墓葬中固定表现了蚂蚱头、琴面起棱昂、补间两朵、令栱长于泥道栱的形制，可见《营造法式》形制在此时已逐步取代了北宋中前期的地方做法，占据了主流地位。

（三）晋东南宋金时期墓葬仿木构建筑史料历史价值的新认识

本文通过对于晋东南地区宋金时期墓葬仿木构建筑史料的考察，深化了对于仿木构建筑史料历史价值的认识。

首先，仿木构建筑史料自身涵盖了丰富的时间和空间信息，是实现地区墓葬分期及判断墓葬年代的重要依据。仿木构建筑史料与墓葬平面形制、墓室壁面装饰布局、壁面装饰题材等其他墓葬中所蕴含的史料信息，一同作为反映地区墓葬发展及演变过程的重要材料。

墓葬仿木构建筑史料作为专门的营造门类，还有助于认识宋金时期的砖制工艺技术。如第一节所述，墓葬仿木构建筑史料“由木到砖”的模拟转化过程蕴含了砖制工匠的设计思想和施工技术。墓葬中模制构件的出现及发展是宋金时期砌墓技术的重要变革。

仿木构建筑史料还是深入认识地面木构建筑大木作形制发展的重要史料。地下所发现的数量众多的仿木构建筑史料，其作用在于：①补充地面木构中不见的形制及形制组合；②强化对地面木构主流形制及形制组合的认识；③更为全面和深入地认识特定形制及形制组合发展变化的过程；④辅助深入理解地区间木构形制及技术的传播关系；⑤有助于探讨《营造法式》等建筑专书的源流及影响问题。

在利用仿木构建筑史料探讨地面木构的相关问题时，必须对仿木构所存在的“滞后性”进行考量，即认为仿木构中所见形制出现的起始时间，一定晚于该形制在地面木构中的起始时间。通过前文的讨论，可以看出在北宋及金代所贯穿的近三个世纪中，不同时段内仿木构相对于地面木构的滞后程度是存在差异的。北宋哲宗以前为墓葬仿木构的发展雏形期，主要表现为斗栱形式简单，木作斗栱中的部分形制及形制组合特征不为仿木构所表现，仿木构斗栱仅耍头形式、补间布置、令栱与泥道栱长度比等形制可以与地面木构对应。北宋哲宗起墓葬仿木构逐渐发展成熟，主要表现为复杂的斗栱形式出现，仿木构技术的发展使得高度模拟地面木作斗栱成为可能。而这类复杂化仿木构斗栱形成之初所反映的形制应与地面木构流行形制相符。金代各地墓葬仿木构基本延续北宋末期的技术做法，局部进行了技术改进，使得仿木构建筑技术逐渐成熟。北宋哲宗以后墓葬所见仿木构斗栱敏感形制的样式变化，与地面木构对应形制几乎同期发生。

此外，仿木构建筑史料的制作材料在一定程度上限制了构件形象的表达，如因跳头横栱表现较为困难，部分墓葬流行做出计心单栱和跳头出翼型栱的形制，此外墓葬中平出昂的流行也同昂头向下形制难以加工有密切关系。这些因材料限制而形成的斗栱形制，不可用来讨论地面木构的相应问题。仿木构中脱离了材料限制、加工中体现刻意修饰的部件，则最具有同地面木构进行对比的价值。

五、小结

本文通过对典型纪年实例的分析，晋东南地区宋金时期墓葬仿木构史料的发展演变分为三期，第一期为北宋哲宗以前，墓葬仿木构建筑史料表现简略，为该地区的发展雏形期；第二期为北宋哲宗至金世宗大定十四年（1174 年），该期墓葬仿木构整体复杂化，实例也体现出了不同形制的并存，仿木构加工方式更为精致，出现了模制构件的使用，为该地区的发展变化期；第三期为金大定十四年（1174 年）至金章宗明昌年间，仿木构建筑史料体现了程式化的面貌，仿木构形制较前期更为统一，为该地区的形制固定期。北宋中期以后商品贸易的发达使得新兴乡绅、地主、商人阶层扩大，在奢侈消费观念的影响下，这些具有雄厚经济实力的群体对于华丽仿木构墓葬的营造需求增加，从而刺激了北宋晚期起仿木构营造技术的飞跃。宋末金初的社会动荡对于营墓活动产生了一定的冲击，但晋东南民众很快对新政权产生了认同，至金海陵王正隆年间，社会生产逐渐稳定，该地区的仿木构墓葬营建活动得到复苏。金世宗、章宗年间，经济繁荣发展，墓葬营建在此前继承北宋晚期技术的基础上进行了改革，新的仿木构形制和技术得到推广。

通过与地面木构斗栱遗存的对比，本文认为，晋东南地区宋金墓葬仿木构斗栱与地面木构斗栱的对比关系方面，体现出三个时段的变化。北宋哲宗以前，仿木构斗栱在技术条件的限制下，对于木构的模仿程度较低；北宋晚期哲、徽宗时期，仿木构的模仿程度显著增高，其所体现的形制变化也与木构斗栱的形制变化几乎同期；金代仿木构斗栱的形象仍与地面斗栱有着高度的对应，但在材料限制下仿木构斗栱在一些细部做法中，体现出对于木构斗栱的简略表达。

墓葬仿木构建筑史料不仅自身含有丰富的时空信息，可作为探讨地区墓葬时代演变、营墓手工业发展的重要史料。其所包含的仿制信息，还可作为补充、佐证地区木构建筑形制发展的重要材料，从而对地区木构建筑技术发展有更为深入的认识。仿木构墓葬作为特殊的地下文化遗产，应该得到足够的关注和重视。

宋金时期山西东南部地区仿木构墓葬统计表　　**附表**

编号	发掘时间（年）	名称	出处	年代（年）	平面形制
1	1988	山西长治故县宋代壁画墓 M1	《山西长治故县宋代壁画墓》，《文物》2005 年第四期	元丰元年左右	砖砌方形带耳室墓
2	1988	山西长治故县宋代壁画墓 M2	《山西长治故县宋代壁画墓》，《文物》2005 年第四期	元丰元年，1079	砖砌方形带耳室墓
3	1984	山西长治五马村墓	《山西长治市五马村宋墓》，《考古》1994 年第九期	元丰四年，1081	砖砌方形单室墓
4	1989	山西壶关南村宋代砖雕墓	《山西壶关南村宋代砖雕墓》，《文物》1997 年第二期	元祐二年，1087	砖砌方形多室墓
5	1999	山西平顺张家洼宋代砖雕墓	《长治宋金元墓室建筑艺术研究》，文物出版社，2015 年 1 月	元祐七年，1092	砖砌方形多室墓
6	2000	山西长治西白兔村宋代壁画墓	《长治市西白兔村宋代壁画墓发掘简报》《山西省考古学会论文集（三）》，山西古籍出版社 2000 年 3 月	元祐三年，1088	砖砌方形带耳室墓

续表

编号	发掘时间（年）	名称	出处	年代（年）	平面形制
7	不明	山西壶关高岸上村宋代砖雕墓	《长治宋金元墓室建筑艺术研究》，文物出版社，2015 年 1 月	政和二年，1112	不明
8	1991	山西壶关下好牢墓	《山西壶关下好牢宋墓》，《文物》2002 年第五期	宣和五年，1123	砖砌方形带耳室墓
9	不详	山西长子特高压北宋砖雕壁画墓	长子文物局提供	宣和五年，1123	砖砌方形单室墓
10	1999	山西屯留宋村墓	《山西屯留宋村金代壁画墓》，《文物》2003 年第三期	天会十三年，1135	砖砌方形单室墓
11	2002	山西长治安昌村金墓 ZAM8	《长治北效安昌村出土金代墓葬》，《文物世界》2003 年第一期	皇统三年，1143	石砌方形多室墓
12	1994	山西长治魏村墓	《山西长治市魏村金代纪年彩绘砖雕墓》，《考古》2009 年第一期	天德三年，1151	砖砌方形带耳室墓
13	1965	山西长治南垂墓	《中国出土壁画全集》，长治市博物馆馆藏	贞元元年，1153	砖砌八边形单室墓
14	1983	山西长子石哲村墓	《山西长子县石哲金代壁画墓》，《文物》1985 年第六期	正隆三年，1158	砖砌方形带耳室墓
15	1999	山西沁源正中村金代砖雕壁画墓	《长治宋金元墓室建筑艺术研究》，文物出版社，2015 年 1 月	大定八年，1165	砖砌八边形带耳室墓
16	2008	山西陵川玉泉村墓	《陵川县玉泉村金代壁画墓》，《中国考古学年鉴》，2008 年《中国出土壁画全集 2》	大定九年，1169	砖砌方形单室墓
17	1994	山西长子小关村墓	《山西长子县小关村金代纪年壁画墓》，《文物》2008 年第十期	大定十四年，1174	砖砌方形带耳室墓
18	1981	山西长治故漳村墓	《山西长治市故漳金代纪年墓》，《考古》1984 年第八期	大定二十九年，1189	砖砌方形带耳室墓
19	1985	山西长治安昌村金墓	《山西长治安昌金墓》，《文物》1990 年第五期	明昌六年，1195	砖砌方形带耳室墓
20	1988	山西屯留李高村砖雕壁画墓	《长治宋金元墓室建筑艺术研究》，文物出版社，2015 年 1 月《中国出土壁画全集 2》	泰和八年，1208	不明
21	1981	山西长治故漳村壁画墓	《山西长治市故漳村宋代砖雕墓》，《考古》2006 年第九期	北宋徽宗	砖砌方形带耳室墓
22	2010	山西壶关上好牢村宋墓 M1	《山西壶关上好牢村宋金时期墓葬》，《考古》2012 第四期	北宋徽宗	砖砌方形带耳室墓
23	2010	山西壶关上好牢村宋墓 M3	《山西壶关上好牢村宋金时期墓葬》，《考古》2012 第四期	北宋徽宗	砖砌方形单室墓
24	不明	山西长子南李村砖雕壁画墓	长子文物局提供	北宋徽宗	砖砌方形带耳室墓
25	不明	山西壶关县杨家池村砖雕墓	《长治宋金元墓室建筑艺术研究》，文物出版社，2015 年 1 月	北宋晚期	不明
26	不明	山西潞城贾村砖雕墓	《长治宋金元墓室建筑艺术研究》，文物出版社，2015 年 1 月	北宋晚期	不明
27	不明	山西沁源县西关砖雕壁画墓	《长治宋金元墓室建筑艺术研究》，文物出版社，2015 年 1 月	北宋晚期	不明
28	不明	山西长治县师庄村砖雕壁画墓	《长治宋金元墓室建筑艺术研究》，文物出版社，2015 年 1 月	北宋晚期	不明

续表

编号	发掘时间（年）	名称	出处	年代（年）	平面形制
29	不明	山西长治郭堡村砖雕壁画墓	《长治宋金元墓室建筑艺术研究》，文物出版社，2015 年 1 月	北宋晚期	不明
30	1988	山西长治北石槽砖雕壁画墓	长治博物馆馆藏，《长治宋金元墓室建筑艺术研究》	金代中期	砖砌方形单室墓
31	1998	山西沁县西林东庄村砖雕墓	《山西沁县发现金代砖雕墓》，《文物》2000 年第六期	金代中前期	砖砌八角形单室墓
32	2001	山西沁县故城镇砖雕墓 M1	《山西沁县出土金代孝行砖雕》，《上海文博》2003 年第四期	金代中前期	砖砌八边形单室墓
33	2001	山西沁县故城镇砖雕墓 M2	《山西沁县出土金代孝行砖雕》，《上海文博》2003 年第四期	金代中前期	砖砌方形单室墓
34	不明	山西沁县故县镇中学砖雕墓	《长治宋金元墓室建筑艺术研究》，文物出版社，2015 年 1 月	金代中前期	不明
35	不明	山西武乡县郊砖雕壁画墓	《长治宋金元墓室建筑艺术研究》，文物出版社，2015 年 1 月	金代中前期	不明
36	2011	山西黎城东水洋村砖雕墓	http：//www.huaxia.com/zhwh/kgfx/2011/04/2389311.html	金代中前期	不明
37	1999	山西屯留县宋村砖雕壁画墓 1999M1	《山西屯留宋村金代壁画墓》，《文物》2008 年第八期	金代中期	砖砌方形带耳室墓
38	不明	山西长子西峪村砖雕墓	《长治宋金元墓室建筑艺术研究》，文物出版社，2015 年 1 月	金代中期	不明
39	1977	山西晋城南社砖雕墓	《山西晋城南社宋墓简介》《考古学集刊·第一辑》	金代中期	砖砌方形前后室墓
40	不明	山西高平汤王头村砖雕墓	现场调查	金代中期	砖砌方形带耳室墓
41	1964	山西长治李沟村砖雕壁画墓	《山西长治李沟村壁画墓清理》，《考古》1965 年第七期	金代中后期	砖砌方形带耳室墓
42	不明	山西长治南寨村砖雕墓	《长治宋金元墓室建筑艺术研究》，文物出版社，2015 年 1 月	金代中后期	不明
43	不明	山西长治瓦窑沟砖雕壁画墓	《长治宋金元墓室建筑艺术研究》，文物出版社，2015 年 1 月	金代中后期	不明
44	2002	山西长治安昌村金墓 ZAM2	《长治北效安昌村出土金代墓葬》，《文物世界》2003 年第一期	不明	砖砌方形单室墓
45	2004	山西长治任家庄砖雕墓	《长治县任家庄出土一批宋代砖雕》，《文物世界》2009 年第四期	不明	砖砌方形单室墓
46	2011	山西长子墓下村砖雕壁画墓	长子文物局提供	不明	砖砌方形单室墓
47	不明	山西黎城县郊砖雕壁画墓	《长治宋金元墓室建筑艺术研究》，文物出版社，2015 年 1 月	不明	不明
48	不明	山西潞城北关砖雕壁画墓	《山西潞城县北关宋代壁画墓》，《考古》1999 年第五期	不明	砖砌方形单室墓
49	不明	山西长治暴马村砖雕壁画墓	《长治宋金元墓室建筑艺术研究》，文物出版社，2015 年 1 月	不明	不明
50	不明	山西长治中村砖雕墓	《长治宋金元墓室建筑艺术研究》，文物出版社，2015 年 1 月	不明	不明
51	不明	山西长治淮海厂砖雕墓	《长治宋金元墓室建筑艺术研究》，文物出版社，2015 年 1 月	不明	
52	不明	山西沁源段家庄砖雕墓	《长治宋金元墓室建筑艺术研究》，文物出版社，2015 年 1 月	不明	
53	不明	山西沁源王陶村砖雕墓	《长治宋金元墓室建筑艺术研究》，文物出版社，2015 年 1 月	不明	

注释：

① 王进先．长治宋金元墓室建筑艺术研究 [M]. 北京：文物出版社，2015.

② 秦大树．宋元明考古 [M]. 北京：文物出版社，2004.

③ 许若茜．山西金墓分区分期研究 [D]. 北京：中央民族大学，2011.

④ 刘耀辉．晋南地区宋金墓葬研究 [D]. 北京：北京大学考古文博学院，2002.

⑤ 任林平．晋中南地区宋金墓葬研究 [D]. 南京：南京大学，2012.

⑥ 长治魏村金墓壁面每边分为三开间，明柱柱头各置斗栱一朵，因此此墓虽每边出斗栱两朵，实并无补间斗栱。

⑦ 实例中见有金泰和八年屯留李高村仿木构砖雕壁画墓，但因笔者未能获取该墓仿木构建筑史料的详细信息，因此在针对晋东南地区宋金墓葬仿木构建筑史料的分期中，仅考虑金章宗承安以前的时代变化。

⑧ 收录于王进先《长治宋金元墓室建筑艺术研究》、资料尚未发表的长治南寨金墓，斗栱形制及构造做法同长治故漳金墓及安昌金墓完全相同，可知该地区到金大定明昌时期已形成固定的斗栱形制及构造做法。

⑨ 徐怡涛．长治、晋城地区的五代、宋、金寺庙建筑 [D]. 北京：北京大学考古文博学院，2003.

⑩ 此墓材料尚未公开发表，现搬迁于长治市博物馆墓葬厅，王进先《长治宋金元墓室建筑艺术研究》一书内有所提及。笔者根据前文分期结论，将此墓年代判断为金代中期。

⑪ 该墓发掘简报见：山西省考古研究所晋东南工作站．山西晋城南社宋墓简介 // 考古学集刊（1）[M]. 北京：中国社会科学出版社，1981。晋城地区位于长治地区和焦作地区中间，三地自古至今一直存在着交通联系。晋城地区不见有已发表的纪年宋金仿木构墓葬实例，因此推测晋城地区的墓葬营建应同时存在与同时期长治地区和焦作地区墓葬的相似关系。就南社村墓而言，该墓墓室斗栱所反映计心重栱、令栱长于泥道栱、栱瓣做柔和曲线、蚂蚱耍头、琴面昂、斗栱整体预制化、跳头横栱脱离壁面等形制特征，在长治地区流行于北宋晚期。但值得注意的是，墓葬后室为了做出孝行图像装饰带做出重檐，这是长治地区金初时期的流行做法。同时，墓室中所见通间双腰串造格子门、《营造法式》型琴面昂和琴面起棱昂型并存等形制，不见于长治地区的宋金仿木构标尺墓葬中，而这两个形制正是金代中期焦作地区的仿木构墓葬的流行做法。综合以上分期，推测该墓年代在金代中期左右，与原报告认为该墓为北宋墓葬的结论不同。

⑫ 该墓发掘于 2010 年，位于长治壶关县上好牢村。发掘简报见：山西省考古研究所，长治市文物旅游局，壶关县文体广电局．山西壶关县上好牢村宋金时期墓葬 [J]. 考古，2012(4)：48-55. 该墓在墓室整体布置、仿木构构造做法以及仿木构彩画装饰等方面同邻近的宣和五年下好牢宋墓十分接近，所不同的是该墓昂型及耍头形制仍见有较早的批竹起棱形制，两墓很有可能是同一批工匠所为，因此推测该墓年代与下好牢宋墓接近或偏早。

⑬ 该墓材料未正式发表，仅在王进先《长治宋金元墓室建筑艺术研究》中见有相关图片和部分文字描述。斗栱为五铺作单杪单昂偷心形式，扶壁泥道重栱，昂为琴面起棱型，耍头不做表现。令栱长于泥道栱，墓室横栱均做栱臂看面抹斜。根据斗栱形制，推测该墓年代也应在北宋哲、徽宗时期。因此可以见得，仿木构斗栱做出横栱抹斜的形制不仅仅在壶关地区存在，在潞州其他地区也有出现。

⑭ 秦大树．宋元明考古 [M]. 北京：文物出版社，2004.

⑮ 程颐《论十事札子》曾批判了北宋中期以来婚丧的奢侈习俗："古者冠婚丧祭，车服器用，等差分别，莫敢逾僭，故财用易给，而民有恒心。今礼制未修，奢靡相尚，卿士大夫之家莫能中礼，而商贩之类或逾王公……"。北宋徽宗年间曾颁布针对婚嫁丧葬奢侈消费的禁令，如《宋会要辑稿》刑法二之七五条记载，宣和元年（1119 年）臣僚奏言："士俗民风，故习犹在，昏丧之礼，务为僭奢"，宋徽宗则要求地方长官重视这类婚丧活动中的奢僭行为。可见北宋晚期，士庶墓葬的营建已没有等级的限制，墓葬营建和丧葬活动以追求奢侈为风气。

⑯ [宋] 徐梦莘《三朝北盟会编》卷一〇三，建炎元年五月六日记载金兵南下时两河地区"田野三时之务，所至一空，祖宗七世之遗，厥存无几"。

⑰ 作为北宋政治经济核心区的河南地区，在宋金之交作为交战前线，社会动荡不安。后金朝政府又扶持刘豫建立伪齐政权，此地区于 1130 至 1137 年处于伪齐政权的统治之下，暴政使得该地区经济生产凋敝。截至目前，河南地区仅见有天眷二年济源龙潭金墓及皇统三年林县金墓若干金初纪年墓葬实例，均不见有复杂的仿木构造，可以作为此地区金初生产凋敝、社会动荡之印证。

⑱ 金熙宗在议和后为了实现社会稳定，采用了文治的治国思想，[元] 脱脱《金史》卷四《熙宗纪》载："太平之世，当尚文物，自古致治，皆由是也。"并注重消除民族间的对立，"四海之内，皆朕臣子，若分别待之，岂能致一。谚不有乎，'疑人易使，使人勿疑'。自今本国及诸色人，量才通用之。"海陵王继承熙宗的治世

思想，实行一系列经济制度改革，进一步恢复和发展北方生产。《金史》卷四六《食货志》载："熙宗、海陵之世，风气日开，兼务远略，君臣讲求财用之制，切切然以为先务。"

⑲ [元]脱脱《金史》卷八《世宗纪》载："世宗久典外郡，明祸乱之故，知吏制之得失。即位五载，而南北讲好，与民休息。……当此之时，群臣守职，上下相安，家给人足，仓廪有余，……号称'小尧舜'……"。卷十二《章宗纪》载"章宗在位二十年，承世宗治平日久，宇内小康"。卷一〇九《许古传》载"世宗、章宗之隆，府库充实，天下富庶。"

⑳ 有关北宋末年至金代初年《营造法式》对于晋东南木构形制的影响，详见徐怡涛．长治、晋城地区的五代、宋、金寺庙建筑[D]. 北京：北京大学考古文博学院，2003.

参考文献：

[1] 长治市博物馆．山西长治市故漳金代纪年墓[J]. 考古，1984（8）：737-743.

[2] 长治市博物馆，王进先，朱晓芳．山西长治安昌金墓[J]. 文物，1990（5）：76-85.

[3] 长治市博物馆，壶关县文物博物馆．山西壶关南村宋代砖雕墓[J]. 文物，1997（2）：44-54.

[4] 长治市博物馆．山西长子县小关村金代纪年壁画墓[J]. 文物，2008（8）：60-69.

[5] 长治市博物馆．山西长治市魏村金代纪年彩绘砖雕墓[J]. 考古，2009（1）：59-64.

[6] 秦大树．宋元明考古[M]. 北京：文物出版社，2004.

[7] 任林平．晋中南地区宋金墓葬研究[D]. 南京：南京大学，2012.

[8] 山西省考古研究所，长治市博物馆．山西屯留宋村金代壁画墓[J]. 文物，2008（8）：55-62.

[9] 山西省考古研究所，长治市文物旅游局，壶关县文体广电局．山西壶关县上好牢村宋金时期墓葬[J]. 考古，2012（4）：48-55.

[10]山西省考古研究所晋东南工作站．山西晋城南社宋墓简介．//《考古》编辑部．考古学集刊（1）．北京：社会科学出版社，1981：224-230.

[11]山西省考古研究所晋东南工作站．山西长子县石哲金代壁画墓[J]. 文物，1985（6）：45-54.

[12]商彤流，郭海林．山西沁县发现金代砖雕墓[J]. 文物，2000（6）：60-73.

[13]王进先，石卫国．山西长治市五马村宋墓[J]. 考古，1994（9）：815-817.

[14]王进先．长治市西白兔村宋代壁画墓发掘简报．// 山西省考古学会，山西省考古研究所编．山西省考古学会论文集（三）. 太原：山西古籍出版社，2000.

[15]王进先．山西壶关下好牢宋墓[J]. 文物，2002（5）：42-55.

[16]王进先，杨林中．山西屯留宋村金代壁画墓，文物，2003（3）：43-51.

[17]王秀生．山西长治李沟村壁画墓清理[J]. 考古，1965（7）：352-356.

[18]王进先．长治宋金元墓室建筑艺术研究[M]. 北京：文物出版社，2015.

[19]许若茜．山西金墓分区分期研究[D]. 北京：中央民族大学，2011.

[20]徐怡涛．长治、晋城地区的五代、宋、金寺庙建筑[D]. 北京：北京大学考古文博学院，2003.

[21]朱晓芳，王进先．山西长治故县宋代壁画墓[J]. 文物，2005（4）：51-61.

[22]朱晓芳，王进先，李永杰．山西长治市故漳村宋代砖雕墓[J]. 考古，2006（9）：31-39.

试论“斜栱”形制之发展演变

Research on the Evolution of Forms of Angled Bracket-arms used in the Dougong System of Ancient Chinese Architecture

徐新云 | XU Xinyun

摘要：本文在探讨明晰斜栱定义的基础上，通过系统梳理建筑考古史料所反映的斜栱形象，以及现存的大木作木构建筑、小木作室内装修、仿木构砖石塔或墓葬等众多实例中的斜栱形制，从斜栱布局、斜栱构造、斜栱栱件三个层面提炼一系列的斗栱形制或形制组合，尝试建立斜栱这一特殊斗栱形制的时空框架，揭示斜栱形制在不同历史阶段发展演变的特征，以期探讨斜栱应用反映的地域特征和区域流变关系，丰富对中国古代建筑斗栱发展的总体认识。

关键词：斜栱；抹角栱；如意斗栱；分期；地域特征

Abstract: Based on the concept definition of angled bracket-arms, and systematic examination of series of cases from historical data of building archaeology, existing carpentry work and joinery work of Chinese wooden architecture, imitating wooden architecture in pagodas and tombs, this article intends to set up a spatio-temporal framework of the special angled bracket-arms used in the dougong system of ancient Chinese architecture, and reveal the evolution characteristic in different historic stages and regional characteristic. The research enrich the general understanding of the development of dougong system in ancient Chinese architecture.

Keywords: Angled bracket-arms; Squinch bracket-arms; Ruyi dougong; Stage-division; Regional characteristic

作者简介：
徐新云，中国建筑设计研究院有限公司建筑历史研究所，副研究员。

一、斜栱定义之辨析

长期以来，在有关中国古代建筑史的诸多论述中，使用斜栱一般被认为是北方地区辽金时期建筑所具有的特征，甚而认为斜栱创始或成熟于辽金，建筑铺作中使用斜栱被认为是中国古代建筑斗栱发展史在辽金时期的创新。由于“斜栱”并未在宋《营造法式》、清《工程工部做法》等建筑营造的经典文献中被准确定义，只是人们对一种建筑构造或构件的笼统称呼，目前对于斜栱的认识与讨论多集中于对斗栱结构的加强意义、对建筑外观形象所带来的装饰效果，及其可能附带的辽金时期少数民族独具的文化意义或审美取向。

古建筑营造术语历来是中国建筑史界最基本而广泛、深入的议题，但较之其他基于经典历史文献文本的营造术语，“斜栱”的定义却较为模糊，在不同语境下包含建筑构造、斗栱组合、斗栱构件等不同层次的含义。陈薇先生在《斜栱发微》[①]一文中，对斜栱如下定义：“斜栱是与正心方向不垂直的栱，从它的做法和构造上分析，当定义为华栱的一个类别，且与正规华栱方向夹角为一锐角的栱。它的功能和华栱一样，起传跳并支承上部结构的作用。”在朱小南先生的《斜栱溯源》[②]一文中，对斜栱有如下描述：“斜栱就是自斗栱中心与华栱或泥道栱呈45度或60度夹角斜向出跳的栱”。两种描述都是从构件的层面进行定义，斜栱应该是与华栱一个类别，也有出跳并支承上部结构的作用。

在进一步的定义辨析中，何雅丽（HARRER Alexandra）学者对“斜栱”的定义进一步区分[③]，提出“斜栱”是统称一系列栱件的通用名词，表示所有斜向出跳的栱构件，并可区分为“狭义斜栱”和“广义斜栱”。“狭义斜栱”或称“真斜栱”，指外檐斗栱（不包括转角斗栱）中斜向出跳的构件。在营造中，它分为向室内外同时出挑的长弓形构件和只出现在室外的半截华栱。“广义斜栱”指其他更大范围的斜向出跳栱构件，它们通常已有名称，如抹角栱和角栱，是以其特殊的结构功能或建筑中的位置命名。同时该文还使用了“横栱斜置”的概念，即某种程度斜栱不一定都是斜向的出跳华栱。

上述“狭义斜栱”“广义斜栱”的区别关键点在于对角铺作的判断，事实上从斗栱自身的发展演变过程来看，斜向出跳的栱件最早就是在角部为承托檐角而出现，比现存木构实例中更早的角部斜栱形象可见于诸多考古材料，一般被研究者称为“角华栱”与“抹角栱[④]”。如果仅仅从斜向出跳的角度考虑，角华栱确实应列为斜栱，而角华栱跳头上的抹角栱似也可视为斜置的横栱。结合《营造法式》造栱之制条目对角华栱的定义：“交角内外，皆随铺作之数，斜出跳一缝。栱谓之角栱，昂谓之角昂。其华栱则以斜长加之。假如跳头长五寸，则加二寸五厘之类。后称斜长者准此。若丁头栱，其长三十三分，出卯长五分。若只里跳转角者，谓之蝦须栱，用股卯到心，以斜长加之。若入柱者，用双卯，长六分至七分。”可见角华栱所代表的斜向出跳构造技术、尺寸计算，在《营造法式》中已有明确规定，确应列入斜栱之列。结合后文对不同历史阶段斜栱形制特征的梳理，可以发现“狭义斜栱”“广义斜栱”并无实质不同，其区别主要在于其施用位置，而这其实只是不同发展阶段的斜栱形制特征，不宜作为定义进行区分。

二、考古史料反映的五代以前（十世纪前）早期斜栱形象

按照冯继仁先生通过考古材料对转角铺作演变的研究[⑤]，战国时转角处已开始使用45度抹角栱（图1，1. 河北平山战国中山国王陵一号墓出土的铜制方形案座）；汉代多是以正、侧二向出跳来承托檐角，也有于45度插栱上复施抹角栱（图1，2~3. 东汉明器陶楼）；三国时仍用抹角栱结构（图1，4. 函谷关东门线刻）；北朝始有单纯的45度角华栱之结构（图1，5. 云冈第六窟），隋代已完全靠45度角栱支撑檐角（图1，6. 洛阳陶屋）。至初唐在正侧二向垂直出跳旧法（图1，7. 敦煌329窟壁画），以及仅靠45度出跳栱支撑（图1,8. 陕西李寿墓壁画）之外，始出现正、侧及45度三向出跳的实例（图1，9. 敦煌321窟壁画）。由盛唐、中唐至晚唐，随着计心手法的逐渐使用，跳头上瓜子栱、慢栱皆已延伸至角出跳相列，成为后世稳定的转角铺作组合形式（图2，盛唐至晚唐的转角铺作形制演变），并在《营造法式》中得以明确记载。

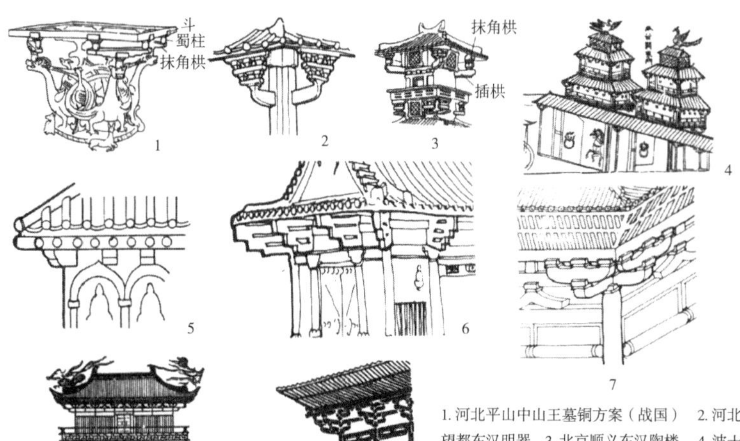

1. 河北平山中山王墓铜方案（战国） 2. 河北望都东汉明器 3. 北京顺义东汉陶楼 4. 波士顿美术馆藏函谷关东门线刻（三国） 5. 大同云冈第6窟北魏塔柱 6. 洛阳陶屋（隋） 7. 敦煌第329窟壁画（初唐） 8. 陕西三原李寿墓壁画（初唐） 9. 敦煌第321窟壁画（初唐）

图1 战国至初唐转角斗栱形制演变

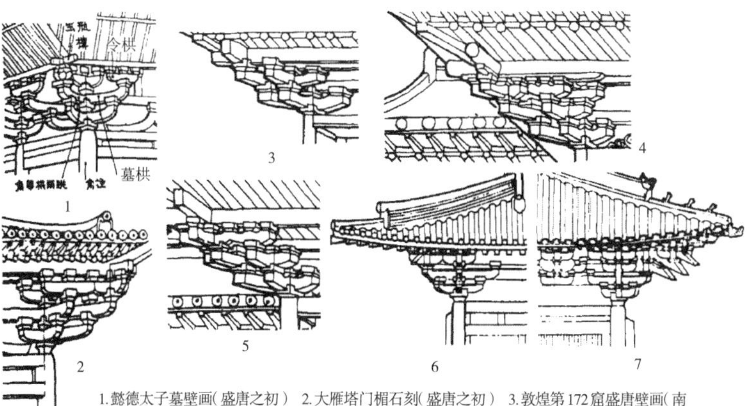

1. 懿德太子墓壁画（盛唐之初） 2. 大雁塔门楣石刻（盛唐之初） 3. 敦煌第172窟盛唐壁画（南壁后殿） 4. 同3（北壁中殿） 5. 同3（南壁中殿） 6. 南禅寺大殿 7. 佛光寺东大殿

图2 盛唐至晚唐转角铺作形制演变

由此可见，角华栱、抹角栱作为斜向出跳的栱件最早见于建筑的角部，但随着斗栱构造的发展完善，45度斜向出跳角华栱成为唐以后解决檐角荷载的普遍形式，抹角栱成为偶尔与角华栱配合使用的构件。因其不再具备明显的时代特征，因此研究者一般将其与其他柱头、补间铺作的斜向栱件区别，并未列入斜栱或“真斜栱”。

那么，角部斜向出跳的栱件何时在补间铺作、柱头铺作开始出现，成为通常意义所指代的斜栱？在已经发现的唐代木构建筑、仿木构的砖石塔和墓葬以及敦煌壁画中的建筑画中，均未发现明确的用于柱头或补间的斜栱形象，甚至用于角部的抹角栱都很少见，目前仅见于四川邛崃花置寺石窟[⑥]中转角铺作的抹角令栱（唐贞元十四年，789年，图3）。目前学界提出的最早实例是敦煌五代洞窟第146窟，

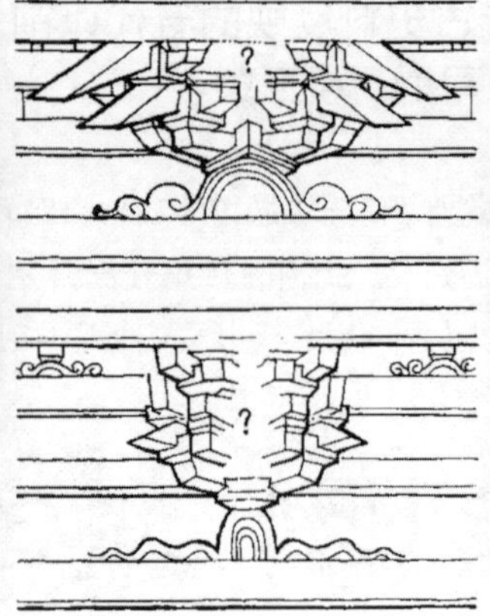

图 3 唐代邛崃花置寺石窟所见转角铺作之抹角令栱（左）
图 4 敦煌第 146 窟壁画[⑦]（中）
图 5 《伯希和敦煌图录》8 窟壁画局部[⑧]（右）

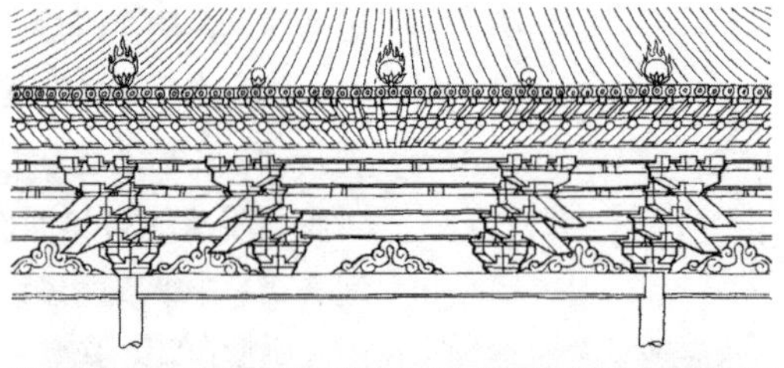

图 6 敦煌壁画 231 窟壁画（中唐）[⑩]

图 7 莫高窟 12 窟北壁壁画[⑪]（晚唐）

认为其南北壁壁画中均绘有明确的斜栱形象（图 4）。因目前未见该壁画的高清原图，仅能将研究者的线画图和伯希和的原始壁画照片（图 5）进行对照，从线图中反映的斗栱形制来看存在诸多疑点：其出斜构件施用的位置仅在明间补间铺作，出现了多层出斜、斜昂等晚至金代建筑中才出现的典型形制，而且从构造上分析因室内空间的局限，出斜构件若为斜昂，其只能是插昂的构造才能满足要求，这与宋代才出现插昂的普遍认识不符。

此外，从线图中表达的绘画内容看，该两图的中心交接部位均表达不详，线图中进行了留白。按照傅熹年先生对建筑画的研究[⑨]，五代北宋时期建筑画成为独立的画种，要求画家对建筑的结构、构造的把握十分准确。146 窟的这两幅壁画采取平视透视的方法表达斗栱结构，参考其他唐代敦煌壁画中的建筑画绘画方式，至居中的明间补间铺作时一般会采取物体遮挡或以不出跳的栱枋进行表达（图 6、图 7），而这两幅图中却绘有出跳的斗栱，其意图并不是为了表达斜栱，可能是属于原绘画作者在绘制建筑画时出现的透视技术表达问题，或者是研究者绘制线图时对原图内容提炼不够准确，亦或是对该洞窟或壁画的年代判定存在其他可能，有待公布该壁画高清原图后才能开展进一步的研究，现有资料不足以成为判断五代时期斜栱施用于补间铺作的标尺案例。

如果我们再观察同期的五代木构建筑和仿木构砖石塔实例，包括北方地区的山西大云院

图 8　云岩寺塔（左上）、闸口白塔（右上）、灵隐寺石塔（左下）与应县木塔（右下）的转角铺作形制对比

大殿、天台庵弥陀殿大殿、龙门寺西配殿、平遥镇国寺万佛殿，以及南方地区的福州华林寺大殿，多边形塔如苏州云岩寺塔、杭州闸口白塔、灵隐寺双石塔等，也均未发现在补间或柱头铺作施用斜栱。值得注意的是，上述五代时期的多座八边形塔，其转角铺作的斗栱形制较为一致，即相邻两壁的华栱均与塔壁面垂直出跳，角华栱自中间斜向出跳，与两个垂直出跳的华栱夹角很小。这种做法与后世辽宋金时期多边形塔角铺作的华栱顺塔身方向出跳的成熟形制明显不同（图 8），并未形成多边形塔的角铺作中意向明确的斜栱形象。

三、大量实例所见的辽宋—明清时期（10 世纪后）的斜栱

（一）斜栱形制或形制组合的分析

辽宋金元时期大量建筑实例的斗栱形制中可见斜栱的应用。为进一步深入讨论斜栱形制的发展演变，我们可以从斜栱铺作布局、斜栱铺作构造、斜栱栱件形制三个层面，综合提炼一系列的特征斗栱形制或形制组合作为分析对象，选取具有明确纪年史料或具有充分研究基础的“标尺性”建筑案例，进行综合排比研究，以期获得更为客观而准确的认识。

（1）斜栱铺作布局是指以使用斜栱为关注点，从面—间—柱三方面分析其具体位置，即前檐、后檐和山面；明间和其他开间；柱头铺作、补间铺作、转角铺作[12]。各种位置之间互相组合，形成三种主要的布局关系（图 9），以符号 X 标记如下：

对称布局（X-1），即前后檐及山面、不同开间的相应位置斗栱使用斜栱的情况一致；

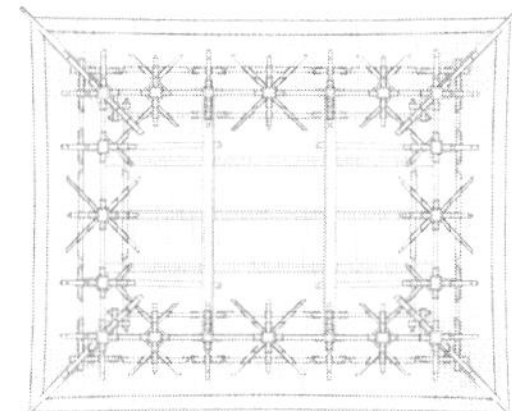

X-1　南吉祥寺大殿铺作布局仰视图

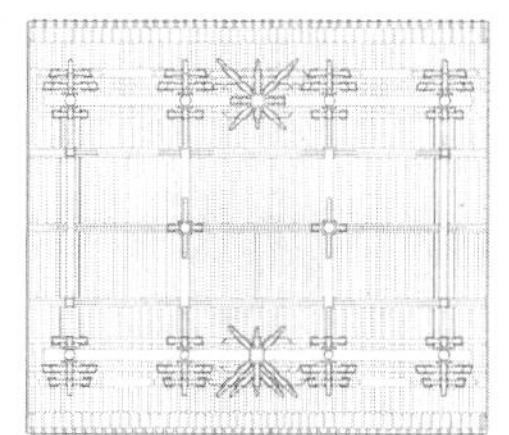

X-3　龙门寺天王殿铺作布局仰视图

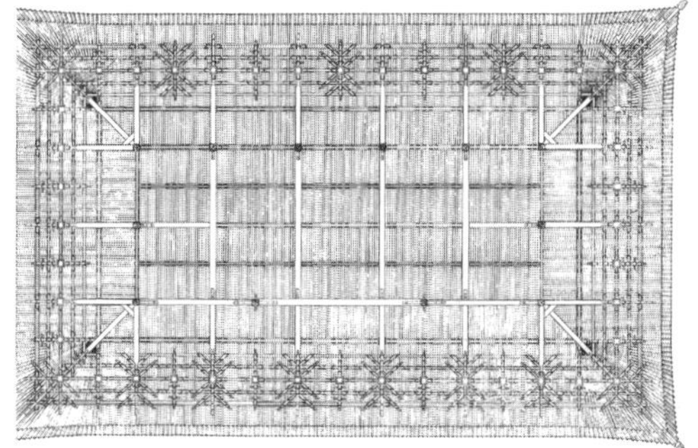

X-2　崇福寺弥陀殿铺作布局仰视图

图 9　铺作布局类型示意图[13]

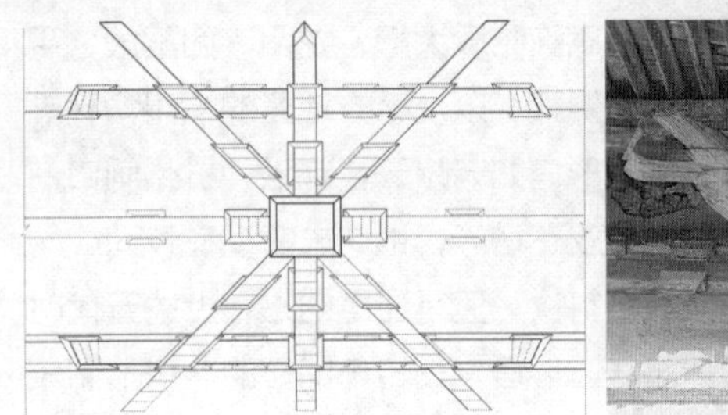

图 10-1 南吉祥寺大殿明间补间铺作斜栱，T-1/D-1/F-1/L-1

图 10-2 应县木塔补间铺作斜栱，(T-1、T-2)/(D-1、D-2)/(F-1、F-3)/(L-1、L-2)

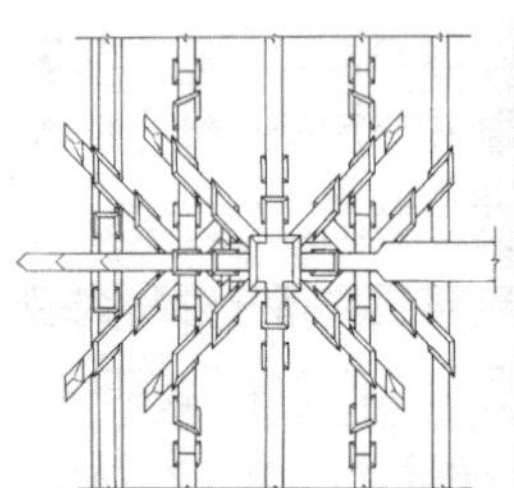

图 10-3 朔州崇福寺柱头铺作斜栱，T-1/D-1/F-2/L-1

图 10-4 善化寺普贤阁角铺作及补间铺作，T-1/D-1/(F-1、F-3、F-4)/L-1

不对称布局（X-2），即前后檐相应位置斗栱使用斜栱情况不一致；

重点位置布局（X-3），即不同开间相应位置斗栱使用斜栱情况不一致。

（2）斜栱铺作构造是指对整朵斗栱的构造进行分析，大体包括：出斜起始跳数、出斜角度、出斜缝数与正向华栱缝数、里外跳出斜等，分别以符号区分标识如下（图 10，1-9.）：

出斜起始跳数（T），区分为：第一跳始出斜（T-1），第一跳以上始出斜（T-2）；

出斜角度（D），区分为：45 度（D-1），60 度或其他角度（D-2）；

出斜缝数与正向华栱缝数（F），区分为：出一缝斜栱（F-1），出两缝或多缝斜栱（F-2），不出正向华栱（F-3），出多缝正向华栱（F-4）；

斗栱里跳（L），区分为：里跳用斜栱与外跳对等（L-1），里跳用斜栱与外跳不对等（L-2），里跳不用斜栱（L-3）。

（3）斜栱构件是指对单个栱件的形制分析，包括斜向华栱或斜向插昂（图 11-1）、横栱平直或横栱抹斜（图 11-2）、方形栌斗或圆形栌斗（图 11-3）等与之有关的构件形象。

（二）辽、北宋时期的斜栱形制

辽宋初年的木构建筑斗栱形制中仍继续沿用角华栱与抹角栱的组合，但抹角栱已经从

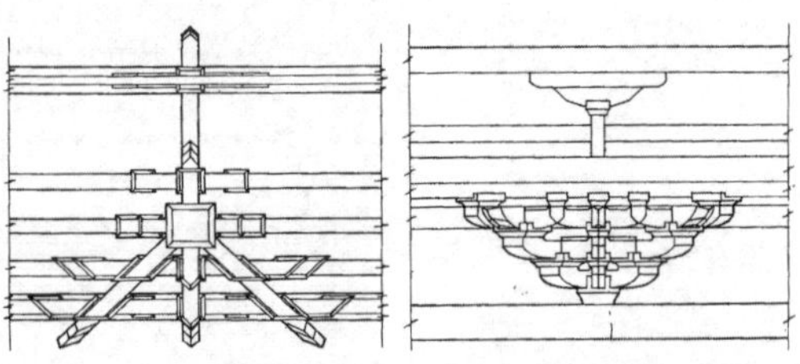

图 10-5 沁县普照寺大殿补间铺作，T-1/D-1/F-1/L-3

图 11-1 长子县北宋村玉皇庙后殿前檐斜栱与斜昂

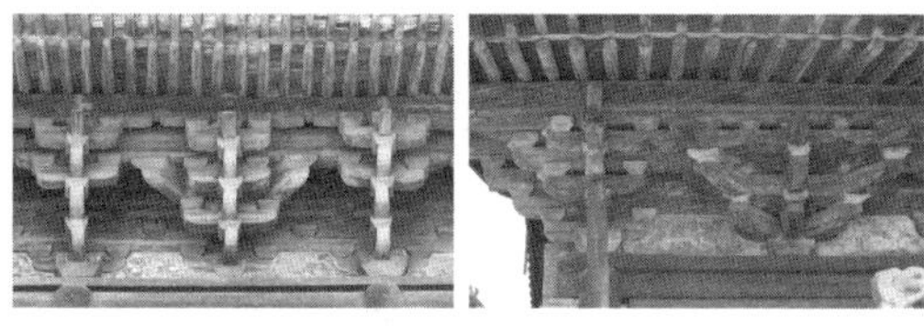
图 11-2 应县木塔（横栱平直）、定襄洪福寺大殿（横栱抹斜）

图 11-3 陵川石掌玉皇庙大殿前檐铺作斜栱与瓜棱斗

图 12 正定隆兴寺天王殿转角铺作（左）

图 13 独乐寺山门转角铺作（右）

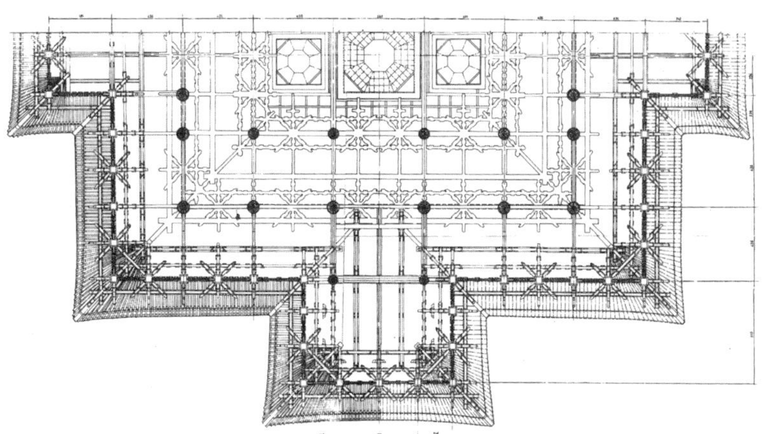
图 14 隆兴寺摩尼殿下檐梁架仰视图[17]

角华栱跳头的令栱位置内移到了角柱上成为抹角华栱，与角华栱、正向出跳华栱共同组成“米”字形的角部斜栱形制，如推测建于宋初的正定隆兴寺天王殿[14]（宋太平兴国七年至宋端栱元年，982—988 年），虽经后代重修，但仍可清晰辨认早期斗栱和晚期斗栱的形制（图 12）；辽代早期建筑独乐寺山门（辽统和二年，984 年，图 13）、独乐寺观音阁（辽统和二年，984 年），甚至到 11 世纪前期的开善寺大殿（辽重熙二年，1033 年）、华严寺薄伽教藏殿（辽重熙七年，1038 年），至辽中后期涞源阁文殊殿[15]（11 世纪中期—12 世纪初），都得以继续沿用。

斜栱构件何时从角铺作转移至柱头铺作、补间铺作？目前发现最早的宋代木构建筑纪年实例是山西陵川南吉祥寺正殿[16]（北宋天圣八年，1030 年），其前后檐和两山的补间铺作均施用了里外跳均等的斜栱（图 9，1. 和图 10，1.），其后在正定隆兴寺摩尼殿（北宋皇祐四年，1052 年，图 14）的补间铺作以及部分柱头铺作使用斜栱。而宋代多边形仿木构砖石塔中最早的纪年实例是河北正定广惠寺华塔中心主塔一层的补间铺作（北宋太平兴国四年，979 年，图 15），而再观辽代木构建筑实例，直到 11 世纪中叶的善化寺大雄宝殿[19]、佛宫寺释迦塔（辽清宁二年，1056 年）、华严寺大雄宝殿[20]（辽清宁八年，1062 年）才开始出现了施用于柱头和补间铺作的斜栱；辽代仿木构砖石塔中最早于补间铺作使用斜栱的纪年实例是智度寺塔[21]（辽太平十一年，1031 年，图 16）。

整体来看，辽宋时期建筑使用斜栱的实例主要集中于以山西、河北为中心的中原北

图 15 广惠寺华塔南立面一层斗栱原状（赫达·莫里逊摄于 1934 年）[18]

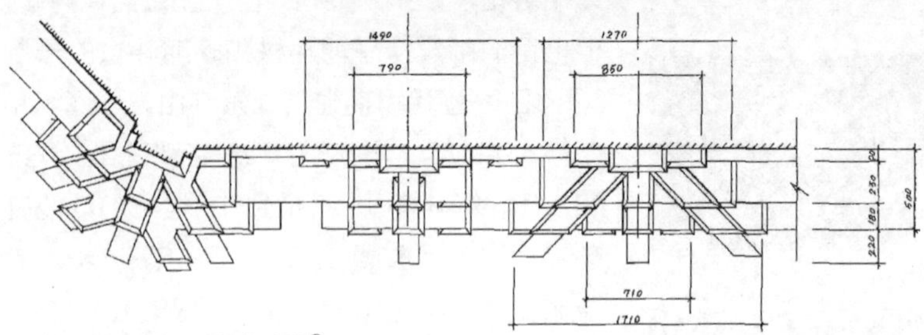

图 16 智度寺塔一层檐部斗栱[22]

图 17 隆兴寺摩尼殿抹角梁与内檐斜栱（左）

图 18 定襄关王庙大殿抹角梁与内檐斜栱（右）

方地区，辽宁、内蒙古等地的仿木构塔中也常见。斜栱铺作布局对称，柱头均施或补间均施；不同位置的斜栱形制较为统一，一般第一跳即始出斜，从出斜一缝发展为出斜两缝，未见出斜多缝，角度以 45 度居多，偶有 60 度出斜且其中缝无华栱出跳，里跳也对等出斜承托顺栿串，具有明显的结构作用；斜栱栱件自身的形象一般与正向出跳的华栱相同，端头抹斜与正中华栱齐平，与之相应的横栱栱件形象也受其影响以两端抹斜相适应，除斜向昂状耍头外，未见斜出下昂。辽宋时期的建筑中对各类斜栱的应用，一方面可通过其整体布局、斗栱造型、构件变化来塑造多样化的建筑外观[23]，另一方面在加强斗栱承托屋檐的结构性能方面发挥重要作用。此外斜栱结构功能还体现在歇山顶或庑殿顶建筑中，斜栱里跳与内檐转角抹角梁的结合，进一步加强了斗栱和梁架的一体性，在正定隆兴寺摩尼殿（图 17）、定襄关王庙大殿[24]（北宋宣和五年，1123 年，图 18）均可见。

辽、北宋是同期对峙的两个政权，如果我们进一步对辽、北宋建筑使用斜栱形制的情况分别进行年代分期，可分别划分为不同的发展阶段，在此基础上进行对比分析，可以发现辽宋两地斜栱应用的区别。

辽代建筑的斜栱应用大致可分为三个时期，10 世纪末的辽代早期建筑在角铺作中使用抹角栱较为常见，如前文所述可见于早期的几座辽代木构建筑，如仔细对比还可发现抹角栱自耍头层逐渐下移至第一跳，形成多跳抹角栱的过程。至辽太平、重熙年间（11 世纪 30—50 年代），开始在补间铺作使用 45 度斜栱，多边形的角铺作也开始变得复杂，顺塔身出跳形成两缝斜栱，如薄迦教藏殿天宫楼阁（辽重熙七年，1038 年，图 19）、涿州智度寺塔（辽太平十一年，1031 年，图 16）、涿州云居寺塔[25]（辽重熙六年或七年，1037—1038 年）。至辽清宁年间斜栱的应用已经相当普遍而成熟，如山西佛宫寺释迦塔[26]（辽清宁二年，1056 年）应用了多种形制的斜栱，在斜栱布局、斜栱构造、栱件形制上有多样的组合形式，体现了高超的营造技巧。而善化寺大雄宝殿（辽代中期，约十一世纪中叶，图 20）及华严寺大雄宝殿（辽清宁八年，1062 年，图 20）在明间补间施用非 45 度出跳斜栱[27]，中缝华栱不出跳，并且铺作里跳的出斜结构比外跳更长，

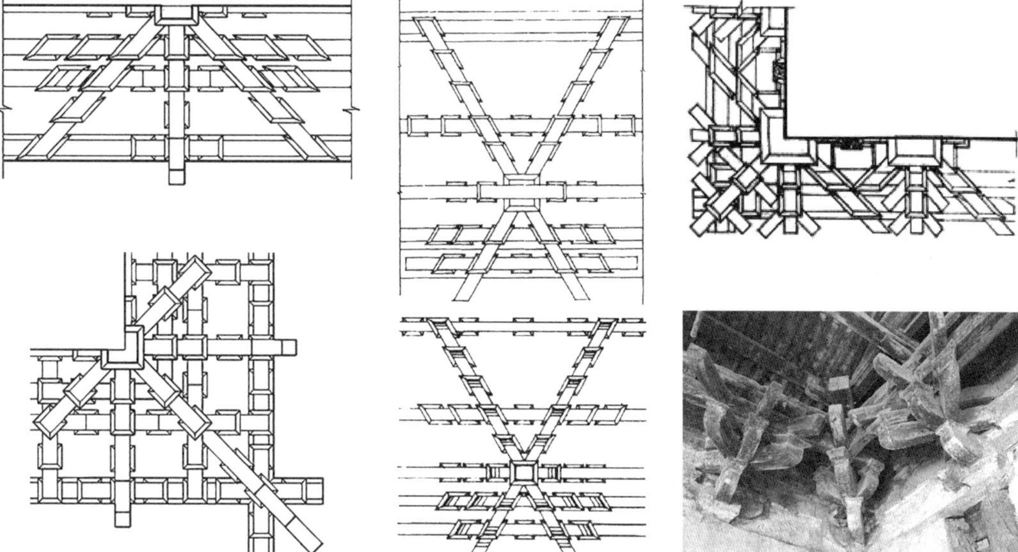

图 19 薄迦教藏殿天宫楼阁补间铺作及角铺作斜栱[30]（左）
图 20 善化寺大雄宝殿及华严寺大雄宝殿明间补间铺作斜栱[31]（中）
图 21 辽宁朝阳南塔斜栱（右上）
图 22 南吉祥寺大殿内檐斜栱（右下）

呈现出非常显著的结构意义，以及对明间补间铺作这一重点位置的关注。辽代中晚期仍可见有角部抹角栱形制，至辽末其斜栱应用一直保持柱头与补间铺作整体布局、多缝出斜的组合形式，如辽宁朝阳南塔[28]（辽大康二年，1076年，图 21）、北京天宁寺塔[29]（辽天庆九年，1119 年）。

北宋建筑斜栱应用大致也可以分为三个时期，10 世纪末的北宋早期建筑仍可见抹角栱的使用，但已是较为完善的多层抹角栱，斜栱也已经开始在补间铺作中出现，跳头横栱端头也已开始抹斜。至北宋中期天圣—皇祐年间（11 世纪 30—60 年代），南吉祥寺大殿和隆兴寺摩尼殿已呈现出十分成熟而完善的斜栱结构，铺作布局对称，前后檐及两山面的补间铺作均出里外跳完全对等的斜栱，形成牢固均匀的铺作层以承托檐部荷载，此外柱头铺作也开始出现斜栱，如南吉祥寺大殿的山面柱头铺作甚至只在里跳用斜栱而外跳不用，是此时期斜栱结构功能的最直接体现（图 22）。北宋中后期至北宋末年开始出现斜栱的不对称布局，如晋东南地区小会岭二仙庙大殿[32]（北宋嘉祐八年前，1063 年前，图 23）仅在前檐明间补间使用斜栱，景县开福寺舍利塔[33]（北宋元丰二年，1079 年）仅在第三层补间铺作使用斜栱，阳泉关王庙大殿[34]（北宋宣和四年，1122 年，图 24）仅在前檐柱头铺作使用斜栱；斜栱构造开始出现出斜两缝的斜栱，如晋城南村二仙庙大殿内天宫楼阁小木作[35]（北宋末年至金代中期，12 世纪初—12 世纪中叶，图 25）、定襄关王庙大殿（北宋宣和五年，1123 年）的明间补间铺作。此外在北宋末年的仿木构砖雕墓中也出现了斜栱[36]，可见于山西平顺县郊宋代砖雕墓（北宋元祐七年，1092 年）、壶关上好牢砖雕壁画墓 M1（北宋宣和五年前，1123 年前），

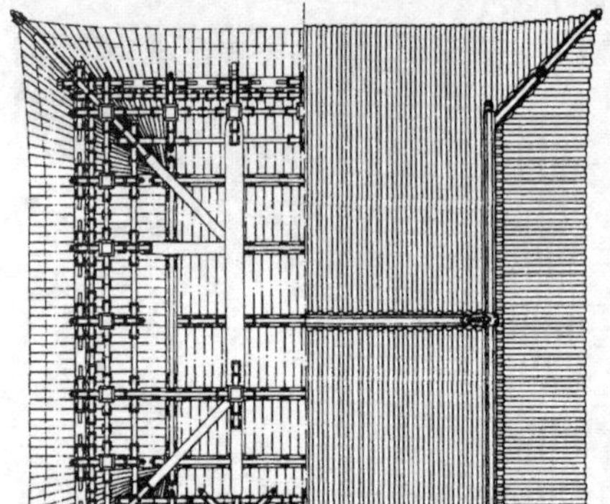

图 23　小会岭二仙庙大殿前檐斜栱（左上）
图 24　阳泉关王庙梁架仰视图（左下）
图 25　南村二仙庙大殿小木作（右上）
图 26　稷山南阳砖雕墓（右中）
图 27　林县小西环路壁画墓（右下）

在稷山南阳砖雕墓（北宋崇宁四年，1105 年，图 26）还出现了斜向插昂，是目前最早的斜昂实例。此外在临近山西的河南林县小西环路壁画墓（北宋大观年以后 1107—1110 年后，图 27）中也出现了斜栱，表明北宋末年斜栱应用地域已经扩展。

由此可见，北宋木构建筑的斜栱形制在诸多方面都早于辽代建筑出现，表现出更为高超的建筑营造技艺及更为和谐的建筑艺术效果，甚至反映对辽代建筑的影响，如多跳抹角栱的出现、补间或柱头开始使用斜栱、斜栱与转角内部抹角梁的结合、横栱端头与斜栱端头进行抹斜取得一致、斜昂的出现、耍头层出斜等。但宋辽时期多边形仿木构砖石塔中斜栱应用的情况却不一样，辽代仿木构多边形砖塔表现出更为明显的忠于木构的形制特征，斜栱应用更为普遍、富于变化，而宋代仿木构实例除少量砖塔或铁塔实例[37]，多数实例均使用出跳短促、连续分布的补间铺作，角部华栱正向出跳而非顺塔身出跳，对木构形制的模仿在形神上均有明显差异。通过以上分析，与通常认为的斜栱是辽代建筑的创新或发明不同，宋代建筑更早完成了斜栱应用于柱头补间铺作的技术革新，但在宋辽长期对峙发展的过程中，两地也各自形成了各自的技术和风格所长并互相影响[38]。事实上如果从历史背景分析，辽宋虽都承唐制，但北宋占据了唐、五代以来原有的文化核心区域，而辽主要占据了唐代北方广大区域，从工匠传承和木作技术的发展来看待这一问题，北宋建筑较辽代建筑在斜栱应用方面体现出领先的营造技艺也是更为合理的解释。

（三）金、南宋、元时期的斜栱形制

金代建筑对斜栱的应用较为普遍，在继承辽、北宋建筑斜栱营造技术的基础上，有了进一步的发展和变化，建筑实例分布的地域从辽宁、河北、山西等主要区域扩展至河南、陕西等交界临近地区。

金代前期的斜栱结构性能已经开始出现明显的装饰化倾向，普遍出现注重前檐和明间的不对称布局、柱头和补间混用、多缝出斜、里外跳均出斜但不对等、抹斜横栱或翼形横栱、斜向插昂的情况，为塑造金代建筑绚丽的建筑外观发挥了重要作用。如佛光寺文殊殿（金天会十五年，1137 年，图 28）的前后檐有所区别，前檐中三间用两缝斜栱而稍间用一缝斜栱；善化寺三圣殿（金天会六年至皇统三年，

图 28　佛光寺文殊殿前檐明间铺作（左）
图 29　善化寺三圣殿次间补间铺作（中）
图 30　稷山马村砖雕墓中的斜昂（右）

1128—1143 年，图 29）在前后檐次间补间铺作使用造型夸张的出斜三缝的斜栱；崇福寺弥陀殿（金皇统三年，1143 年）在柱头铺作、补间铺作均用斜栱，角铺作也沿用了多跳多缝抹角栱；善化寺普贤阁（金贞元二年，1154 年）二层檐下明间补间铺作用斜栱而正中华栱不出跳，但角部却用抹角栱并出多缝华栱。这种多缝斜栱的构造意味着必须在斗上开更多的槽，降低了构件本身的强度，而且使得铺作的体积和荷载加大，自身所具有的增加檐下支点的结构作用反而被减弱；而且里跳出斜相比外跳的出斜长度明显缩短，原有的结构性减弱。此外在金代前期的仿木构砖室墓里开始使用斜向出跳的插昂，如山西稷山马村砖雕墓[39]（金代前期，图 30）M1、M2、M5、M8 均大量使用斜昂，此外还受其影响创造性地使用翼型横栱、昂状令栱以取得一致的装饰效果；又如正定临济寺澄灵塔[40]（金大定二十五年，1185 年）通过不同层数的斜栱位置、出斜缝数、正中华栱出跳等细节的变化（图 31），形成了墓葬或塔身绚丽夸张的立面效果。

图 31　正定临济寺澄灵塔立面图

金代中后期至末年，相对于此期的建筑实例数量，斜栱的应用普遍性有所降低，也不再具有金代前期多样化的布局和夸张的造型。常见的斜栱铺作布局是通过斜栱的使用对前檐明间补间进行点睛重点装饰，铺作构造方面除里外跳不对等出斜外，开始出现里跳不出斜、无后尾的斜栱[41]，丧失结构意义而只具备装饰建筑立面功能。与此相应斜向昂状构件、圆形栌斗或瓜棱斗等构件装饰性也开始加强，如泽州县高都东岳庙天齐殿[42]（金大定年间，1161—1189 年，图 32）、沁县普照寺大殿[43]（金大定年间，1161—1189 年）、盂县大王庙后殿[44]（金承安五年，1200 年，图 33），都是在前檐明间铺作使用了装饰意向突出的斜栱，在建筑整体立面效果中较为醒目。甚至还出现昂状令栱与斜昂同时在一朵斗栱中使用的情况，如丹凤县二郎庙大殿（金大安三年，1211 年，图 34）。此外在河南地区的金代仿木构中也出现了类似的情况，如三门峡市崤山西路古墓 M1[45]（金大定七年，1167 年），其栌斗使用圆形栌斗。

与金代相比，南宋建筑中使用斜栱的情况较少受到关注，一般常被提及的四川江油云岩寺飞天藏小木作作为南宋斜栱营造技术的实例，已有研究者指出其为元代实例[47]。从保存数量有限的南宋建筑实例来看，其对斜栱的使用情况远不及金代建筑。最早使用斜栱的南宋建筑实例为山东广饶关帝庙[48]（南宋建炎二年，1128 年），仍属于北方地区的实例，其使用斜栱的位置较为特殊，在后檐明间补间施用 45 度一缝斜栱。南宋中后期在四川地区的仿木构砖石塔或墓葬中可见有简单的斜栱出现，如华蓥安丙墓的 M1、M2、M5[49]（南宋嘉定年间 1209—1221 年，图 35）中均使用布局对称、造型简单的五铺作斜栱；广安白塔[50]（南宋嘉定二年至七年，1209—1214 年，图 36）下五层的柱头、补间铺作均使用四铺作斜栱，直接承替木，不施令栱。

至元代，斜栱仍然在建筑立面装饰中发挥重要作用，使用地域也在元代后期进一步在河南、四川等地普及，其形制延续了金代中后期以来的注重前檐明间补间铺作、斜昂的应用、圆形栌斗或翼形栱等装饰性构件的使用、里跳弱化或不出斜等主要特征，如山西明应王庙水神殿[51]（元延祐六年，1319 年）、武乡真如寺大殿[52]（元至治三年，1323 年）、汾阳北榆苑五岳庙五岳殿[53]（元大德十年，1306 年），河南博爱汤帝庙大殿（元代）、逢石汤帝庙大殿（元代）、四川眉山报恩寺大殿（元泰定四年，1327 年）、阆中五龙庙文昌阁（元至正三年，1343 年）、芦山青龙寺大殿（元至正年间，1341—1370 年）[54]。同时元代斜栱的应用在以下几方面又有所变化，一是外檐大额的使用使得明间开间尺寸扩大，并且为斜栱布局提供更为牢固的支撑，明间补间铺作或柱头铺作开始出现多缝斜昂，体积巨大、造型夸张，如临晋县衙大堂（元大德年间，1279—1307 年，图 37）、玉皇观五凤楼（元代，图 38），而四川江油云岩寺飞天藏（元至正年间重修，图 39）的小木作中多缝出斜、繁复交错的斜栱结构，可视为明清时期网状出斜如意斗栱的

图 32　泽州县高都东岳庙天齐殿补间铺作（左）

图 33　盂县大王庙后殿补间铺作（中）

图 34　丹凤县二郎庙大殿[46]明间补间铺作（右）

图 35　华蓥安丙墓 M2 前室右壁斗栱（左）

图 36　广安白塔 2~3 层斜栱（右）

图 37　临晋县衙大殿明间补间铺作（左）

图 38　长子五凤楼玉皇观上檐补间铺作（右）

图 39 云岩寺飞天藏中的斜栱（上左）

图 40 显圣王庙前檐铺作[57]（上右）

图 41 魏村牛王庙戏台梁架仰视图（右）

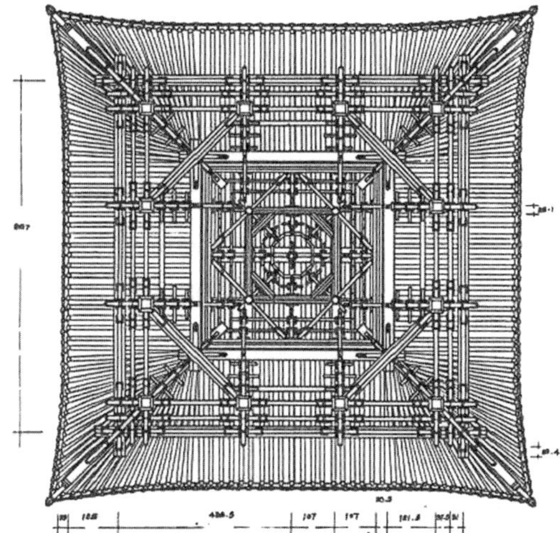

图 42 万荣东岳庙飞云楼（左上）

图 43 解州关帝庙春秋楼首层斗栱（右上）

图 44 广西容县真武阁如意斗栱（左下）

图 45 佛山祖庙前殿如意斗栱[65]（右下）

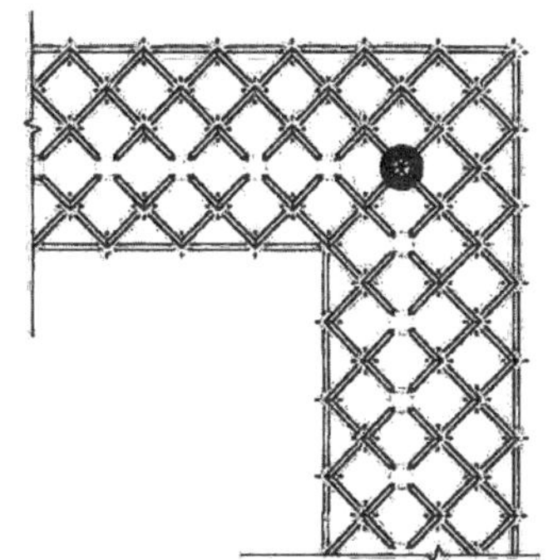

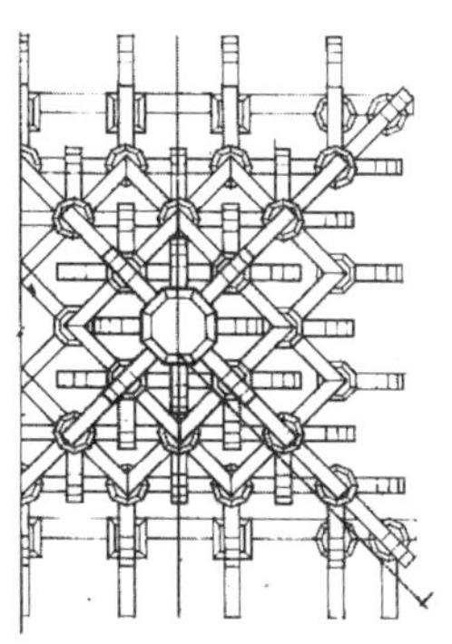

最早实例；二是斜栱在元代较多的悬山殿宇的前檐铺作中得以应用，甚至在角部呈现出模拟角铺作的特征单向出斜，如孟州显圣王庙（元至正十年，1350 年，图 40）；三是少量歇山建筑的转角部位仍然可见抹角梁与里跳斜栱的结合，如定兴慈云阁[55]（元至元十年至十七年，1273—1280 年）、魏村牛王庙戏台[56]（元元至元二十年，1283 年，图 41）、临汾东洋村后土庙戏台（元至正五年，1345 年），都使用此结构形成角部的结构。

（四）明清时期的斜栱：装饰性的网状如意斗栱

明清时期的斜栱应用地域性不再明显，虽然在明代和清早期的一些建筑中仍可见对元以前斜栱形制的模仿和延续，如万荣东岳庙飞云楼[58]（明正德年间，1506—1521 年，图 42）在首层使用加厚的普拍枋以放置多缝华栱出跳的斜栱，北京慈寿寺塔[59]（明万历四年，1576 年）的仿木砖雕斗栱与辽塔斜栱形制相似，而解州关帝庙春秋楼[60]（清同治九年，1870 年，图 43）廊下斗栱，还出现了各种龙首、云形、象鼻的构件装饰形象。但明清时期斜栱最为明显的特征是如意斗栱的出现和普及，即相邻两攒斗栱坐斗左右分别出若干跳斜栱，这些斜栱左右彼此搭连，交织成网状，成为一个整体。这种网状的如意斗栱存在两种形式[61]，一是无正心出跳全部由斜栱组成，二是有正心出跳。前者实例可见于广西容县真武阁[62]（明万历四十八年，1573 年，图 44），后者可见于佛山祖庙前殿[63]（明宣德四年，1429 年，图 45）、北京北海智珠牌楼[64]（清乾隆十六年，1751 年），此外还有两种结构形式的结合体，如解州关帝庙威震华夏牌坊（清末）等。很明显，元以前的多缝斜栱营造技术发展为明清时期如意斗栱的出现奠定了基础，其实例多见于戏楼、牌楼、门楼等特定的建筑类型，主要作用是以其烦冗复杂的造型吸引视线关注和空间引导。

图 46 斜栱发展演变示意图

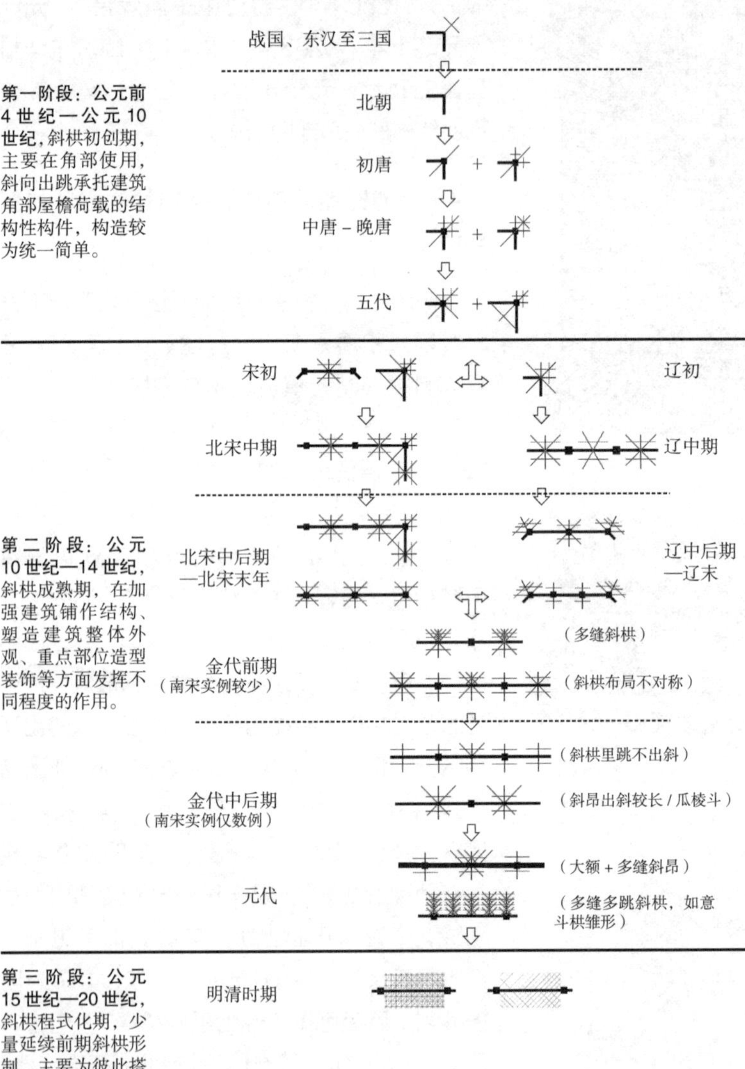

四、主要结论及相关问题探讨

（一）斜栱的主要发展演变过程

斜栱并非起源于辽代也并非辽构中的独创，而是从战国至汉代即已开始使用，从初创到变化都与角铺作结构作法紧密相关，有着长期的营造技术发展过程。如同中国古代建筑斗栱的总体发展演变趋势一样，斜栱也经历了结构性到装饰性的转变过程，呈现出铺作布局、铺作构造、栱件形象等方面的明显变化，其主要发展演变过程可以分为以下几个阶段（图 46）：

第一阶段：公元前 4 世纪至公元 10 世纪，斜栱初创期，主要在角部使用，作为斜向出跳承托建筑角部屋檐荷载的结构性构件，构造较为统一简单。

前期（公元前 4 世纪—公元 3 世纪），斜栱最早是为了解决建筑檐角的荷载而出现，自战国、东汉至三国一直沿用角部 45 度出跳的角华栱和跳头垂直的抹角令栱这一组合形式。

后期（公元 4 世纪—公元 10 世纪），北朝以后逐渐发展以 45 度斜向出跳的角华栱为主体独立支撑檐部的转角铺作结构，至唐代晚期已经形成角华栱和瓜子栱、慢栱出跳相列的稳定转角铺作组合形式，跳头的抹角令栱不再成为必要构件，仅在少量实例中可见，至五代时期仍得以延续，多边形仿木构塔的转角铺作也主要使用角华栱和正向出跳的华栱的组合。

第二阶段：公元 10 世纪—14 世纪，斜栱成熟期，在加强建筑铺作结构、塑造建筑整体外观、装饰重点部位等方面发挥不同程度的作用。

前期（辽、宋初年—辽、宋中期，10 世纪—11 世纪中叶），抹角栱自跳头内移至栌斗形成角部“米”字形结构以加强角铺作，又向中部转移形成补间铺作、柱头铺作的斜栱，向内檐转移形成转角部位内部的抹角梁，两者交接形成角部的三角形构架进一步加强结构。此期的斜栱铺作布局对称，形制统一，里外跳均对等出斜，对塑造建筑的整体外观、加强铺作层整体结构发挥重要作用。

中期（辽宋后期—金代、南宋中期，11 世纪中叶—12 世纪下半叶），斜栱的构造和造型取得诸多创新，注重通过斜栱的差异化布局和单朵斜栱的造型营造建筑外观立面的艺术效果，出现了多种样式的不对称斜栱布局和组合、出两缝或多缝的斜栱、里外跳不均等、斜向插昂等多种形制，斜栱开始从结构性转向装饰性。

后期（金代、南宋中后期—元末明初，12 世纪下半叶—14 世纪），斜栱的应用表现出对前檐明间补间的重点关注，在中期的基础上斜栱装饰性进一步加强，如多缝出斜、斜昂构件、圆形栌斗、外跳出斜里跳无后尾等。此期斜栱的应用地域开始扩展到南方地区，并且出现了网状出斜交织的斜栱结构，是明清时期如意斗栱的最早雏形。

第三阶段：公元 15 世纪—20 世纪，斜栱程式化期，少量延续前期斜栱形制，主要为彼此搭连、网状交织的如意斗栱。

明代中后期至清代（15 世纪—20 世纪），斜栱应用的地域进一步扩展至南北方大部分地区，地域差异较小。除少量木构和仿木构实例仍延续前期的斜栱形制外，此期斜栱主要表现为彼此搭连、网状交织的如意斗栱，且主要用于戏楼、牌楼、门楼等特定的建筑类型。

（二）斜栱转移的动力：外观模仿还是结构创新？

角部斜向出跳的栱件为何会向柱头铺作、补间铺作转移，成为通常意义所指代的斜栱？一般认为这一过程是由于斗栱发展成熟后与梁枋的结合，基于建筑立面外观统一的需求，柱头铺作、补间铺作对角铺作的形制趋同模仿而开始施用斜栱[66]。这种转移主要的途径有两种可能的方式：一种是普通的四方形建筑中，柱头铺作、补间铺作对由角华栱、抹角栱和正侧两面垂直出跳华栱共同组成的“米”字形结构角铺作的模仿；另一种是由于多边形塔的出现，相邻壁面的华栱顺塔身方向而非垂直塔身方向出跳，客观上形成了角部斜栱的构造而被柱头铺作、补间铺作模仿，并因为六边形、八边形的区别而产生 45 度、60 度的斜栱[67]。

也有学者提出斜栱出现于补间铺作这一加强结构功能得以实现是因为普拍枋的出现，为补间铺作趋同柱头铺作或者超越之提供了条件，使得在补间铺作安排大体量的补间铺作成为可能[68]，换言之柱头铺作出现斜栱应比补间铺作更早。从目前的实例来看，木构建筑中使用普拍枋最早的实例为平顺大云院大殿（五代后晋天福三年，938 年），但均未使用斜栱；而年代最早的几处补间铺作使用斜栱的木构建筑实例确定都使用了普拍枋，但北宋初年的广惠寺华塔主塔一层补间铺作使用斜栱，却并未使用普拍枋。由此观之，普拍枋确实早于斜栱出现，但普拍枋与斜栱转移至补间铺作并无直接明确的因果关联。从技术角度辨析，普拍枋可能为补间铺作的出现创造了条件，但并非促使补间铺作使用斜栱的直接原因。从前文的分析来看，补间铺作出现斜栱应早于柱头铺作，因形制趋同于柱头铺作的设定并不成立。

以上的推测都是基于“立面外观的统一需求而趋同模仿”这一基本点，但这种“现代设计者的代入感”是否符合真实的动因，还需要从实例中继续探寻。一方面因《营造法式》明文主张“铺作分布令远近皆匀”，宋以后外观统一的外檐斗栱才成为官式木构建筑的重要特征，相反差异化的铺作布局、铺作形制所体现的多样化斗栱意匠在唐、五代、辽、宋的早期建筑实例中更为普遍[69]；另一方面从多边形塔实例中的斜栱应用来看，其补间铺作出现斜栱并不早于四方形的木构建筑，都是在北宋初年出现，五代时期多边形塔的角铺作也没有出现可供补间铺作模仿的斜栱形象。

如果我们将“立面形式统一”的设计视角转向“解决结构需求”的构造视角，会发现补间铺作斜栱的出现有另一种可能的解释。斜栱最初出现在角部是为了解决角部屋檐部荷载的结构性功能，发展出了抹角栱和角华栱共同组成的“米”字形转角铺作结构，以及抹角栱转移至角华栱后尾成为内部抹角梁形成的“三角形”结构。这两种结构在宋代初年正定隆兴寺天王殿中已经同时得见（图 47），到北宋中期的隆兴寺摩尼殿将抹角梁与补间铺作里跳进行结合，并延伸至外檐，同时解决外檐的屋檐承托和内部梁架承托的问题。此外，抹角梁在五代时期的正定文庙的转角内檐已经得见（图 48），其与补间铺作结合形成 45 度斜栱的时间可能更早，但目前在实例中尚未见早于隆兴寺摩尼殿的实例。从此角度也可以理解 45 度斜栱比其他角度的斜栱应用更为普遍、出现时代更早的原因，并非因对八边形塔、六边形塔的角铺作的模仿，而是基于角铺作构造加强之缘故。

（三）斜栱应用的地域特征

斜栱因在较多早期建筑实例中得见而被关注，但其实仍是具有明显地域特征的斗栱形制。从使用斜栱的元以前早期建筑实例分布来看，具有显著的南北方区域差别，即使用斜栱实例主要集中于北方地区，以河北、山西地区为核心区域，不断扩展至辽宁、内蒙古、河南、陕西、山东等区域；而南方地区从五代至北宋时期，无论是仿木构砖石塔或是木构建筑均极少见，到南宋、元代以后在南方四川地区开始出

图 47 正定隆兴寺天王殿抹角梁（左）
图 48 正定县文庙大成殿抹角梁[70]（右）

现。至明清时期斜栱应用已不再具有明显的地域特征。

这一明显的地域差别可能和南北方的建造传统有一定关联，即北方地区殿阁式构架形成了相对独立的铺作层，为斜栱在斗栱布局、斗栱构造和栱件造型等方面提供了条件，而南方江浙地区以江南厅堂式井字形构架为范式的建造逻辑则更早建立外檐斗栱均质的特征。此外这一地域分布特征还揭示了斜栱形制自北向南的传播方向，如果再结合与之相关的横栱抹斜、瓜棱斗、翼形横栱等斗栱形制组合来观察这一传播过程，会发现更加生动而具体的区域流变关系，对于建立完整的中国古代建筑斗栱技术发展史具有重要意义。

（本研究基于北京大学考古文博学院徐怡涛教授所开设研究生课程“中国古代木构建筑年代学研究纲要”的2006年课程作业研究积累，结合近年来学界的研究进展修改完善成文。得益于该课程的课件传授与学术考察，本文通过建筑形制年代学的理论和方法尝试初步建立斜栱这一斗栱形制组合的时空发展框架，总结发展演变特征。限于文章篇幅，对于斜栱所体现的区域流变、区域文化影响等进一步的论述，有待今后开展进一步的研究，进行更为具体的论述）。

注释：

① 陈薇．斜栱发微 [J]. 古建园林技术，1987（4）：40.

② 朱小南．斜栱溯源 [J]. 文博，1987（3）：65.

③ 荷雅丽著，俞琳译．两种使用斜栱的重要且成熟的设计概念：“扇式斗栱”和“如意斗栱”[J]. 古建园林技术，2012（2）：11-18.

④ 关于抹角栱的描述最早可见于梁思成：蓟县独乐寺山门考 [M]// 梁思成全集（第一卷）. 北京：中国建筑工业出版社，2001：184，“屋角四十五度斜线上，有角栱三层，最上者与跳头令拱平，以支角梁。与角栱成正角，而施于柱中线上者，有长栱一道，与令栱平，唯安于二层跳头之瓜子栱（今称外拽瓜栱），故名之曰抹角慢栱。”

⑤ 冯继仁．中国古代木构建筑的考古学断代 [J]. 文物，1995（10）：43-68，图1、图2均引自该文P48、P47。

⑥ 辜其一．四门唐代摩崖中反映的建筑形式 [J]. 文物，1961（11）：65.

⑦ 萧默．敦煌建筑研究 [M]. 北京：文物出版社，1989：240.

⑧ 该壁画为莫高窟五代第146窟主室北壁东起第一铺“思益梵天请问经变”，该窟现编号146，对应原伯希和编号8。该壁画照片收录于《伯希和敦煌图录》，本研究所引用图片下载自数字丝绸之路网站中国石窟数据库敦煌莫高窟的相关页面，网址为 http：//dsr.nii.ac.jp/toyobunko/VIII-5-B6-3/V-1/page/0055.html.en.

⑨ 傅熹年．中国古代的建筑画 [J]. 文物，1998（3）：75-94.

⑩ 萧默．敦煌建筑研究 [M]. 北京：文物出版社，1989：234.

⑪ 图引自樊锦诗主编，孙毅华，孙儒僩著．解读敦煌：中世纪建筑画 [M]. 上海：华东师范大学出版社，2010：203.

⑫ 按前文所述，唐以后建筑的转角铺作中均使用角华栱，不具备时代特征意义，因此本分析中主要以转角铺作中是否还施用抹角栱作为判断标准。

⑬ 图9-1和图9-3改绘自《上栋下宇：历史建筑测绘五校联展》，天津大学出版社，2006年，北京大学考古文博学院文物建筑专业测绘实习图纸。图9-2引自：柴泽俊．中国古代建筑朔州崇福寺 [M]. 北京：文物出版社，1996：143.

⑭ 王素辉．正定隆兴寺天王殿建造年代再认识 [J].2016（Z1）：79-83.

⑮ 徐怡涛．河北涞源阁院寺文殊殿建筑年代鉴别研究．建筑史论文集，2002（2）：82-94.

⑯ 据寺内所存《吉祥院碑文并序》碑记载，南吉祥寺于北宋淳化三年（993年）敕赐院额，北宋天圣八年（1030年）迁至今址。

⑰ 图引自：河北省正定县文物保管所，编著．中国古代建筑：正定隆兴寺 [M]. 北京：文物出版社，2000：56.

⑱ 图引自：崔金泽．河北省中南部地区明以前寺庙建筑

研究 [D]. 北京：北京大学，2012：96。文中以广惠寺花塔维修记录为依据，通过对比历史照片，确定仅有一层主塔外檐斗栱为宋初原构。

⑲ 郭黛姮 . 中国古代建筑史（五卷本第三卷）—宋辽金西夏建筑 [M]. 北京：中国建筑工业出版社，2003：332. 善化寺大雄宝殿并无确切纪年，但其主要形制与寺内普贤阁、三圣殿差别较大，而与华严寺中主要辽代建筑接近。按照该寺山门中金大定十六年重修记载，其当为“前日栋宇所存者，十不三四”中的幸存者，其可能为幸存的辽构。

⑳ 柴泽俊 . 大同华严寺大雄宝殿结构形制研究 [C]// 柴泽俊古建筑文集 . 北京：文物出版社，1999：96-119. 按照此篇文章的观点，此殿创始于辽，重建于金，现存实物在许多方面保存着辽代形制。根据实物现状分析，金天眷三年（公元 1140 年）重建，实为原件重构。基于此种情况，本文中将华严寺大雄宝殿的年代定为其创始年代。

㉑ 曹汛 . 涿州智度寺塔的史源学考证 [J]. 建筑师，2007（2）：184-193.

㉒ 图引自：田林，杨昌鸣 . 涿州智度寺塔初探 [J]. 文物，2004（5）：89-96.

㉓ 温静 . 论多样化外檐斗栱的外观与布局：日本和样佛堂与中国北方辽宋金建筑的比较研究 [J]. 中国建筑史论汇刊，2014（2）：291-316.

㉔ 参见：李有成 . 定襄县关王庙构造浅探 [J]. 古建园林技术，1995（4）：4-8；王子奇 . 山西定襄关王庙考察札记 [J]. 山西大同大学学报（社会科学版），2009（4）：23-27.

㉕ 曹汛 . 涿州云居寺塔的年代学考证 [J]. 建筑师，2007（1）：97-102.

㉖ 陈明达 . 应县木塔 [M]. 北京：文物出版社，1966

㉗ 善化寺大雄宝殿及华严寺大雄宝殿还分别在前后檐次间和第二次间使用 45 度斜栱，前者里跳并未使用斜栱，后者里跳使用加长的斜栱。辽代中期是否会出现无里跳的斜栱？从该二殿的斜栱形制来看还存在一些疑点，包括：1. 两殿补间铺作的横栱抹斜面朝里，而其他未使用斜栱的横栱、同期的其他辽代建筑横栱多未抹斜，另外补间铺作的耍头与柱头铺作也存在差别；2. 善化寺大雄宝殿斜栱的布局位置、出斜角度以及横栱抹斜方式，与寺内的普贤阁、山门颇有相似之处。因此两殿的斗栱是否存在后世金代扰动的情况，还有待进一步深入分析。

㉘ 朝阳南塔的年代原多根据碑志记载，认为其始建于辽圣宗太平九年（1029 年）。但在 1999 年至 2001 年维修南塔时，维修过程中发现建塔砖铭，证实该塔建于辽大康二年（1076 年）。参见：佟强 . 浅谈朝阳城内的七座辽代砖塔 [C]// 辽宁省辽金契丹女真史研究会编 . 辽金历史与考古 第 3 辑 . 辽宁教育出版社，2011：226.

㉙ 王世仁 . 北京天宁寺塔三题 [C]// 当代中国建筑史家十书：王世仁中国建筑史论选集 . 沈阳：辽宁美术出版社，2013：143-158.

㉚ 图引自：刘翔宇 . 大同华严寺及薄伽教藏殿建筑研究 [D]. 天津：天津大学，2015：165-167.

㉛ 图引自：郭黛姮 . 中国古代建筑史（五卷本第三卷）：宋辽金西夏建筑 [M]. 北京：中国建筑工业出版社，2003.

㉜ 王书林，徐怡涛 . 晋东南五代、宋、金时期柱头铺作里跳形制分期及区域流变研究 [J]. 山西大同大学学报（自然科学版），2009（4）：79-85.

㉝ 崔金泽 . 河北省中南部地区明以前寺庙建筑研究 [D]. 北京：北京大学，2012.

㉞ 史国亮 . 阳泉关王庙大殿 [J]. 古建园林技术，2003（2）：40.

㉟ 吕舟，郑宇，姜铮著 . 晋城二仙庙小木作帐龛调查研究报告 [M]. 北京：科学出版社，2017：108。该报告综合形制分析、事件逻辑以及科技测年等手段，认为该小木作的修造时间为 12 世纪初—12 世纪中叶。图 25 引自该报告。

㊱ 相关实例参见：俞莉娜 . 宋金时期墓葬仿木构建筑史料研究：以河南中北部、山西南部地区为例 [D]. 北京：北京大学，2015 年。图 26、图 27 引自该文。

㊲ 如河北正定广惠寺华塔、天宁寺凌霄宝塔、景县舍利塔、山西潞城原起寺七圣塔、湖北玉泉寺铁塔等。

㊳ 张晓东 . 辽代砖塔建筑形制初步研究 [D]. 长春：吉林大学，2011：33-40.

㊴ 俞莉娜 . 宋金时期墓葬仿木构建筑史料研究：以河南中北部、山西南部地区为例 [D]. 北京：北京大学，2015.

㊵ 刘友恒 . 正定四塔名称及创建年代考 [J]. 文物春秋，1996（1）：53-56.

㊶ 此时期较少出现多缝斜栱，可能与铺作里跳不用斜栱有关，若在外跳还用多缝斜栱，恐其自重过大而不能稳固。

㊷ 该殿存有金大定十八年石柱题记、金大定二十五年门楣题记及金大定二十九年佛坛题记，结合其建筑形制判断大殿建筑年代为金大定年间。

㊸ 滑辰龙 . 沁县普照寺大殿勘查报告 [J]. 文物世界，1996（1）：36-43.

㊹ 徐怡涛 . 北京大学文物建筑导论课程讲义：文物建筑

踏查示例 · 盂县大王庙。

㊺ 三门峡市文物工作队．三门峡市崤山西路发现三座古墓 [J]. 华夏考古，1993（4）：80-86.

㊻ 国家文物局，主编．中国文物地图集（陕西分册，下册）[M]. 西安：西安地图出版社，1998：1189。图片由陕西省文化遗产研究院白海峰先生提供。

㊼ 王书林．四川宋元时期的汉式寺庙建筑 [D]. 北京：北京大学，2009：94.

㊽ 颜华．山东广饶关王庙正殿 [J]. 文物，1995（1）：59-63.

㊾ 四川省文物考古研究所，广安市文物管理所，华蓥市文物管理所．华蓥安丙墓 [M]. 北京：文物出版社，2008。图 35 引自图版 36。

㊿ 蔡东洲．安丙遗记考述 [J]. 四川师范学院学报，1999（4）：4.

(51) 柴泽俊，任毅敏著．中国古代建筑：洪洞广胜寺 [M]. 北京：文物出版社，2006：68.

(52) 吴静品．山西省武乡县真如寺大殿勘查报告 [J]. 古建园林技术，1998（1）：31-35.

(53) 刘永，商彤流．汾阳北榆苑五岳庙调查简报 [J]. 文物，1991（12）：1-15.

(54) 四川地区的几座纪年建筑实例均引自：王书林．四川宋元时期的汉式寺庙建筑 [D]. 北京：北京大学，2009.

(55) 崔金泽．河北省中南部地区明以前寺庙建筑研究 [D]. 北京：北京大学，2012.

(56) 柴泽俊．临汾魏村牛王庙元代戏台剖析 [C]// 柴泽俊古建筑文集．北京：文物出版社，1999：274-283.

(57) 图引自：王敏．河南宋金元寺庙建筑分期研究 [D]. 北京：北京大学，2011：64.

(58) 孙大章．万荣飞云楼 [C]// 建筑历史研究（第二辑）.P94-117.

(59) 汪艺朋，汪建民．北京慈寿寺及永安万寿塔（I）[J]. 首都师范大学学报（自然科学版），2012（2）：87-96.

(60) 柴泽俊．中国古代建筑：解州关帝庙 [M]. 北京：文物出版社，2002：86.

(61) 焦洋．探寻如意斗栱 [J]. 华中建筑，2010（8）：177-179.

(62) 欧阳雨．广西容县真武阁如意斗栱分析 [J]. 建筑与文化，2017（7）：129-130. 图 42 引自该文。

(63) 吴庆洲．广东佛山祖庙建筑研究 [J]. 古建园林技术，2011（1）：46-50.

(64) 任明杰．北海公园智珠牌楼 [J]. 古建园林技术，2007（1）：21-62.

(65) 图引自：程建军，编．岭南历史建筑测绘图选集 [M]. 广州：华南理工大学出版社，2013：121.

(66) 参见陈薇先生《斜栱发微》，朱小南先生《斜栱溯源》文中相关论述。

(67) 事实上对于斜栱出斜的角度，可能并非仅有 45 度、60 度两种角度，在部分建筑测绘数据中还出现过 67.5 度、40 度等数据。出斜的角度有待在对相关建筑的精细测绘中进行核实明确。

(68) 沈聿之．斜栱演变及普拍枋的作用 [J]. 自然科学史研究，1995，14（2）：176-184.

(69) 温静．论多样化外檐斗栱的外观与布局：日本和样佛堂与中国北方辽宋金建筑的比较研究 [J]. 中国建筑史论汇刊，2014（2）：301.

(70) 梁思成．正定古建筑考察记略 [C]// 梁思成全集（第二卷）. 北京：中国建筑工业出版社，2001：36.

建筑考古与保护：有形的阿姆斯特丹黄金时代（1585—1700）

Building Archaeology and Preservation: The Tangible Golden Age of Amsterdam (1585-1700)

Gabri VAN TUSSENBROEK

摘要：阿姆斯特丹是荷兰的首都，其名初见于 1275 年。经过 14 到 15 世纪的适度增长，居民人数增长至约 20 万。在 17 世纪，这个城市空前繁荣，成为国际贸易的领导者。城市大规模扩张以解决更大空间需求。

如今，阿姆斯特丹大都市区的人口约为 240 万。这座城市仍然以它 17 世纪的城市为标志，向世界展示了它的独特形象。历史建筑被认为是这个城市文化身份的重要载体。对登录建筑物的保护，确保了大部分可以追溯到 17 世纪甚至更早期的阿姆斯特丹市中心的建筑物能够得到保护。建筑的延续机会应当与材料真实性的保护密切相关。这种保护主要依靠知识，为了获得关于阿姆斯特丹遗产的知识，研究至关重要。

阿姆斯特丹市有着悠久的建筑考古研究传统。古迹和考古管理办公室（The Office for Monuments and Archaeology）强调，为了保护城市历史景观，关于建筑的知识是必要的。建筑考古研究提供关于城市及其建筑的历史知识，并创造公众对城市环境的欣赏。该研究为阿姆斯特丹遗产的评估和保护做出了重要贡献。

关键词：建筑考古；遗产保护；荷兰

Abstract: Amsterdam is the capital of the Netherlands and was first mentioned in the year 1275. After modest growth in the 14th and 15th centuries, the number of inhabitants grew to *ca*. 200,000 during the course of the 17th century as the city prospered as never before and became a world leader in international trade. Large-scale urban expansion was the solution to the demand for more space.

Nowadays, the Amsterdam Metropolitan Area has a population of about 2.4 million. The city still identifies itself with its 17th-century city, and presents this particular image to the world. Historic buildings are considered to be essential bearers of the city's cultural identity. The protection of listed buildings has ensured that large parts of Amsterdam's city centre, which date back to the 17th century or before, have been preserved. Material authenticity should be preserved if it is to stand a chance of survival. This preservation primarily depends on knowledge, and to obtain knowledge about Amsterdam's heritage, *research* is crucial.

作者简介：
Prof.Gabri VAN TUSSENBROEK, University of Amsterdam, Office for Monuments and Archaeology of the City of Amsterdam.

The City of Amsterdam has a long tradition of building archaeological research. The Office for Monuments and Archaeology emphasises that for the protection of the historic urban landscape, knowledge of buildings is required. Building archaeological research provides knowledge about the history of the city and its buildings, and creates public appreciation for the urban environment. This research is an important contribution to the assessment and preservation of Amsterdam's heritage.

Keywords: Building archaeology; Heritage conservation; Holland

As the capital of the Netherlands, Amsterdam is the country's largest city. It is situated in the heart of the Amsterdam Metropolitan Area, which has a population of about 2.4 million. The city was first mentioned in the year 1275 and, after modest growth in the 14th and 15th centuries, the number of inhabitants grew to *ca.* 10,000 in the year 1500. The city then expanded to a population of *ca.* 50,000 around the year 1600, and increased to *ca.* 200,000 during the course of the 17th century as the city prospered as never before and became a world leader in international trade. Large-scale urban expansion was the solution to the demand for more space. Amsterdam is still widely known for its 17th-century canal belt [Fig. 1].

Fig.1 The Herengracht, close to the Leidsegracht [© Monumenten en Archeologie Amsterdam/ Han van Gool].

Preservation of the Historic Urban Landscape

Today, the city of Amsterdam has 853,000 inhabitants and 180 nationalities. Occupancy levels and population increase are extremely topical issues. Middle income bracket households are experiencing difficulty finding housing, investors are getting their hands on a growing proportion of Amsterdam's real estate and time and again, tourism prognoses are being adjusted upwards. Every year, the Amsterdam museums break their attendance records and the influx of tourists has led to the 'industrialisation' of heritage.[1] This creates an increased demand for tourist accommodation, leads to a rise in Airbnb rentals, and worsens cycling and traffic issues, resulting in a great deal of nuisance, congestion and a decrease in the quality of life for the inhabitants of the city.[2]

The popularity of Amsterdam's city centre poses the threat that the city will consume itself; that the heritage industry and tourism will damage historic buildings. This popularity could create a single-sided legitimisation of the past: heritage serves economic interests. If this happens, the city will basically be disconnected from its uniqueness; it will become a product that meets consumer demand. Its uniqueness will start to serve a globalised economic mechanism, adapting to meet the needs of visiting tourists. In this way, commercial motives infiltrate the heritage value system in the same way nationalist motives did for quite some time during the nineteenth and twentieth centuries.[3] Apart from the heritage industry, the global sustainability drive will also have far-reaching consequences for the pool of listed buildings over the coming years. A generic standardisation process will develop that leaves less and less room for uniqueness and identity. The city government is trying to deal with all the changes resulting from the industrialization of heritage while at the same time trying to concentrate large-scale developments in the fringe belt of the city, in order to preserve the historic urban landscape.

As early as the 17th century, Amsterdam's cityscape was praised by famous poets such as Joost van den Vondel (1587-1679) and Laurens Jansz Spieghel (1575-1623),[4] in descriptions of the city and in drawings, paintings and prints. The city's impression of itself was far from static and over the course of the 17th century, this shifted towards a more cosmopolitan and multiform entity, with the focus shifting from the old city centre to the canal belt.[5] However, until the last quarter of the 19th century, no one reflected on whether part of the city should be *preserved*, even though it was considered picturesque by individuals. The city was and remained a *thing* that could be modified to suit people's needs when conditions demanded it: the city as a utilitarian object.

Generally speaking, this continued to be the case until well into the 20th century. New architecture, the cleaning-up of decrepit neighbourhoods and the creation of a new ideal for life dominated the debate on public spaces at the start of the 20th century.[6] A movement developed that wished to do away with the past and abolish all the drawbacks associated with tradition: dark, unhygienic houses, the exploitation of the working class, the huge difference between rich and poor and the conceptual vacuum regarding new architecture. Old and new battled it out in the arena provided by magazines, societies, discussion fora and politics. This new movement was a widely supported, properly thought-out, convincing attempt to halt the decline.

Yet, there were also other voices.[7] Under the influence of the Romantic era a sentimental love for everything that seemed old and even slightly picturesque developed. Since 1953, this love has been solidified by an official municipal heritage care. In the year 1961, a government act on listed buildings was issued for the protection of historic buildings and sites, which in Amsterdam alone lead to the protection of 7,484 individual buildings. Since the renewal of the monument act in 1988, 1,379 municipal monuments have been added. This has led to a large variety of protected buildings, ranging from the late middle ages to the post-war period up until 1990. Apart from the individually protected buildings, Amsterdam has six protected areas meant to put restrictions mainly on large scale developments that could affect the urban landscape. Individual buildings are now analysed in their historic cultural context because of defined zoning plans. For these protected areas, strict requirements exist for parcel zoning, building heights, roof design and façade design. By doing so, Amsterdam also takes care of the preservation of archaeological values.[8]

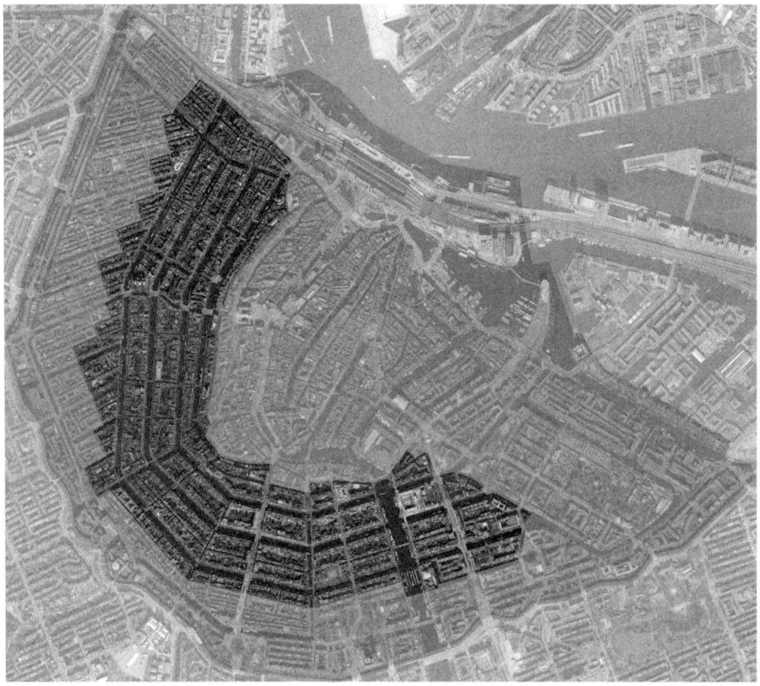

Fig.2 Aerial view of the canal belt, the area inscribed on the UNESCO World Heritage List in 2010[© Aerodata international surveys in cooperation with the Municipality of Amsterdam].

The most prominent historic feature of Amsterdam, the 17th-century canal district, was inscribed on the UNESCO World Heritage List in 2010 [Fig. 2]. This canal belt was laid out around the medieval city centre in two stages: one in 1613, the other in 1660. The canal district and Amsterdam's 17th century are seen as a symbol of an open, liberal society, in which the people — in fact a small group of oligarchs — held the power, independent from kings or emperors. There was relative freedom of speech and philosophers who were persecuted in other countries found a free haven in Amsterdam and could print their work there.

Protection and Interpretation

The romantic appreciation of buildings from the past has social consequences, namely that these buildings — if they are preserved — have to be useable. This has led to thousands of restorations in Amsterdam alone. Restoring basically means repairing to a previous condition; augmenting what has been lost, repairing what is broken. In practice however, this virtually always means something new is being added and the buildings are being modified to meet modern requirements and common perceptions of the past. Buildings outlive their builders, users and the era they were built in. Moreover, they are subject to use, wear and deterioration. If we limit ourselves to listed buildings, every single one is an adaptation and interpretation of what once was, made by later generations projecting their own ideas onto them.[9]

Fig.3 The layout of the metro, seen towards the north [© Pieter Boersma, 1975].

Amsterdam identifies itself with its 17th-century city, and presents this particular image to the world, not the medieval city centre, nor the 19th-century expansions, let alone the post-war expansions. The fact that so much of the 17th century city still exists today is, however, not self-evident. It primarily thanks to the old inhabitants of the different neighbourhoods that so many historic houses remain in Amsterdam. These inhabitants protested against demolitions and the loss of social cohesion in the old city. If certain visionaries had had their way, the city centre would have had a very different appearance today. The western part of the city would have been demolished and a section of the medieval city would have been transformed into a model housing project. In 1972, one alderman declared that he 'didn't give two cents' about the old neighbourhoods.[10] During post-war reconstruction, cheap, standardised pre-fab buildings became the norm; [11] the old, dilapidated city no longer suited the modern utopia of the exemplary ideal society. The building of a subway in the eastern part of the city lead to the demolishing of even more houses and structures, losses that were very hard to recuperate [Fig. 3].

Fig.4 Construction works for the new metro in the inner city [© Edwin van Eis, 2006].

Nowadays, Amsterdam looks back from a certain distance on the 1970s as a tumultuous period in the city's history. A subway line is once again being built, but this time historic houses are being spared from demolition [Fig. 4]. Not a single house has been demolished for the present construction works.[12] This is a lesson that was drawn from the seventies. Contemporary society now emphatically appreciates the old city; in fact, this appreciation is increasing exponentially. The plans for demolishing the historic city centre have been scrapped a long time ago. We now think of historic buildings as essential bearers of the city's cultural identity. With the loss of old buildings, we lose a part of our collective identity.

The city's architectural heritage is a finite collection of historic buildings; a fragile archive exposed to the elements, to which only younger models can ever be added. The city takes good care of many of these buildings by listing them and incorporating them into its cultural heritage. The suggestive power of historic buildings is such that we can be convinced that we are looking at something real.[13] In this respect, visitors are sometimes terribly deceived. Walking around Amsterdam, it seems as if there is an old building on every corner. Upon a closer look, it becomes clear that, for example, the buildings on the corners of Vijzelgracht and Prinsengracht, Reestraat/Keizersgracht, Nieuwe Kerkstraat/Amstel do not date back to a distant past, but are basically the results of the post-war movement that wished to retain the historic cityscape [Fig. 5].

Fig.5 Reestraat2/corner Keizersgracht in 1957, 1969 and 1970 [© Monumenten en Archeologie Amsterdam].

Nevertheless, the protection of listed buildings has ensured that large parts of Amsterdam's city centre, which date back to the 17th century or before, have been preserved. This is of enormous importance for the academic, 'historic' history of the city. Clearly, those who wish to know how the city was built and used cannot do so without the source material of these old buildings. If the city becomes a mere backdrop, it may perhaps be possible to elicit a sense of history, but what that history actually *means* can in this case no longer be studied and determined.[14] The verifiability of the past is encapsulated in its material and written transmittal. In this sense, the past feeds our curiosity and a need for history, which we believe we can satisfy increasingly well thanks to innovations in research methods and techniques.

It is therefore of crucial importance that we are *able to* know our history; that old buildings are preserved in their material state, even though they are endangered by multiple external factors. Our understanding of 'authenticity' has become less stable since the ICOMOS *Nara Conference on Authenticity* in 1994. We are seeing a global heritage movement that shapes and 'improves' to its heart's content. According to Nara, everything is possible as long as the narrative of the 'outstanding values' can be *told* in a believable, truthful manner. However, images and narratives are not value-free. This is why, materially speaking, we need history so badly; to allow everyone, today and in the future, to glean their own stories from the past, and time and again. Material authenticity should be preserved if it is to stand a chance of survival. This preservation primarily depends on knowledge, and to obtain knowledge about our heritage, *research* is crucial.

Architectural Evidence

Amsterdam has a long tradition of building archaeological research. The Office for Monuments and Archaeology emphasises that for the protection of the historic urban landscape, knowledge of buildings is required. And this knowledge can only be obtained by surveys and research of the buildings themselves. Unlike other cities, Amsterdam has a tremendous archive, which contains about 20 km of archive boxes recording the city's past. Written documents going back to the 13th century, but also drawings, building plans and old publications contain information about Amsterdam's origins and past [Fig. 6]. Thanks to these sources, researchers can go back to the past and distillate a great deal of knowledge about Amsterdam's development. But these documents can never replace the historic buildings themselves. The facade and old beams provide us with knowledge

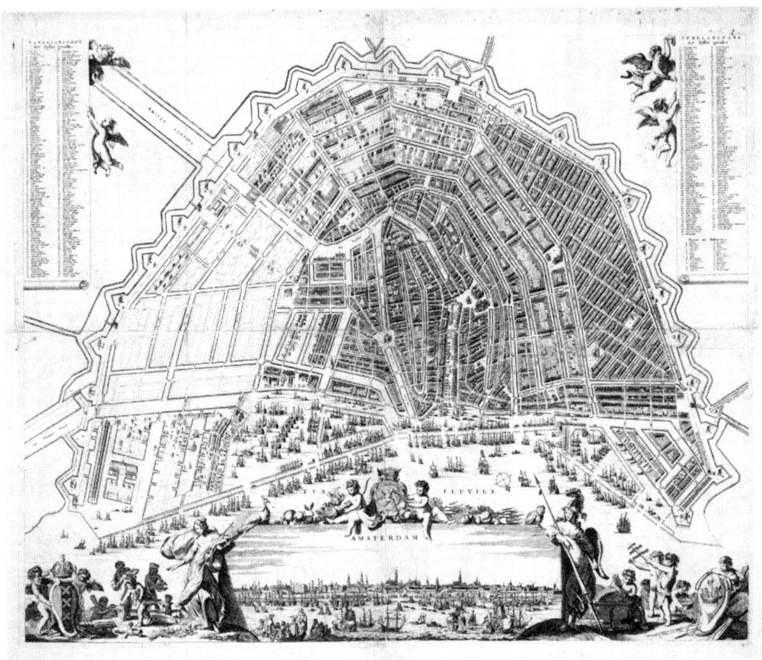

Fig.6 Plan of Amsterdam, published by Covens and Mortier, 1676-1680 [© Stadsarchief Amsterdam].

that would be untraceable without them. The old building materials, for example, teach us about the way the people of Amsterdam coped with massive water problems [Fig. 7]. The city's growth resulted in pressure to utilise the available space in merchants' houses as effectively as possible. It was more economical to deepen existing buildings than to purchase scarce building land, but a recurring problem was that cellar floors had a tendency to burst open due to rising groundwater caused by storm tides. The first watertight floating cellars and basement water cisterns were built during the second half of the 17th century. Trass mortar, [15] or hydraulic cement, was needed in order to build these floating cellars: brickwork basins that could be moved up and down with the groundwater level.[16] These cellars were in use until 1871, when the city's water level was stabilised by the construction of the Oranje sluices. Up until fifteen years ago, however, these unique floating cellars were never recorded. We only gained knowledge about these cellars by doing research in the old canal houses themselves.

Fig.7 Floating cellar in Herengracht 60 [© Dik de Roon /Monumenten en Archeologie Amsterdam].

Another example: One of the most essential expressions of human culture — building a roof over your head — is characterised by enormous diversity. The development of roofing constructions was a process of natural selection using the materials available in a particular area at a specific time. By having the historic constructions at hand — like the roof construction of the Portuguese Synagogue of 1672 — we can actually examine an almost 350-year-old construction. We learn about the way the wood was processed in sawing mills and how it was applied in this specific building, but

Fig.8 Amsterdam, Portuguese synagogue. Drawing of the roof in the architectural mass [©Dik de Roon /Monumenten Archeologie en Amsterdam].

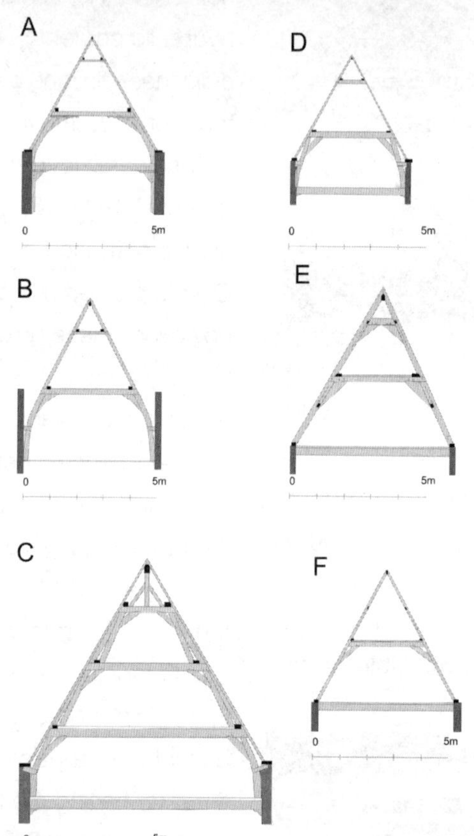

Fig. 9 Amsterdam roof constructions: A. Damrak 57 (*ca.*1535), B. Nieuwmarkt 28 (1550-1600), C. Herengracht 12 (1614d), D. Herengracht 78 (1585d/1614a), E. Oudezijds Voorburgwal 40 (1656d), F. Oude Schans 11 (*ca.*1725d) [© Gabri van Tussenbroek/Monumenten en Archeologie Amsterdam].

also about the constructive solution that was found, in order for the roof *not* to be visible above the building itself [Fig. 8], because that would have been seen as inappropriate in the classicist architecture of the synagogue. By surveying, measuring, drawing and analysing the roof of this building, we gain insight into one of the masterpieces of Amsterdam carpentry of the 17th century. We learn about statics in the past, but also in the present, because the knowledge that is obtained during building archaeological research is highly essential for restoration plans, when problems with the statics of the buildings have occurred.[17]

Our old roof constructions show a great variety in detail. They were built with oak and pine wood, had different roofing materials like pan tiles or slates on them, and they could differ depending on whether the building was smaller or taller, or whether the builder had more or less money to spend on his house.[18]

Due to our building archaeological research, especially documentation of old constructions, we have been able, in the past ten years, to start compiling a typology of roofing constructions in Amsterdam [Fig. 9]. With this, we are much more capable of assessing the historical value of a construction. In other words: how many of a certain type are still left? How rare are they? And how should we proceed during a restoration campaign? On top of that, we managed to obtain reliable dating of our constructions, thanks to the method of dendrochronology. For the last ten years, the Office for Monuments and Archaeology has been taking wood samples from old constructions in order to determine when exactly houses were built. These samples are analysed in a laboratory and supply us with a dating, so we can put the building or construction in its historical context.[19] Apart from that, the analysis gives us information about where the wood came from. And with that knowledge, we can understand more about the whole context that played a role as the Amsterdam canal belt was being built.

Most passers-by in Amsterdam's canal belt do not realize that the canal-side houses were built using materials imported from many parts of the world. Yet, international trade conducted in Amsterdam had visible effects on the residences in the city. Construction and developments in the building trade were only possible because of the international building materials market. Sandstone from Germany and bluestone from the Ardennes or Hainaut gave façades a more prestigious appearance than could be achieved by using only bricks. Timber from half the countries of Europe was needed for piles, beams and roof structures. Iron from Spain, Sweden and the Harz mountains was the raw material for wall anchors, nails, fire backs and stoves[20] [Fig. 10]. Luxury marble from Italy and expensive types of wood from even further afield were used to adorn interiors and give an international flavour to the lifestyle on Amsterdam's canals.

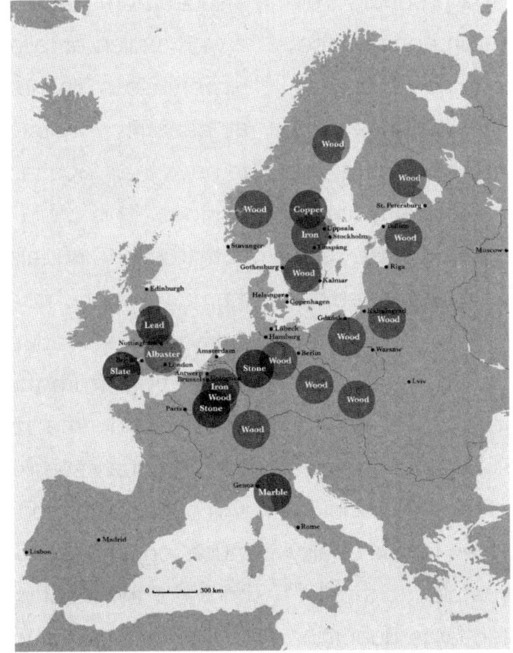

Fig.10 Map showing the most important regions producing building materials needed for the Amsterdam canal belt [© Monumenten en Archeologie Amsterdam].

Trade in timber on a large scale was an essential condition for enabling the construction of so many residences in the canal belt. This colossal construction programme called for massive flows of building materials and in Amsterdam timber and bricks were among the most important construction commodities. During the seventeenth and eighteenth centuries, approximately 2,500 large houses were built on the main canals. A residence that was eight metres wide and twenty metres deep needed at least 120 piles. On top of that, timber was needed for joists and floors, staircases and roofs, and for windows, doors and wainscoting. Huge numbers of bricks were also required to create the ideal 17th-century way of life along the canals. Brick was the right material for foundations, walls, façades and basement cisterns. Stone was indispensable for decorative elements in façades, doorsteps, fireplaces, floor tiles and sinks. Virtually none of the materials needed for constructing the canal ring were available locally, so the exclusive right to sell building materials, for example Norwegian pine tree trunks, was extremely lucrative.

The bricks used in Amsterdam façades came from various areas. There was no suitable clay in Amsterdam's environs, so brick making was impossible and the city depended on imports from other parts of the country.[21] Although the products from these sources could differ in appearance, they all seemed to be about the same quality. On 3 October 1613, for instance, City Mason Cornelis Danckertsz said that the bricks made by Arent ten Grotenhuys in his brick-making kiln in Breukelen were usually just as good as bricks from Leiden.[22] It was important, however, to ensure the bricks were properly sorted by quality and size. The ones used for façades were of the highest quality. The substantial volumes that were exported testify to the appreciation that existed in other countries for the quality of Dutch bricks.[23] For example, in the 17th century, England imported large quantities of bricks and roof tiles from the Dutch Republic.[24] It was the same story in Denmark, where Dutch bricks were used to build the Copenhagen Stock Exchange and to restore Kronborg Castle, the Danish king's palace. Dutch bricks were imported and used by bricklayers who went from the Netherlands to Sweden.[25] They were also used along the Baltic coast in Rostock, Wismar, Danzig (present-day Gdansk) and elsewhere.[26] Dutch bricks were even exported as far afield as Sri Lanka for building Dutch colonial forts.[27]

Brick was not the only product used to build façades in Amsterdam. Stone was also popular. Anyone who wanted a stone façade had to have his building material shipped from places hundreds of kilometres away, which entailed significant expense. Nevertheless, in the 17th and 18th centuries, at least fifty Amsterdam residents decided to have their façades on Herengracht made in stone. This could be done at the time of construction, but also at a much later time if a new owner chose to have his newly acquired property radically altered.[28]

Almost from the outset, Amsterdam depended on imports for its structural timber. Generally speaking, the distances over which the timber had to be transported were much longer than those for the majority of bricks or the most common types of stone. Moreover, the history of the timber trade reflects a much greater changeability and unpredictability than the relatively stable commerce in stone, where shifts in demand were more determined by fashion.[29]

The huge volumes of timber imports were accompanied by transhipment and onward transportation, though much of the timber that arrived was used in Amsterdam. Demand was massive, particularly during the Third and Fourth Stages (1613 and 1660), and this caused periods of scarcity. On 4 August 1619, the glass-maker Jan Hendricksz Soop complained that he had to use pine trunks as firewood and for four months he did not have any wood at all for heating.[30] In some building projects — such as the Munttoren (Mint Tower) — the available construction timber was in fact not thick enough, so undressed tree trunks were used instead. In some cases old timber was reused, for example in the Noorderkerk (North Church), which was consecrated in April 1623 but for which construction timber dating from 1497 was used.[31] There were periods of short supply in later years too; in 1659, for example, the scarcity of piles was so severe that the city authorities decided to send two ships to Fredrikstad in Norway immediately with instructions to bring back as many piles as possible.[32]

The demand on the Amsterdam market and the timber trade in Holland should be seen in a European context. As the demand for timber in one region grew, the strength of the economy in another region — where the construction timber came from — grew as well.[33] The different areas that exported to the Amsterdam timber market varied in importance, depending on the period and the circumstances.[34] Quality was the buyer's prime concern, although price also played a part. Whenever the prices in a particular region increased and timber became harder to obtain, buyers looked for alternatives.[35] This brought about regular shifts in the geographical centres of gravity in the timber trade. People on the supply side wanted the best possible returns, while those on the demand side wanted the lowest prices. A close eye was kept on every step in the production process, as is evidenced by the fact that in the 17th century, Hollanders purchased short planks in Norway, but transported longer unsawn beams to Holland. The sawing costs to produce short planks were lower in Norway than in the Netherlands. The fact that the waste material did not have to be transported was an additional advantage. The dressing costs increased if larger dimensions were needed, however. In the producing regions, investments in much larger sawmills had to be made, which made working the timber substantially more expensive. As a rule, Norwegian suppliers were not prepared to make such investments. In those cases, the choice was to import undressed products and to have them sawn up in Holland, where it could be done relatively cheaply as a result of the well-developed timber-sawing industry.[36]

Some of the wood came from very far away. Deal was imported from Scandinavia, whereas split oak was sourced from the Baltic coast. Walnut came from Southern Europe. Ebony, rosewood and marblewood, however, were tropical products. So too was the hard, self-lubricating lignum vitae, which was used to make pulleys. Ebony came from Sri Lanka, Mauritius, Madagascar, Indonesia and India, and one example dates from as early as 1619. Rio rosewood was shipped from Brazil.

Needless to say, the trade in building materials left its mark on Amsterdam houses. Recognizing these materials is the first step to understanding their origins. These origins were changeable though. The international trade in building materials was subject to continual changes in the economic climate. It was a complex cocktail of supply and demand for products of differing qualities, with dealers keeping a close eye on their profit margins. Merchants and administrators used their extensive international networks to optimize the profitability of the trading in Amsterdam. This could ultimately lead to shifts in the source of a particular product. Armed conflict, boycotts, competition or shortage of supply in the source areas could also result in changes in the trading pattern. And we find evidence of all of these factors back in our houses on the canals.

Fig.11 Building-historical map, indicating cultural-historical values in buildings (detail). In *red*: buildings where historical values are present with certainty. In *yellow*: buildings where they are expected.In *blue*: buildings that — as far as wa know or expect right now — do not have cultural-historical values [© Monumenten en Archeologie Amsterdam].

Practical Use of Knowledge

As interesting as the above-mentioned historical knowledge may be, it is used first and foremost to improve the quality of preservation [Fig. 11]. Cultural-historical assessment is an important part of the research conducted by Monuments and Archaeology, making it possible to assess historical values early on in a spatial process.[37] The building-historical map is a strong instrument to define these values on a general level. It starts from an area-oriented approach analysing both already protected and unprotected areas and shows in red the buildings where historical values are present with *certainty*, in yellow the buildings where they are *expected* and in blue the buildings that — as far as we know or expect right now — do not have cultural-historical values.

On the individual building level, we draw up value assessments, starting with the collection of data; photographs, drawings, archival materials and of course, the survey of the building itself. With these tools, an analysis of the building is made in order to come to a better understanding of its historical development, so that different building phases and layers can be discerned that contribute to the present appearance and the historical significance of the building. In order to come to a value assessment [Fig. 12], the building is analysed on different value levels: general historical values, ensemble values, architectural and building archaeological values as well as values based on the history of use. This assessment is then used to make recommendations on how to treat the object during an alteration or restoration.

It is crucial for the research and assessment to be executed during the initial phase of the development project. Therefore, the heritage office provides as much information as possible as early in the alteration process as possible. An assessment of historical values is already necessary in the initial phase, which means: research. This research leads to understanding and prevents unwelcome surprises later on in the planning process; it inspires designers and architects and leads to a better preservation of heritage.

Conclusion

Building archaeological research provides knowledge about the history of the city and its buildings, and creates public appreciation for the urban environment. One of the spearheads of Amsterdam's municipal government policy is — like almost everywhere on the world — to increase economic benefit. The historic urban landscape serves as

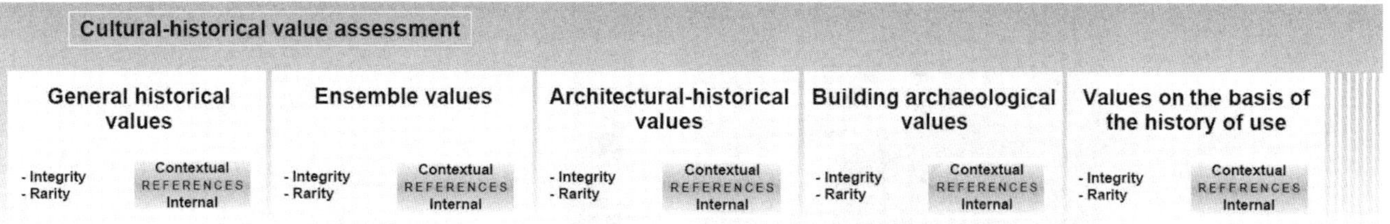

Fig.12 Cultural-historical value assessment; the building is analysed on different value levels [from: *Guidelines*, 2009].

an environment that attracts people: residents, companies and tourists alike. The city is a valuable environment for this, and that is one of the reasons the municipality wants to preserve our historic urban landscape.

The materiality of the urban environment, the housing culture, the objects and their tangibility make up the frame of reference that feeds our field and constitutes the core of our efforts. Without physical, historical material, it will become virtually impossible for future generations to generate an impression of the past with their own eyes. The more historical material we lose, the more the tangibility of the past is lost and the higher the level of abstraction our narrative constructions take on. Building archaeological research is an important contribution to the assessment and preservation of our collective heritage. We make sure the quality of our daily environment is maintained as this constitutes our identity and is an important asset for our place in the world.

Fig.13 The ballroom in Herengracht 502, with an interior dating from around 1870 [© Edwin van Eis].

Amsterdam is, however, not a museum: the city is in transition every day and is modernised by every generation [Fig. 13]. Nevertheless, we should recognise the past in the city of today and building archaeology is an essential contribution to the preservation of that past, as well as the quality of our present environment.

notes

① Glendinning, Miles, *The Conservation Movement. A History of Architectural Preservation*, Abingdon: Routledge, 2013, p. 420; van Tussenbroek, Gabri, 'The Politics of Attraction. About Competing Heritage Experiences', *Pharos. Journal of the Netherlands Institute at Athens*, 21/1, 2015, p. 125-132.

② Madden, David; Marcuse, Peter, *In Defense of Housing. The Politics of Crisis*, London/New York: Verso, 2016.

③ Glendinning, *The Conservation Movement*…, as in note 2, p. 420.

④ Gelderblom, Arie Jan, *'k Wil rijmen wat ik bouw. Twee eeuwen topografische poëzie*, Amsterdam, 1994, p. 9-11.

⑤ Janssen, Geert H., *Nieuw Amsterdam*, Amsterdam, 2014, p. 10. http: //oratiereeks.nl/upload/pdf/PDF-2082weboratie_Janssen_-_DEF.pdf [22 September 2015].

⑥ van Rossem, Vincent, *The Rape of Cities. The disastrous impact of urban renewal*, Amsterdam, 2014; van der Woud, Auke, *Koninkrijk van sloppen. Achterbuurten en vuil in de negentiende eeuw*, Amsterdam, 2010.

⑦ Veth, Cornelis, 'Aan het gezond verstand', in: Veth, C.; Tillema J.A.C.; Jans, J., *De ontluistering van ons land*, The Hague, 1936, p. 5-23.

⑧ van Sprew, Bas; Gawronski, Jerzy, *Ar-*

cheologische signaleringskaart Amsterdam, Amsterdamse Archeologische Rapporten 54, Amsterdam, 2010; van Tussenbroek, Gabri; van Drunen, Ad; Orsel, Edwin, 'Bouwhistorische waardenkaarten. Een gebiedsgerichte benadering van bouwhistorisch erfgoed', *Bulletin KNOB*, 111/1, 2012, p. 40-53. The Office for Monuments and Archaeology (MenA) has approximately forty employers, in the field of archaeology, building history, architecture and back office. MenA produces circa 1.200 permits a year for the transformation of listed buildings, and 150 archaeology reports a year, in order to monitor, supervise and document transitions.

⑨ van Leeuwen, A.J.C., *De maakbaarheid van het verleden. P.J.H. Cuypers als restauratie-architect*, Zwolle: Waanders, 1995; van der Laarse, Rob, 'Erfgoed en de constructie van vroeger', in: van der Laarse, R. (ed.), *Bezeten van vroeger. Erfgoed, identiteit en musealisering*, Amsterdam: Het Spinhuis, 2005, p. 1-28 (esp. p. 5).

⑩ de Liagre Böhl, Herman, *Amsterdam op de helling. De strijd om stadsvernieuwing*, Amsterdam: Boom, 2010, p. 27.

⑪ Abrahamse, Jaap Evert; Noyon, Roger, *Het oude en het nieuwe bouwen. Amsterdam, de markt en de woningbouw*, Bussum, 2007, p. 84-87.

⑫ van Tussenbroek, Gabri, *In het voorbijgaan. Zeven eeuwen bouwen langs de Noord/ Zuidlijn*, Bussum: Toth, 2014.

⑬ "Het oudste is het mooiste als wij het zelf gemaakt hebben". Peeters, C., 'Een oud verlangen naar het nieuwe', in: *Jaarboek Monumentenzorg 1991*, Zwolle: Waanders / Zeist: RDMZ, 1991, p. 8-25 (esp. p. 15).

⑭ de Vries, Dirk Jan, *Verbrokkeld verleden*, Leiden: Leiden University, 2001, p. 4.

⑮ Trass is ground tuff from Germany and when used in mortar it prevented water from getting into cellars, which made them suitable for storing goods without risk, even in time of high tides.

⑯ de Roon, Dik, 'Gedragen door water. Drijvende kelders in Amsterdam en omstreken', *Bullctin KNOB*, 106/4-5, 2007, p. 162-178.

⑰ Krabbe, Coert Peter; de Roon, Dik, 'Construction and maintenance (1671-2000)', in: Vlaardingerbroek, Pieter (ed.), *The Portuguese Synagogue in Amsterdam*, Zwolle, 2013, p. 73-110 (esp. p. 79-82).

⑱ Derksen, David, 'Dachwerke der Amsterdamer Bürgerhäuser im 17. Jahrhundert', *Hausbau in Holland. Baugeschichte und Stadtentwicklung. Jahrbuch für Hausforschung*, 61, 2010, p. 95-112.

⑲ van Tussenbroek, Gabri, *Historisch hout in Amsterdamse monumenten. Dendrochronologie - houthandel - toepassing*, Publicatiereeks Amsterdamse Monumenten 3, Amsterdam, 2012.

⑳ Hoving, A.J., *Nicolaes Witsens Scheeps-bouw-konst Open Gestelt*, Franeker, 1994, p. 47-48.

㉑ In Amsterdam bricks from the area around Leiden and the Vecht region, and also from Gouda and Friesland, were used. Gawronski, Jerzy; Veerkamp, Jørgen, 'Bakstenen. Bouwstenen van Amsterdam', in: Gawronski, Jerzy; Schmidt, Freek; van Thoor Marie-Thérèse (eds), *Amsterdam. Monumenten & Archeologie 3*, Amsterdam, 2004, 10-2 (esp. p. 15-16).

㉒ van Dillen, J.G., *Bronnen tot de geschiedenis van het bedrijfsleven en het gildewezen van Amsterdam. Tweede deel 1612-1632*, Rijks Geschiedkundige Publicatiën 78, The Hague, 1933, p. 63, no. 118.

㉓ Arntz, W.J.A., 'Export van Nederlandsche baksteen in vroegere eeuwen', *Economisch Historisch Jaarboek*, 23, 1947, p. 53-133 (esp. p. 73).

㉔ Louw, Hentie, 'Dutch Influence on British Architecture in the Late-Stuart Period, c. 1660-c. 1714', *Dutch Crossing*, 33/2, 2009, p. 83-120 (esp. p. 85-86); Clifton-Taylor, Alec, *The Pattern of English Building*, London: Jack Simmons, 1972, p. 275.

㉕ van Dillen, J.G., *Bronnen tot de geschiedenis van het bedrijfsleven en het gildewezen van Amsterdam. Derde deel 1633-1672*, Rijks Geschiedkundige Publicatiën, Grote Serie 144. The Hague, 1974, p. 553, no. 1093.

㉖ Arntz, 'Export van Nederlandsche baksteen…',

as in note 23, p. 79-85 and 91-93; Noldus, Badeloch, *Trade in Good Taste. Relations in Architecture and Culture between the Dutch Republic and the Baltic World in the Seventeenth Century*, Turnhout: Brepols Publishers, 2004, p. 64 and 164.

㉗ Jayasena, Ranjith; Floore, Pieter, 'Dutch Forts of Seventeenth Century Ceylon and Mauritius: an Historical Archaeological Perspective', in: Klingelhofer, E. (ed.), *First Forts. Essays on the Archaeology of Proto-colonial Fortifications*, Leiden-Boston: Brill, 2010, p. 235-260 (esp. p. 240).

㉘ van Tussenbroek, Gabri, 'Assembling the World. The International Building Materials Trade in Amsterdam (1613-1795)', in: Vlaardingerbroek, Pieter (ed.), *The Amsterdam Canals: World Heritage*, Amsterdam: Bas Lubberhuizen, 2016, p. 108-147 (esp. p. 114-118).

㉙ van Tussenbroek, *Historisch hout*…, as in note 19.

㉚ van Dillen, *Bronnen tot de geschiedenis*…, as in note 22, p. 300, no. 485.

㉛ van Tussenbroek, Gabri, 'Dendrochronologisch onderzoek in Amsterdam (1490-1790). Bouwhout als materiële bron', *Stadsgeschiedenis*, 4/2, 2009, p. 135-164 (esp. p. 148).

㉜ van Eeghen, I.H., 'Buitenlandse monopolies voor de Amsterdamse kooplieden in de tweede helft der zeventiende eeuw', *Jaarboek Amstelodamum*, 53, 1961, p. 176-184 (esp. p. 179-180).

㉝ For this interaction in detail see: van Bochove, Christiaan, *The Economic Consequences of the Dutch. Economic integration around the North Sea, 1500-1800*, Amsterdam: Amsterdam University Press, 2008.

㉞ For the most important literature see Buis, Jaap, *Historia Forestis. Nederlandse bosgeschiedenis. II. Houtmarkt en houtteelt tot het midden van de negentiende eeuw*, Utrecht: Hes & de Graaf Publishers, 1985, 487-518; Lesger, Clé, 'Lange-termijnprocessen en de betekenis van politieke factoren in de Nederlandse houthandel ten tijde van de Republiek', *Economisch- en sociaal-historisch jaarboek*, 55, 1992, p. 105-142.

㉟ van Bochove, *The Economic Consequences of the Dutch.*…, as in note 33, chapter 2.

㊱ van Bochove, *The Economic Consequences of the Dutch.*…, as in note 33, p. 217.

㊲ *Guidelines for Building Archeological Research. The interpretation and analysis of cultural-historical heritage*. Government Buildings Agency and The Netherlands Cultural Heritage Agency, The Hague, 2009.

人造天穹：
中国教堂中的哥特拱顶

Building the Sky:
Gothic Vaults in Chinese Churches

[比]高曼士 | Thomas COOMANS
崔金泽 译 | Translated by CUI Jinze

摘要：19 世纪的基督教传教士们在全世界范围内推崇哥特建筑，包括有着全然不同建筑传统的中国在内。本文对传教士们在中国实践的多种多样的哥特状拱顶系统进行概述[①]，同时也将中国哥特教堂还原到诸如建造技艺、建筑材料、建筑风格、经济、基督教文化认同等多种复合的建筑语境中来考察。

本文检视了传教士们如何通过建造仿砖木拱顶的方式解决砖石技术问题。根据在中国进行的现场踏查和在西方进行的文献研究，揭示出除了拱顶的技术性方面以外，同样存在着经济和审美考量。再者，在 19 世纪的建筑界，用木板、木框架和灰泥模拟石质的哥特拱顶，也被秉持纯粹主义的建筑师们在真实与模仿的对立层面上提出质疑——今天我们也许可以称之为“真实性”。

关键词：中欧技术交流；教堂建筑；哥特建筑；拱顶

Abstract: 19th-century Christian missionaries promoted Gothic architecture worldwide, including in China, a country with a totally different building tradition. The present chapter gives an overview of the various Gothic looking vaulting systems that missionaries experienced in China. It also contextualises China's Gothic churches in the complex architectural debate on construction techniques, building materials, style, economy, and Christian identities.

This research examines how missionaries circumvent the issue of stone and brick rib vaults by building wooden imitations of brick vaults. Based on fieldwork in China and archival research in the West, this research reveals that besides the technological aspects of the vaulting issue, there were economic and aesthetic considerations as well. Moreover, in 19th-century architecture, imitating Gothic stone vaults with planks, lattice and lime was contested by purist architects in the context of the debate on truth and imitation — today, we would say 'authenticity'.

Keywords: Technical transfers between Europe and China; Church architecture; Gothic architecture; Vaults

作者简介：
[比]高曼士（Thomas COOMANS），比利时鲁汶大学建筑工程学院，雷蒙·勒迈尔国际保护中心，教授；北京大学人文社会科学研究院访问学者

19 世纪，许多基督徒把哥特式看作是教堂建筑的普世性风格，因此天主教、英国公教以及其他基督教传教士们将哥特式从欧洲出口到美洲、非洲、亚洲和澳洲②。哥特以及哥特复兴式建筑的主要特征是模块重复的结构、扇形肋拱顶、充满装饰的扶壁系统、尖拱以及带有装饰窗格的大型花窗。从审美及隐喻的角度来讲，一座哥特教堂的拱顶象征了上帝在人间宫殿的天穹。他的宫殿向着光的方向大面积开敞，也是上帝本身的象征。

从 19 世纪 60 年代到 20 世纪 30 年代，中国建造了数百座教堂，其中很多都具有哥特式的风格③。中国并不熟悉扇形肋拱顶筑造的技术，以及通过扶壁系统、墙壁内嵌拱券和阶梯形地基传递受力的原则，那么，传教士们是否成功地在这里建造了哥特肋拱？

本研究检视传教士们如何通过筑造仿砖木拱顶的方式解决砖石技术问题。这种方式只有在中国木匠的协助下才有可能实现，而他们同时一定接受了哥特风格和西方木屋架方面的指导，又将中国木构建筑传统的元素融合其中。这种技术上的融合又在中国引起了怎样的结构创新呢？

图 1 广东省广州市，圣心主座教堂（石室）：主殿的哥特肋拱顶，1874-1875 年（© THOC 2017）（左）

图 2 广东省广州市，圣心主座教堂（石室）：一块空心砖的细部（© 岭南建筑设计研究所）（右）

一、砖石哥特拱顶

我国香港圣公会圣约翰主座教堂是 1844~1850 年之间中国境内建造的第一座重要哥特教堂。教堂里没有拱顶，而是一个取材自英国哥特模型的开敞式木梁结构屋顶。

1861~1879 年，法国传教士们在广州建造了一座主座教堂，也被称作“石室”，采用了法国 13 世纪主教堂风格④。两位法国建筑师从巴黎来到广州，却遭遇了极大的技术及用工难题。在这项工程中，一些客家人扮演了重要的角色，如魏亚义、蔡亚考、曾泰源等。花岗岩石只能由香港引入，石雕工匠被招募到广州。中国的石雕工匠和泥瓦匠从来没有建造过哥特拱券、飞扶壁拱、扇形肋拱顶以及其他带有内应力的构件。施工人员和匠人们需要从头学习哥特的形式、结构以及其他西方的建造技术。拱券及拱肋由花岗岩建成，而拱顶的扇面则由法国进口的红色空心砖块砌筑（图 1、图 2）⑤。这些完美的扇形肋拱顶是 1874~1875 年在魏亚义的指导和爱尔兰人麦克纳马拉的控制下而完成的⑥。它们是中国乃至东亚最早的真实哥特风格实例。

这些拱顶需要由带扶壁的墙体和深深的地基来支撑，即便是在条约口岸，来华的基督传教团体并没有钱来建造如此昂贵的拱顶，也不愿意承担由不熟练的工人来建造的风险。广州主座教堂的拱顶虽然例外地出色，但并不是独一无二的。山东济南的主座教堂，是由蒂罗尔

（Tyrolian）庶务修士建筑师庞会襄（Korbinian Paugger OFM）和中国泥瓦匠卢立成于1901-1905年合作建造的，卢立成在其中负责协调石雕及泥瓦匠人们的工作⑦。这座卓越的砖石建筑有着飞扶壁拱，以及充满彩绘的砖造盝顶（图3）。

图3 山东省济南市，洪家楼教堂：耳堂拱顶，1901-1905（© THOC 2018）

图4 江苏省扬州市，圣心教堂：哥特托臂梁屋顶，1863—1873年（© THOC 2014）

图5 上海市，圣三一主座教堂：圣所和后殿的木质拱顶，1866—1869年（© THOC 2011）

二、木质哥特拱顶

一个中式的屋顶是最简便、最经济的选择，因为它以本地的建筑传统建成，而且不需要承重墙。然而这种屋顶却不可能容纳比例相对固定的哥特式拱顶。因此，很多传教士更喜欢采用具有良好地基的承重墙，然后在其上安置西式桁架和开敞的木屋顶，看起来就像早期基督教的巴西利卡一样。哥特式的柱头和外轮廓可以作为纯粹的装饰添加上去。例如带有红色木构梁架、垂莲柱和铁箍拉牵的扬州圣心教堂，看起来很像中国式，但实际上却是带有拉纤的西式桁架（图4）。

在与宗教认同相联系的19世纪国家认同的语境中，英国圣公会的传教士们喜欢采用英国哥特式木工营造，而天主教徒，正如我们看到的那样，喜欢采用扇形肋拱顶。在1865年，建筑师乔治·基尔伯特·斯科特设计了上海圣公会圣三一主教堂的平面。这个优秀的建筑混合使用了石材和不同颜色的砖块，并带有一个开敞的木屋顶。⑧教堂最神圣的部分——圣所的多边形后殿上，建有一个装饰哥特式的木质星星拱顶（图5）。到底是谁建造了这个精细的拱顶并无人知晓，但是可以肯定的是，在当时的上海找到一位西方木匠比中国其他的任何地方都要简单。

由于冬天的寒冷和夏天的炎热，开敞的木屋顶在中国的北方并不理想。气候使得北方的房屋应当有所隔热，理想的方法是在屋顶下加盖天花板。20世纪早期著名的传教士建筑师、比利时人和羹柏，无法在华北地区建造砖石拱顶，并且他拒绝模拟。他曾在根特的圣路加学校接受教育，那里推崇奥古斯塔斯·普金天主教哥特式风格的极端世界观。⑨因此，和羹柏设计了木板构成的桶状拱顶来配合自己的哥特风格。为了实现自己的设计并监督施工，他培训了一些有技能的中国工匠。其中有两个人，王师傅是细木匠，姚师傅成为工头。和羹柏建造的大部分带筒形拱顶的大型教堂都已经拆毁，现存最为完整的作品是日后升为主座教堂的宣化教堂。⑩从后殿木质多边形拱顶的复杂程度、桁架的完美组装，以及屋顶十字交叉处的西式筑拱来看，这些木工的技能非常高超（图6）。

三、用木板、板条和灰泥模拟的哥特扇形肋拱顶

将一座教堂的中殿用模仿石扇形肋拱顶的木构拱顶覆盖，会为其内部空间带来良好的哥特效果。这是隐藏屋顶结构，并在屋顶下创造隔热层的另一种方法。模拟出的哥特扇形肋拱顶，其实是一个由木板、板条构成，由灰泥涂覆并覆盖装饰的轻质木结构。中国大部分的重要哥特教堂和主教堂都具有此类的拱顶。

根据教堂的建造类型，有两种主要形式的拱顶必须得到区分：一个在殿式教堂中，另一个在巴西利卡中。

（一）带有木质框架结构的殿式教堂

在一个殿式教堂中，侧廊与中殿具有近似的高度和宽度。光线并非直接射入中殿，而是要透过侧廊墙上的窗户。中殿与侧廊之间，由两排高大开敞的立柱支撑拱顶。在欧洲，中世纪的殿式教堂由不同种类的屋顶覆盖（双坡屋顶，几组勾连搭的双坡屋顶，在侧廊上出山面向前的双坡屋顶抱厦等）。

在中国，当需要一个大型教堂时，传教士们通常采用殿式教堂的类型，因为它是最简便且便宜的结构。只有外墙采用砖砌，而柱子、屋顶结构和拱顶则采用木构。两排立柱为巨大的木柱，构筑起桁架的主要框架（图7）。侧廊比中殿稍低，在同一片坡屋顶之下。通常没有十字形的耳堂。中国的殿式教堂实例有：北京的五座主要天主教堂（南堂、北堂、西堂、东堂以及圣弥厄尔堂），还有天津的望海楼教堂等。

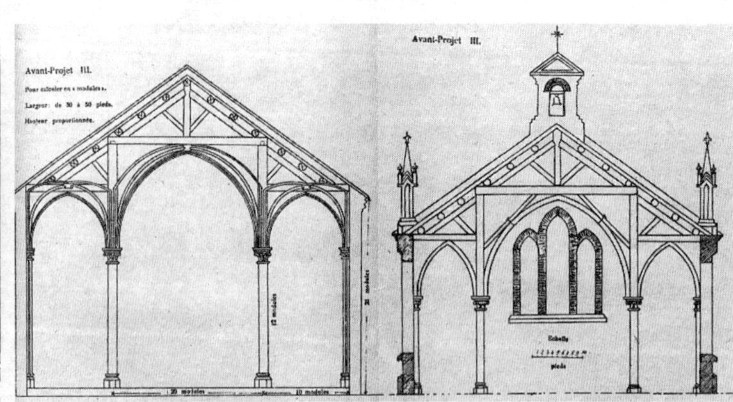

图6 河北省张家口市宣化区圣十字教堂：圣所和后殿的木质拱顶，1903—1906年（© THOC,2017）（左）

图7 带有木质框架结构的殿式教堂剖面图（《传教士建造师》，1926，图版35）（右）

图 8 北京市，北堂（西什库教堂）：1877—1888 年建成的殿式主殿（© THOC 2018）（左）

图 9 北京市，东堂：主殿木质肋拱顶与侧廊筒形拱顶相结合，1912（© THOC 2017）（右）

木板、板条和灰泥拱顶被安插在主框架结构之下。从中殿的角度看，柱子好像承托着柱头和拱顶的起拱石（图 8），而实际上这些木柱穿过拱顶，直达框架桁架的横梁之下（图 9）。

拱顶的拱和肋由板条和灰泥覆盖的木板做成。各条拱肋汇聚在拱顶中心。这个伞状的结构结实而独立，所以拱顶木板不需要挂在檩条之下，由板条和灰泥构成。拱顶的顶端通常要稍微高于横梁（图 10）。

2014 年 7 月 28 日，一场大火摧毁了宁波江北教堂，这正是一座如前所述的木构哥特拱顶殿式教堂。只有砖塔和砖墙在大火中幸存。在烧焦的中殿的照片上可见立柱顶端附近碳化了的框架结构（图 11）。

（二）带有天窗的巴西利卡教堂和单一中殿教堂

在一座巴西利卡中，中殿高于侧廊并在高处开有窗户（图 12）。从空间和结构两个方面来看，巴西利卡类型都与殿式教堂截然不同。

在中国，巴西利卡比殿式教堂建造起来更加困难且昂贵。不仅是侧廊的外墙、立面和后殿必须采用砖砌，而且柱子、侧墙和中殿的天窗也是如此。因此这种类型主要用于建造 1900 年以后的重要教堂和主座教堂，这些教堂通常带有后殿，如上海徐家汇主座教堂，以及佘山巴西利卡、吉林、沈阳、芜湖、济南、青岛和香港的天主教主教堂等。像北京的中华

图 10 北京市，北堂（西什库教堂）：北侧小礼拜堂木质桁架上悬挂的木板、板条和泥灰制拱顶（© THOC 2017）（左）

图 11 浙江省宁波市，江北教堂：主殿碳化了的木质框架结构（© Reuters 2017）（右）

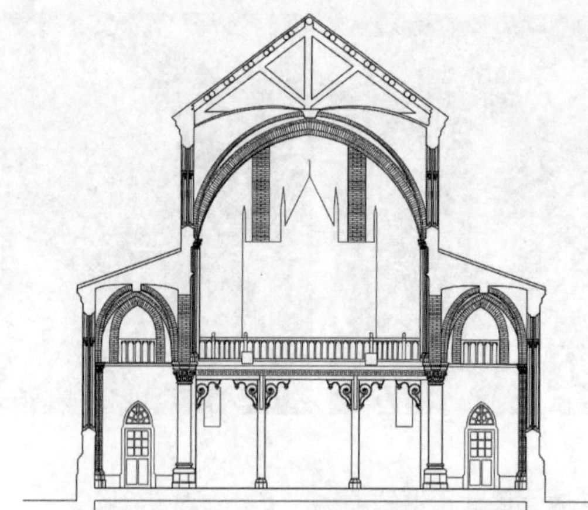

图12　河北省大名县，圣母教堂：一座巴西利卡教堂的横剖面图，1917—1921年（©北京大学考古文博学院）

图13　上海市徐家汇，圣依纳爵主座教堂：主殿的轻质勒拱顶，由木板、板条和泥灰构成，约1910年（© THOC 2016）

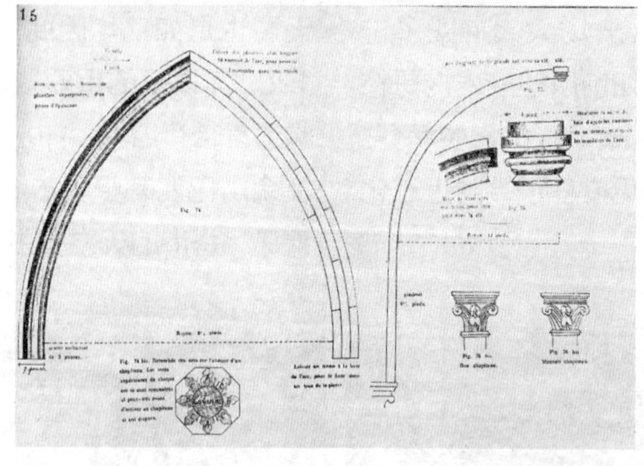

图14　带有木质框架结构的殿式教堂剖面图（《传教士建造师》，1926，图版15）

圣公会教堂（1907年）那样，带有木质柱子和纵向天窗的巴西利卡是比较例外的案例。

巴西利卡类型没有框架结构。拱顶横跨于中殿的两堵高墙和横向拱券之间（图13）。他们的起拱木块被放在沿墙面布置的托柄上。横向的或者隔断拱券既可以是砖砌的也可以是板条灰泥构成。如果是砖砌，边墙的受力要求使用扶壁拱。因为扶壁拱复杂而昂贵，大部分的横向拱券由木板、板条和灰泥构成，并且与拱顶同时建造（图14）。横向拱券位于桁架的横梁之下，但是不与它们相连。屋顶与拱顶完全各自独立，拱顶总是在屋顶之后建造，因为它不能被雨淋。

单中殿式教堂以及没有侧廊的小教堂与巴西利卡的上部相似。因为没有侧廊，建造带扶壁拱的边墙以及较大的开窗则更为容易。

（三）用木板建造拱顶

1926年，法国耶稣会传教士们出版了一部指导如何在华北地区建造教堂的建筑手册。[11]手册包括全部关于建造方面的技术建议和图纸，从地基到屋顶，系统地将中国技术与西方技术相比较。我们研究并翻译了这份无与伦比的材料，作为北京大学与鲁汶大学共同研究的结晶[12]。这部手册的作者们在1917—1921年大名圣母堂的建造中获得了众多的经验（图12~图14）。

这部手册包含一些关于如何用木板、板条和灰泥建造拱顶的描述和一份详细的技术图纸：

“你应该在地上画出要做成的拱的弧度，接着就按照这个弧度来切割木板。这些木板用钉子钉在一起，交接的地方要轮换变化。木板之间的交接边不能方方正正地切割，而是应该沿着弧的半径方向切割。在用钉子钉之前，要将木板塑形，像左图所示那样”（图14）。

“假的哥特式拱，用木头做成，有两种：大的那种是与教堂中轴线平行或垂直的（墙拱和横向拱）；小的是交叉拱（拱顶肋骨）。这些交叉拱相交于‘间’中心处的拱顶木上。这种拱顶木是用单块圆形木做成的，有着与拱一样的轮廓。在拱顶木的底面钉上木板，这些木板事先被雕刻成具有装饰性的花朵形状、字母图样等。”

“在拱顶木与拱交接的地方，你应该做一个榫槽，使得拱的榫头能插入。拱需要雕刻一定的轮廓与拱顶木相协调。教堂侧廊上方的拱顶木，尺寸会小一点（举个例子，如果中殿的拱顶木是1英尺，那么侧廊的拱顶木是8英寸）。但是它们应该在同一高度而且要有同样的轮廓。如果有足够大的板条，应该在其上直接雕刻出拱顶木”（图14）。

“由拱顶木绞接的各拱，必须为由板条和石灰做成的拱顶提供一个绝对结实的支撑。不需要在屋架上附加任何东西。”

“在钉板条时，你应该赋予它们稍微向上的弯曲，这样拱顶板自己就会形成更牢固的拱顶。如此的预防措施只需要用在拱的上端，那些变得水平从而形成天花板的拱顶板上[13]。”

图15 吉林省长春市，正在建造中的教堂，时代不明（©法国巴黎对外传教档案馆）

（四）用板条、灰泥和彩绘来覆盖拱顶

手册的描述在此继续：

“要想给拱顶面抹上石灰，必须在板条之间留够足够空间以保证石灰能够穿过。一个工人站在拱顶上面，涂抹石灰使其覆盖板条。通常，拱的中点会在教堂的‘纵向剖面图’标出来。原则上，拱顶木必须至少与其周边的横向拱和墙拱的拱尖在同一高度。同样，那些形成拱顶肋骨的交叉拱（那些与拱顶木相交的）必须是圆拱（半圆形），不是通常所说的‘ogees’（尖形拱）。在哥特样式里，墙拱和横向拱都是尖形拱。兰斯教堂是为数不多的例外：那里的交叉拱也是尖形的。”

“如果在交叉肋上使用圆拱的话，拱顶石就会太低（见上述第一条规则），你可以通过使圆拱的中心高于柱头所在的水平线而加以补救。只有在这般加高法变得过于夸张时，你才应像兰斯大教堂那样做尖形拱。”

“如果想要做一个非常牢固的天花板（拱顶面板），两层板条应该互相交叉安放：第一层板条与墙拱和横向拱垂直，第二层板条与第一层板条十字交叉[14]。”

长春教堂的一份引人注目的文献照片，显示了正在建造中的教堂的内部，拱顶在完成木板和板条构筑之后尚未抹灰的状态（图15）。这座教堂属于带有木柱的殿式类型。柱头、起

图16 河北省大名县，圣母教堂：从主殿拱券的破损处可见板条和泥灰涂层，1917-21（©THOC 2014）（左）

图17 北京市，北堂（西什库教堂）：北侧小礼拜堂，修复前的彩绘拱顶（THOC）2017（右）

拱构件、拱券、拱肋和顶板都是由板条做成。这证明了完美掌控的灰泥涂覆技术可以模拟一个完整的哥特拱顶。

最后，灰泥层必须由可以模拟砖块的好看涂层覆盖（图16），或者用较浅的颜色突出拱顶木块和拱肋（图17）。

（五）板条与钢筋混凝土框架相结合

值得一提的是，手册从未提及铁和钢筋混凝土的屋顶结构和拱顶。在1920和1930年代，如此的现代化结构主要出现于西方工程技术存在的条约口岸。在南华的亚热带气候条件下，水泥和钢筋混凝土提供了不同于木材的另一种可持续性的选择。1933年，广州主座教堂那著名的拱顶上部，木质的屋顶被法国工程师设计的现代化钢筋混凝土屋顶结构所取代[15]。在其他地方，新的哥特教堂由钢筋混凝土结构骨架与填充其中的砖砌墙体相结合建成，表面再由板条和灰泥装饰覆盖。浙江嘉兴的大教堂建于1920至1930年代初，由法国传教士建筑师韩日禄（Ange Asinelli C.M.）设计，其建造获益于全球化的市场：水泥购自华商上海水泥股份有限公司（The Shanghai Portland Cement Works），俄勒冈州松购自上海祥泰木行（The China Import and Export Lumber Co, Shanghai）。今天，教堂的废墟上，板条尖拱和拱顶与建筑的主体框架相切，混合的构造方式清晰可见（图18）。在主殿的侧廊中，板条拱顶被放置在水平的钢筋混凝土屋顶下（图19）。这种混合设计将新材料和结构的现代性与旧的造型传统相结合，并将其贬为纯粹的装饰。

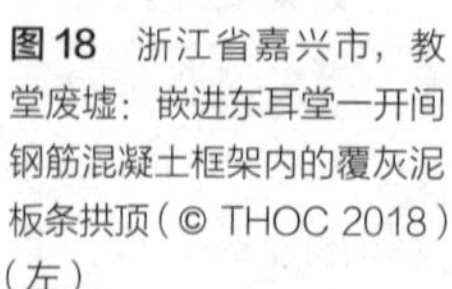

图18 浙江省嘉兴市，教堂废墟：嵌进东耳堂一开间钢筋混凝土框架内的覆灰泥板条拱顶（© THOC 2018）（左）

图19 浙江省嘉兴市，教堂废墟：残破的板条拱顶悬挂在东侧廊的水泥屋顶下（© THOC 2018）（右）

四、关于模仿的道德问题

在奥古斯塔斯·普金的两部主要理论著作《差异》和《尖拱或基督教建筑的真实原则》中，他表述了真正的信仰和真正的建筑之间必须有关联这样的观点[16]。对于他来说，唯一至真的教堂建筑应由砖、石和木头等真实的材料来建造。因此他谴责任何类型的模仿行为，包括当时在新古典主义建筑上使用的板条和灰泥技术，以及工业建筑上用金属材料对其他形式的模仿。前往教堂的信徒们怎么可能在充满谎言的房子中拥有真实的信仰？作为基督教普世风格的哥特式建筑，必须要遵循中世纪的技术来建造。

普金的理论在当时具有极大的影响力，他的哥特范本被圣公会和天主教的传教活动传播到世界各地。在华北地区建造哥特教堂的和羹柏神父在上文中已提及[17]。一些声音反对此类逐字逐句遵从普金理论的传教士建筑师们，更加务实的人则已经做好准备，在不可能建造真实拱顶的传教地区接受用木板、板条和灰泥仿造哥特肋拱的手段。

在普金的理论发表大约一个世纪以后，1926 年的《传教士建造师》手册还是引起了一个有关华北地区真实拱顶的微妙问题：为了使我们带有纪念意义的教堂更有风格性而加筑拱顶是否合适？

这位耶稣会神父对支持与反对仿造哥特肋拱的两方意见进行了评估：

“那些纯粹主义者们微带愤怒地回答，考虑到财政情况，要做一个真正的有着雕花拱顶石、密集的扶壁、石柱和奢华柱头来支撑的石头或者砖头拱顶，这样的想法是愚蠢的。然而因此你就用木板和石灰做一个拱顶仿制品，准备用这去欺骗谁？如果不能做真的，就什么也别做。”

“然而，那些寒酸的仿制拱顶，那样的假拱顶，却有很多优点这点不容置疑，那就是它使教堂更有特点、更有造型。除了更有造型外，它会看起来更整洁；你不会注意到那些木结构的微小裂纹的。它也将会更干净（令人羞愧的细节），因为那些足以让这些地区最好的传道者也焦头烂额的麻雀，不会在欧式的拱顶下感到方便，它们无处筑巢啊。此外，拱顶使得教堂内夏天更亮、冬天更暖。尤其是在用普通板条架做的拱顶做得很好的情况下，教堂的音响效果将彻底改善[18]。”

手册的耶稣会传教士作者倾向于筑造模拟的拱顶，特别是在没有钱建造石拱顶的传教国。他们强调了技术上的优点——美观、实用、拢音、隔热并且经济，谴责了强求真实性和中世纪石造结构的纯粹主义者们。

最后，值得一提的是，手册从未提及铁和钢筋混凝土的屋顶结构和拱顶。即便是在 20 世纪 20 年代，这类现代结构还仅仅存在于诸如香港和上海之类的条约口岸，并且传教士们无力承担其费用。

五、结论

由和羹柏神父于 20 世纪 20 年代早期设计的上海佘山哥特式巴西利卡，在 1924 年至 1935 年之间建成。[19] 位于山顶的佘山巴西利卡需要抵抗强风，因此其屋顶和拱顶均使用了钢筋混凝土结构。在扇形肋拱顶和墙盘之间的圆形的横向拱券，与钢筋混凝土的桁架相连。

这个刚硬的框架结构使得建造者们可以避免使用沉重的扶壁拱和飞扶壁拱。

佘山教堂的现代屋顶和拱顶结构，是自1875年左右广州主座教堂的石造拱顶起，拱顶结构之演进的最后一步。本论文对中国不同类型的哥特状拱顶系统进行了概览，并且将它们的建造置于关于技术、风格、经济与认同等讨论的复杂建筑语境中。

"在中国建造基督教上帝宫殿的天穹"曾经不仅仅是一个信仰问题，最重要的这也是一项对于传教士建筑师和中国工匠来说共同的技术挑战。建造的工作本身，即是一种强烈的创新，以及形式、材料和技术的交流。

注释：

① 本课题在以下的研究中另有深入探讨：Coomans，Thomas，"Vaulting Churches in China：True Gothic or Imitation?"， 见：Van Balen，Koen & Verstrynge，Els（eds）. *Structural Analysis of Historical Constructions - Anamnesis，Diagnosis，Therapy，Controls（*International conference on structural analysis of historical constructions，SACH 2016，鲁汶，13-15 September 2016）. 伦敦：Taylor & Francis Group，2016：535-541.

② Brittain-Catlin，Timothy；De Maeyer，Jan & Bressani，Martin（eds）. *Gothic Revival Worldwide：A.W.N. Pugin's Global Influence（*KADOC Artes 16），鲁汶：Leuven University Press，2016；Bremner，Alexander，*Imperial Gothic：Religious Architecture and High Anglican Culture in the British Empire c.1840-1870.* 纽黑文 - 伦敦：Yale University Press，2013.

③ 高曼士，从西式基督教风格到中式基督教风格：作为在华本土化文化适应手段的建筑，1919-1939年，见：贾珺等. 建筑史. 北京：中国建筑工业出版社，2016：190-200；Coomans，Thomas，"Die Kunstlandschaft der Gotik in China：eine Enzyklopädie von importierten，hybridisierten und postmodernen Zitaten"， 见：Brandl，Heiko；Ranft，Andreas & Waschbüsch，Andreas（eds）. *Architektur als Zitat. Formen，Motive und Strategien der Vergegenwärtigung.* 雷根斯堡：Verlag Schnell & Steiner，2014：133-161；Coomans，Thomas，"Gothique ou chinoise，missionnaire ou inculturée? Les paradoxes de l'architecture catholique française en Chine au XXe siècle"，*Revue de l'Art*，189，2015：9-19.

④ Masson，Mathieu. *The Sino-French cooperation on the site of the cathedral of Guangzhou. Technical，financial and cultural aspects from 1861 to 1879.* 西学东渐研究，第7 vol，2019（即将发表）；汤国华. 岭南历史建筑测绘图选集（一）. 广州：华南理工大学出版社，2001: p. 199-211；Wiest，Jean-Paul，"The Building of the Cathedral of Canton：Political，Cultural and Religious Clashes"，见：*Religion and Culture：Past Approaches，Present Globalisation，Futures Challenges.* 澳门：Instituto Ricci de Macau，2004：231-252.

⑤ 尺寸：11 × 11 × ca 30 cm. 感谢汤国华教授提供，广州大学，岭南建筑设计研究所。

⑥ 感谢 Matthieu Masson（马崇义）提供.

⑦ Coomans，Thomas，'East Meets West on the Construction Site. Churches in China，1840s-1930s'，*Construction History*，33-2，2018: 69-75.

⑧ Shu，Chang-Xue（舒畅雪），'La 'constructional polychromy' dei mattoni nella moderna Shanghai'，见：Fabian，Lorenzo & Marzo，Mauro（eds），*La ricerca che cambia.* 叙拉古：Lettera Ventidue Edizioni，2015：156-167.

⑨ Coomans，Thomas，'Pugin Worldwide：From *Les Vrais Principes* and the Belgian St Luke Schools to Northern China and Inner Mongolia'，见：Brittain-Catlin，Timothy；De Maeyer，Jan & Bressani，Martin（eds）. *A.W.N. Pugin's Gothic Revival：The International Style*（KADOC-Artes，16）. 鲁汶：Leuven University Press，2016：156-171.

⑩ Coomans，Thomas & Luo，Wei（罗薇），'Exporting Flemish Gothic Architecture to China：Meaning and Context of the Churches of Shebiya（Inner Mongolia）and Xuanhua（Hebei）built by Missionary-Architect Alphonse De Moerloose in 1903-1906', *Relicta. Heritage Research in Flanders*, 9, 2012: 219-262.

⑪ [Jung, Paul], *Le missionnaire constructeur, conseils-plans.* 献县: Imprimerie de Sien-Hsien, 1926.

⑫ 高曼士（Coomans Thomas）& 徐怡涛（Xu Yitao）. 舶来与本土——1926年法国传教士所撰中国北方教堂营造之研究 / *Building Churches in Northern China. A 1926 Handbook in Context.* 北京: 知识产权出版社, 2016: 73-76, 213-217; Thomas Coomans & Xu Yitao（徐怡涛）, "Gothic Churches in Early 20th-Century China: Adapting Western Building Techniques to Chinese Construction Tradition", 见: Brian Bowen, Donald Friedman, Thomas Leslie & John Ochsendorf（eds）. *Proceedings of the Fifth International Congress on Construction History. Chicago*: Construction History Society of America, 2015, vol. 1: 523-530.

⑬ 高曼士（Coomans Thomas）& 徐怡涛（Xu Yitao）. 舶来与本土——1926年法国传教士所撰中国北方教堂营造之研究 / *Building Churches in Northern China. A 1926 Handbook in Context*. 北京: 知识产权出版社, 2016: 214-215（吴美萍译, 崔金泽校订）.

⑭ 同上: 215-216.

⑮ Coomans, Thomas, 'East Meets West on the Construction Site, Churches in China, 1840s-1930s', *Construction History*, 33-2, 2018: 77-79.

⑯ Pugin, Augustus W.N.. *Contrasts or a Parallel between the Noble Edifices of the Middle Ages and Corresponding Buildings of the Present Day, showing the Present Decay of Taste.* 伦敦: Charles Dolman, 1836; Pugin, Augustus W.N. *The True Principles of Pointed or Christian Architecture*. 伦敦: John Weale, 1841.

⑰ 高曼士（Coomans Thomas）& 徐怡涛（Xu Yitao）. 舶来与本土——1926年法国传教士所撰中国北方教堂营造之研究 / *Building Churches in Northern China. A 1926 Handbook in Context*. 北京: 知识产权出版社, 2016: 213-214（吴美萍译, 崔金泽校订）.

⑱ 同上: 213-214.

⑲ Coomans, Thomas, 'Notre-Dame de Sheshan à Shanghai, basilique des Jésuites français en Chine, 1867-1935'. *Bulletin monumental*, 176 巴黎, 2018: 129-156.

保护研究

Conservation Studies

物质之生：
保存与研究建筑物的演变

The Life of Things：
Conservation and the Investigation of Architectural Palimpsests

Carolina DI BIASE

摘要：如果想了解建成环境的物质历史，必须利用更加深入的跨学科研究方式，从而记录他们在历史时期的存续情况。本文旨在审视建筑中物质之存续(“物质之生”)。本文讨论分为两部分。第一个是对意大利“建筑考古学”方法的概述；讨论了在过去30~40年中，该领域的研究如何将后古典考古学的专家和致力于保护建成环境的建筑师聚集到一起。第二部分通过两个案例来展示可以如何通过建筑考古学的方法和工具梳理建筑物不同部分建造、改造的时间先后顺序，从而决定建筑保护的方案。第一个案例研究涉及一个实际项目的保护和再利用。第二个案例研究是由来自米兰理工大学的一个研究小组，该小组的研究关注了一个多层历史叠压的建筑，而这一点已被考古证实。

关键词：建筑利用；知识；保护；意大利

Abstract：If one is to ‘read’ the material history of built environments，one must draw upon ever more advanced forms of interdisciplinary research in order to chart their existence over time. Such tracing of the ‘life of things’ is what this paper aims to examine. The discussion falls into two parts. The first is an outline of the Italian approach to ‘the archaeology of architecture’；it shows how，in the last 30-40 years，research in the field has brought together experts in post-classical archaeology and architects who specialise in the conservation of the built environment. The second part discusses two case studies that reveal how the methods and instruments of architectural archaeology enable one to establish time sequences in the construction and modification of buildings，thence make decisions regarding their conservation. The first case study concerns an actual project for conservation and re-use. The second case study is a research project by a group from the Politecnico di Milano，which focuses on a structure whose multi-layered history had yet to be examined.

Keywords：Architectural palimpsest；Knowledge；Conservation；Italy

作者简介：
Prof. Carolina DI BIASE，Politecnico di Milano，Italy，Department of Architecture and Urban Studies，Architectural Conservation Unit，head of the PhD Programme in ‘Preservation of the Architectural Heritage’.

The Life of Things

Various sources inform our knowledge of the architecture and settlements of the past: descriptions and accounts that have survived in either manuscript or published documents; the legendary topographies made up by collective memories; cartographical representations or depicted views; drawings, photographs and films; the building traditions that are a feature which defines the very culture of their inhabitants. However, the architecture and cities of the past survive into the present mainly as physical entities: as settlements which, after centuries underground or underwater, are brought to life through excavation, providing us with accounts of lost civilizations; as the remains of more recently abandoned villages; as ancient ruins, whose presence in the very heart of our own cities testifies to their stratified history; in the ancient or medieval layout that determines the form of our own roads and streets; in foundation structures and walls which form the buildings we still use; in modern additions we have made to age-old urban fabrics, particularly noticeable over the last two centuries; in manufacturing sites and facilities, abandoned or redeveloped for new use. All this makes it clear that, if one is to 'read' the material history of buildings and built environments, one must draw upon ever more advanced forms of interdisciplinary research in order to chart their existence over time. Such tracing of the 'life of things' is what I aim to examine in this chapter.

The discussion will fall into two parts. The first is an outline of the Italian approach to 'the archaeology of architecture'; it will show how, in the last 30-40 years, research in the field has brought together experts in post-classical archaeology and architects who specialise in the conservation of the built environment. The second part will discuss two case studies that reveal how the methods and instruments of architectural archaeology enable one to establish time sequences in the construction and modification of buildings, thence make decisions regarding their conservation: the first study concerns an actual project for conservation and re-use, the second a research project by a group from the Politecnico di Milano which focused on a structure whose multi-layered history had yet to be examined.

For some time now, the archaeology of architecture has been recognised as a fundamental area of research for all those engaged in the conservation of architectural heritage. But what logic inspires such an analytical 'breakdown' of buildings? Why do we aim to identify the 'actions of construction' that have produced the artefact as it now stands? The chief reason for this form of research is the awareness that the meaning and significance of a building are not to be found solely in the period in which it originated, however essential that might be for our understanding of the structure. In effect, there is more to any building than its initial design and construction, than the cultural context within which it was conceived and created. After just a few decadesands — even more so, after the course of centuries — any building presents scholars, conservation experts, technicians and end-users with an entity that has been modified by the sequence of uses and also by the range and kind of intervention it has already undergone. Each structure with a history is an embodiment of change; it raises the issue of duration over time, with regard to both the structure itself and its urban environment. It is this which we must examine in order to chart the life that structure has lived; in order to understand the impact of the different generations who have used it since its construction.

The title of the English edition of a short but insightful book by the philosopher Remo Bodei (1938-...) is significant here: *The Life of Things*, *The Love of Things* makes it clear that to understand the life of things is to love them (thence to wish to protect them) .[2] Once again one sees that knowledge is linked with a concern with protection; that attempts to understand the significance of a building are inevitably bound up with the preservation of its existence.

"The meaning of 'thing' is richer than that of 'object', which is something that is manipulated with indifference or according to impersonal technical procedures. Things, in the philosophical sense, are nodes of relationships with the life of others, chains of continuity among generations, bridges that connect individual and collective histories, junctions between human civilizations and nature. Things incite us to listen to reality. Things are the repositories of ideas, emotions, and symbols. The more we are able to recover objects in their wealth of meanings and integrate them into our mental and emotional horizons, the broader and deeper our world becomes. It is very important to increase a fruitful dialogue with that which already exists and 'let things speak for themselves'. [...] We must take the history of such things as part of our own history [...]. Because when approached with openness and attention each thing can reveal new trajectory of research and curiosity, in the noble sense of that term indicated by its etymological origin in the word *cura*, care (to take care of the things, to preserve them)" .[3]

On another occasion, Bodei indirectly approached the same issue from the opposite direction — that is, when discussing the sudden loss of a 'thing' due to a devastating fire. Like any such destructive trauma, this raised important questions regarding not only what had been lost but also with regard to the future, an issue of key importance when the lost building had served the community as a whole. What was to be done with the 'new' site created within the old city fabric? How was one to treat what had escaped destruction? The case in question was the 1996 fire in Venice that had destroyed the city's main opera house, La Fenice, a phoenix that had already risen once from its ashes after an 1836 fire. The 1996 fire was followed by a vigorous debate regarding reconstruction, with most Venetians — including the then mayor, philosopher Massimo Cacciari (1944-...) — arguing that the theatre should be rebuilt "as it had been, where it had been". Reviewing the centuries-old debate regarding such issues as 'the copy' and 'the original', authenticity and identity, Bodei himself asked: "To what extent can one reconcile fidelity to the past, to the identity, of a historic city such as Venice with the ability to innovate in a creative and aesthetically acceptable manner?" In effect, the illusion of being able to exorcize the catastrophic event — by turning the clock back to a state of affairs which existed before it had occurred — was tantamount to negating history. Bodei wrote: "In my opinion, an ideal reconstruction should be able to combine elements of historical continuity with innovation that is both clear and creative; that bears the mark of discontinuity, of the trauma suffered. Within certain limits, one must accept history and its irreparable events. It makes no sense to imagine that one can stop time, restoring something that has been erased either through neglect or crime to its ancient, unchanging, splendour. Wounds should leave scars. Even works of art should bear traces of their history; they should absorb caesurae and discontinuity, making them a part of continuity. It is through innovation, through the difference to be seen between what arises and the original which had been destroyed, that one keeps the memory of a community alive".[4]

Wounds, scars and the traces left by destructive forces are thus important: as archaeologists have shown, they have a tale to tell even centuries after the event. And acknowledging the existence of caesurae means that we have to describe and interpret any rupture in continuity, to 'read' the traces left by materials and features that no longer exist.

The Palimpsest of Architecture, City and Territory

Buildings and urban sites bear marks left by the individuals and social groups that have used and re-used them, continually adjusting their relationship with the surrounding environment and context. Such buildings can be modified by changes in ownership and function; by change in ideas regarding construction; by the advent of new forms and new languages, which generally spread from 'learned' to 'vernacular' architecture. As such, they can be seen as texts written by a range of different cultures, which means the traces left by these superimposed texts must be painstakingly deciphered. Whether clearly visible [Fig. 1] or less apparent, the stratifications that one finds in each building, settlement, city or human landscape make them comparable to a *palimpsest* created over time.

In some buildings, the layers that one finds from underground right up to the level of the present-day city are a clear reflection of the different phases in the construction of the urban fabric: this can be seen, for example, in the church of San Clemente in Celio, in the area of the Rome Forum, where one read the different stratifications vertically. In that church, the building techniques used and the size, decoration and style of the components in the construction change from level to level, 'narrating' the move from Late Roman to Medieval architecture. So, beneath the 12th-century structure one has: a structure, perhaps used as a goods warehouse, which dates from the 1st century A.D.; a private house (*domus*) dating from the 2nd century A.D.; and, within this latter, a sanctuary of the cult of Mithras (*mithraeum*) dating from the 3rd century. It was upon the *domus* that the first Christian church (*basilica*) was built, with an apse dating from the 4th century.

In other cases, one finds buildings that are a result of the intersection and juxtaposition of parts built at different times, all of which go to form its composite identity. Think, for example, of the Palace of Diocletian in Spalato, which was built in the 3rd century A.D. but subsequently underwent a number of alterations in the Middle Ages and Early Modern periods. It was this composite which Alois Riegl (1858-1905) and Max Dvořák (1874-1921) — not only great art historians but also major exponents of the theory underlying architectural conservation — argued should be protected, recognising

Fig.1 Architectural palimpsests: original medieval structures in Venice (left) and Genoa (right) modified over the following centuries [© C. Di Biase (left), courtesy of D. Pittaluga, ISCUM, Genoa (right)].

it as a single whole created by the co-existence of different material and artistic cultures.[5]

It is not only in great architectural artefacts that one finds different historical phases surviving alongside each other within a single construction. This is often to be found in 'minor' architecture. And given the relative rarity of detailed written sources with regard to the life associated with such 'lesser' buildings, these structures make a huge contribution not only to our understanding of the history of constructions and their use, but also to our knowledge of the rural settlements or urban/territorial contexts within which they were located.[6] Here, the co-existing elements dating from different periods might include changes to walls (both the creation of new openings and the blocking-in of previous openings) and stratified alterations apparent in wall surfaces themselves, with different overlaid stretches of plaster often exposed by decay [Fig. 2].

Fig.2 Overlaid strata of plaster on the wall surfaces of residential palazzi in Venice and Genoa. The intermediate layer of plaster has been 'scored' (nicked in a regular manner using a small pickaxe) in order to improve its adherence with the plaster applied over it [© C. Di Biase (left), courtesy of D. Pittaluga, ISCUM, Genoa (right)].

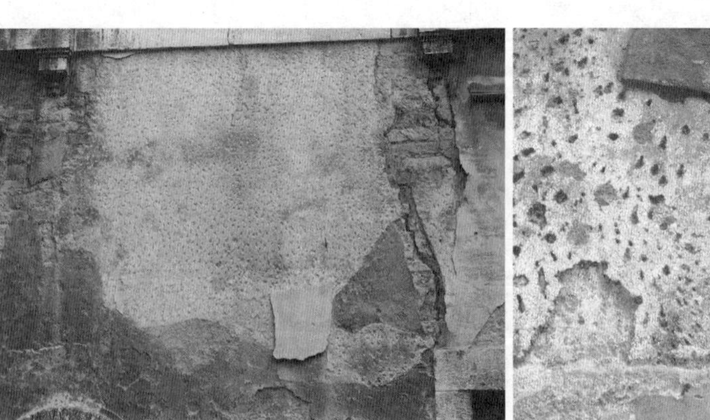

The term *palimpsest* derives from the Greek word παλίμψηστος, which referred to a parchment that, either in Classical Antiquity itself or during the Middle Ages, had been scratched and washed so that it might be reused for the writing of a new text. The decoding of such palimpsests is a fascinating activity and nowadays can draw upon a range of non-destructive techniques — from photography to spectroscopy — to identify the different layers of writing and thus reconstruct the various texts that co-exist on the surface of a single 'thing'. Similarly, various skills and fields of knowledge are brought to bear in deciphering an architectural palimpsest, with the results of different methods of research and investigation being compared and combined.[7]

Archaeology and Conservation: The Italian Approach to 'Building Archaeology'

From some decades now, archaeological research in Italy has espoused an approach that combines available written texts with the 'text' formed by the building itself. Hence, excavation, which always destroys as it unearths, is flanked with non-destructive stratigraphic observations and analysis of the body of buildings themselves; in addition, virtual reconstructions are used to break down the structure into its different layers, and thus make it possible to map out its construction over time. The result of this is that the writing of a building's history is based upon a study of the different material cultures it embodies, with each component bearing witness to a specific phase. This material history can be of decisive importance when it comes to drawing up and implementing a project for the conservation and appropriate re-use of existing structures. This is why the method has been espoused by so many conservation architects, whose priorities are to reduce alterations to a minimum; carefully preserve the material, cultural and economic resources embodied in our built heritage; make additions thereto which will be clearly recognisable as layers in a process of stratification that runs from past to future.

As far back as 1974, the medievalist and archaeologist Riccardo Francovich (1946-2007) would found the journal *Archeologia Medievale*, whose very subtitle *Cultura Materiale*, *Insediamenti*, *Territorio* [Material Culture, Settlements, Territory] revealed the focus of a publication that looked towards the range of interesting work being done from Poland to the United Kingdom. In the latter, for example, the journal *Medieval Archaeology* was inspired by a keen interest in historical geography and 'local history', and the school of work based upon the methods promoted by Edward C. Harris in his successful *Principles of Archaeological Stratigraphy*.[8] Francovich was clear about the need for interdisciplinary studies in the examination of human settlements and in decisions regarding urban planning and building. For example, the 1979 issue of *Archeologia Medievale* dedicated to the theme of archaeology and the planning of inhabited areas, defines such areas as "multi-layered sites that are still in use [...] living urban fabrics that, more than ever, are undergoing continual transformation", and discusses the issue with contributions from architects and city historians.[9] The very concept of 'archaeology' is expanded to cover to the study of evidence that bears witness 'to any period in history, regardless of aesthetic quality'. Above all, such studies are seen in relation to the complex social and scientific reality of "the historical heritage with which we come into contact every day and yet which we overlook... [a heritage] that is not set aside for quiet excavation, which can be carried out over a long period of time, but is continually being eroded" . Hence, what one must bring to bear is so-called 'emergency or rescue archaeology'. For example, in areas that have been cleared for the creation of new urban infrastructures, the archaeologists intervene so that any data or material that might have been unearthed, and is about to be lost, can be recorded and documented. But they should also participate in the planning process, working with local authorities to propose programmes of action that promote planned 'preventive archaeology'.

The year 1979 saw the publication of another work well-known amongst architects working in the field of conservation: *Archeologia e cultura materiale* [Archaeology and material culture. Towards a policy for cultural heritage] by Andrea Carandini (1937-...) .[10] He argued for a new approach to historical studies which would look beyond the history of art and the aesthetic qualities of objects. Attention was now to be focused on the fruits of human labour in order to reconstruct a 'history of manufacture'; the 'fossils of human effort (from prehistorical times to the industrial age) ' became part of our cultural heritage. Such an approach paid particular attention to the different technologies and tools of work to be found in different cultural contexts, opening up new directions in the analysis and study of the processes and means of production and manufacture.

In 1988 Francovich himself would publish a book dedicated to the relation between archaeology and the restoration of monuments.[11] Here, he points out that "the conservation of historical structures is a problem that concerns both the archaeologist and the architect-restorer", both of whom must be conscious of working in a stratified environment, of the need to apply the new methods available in describing original (and subsequent) construction work and dating different strata. Derived from geology and first put to use in archaeological excavation, these methods were now to be used upon the elevation of structures — the cover of the book had an illustration that shows how stratigraphy might identify overlaps, additions, intersections and chronological sequences within walls. Such an approach meant that the reading and dating of structural components drew upon a range of different instruments: macroscopic examination of how components were assembled; study of surface treatments in the various elements within a construction; consideration of the size of wall components (for example, regulations governing the manufacture of bricks, measurements and the application of mensiochronological analysis); archaeometrical analyses; laboratory testing of materials. The work carried out at the ISCUM (Ligurian Institute for Material Culture) would, in its turn, differentiate between urban contexts and minor settlements where innovations in technology and form arrived with a certain delay and thus 'chronotypologies' of buildings and the stratigraphies of the 'volumes' added to the previous constructions are more effective instruments of examination. For many years the director of the ISCUM was Tiziano Mannoni (1928-2010), a leading figure in this sort of research. He often stressed the interdependence of conservation and knowledge ('conserve in order to know/ know in order to conserve') and the need to focus as much as possible upon non-destructive methods for 'reading' individual buildings and extra-urban settlements.[12] As a result of this new focus, the relation between archaeologists and the architects working in the conservation area would become closer and more fruitful. This was exemplified in 1996 by the publication of *Archeologia dell'Architettura* [Archaeology of Architecture], edited by Gian Pietro Brogiolo.[13] This supplement to *Architettura Medievale* aimed to be a point of reference for the different schools of stratigraphic archaeology that had been founded in some Italian universities. A discussion forum for archaeologists and restorers who had adopted the stratigraphic method, the journal would host lively discussion of such important issues as: the use of stratigraphic data in projects concerning buildings or sites; the study of building techniques in relation to developments in technical know-how; the controversial relationship with art historians, who played no role in the on-going debate between restorers and archaeologists; the widening horizons resulting from an archaeology of urban planning and layout; the autonomy of stratigraphic analysis of structures both above and below ground. This latter issue concerned primarily the standing of stratigraphy as more than just a practical instrument at the service of other disciplines; as a constituent part of archaeology *tout court*, it was seen as necessarily drawing upon a range of disciplines.

In Italy, a country that was at high risk of earthquakes, one question of particular interest was the application of stratigraphy to a reading of the cracking suffered by structures, something which made it possible to establish the effects of earthquakes and the vulnerability of settlements. The 2010 issue of *Archeologia dell'Architettura* dedicated one of its four sections entirely to the matter of the relationship between archaeological research and the prevention of earthquake damage, with contributions from structural engineers, archaeologists and architects working in the field of conservation.[14] The theme would then be returned to in the 2014 issue of the journal dedicated to the topic of archaeo-seismology in architecture.[15]

Architects working in the field of conservation would also be active in universities, making such questions a central feature of the process that leads from the collection of information to the planning of intervention. The experience such figures had acquired was reflected in books and collective publications that aimed not only to make a contribution to an ongoing debate but also to the approach adopted in both planning and intervention within historic buildings. The dominant line of research was now one that focused on the need to 'manage the process of modification' — a recognised necessity if intervention is aimed to prolong the life of existing structures and add layers both new and yet compatible to the previous stratifications. Amongst the most wide-ranging publications dealing with the application of archaeological research in the process of fact-gathering that should precede any plan of intervention, one might mention those by Francesco Doglioni,[16] Gian Paolo Treccani,[17] and Anna Boato,[18] while Stefano della Torre pursued a similar line of research in his study of the building techniques employed in the construction of walls.[19] In effect, by the first decade of the 21st century, it was architects that were most active in exploring the role of archaeology and stratigraphy in the conservation of our architectural heritage.

As for the archaeologists themselves, adopting different approaches, they returned to issues that were integral to the discipline. In a special issue of 2014 that celebrated forty years of Italy's *Archeologia Medievale*, edited by Sauro Gelichi, various non-Italian archaeologists amongst others Martin O. H. Carver, Richard Hodges, Chris Wickam were invited to discuss possible developments in such work.[20] The aim was to "offer a critical account of the history of medieval archaeology in Italy as seen through the lens provided by a journal that had been both a reflection of such studies and a source of guidance for them". The Italian archaeologists who contributed to the special issue were asked to discuss "a series of themes that had been pursued by the discipline over these years, and to analyse the relationship between medieval archaeology and other areas of scientific research".

Building Archaeology: Applications

The two cases that we will now discuss bear certain similarities, given that both concern fortified structures that had long been abandoned. In both cases, the results of neglect — the structural lesions, the partial collapses and the fractures within components — were factors which actually revealed evidence regarding the techniques and materials used in construction. Furthermore, neither structure was widely discussed in the existing literature, even public archives, the most readily available source of information, contained relatively little data; hence one might say that each of them was awaiting the rediscovery of its identity (as well as a new lease of useful life) . In both cases, the total absence or slight traces of plastering exposed the fabric of the external walls. Thus it was possible to study, identify and map the USM (Unità Stratigrafiche Murarie - Stratigraphic Wall Components) and then frame them within the geometries and forms recomposed on the basis of topographical and longimetrical measurement. The direct knowledge acquired through the 'archaeology' of the structures' elevations, therefore, made it possible to reconstruct the warp and weft in the history of both their construction and their use; to cast light on the past of architectural entities that had long been ignored and forgotten.

Fig.3 The Charles V Tower. Martinsicuro: the east facade during work to strengthen the structures and clean the facades; Charles V's coat-of-arms in the centre [© C. Di Biase].

Preliminary and Archaeological Investigation: a case history [21]

The so-called Charles V Tower was close to falling down completely in the late 1980s when, after more than a century of use as a private residence, it was purchased by the public authorities. The name of the location, Martinsicuro (Abruzzo), which also applies to the bordering territory of the local council, derives from that of the tower's builder, Martin de Segura, which, together with the date of the completion of construction (1547), figures on a plaque to be found on the main façade, facing onto the sea. No doubt is possible as to the origins of the structure, as it was part of the system of 380 look-out towers that had been ordered by the Spanish viceroys Pedro de Toledo in 1532 and Parafran de Ribera in 1565 to protect the southern coats of Italy against Saracen attack. Standing in the border area between the Kingdom of Naples and the Papal States, the tower stills bears, at the centre of its eastern façade, a stone tabernacle [Fig. 3] that is dedicated to Charles V (1500-1558), Emperor of the Romans (*Romanum Imperator*), and contains his coat-of-arms.[22]

By the 1960s the stability of the structure was a cause for concern, and it had clearly worsened some twenty years later: substantial cracks were to be seen in three of its facades; the rib vaulting was in parts fissured, in parts sagging; the sloping roof had caved in at various points. As provisional work was necessary immediately to prevent the collapse of the structure, external bracing was fitted at two levels of the tower and the vaulting was propped up. This work to make the building safe also made it possible to plan and execute a detail range of preliminary studies, the aim being to determine the causes of the structure's instability and thence identify the most appropriate and effective measures for its consolidation.

Working together with Lorenzo Jurina (structural engineer and a professor at the Politecnico di Milano) and the afore-mentioned prof. Tiziano Mannoni (who coordinated the stratigraphic and archaeometric studies), I oversaw the programme of exploratory studies, which draw upon a range of different experts, research laboratories and specialist companies. The need to carry out geotechnical tests and to assess the state of the foundations meant that — in collaboration with the Superintendence for Archaeological Affairs within the region of Abruzzo — we performed stratigraphic tests at the foot of the escarped walls. These revealed the presence of pre-existing structures on the western side of the tower, whilst excavation of the internal ground level unearthed ceramics that were contemporary with the original construction work.

As for the facades, stratigraphic testing made it possible to draw up a clear map of the phases of construction. These included: repairs to the base of the walls; additions (the walls of the double slope roof above the level of the corbels); removals (the windows created by breaking through existing walls) and various repairs intended to fill in gaps (for example, within the niche of the *bolzone*, the wooden beam used to support the drawbridge on the north side of the tower). On the basis of the USM identified [Fig. 4], tests were carried out to sample building materials and mortars. As a result, distinctions between the 16th-cen-

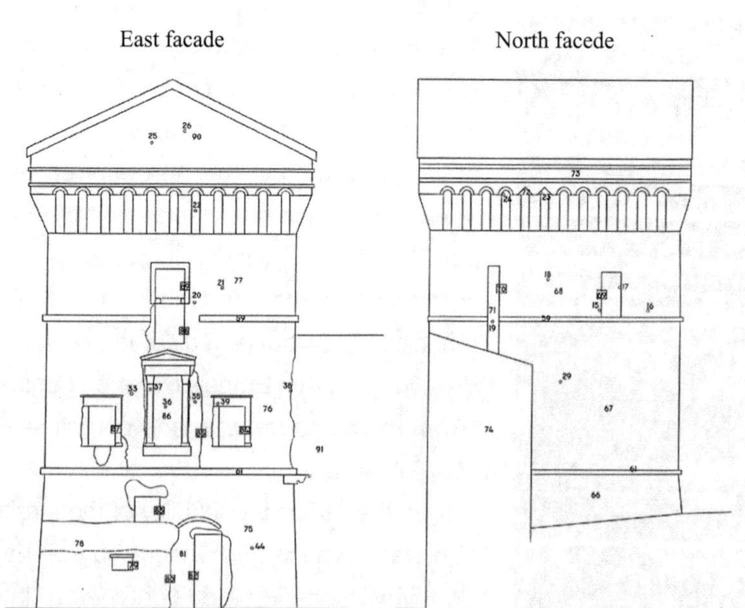

Fig.4 The Charles V Tower, Martinsicuro: stratigraphic surveys of the east and north facades; the representation indicates USM removed or added to the existing fabric, and the points where samples were taken[© T.Mannoni, ISCUM].

tury and later parts could be established on the basis of the types of binding agent and sand (river or coastal) that were used in the mortars; hence the binding agents and the aggregates for the repair mortars could be chosen accordingly, in order to guarantee both reliability and compatibility with existing materials — something which was fundamental if the 'patching' and in-depth strengthening of the walls was to be effective.

The approach chosen by the project[23] was predicated upon the maintenance of traces that revealed the discontinuity resulting from the previous static instability, even when repairing the cracks in the upper part of the north wall. After consolidation, these looked like scar tissue [Fig. 5], bearing witness to the previous state of the structure. Once more a 'lookout over the sea', the building is now extensively used.

Fig.5 The Charles V Tower, Martinsicuro: the coping of the north facade after consolidation work; the'scars'left by the substantial cracks are clear[© C.Di Biase]

A research programme for Rangoni Castle, Spilamberto [24]

From the 14th century onwards, Rangoni Castle was the centre of the fiefdom of the Rangoni family, one of the most powerful in the Duchy ruled by the Este family. For more than five centuries it was property of that family. In 2006, the castle and the associated buildings passed to the ownership of the town council of Spilamberto (Modena, Emilia-Romagna), being opened up for public use for the first time. Long unused, the castle had a complex internal layout, with rooms at different levels and ceilings of varying heights and decoration — all damaged by neglect, whose effects on the upper floor had been compounded by the infiltration of rainwater over a long period. There was no extensive information regarding the structure: the archives of the Rangoni family had been shut for years to undergo reorganization. Thus, without on-site surveys to determine the actual size of the complex, any attempt to reflect upon conservation works of the castle and how it might be used in the future would be essentially ill-informed. The town council, therefore, called for tenders from various Italian universities to carry out exploratory work on the Castle and its surroundings. Ultimately, the work was commissioned from a research group at the Politecnico di Milano, which immediately set in motion various kinds of on-site examination (laser scanning and topographical and geometrical surveys). The results from this initial work provided the essential basis for the 'reading' of the structures and all the subsequent phases of investigation. Given that the few available documents made no reference to the building work or to how the castle had taken on its present form through the construction of its different parts, it was the building itself that had to be our prime source of information. Data, therefore, was gleaned through a complex and extensive campaign of observations, measurements and analyses. And one of the main tools in this work was examination of the 'archaeology of elevations'.

Fig.6 Rangoni Castle Spilamberto: elevations and sections [© Architectural Conservation Unit, DASTU, coordination: C. Di Biase].

At each of the different levels of the castle, the floor plan shows a fortified enclosure with four corner towers and two central towers on the east and west facades; but these plans also show that the geometry and development of these walls is not entirely uniform. As for transverse and longitudinal sections, they revealed substantial difference between single and compound spaces that make up the castle within the perimeter walls [Fig. 6].

One point that immediately attracted attention when studying the plans of the ground and mezzanine levels was the incorporation within the north building of two thick walls for which there was no comparable counterpart (in either size or component material) in the other walls of the castle [Fig. 7]. Tests involving the removal of small portions of the wall plaster at the joins between the large and smaller walls revealed the scale and particular finish of the surfaces of the former. It was thence suggested that there might have been a previous tower, which was half demolished in order to permit the creation of the internal courtyard whose colonnaded loggias (along the east and west sides)

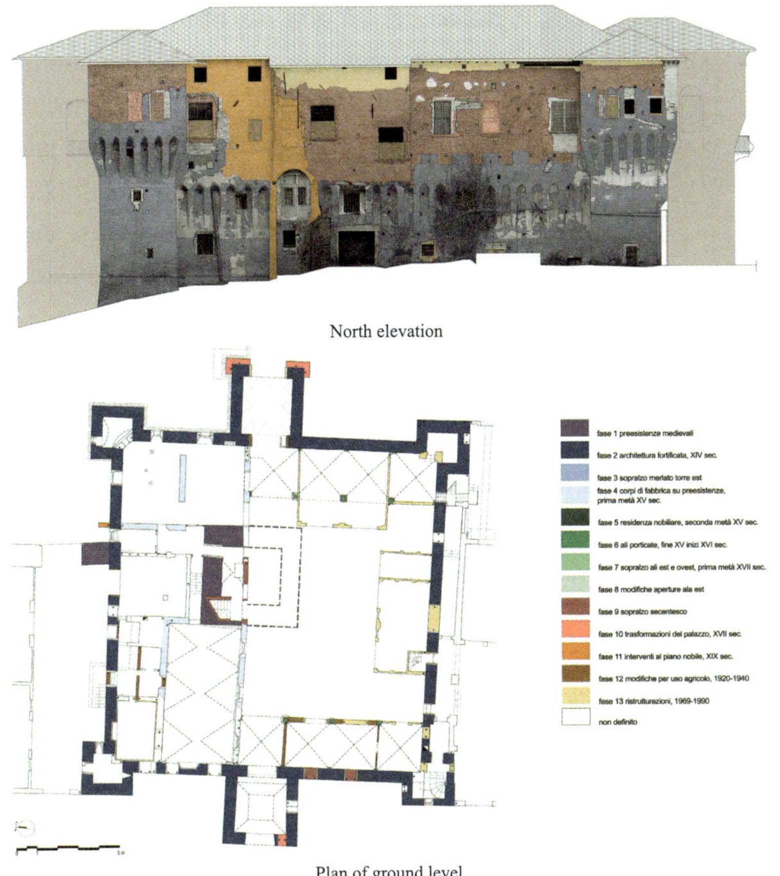

Fig.7 Rangoni Castle, Spilamberto: north elevation and plan of ground level, with indications of main phases of construction work. At the centre of the ground plan one can see the thickness of the two surviving walls (around 190 cm) of a previous tower [© Architectural Conservation Unit, DASTU, coordination: C. Di Biase].

were built in the second half of the 15th century. This hypothesis was confirmed by two pieces of evidence. The first was the discovery of the 1501 will of the feudal lord Nicolò Rangoni, which amongst the property bequeathed describes the Castle, complete with its courtyard and two porticoes. The second confirmation came from stratigraphic tests of the ground level in the courtyard, carried out by archaeologists from the University of Bologna: in the area corresponding to the surviving walls of the supposed tower, these revealed the presence of the foundations of the demolished walls [Fig. 8].

Using various methods, long and patient archaeological analyses produced approximate chronology which, combined with the few 'absolute' dates, made it possible to reconstruct the main phases in the building and subsequent transformations of the complex. For example, on the walls of a spiral staircase there is an inscription in the plaster made 1514 — that year thus serving as *terminus ante quem* — and the text tells us that Giuliano de' Medici, brother of Giovanni de' Medici (Pope Leo X, reign 1513-21), stayed in the Castle after having attempted to avert a duel between Guido Rangoni, '*condottiero* of Leo X', and his cousin and rival, Count Ugo Pepoli. Together with documentary evidence regarding the life and work of the main artists active in the Early Modern period, local chronicles and the literature on the political and artistic life of Modena and the territories of the Este duchy have also provided precious points of references for the identification and dating of the internal spaces and the decorative schemes that have survived neglect. Many possible links were established between those (both noblemen and servants) who inhabited the various quarters within the Castle and the characteristic features of their construction

Fig.8 Rangoni Castle, Spilamberto: corresponding with a gateway (above), the thickness of the wall of a previous tower is 192 cm; below one can see the excavation in the courtyard area that brought to light the foundations of the two walls of that tower that had been demolished [© Architectural Conservation Unit, DASTU, courtesy of L. Balboni].

and decoration (remains of ceilings, lath vaulting, floors and the decorations overlaid on earlier walls). These features can be seen also in the sequence of rooms created in the second half of the 17th century. It was during this later period that all the walls — with the exception of the towers — were raised beyond the level of the crenellation and a new broad staircase was added at the centre of the north building; this linked the courtyard and the entrance hall of the new *piano nobile* of a castle which was now transformed into a 'delightful palace'. Repeated exploration of the areas beneath the roofing also revealed other, previously unsuspected, phases in the life of the building. As for the final period in which the Castle was a private residence, this could be further understood by comparing the picture of life that might be deduced from 18th-century inventories with the plans of the castle which were drawn up at the beginning of the 20th century (from Rangoni family's archive). The body of information available was completed by: an analysis of the form, wood type and method of working to be seen in the plank floors (whose structural solidity was also tested); inspection and testing of the lath vaults and the fabric of the roofs; stratigraphic examination of surfaces; laboratory testing of mortars, bricks, plasterwork and paints.

At the end of this programme, the Spilamberto Town Council was provided with a complex and fascinating account of the Castle, a sketch of the structure's material history, [25] which would subsequently be developed upon in two PhD thesis projects that have since been published in the same volume.[26] Not only had the research revealed that the castle had come about through a sequence of construction phases, it had also identified the portions and areas put to different uses during the time. It was this which suggested that it should also be reused as different parts; that the redevelopment of the Castle should make it possible to site various activities within the different floors and buildings of the complex, thus respecting its original layout and encouraging a mix of new functions. Inspired by this logic of proceeding through additions, the plan for the new structure within the complex — giving onto the garden grounds and corresponding with the wing added to the Castle in the 18th century — should resolve the problems raised by certain contemporary requirements: emergency stairs, lift, service facilities for visitors and guaranteed accessibility for all.

Notes

① Original Italian edition: Bodei, Remo, *La vita delle cose*, Rome-Bari: Editori Laterza, 2009.
② Bodei, Remo, *The Life of Things, the Love of Things*, (transl. by Murtha Baca), New York: Fordham University Press, 2015, *presentation*.
③ Bodei, Remo, 'La Fenice. L'ossessione di copiare il passato', *La Repubblica*, 23 October 2003.
④ Scarrocchia, Sandro, *Max Dvořák. Conservazione e Moderno in Austria (1905-1921)*, Milano: FrancoAngeli Edizioni, 2009: 92-96.
⑤ Corboz, André, 'Il territorio come palinsesto', *Casabella*, 516, September 1985: 22-27.
⑥ "... architects, archaeologists and design historians sometimes use the word to describe the accumulated iterations of a design or a site, whether in literal layers of archaeological remains, or by the figurative accumulation and reinforcement of design ideas over time. Whenever spaces are rebuilt or remodeled, evidence of former uses remain. Examples include: tarred rooflines remain on the sides of a building after the neighboring structure has been demolished and dust lines after an appliance is relocated [...] some historians are beginning to use the term as a description of the way people experience times, that is, as a layering of present experiences over faded pasts [...] In landscape archaeology the concept of palimpsest is used to describe the way different generations alter the landscape of their ancestors". https://ipfs.io/ipfs/QmXoypizjW3WknFiJnKLwHCnL72vedxjQkDDP1mXWo6uco/wiki/Palimpsest.html More recently, in: Aksamija, Nadja; Maines, Clark; Wagoner, Philip, *Palimpsests: Buildings, Sites, Time* (*Architectural Crossroads* 4), Turnhout: Brepols Publishers, 2017: "As a hermeneutic tool, the concept of the palimpsest embraces the totality of time 'compressed' in a given monument or site, while permitting the extraction of a series of legible and meaningful episodes that allow us to read those palimpsests as a narrative of historical processes, whether that narrative is one of deliberate revision, or one of unintended effect. [...] the notion of the palimpsest can become a paradigm-shifting framework for future, collaborative research in architectural and landscape history".
⑦ Harris, Edward C., *Principles of Archaeological Stratigraphy*, 1979, Academic Press 1989 -2nd edition. It has been translated into Italian, Spanish, Polish, Japanese, Slovene, German, Hungarian and Czech. Chinese, Arabic and French translations are in progress http://harrismatrix.com/about-the-book/ (consulted 16 March 2018).
⑧ *Archaeology and the Planning of Inhabited Areas*, thematic issue of *Archeologia Medievale. Cultura Materiale, Insediamenti, Territorio*, 6, 1979.
⑨ Carandini, Andrea, *Archeologia e cultura materiale. Dai lavori senza gloria nell'antichità a una politica dei beni culturali*, De Donato, 1979. Andrea Carandini, a student of Ranuccio Bianchi Bandinelli, was then director of the Istituto di Archeologia, Storia dell'Arte, della Musica e dello Spettacolo at the University of Siena.
⑩ Francovich, Riccardo; Parenti, Roberto (eds), *Archeologia e restauro dei monumenti. I Ciclo di lezioni sulla Ricerca applicata in archeologia (Certosa di Pontignano, Siena, 28 settembre-10 ottobre 1987)*, Quaderni del Dipartimento di Archeologia e Storia delle Arti - Sezione Archeologia, Università di Siena, Florence: All'Insegna del Giglio, 1988.
⑪ Amongst his numerous publications, see the series *20 anni di archeologia globale* [Twenty Years of Global Archaeology]: Mannoni, Tiziano, *Archeologia dell'urbanistica*, Genoa: ESCUM (Edizioni di Storia della Cultura Materiale), 1994; Mannoni, Tiziano, *Insediamenti abbandonati. Archeologia medievale*, Genoa: ESCUM, 1995; Mannoni, Tiziano, *Caratteri*

costruttivi dell'edilizia storica, Genoa: ESCUM, 1996; Mannoni, Tiziano, *Archeologia delle tecniche produttive*, Genoa: ESCUM, 1994; Mannoni, Tiziano, *Archeometria: geoarcheologia dei manufatti*, Genoa: ESCUM, 1994.

⑫ Brogiolo, Gian Pietro, 'Prospettive per l'archeologia dell'architettura', *Archeologia dell'Architettura*, I (supplement to *Archeologia Medievale*, 22), Florence, 1996: 11-16. Also: Brogiolo, Gian Pietro, *Archeologia dell'edilizia storica*, Como: New Press, 1988.

⑬ Brogiolo, Gian Pietro (ed.), *Temi e prospettive di ricerca Archeologia dell'Architettura*, XV, Sesto Fiorentino: All'Insegna del Giglio, 2010. Especially the contributions by: Lagomarsino, Sergio; Boato, Anna, 'Stratigrafia e statica', p. 47-53; Faccio, Paolo; Brogiolo, Gian Pietro, 'Stratigrafia e prevenzione', p. 54-63.

⑭ Faccio, Paolo (ed.), *Ricerche di Archeosismologia in Archittettura Archeologia dell'Architettura*, XIX, Sesto Fiorentino: All'Insegna del Giglio, 2014.

⑮ Doglioni, Francesco, *Stratigrafia e Restauro. Tra conoscenza e conservazione dell'architettura*, Trieste: Lint, 1997.

⑯ Treccani, Gian Paolo (ed.), *Archeologie, restauro, conservazione. Mentalit à e pratiche dell'archeologia nell'intervento sul costruito*, Milano: Edizioni Unicopli, 2000.

⑰ Boato, Anna, *L'archeologia in architettura. Misurazioni, stratigrafie, datazioni, restauro*, Venice: Marsilio, 2008; Boato, Anna; Pittaluga, Daniela, 'Building Archaeology: A Non-Destructive Archaeology', in *Proceedings of 15th World Conference on Nondestructive Testing*, Rome, 15-21 October 2000 http://www.ndt.net/article/wcndt00/papers/idn365/idn365.htm (consulted 15 March 2018).

⑱ Della Torre, Stefano (ed.), *Storia delle tecniche murarie e tutela del costruito. Esperienze e questioni di metodo*, Milano: Guerini studio, 1996.

⑲ Gelichi, Sauro (ed.), *Quarant'anni di Archeologia Medievale in Italia. La rivista, i temi, la teoria e i methodi*, special issue, of *Archeologia Medievale*, Sesto Fiorentino: All'insegna del Giglio, 2014. https://www.researchgate.net/profile/Chiara_Bonacchi/publication/285593196_Archeologia_Pubblica_e_Archeologia_Medievale/links/5661612b08aebae678aa7ec2/Archeologia-Pubblica-e-Archeologia-Medievale.pdf (consulted 12 February 2018).

⑳ *Conservazione e riuso della Torre di Carlo V* (Martinsicuro, Italy). Design and planning supervisor, Carolina Di Biase.

㉑ The coat of arms, in marble-effect stucco, shows the chain of the Order of the Golden Fleece, and the Pillars of Hercules with the inscription *plus ultra*; stratigraphic mapping revealed that it was installed on the facade in the last phase of the construction work.

㉒ Di Biase, Carolina, 'La Torre di Carlo V in Martinsicuro. Progetto e cantiere in un luogo di margine', *TeMa. Tempo, Materia, Architettura* [restoration journal], 2, 1998: 6-17.

㉓ *Campagna di indagine architettonica e di prima diagnostica mirata all'approfondimento conoscitivo della Rocca Rangoni di Spilamberto e delle relative pertinenze*; the Research Programme was developed in 2007 by the Architectural Conservation Unit of the Department of Architecture and Urban Studies, Politecnico di Milano (scientific coordination: Prof. Carolina Di Biase).

㉔ Di Biase, Carolina, et al., *La Rocca Rangoni*, in Corni, Paola; Vandelli, Vincenzo (eds), *Spilamberto e la sua Rocca. Atti della Giornata di studi (28 ottobre 2006)*, Cinisello Balsamo: Silvana ed., 2008: 109-153.

㉕ Balboni, Laura; Corradini, Paolo, *Rocca Rangoni a Spilamberto. Storia e destino di una fortezza*, Maggioli: Santarcangelo di Romagna, 2017.

雅安观音阁修缮工程中的调查研究

Investigation and study during the conservation project of the Guanyin Hall in Ya'an

赵元祥 李林东 蔡宇琨 | ZHAO Yuanxiang，LI Lindong，CAI Yukun

摘要：雅安观音阁位于四川盆地西端的雅安旧城内，是一座方三间重檐七檩歇山的明代木构建筑。因年久失修，建筑严重倾斜，自2002年临时加固支撑以后，长期没有得到保护。2012—2014年，成都文物考古研究所在勘察设计和施工阶段多次调查观音阁文物本体，并记录了施工过程。本文介绍雅安观音阁的基本情况和结构形制，梳理文献资料，整理新发现的碑记、题记等文字材料，调查研究建筑台基、木结构、瓦屋面的构造和遗痕，还原出观音阁建筑在历史上经历的多次改扩建和维修过程，并推想出建筑室内原有像设布局情况。

关键词：建筑考古学；明代建筑；榫卯；千手观音

Abstract：The Guanyin Hall in Ya'an is located on the western end of Sichuan basin. It's a wooden hall built in 15th century with 3 by 3 bay plan and double eaves. It became inclined severely and was reinforced by timber and nails since 2002. Our team began investigating this hall in 2012 and continued to investigate it in 2014 during the conservation project. In this paper，we introduce the background and structure of the hall，arrange the context and the newly discovered inscriptions and tablets，do some investigation and study on the base，structure and roof. We attempt to look back to the history of the construction，restoration and reconstruction of the hall.

Keywords：Building archaeology；Ming Dynasty architecture；Mortise and tenon joint；Thousand-Hand Guanyin

作者简介：
赵元祥、李林东、蔡宇琨，成都文物考古研究院古代建筑研究所文博馆员。

一、概况

四川盆地最西端的城市雅安，历史上是汉族地区与少数民族地区交界之地，是经四川进入藏区的咽喉要道，是川藏茶马古道上的贸易集散中心。雅安观音阁位于今雅安旧城内的县前街南侧，原商业局车队（后改组为储运公司，已破产倒闭）大院内。建筑坐西南朝东北，背靠月心山（图1）。

商业局车队时期，观音阁曾长期作为仓库和职工宿舍使用，20世纪80年代时，结构尚较为完好，当时的文物档案中，根据旧志中“事传旧梁书洪武甲子岁建”的记载[①]，认为其建于明洪武十七年（1384年）。2002年，观音阁因年久失修，出现梁柱整体倾斜、屋面大面积垮塌的险情，雅安市文物部门得到四川省文物局拨款5万元，立即进行了临时支护。2007年，观音阁被公布为四川省文物保护单位。2008年“5·12”汶川地震中，雅安震感强烈，观音阁在临时支撑的保护下幸运地保存下来。2012年3月至8月，成都文物考古研究所对观音阁进行勘察测绘，编制了修缮方案。然而2013年方案准备实施时，又发生了“4·20”芦山大地震。国家文物局高度重视灾后重建工作，紧急拨款搭建了保护棚，将雅安观音阁增补为全国重点文物保护单位，并将其作为灾后首个实行抢救保护工程的项目，指定北京国文琰文物保护发展有限公司勘察设计，修改完善原有方案。2014年3月，观音阁修缮工程开工，成都文物考古研究所进驻工地开展调查，至11月文物本体基本竣工，调查结束。

图1 雅安观音阁位置图

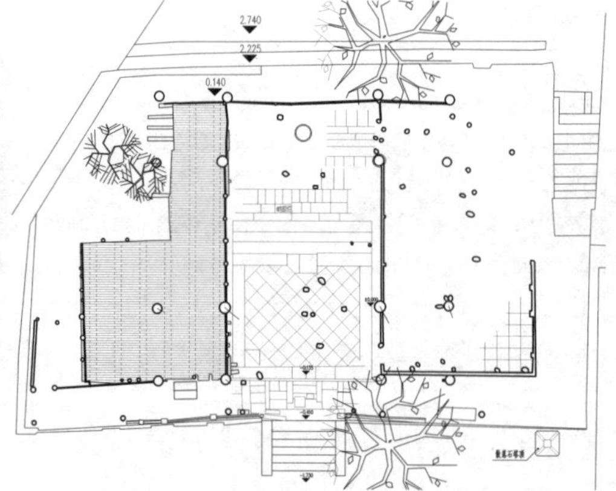
图2 观音阁修缮前平面图

二、修缮前建筑结构形制

雅安观音阁依山而建，台基前高出地表，台帮由条石砌筑，其间嵌有6通石碑，阶条上立石栏杆，中间砌垂带踏跺。台基后则与基岩齐平，压在卵石砌筑的现代建筑基础下。台基上建观音阁及左右厦屋。

观音阁实际并非楼阁式建筑，为重檐七檩歇山的单层殿宇，平面接近正方形，面阔三间，通檐用四柱，形成4×4的柱网，明间面阔约为次间的二倍。柱础为鼓径式，部分柱础上有后期垫入的石盘或鼓墩式柱础。地面为石板铺砌，明间后进有一口水井。原有门窗墙体均已不存，殿内有现代添加的木板隔墙与木地板（图2）。

殿内由4根金柱以两层额串拉结组成木构架的核心，左、右、前三面的下层额串下有雀替痕迹，右缝上层额串下存隔架科雀替。外圈由12根檐柱围合，檐柱之间，柱脚仅前檐存下槛，柱头除前后檐明间只施一道大额枋外，其余各间都施大额枋、由额垫板、小额枋。檐柱与金柱间以桃尖随梁枋相拉结。

檐柱上施平板枋，平板枋上施五踩重昂斗栱，平身科明间用4攒，次间用1攒。柱头科及角科上承桃尖梁，梁尾入金柱。桃尖梁上施瓜柱及角背，瓜柱即上檐柱，柱头之间以上额枋、围脊板、承椽枋相拉结，柱头与金柱间以桃尖随梁枋相拉结。上檐柱上施平板枋，平板枋上施五踩重昂斗栱，柱头科及角科上承桃尖梁，梁尾入金柱。

金柱头上叠摞一根短柱，左右缝短柱之间施下金枋，短柱上承五架梁，五架梁之间施下金垫板，梁头上承下金桁。五架梁上承2根金瓜柱，并施通长的角背。左右缝金瓜柱间施上金枋，金瓜柱上承三架梁。三架梁间施上金垫板，梁头上承上金桁。三架梁上施脊瓜柱及角背，脊瓜柱前后施叉手，左右脊瓜柱之间施脊枋、脊垫板，柱头上承脊桁。下金桁出际处上搭踏脚木，踏脚木上承草架柱子及穿枋。

上下檐桃尖梁头上各施一圈正心桁和挑檐桁。桁上交角处搭角梁，下檐角梁尾插入角瓜柱，上檐角梁尾搭在五架梁头上。角梁上施大刀木[②]，大刀木与挑檐桁之间钉虾须[③]。桁上钉椽，椽断面呈扁长方形。承椽枋和五架梁上通角背都开有椽碗，但修缮前椽子并未插入椽碗，椽间距也比椽碗间距要小。翼角处采用平行布椽。椽上钉飞子，椽飞之间钉有望板。下檐两山屋面与厦屋相接，因此不用飞子。椽、飞头均钉吊檐板。草架柱子外钉山花板。出际端头钉博风板、悬鱼。

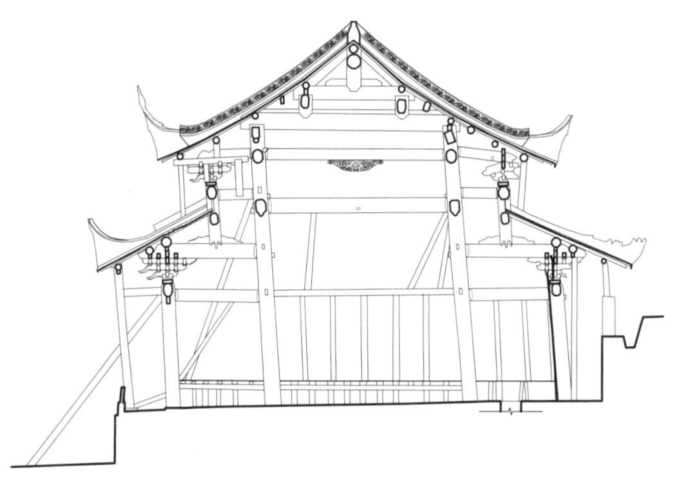

图3 观音阁修缮前剖面

前檐柱前有后期增加的一排擎檐柱，共4根，明间两根与前檐柱间以穿枋相连，另两根位于角梁下方。擎檐柱柱头之间施挂枋[④]，挂枋下各施雕花挂落一对。柱头上承檩条，檩条上承檐椽，至转角处在檩上加垫块承角梁。

主殿两侧后期加建有厦屋，即山面屋檐向外延伸一间，在四川又称之为批檐。右山接出批檐存前半部分，深四步架，前檐出翼角。左山接出批檐残损严重，从残存构件看，原来应与右山对称。

屋面经后期多次维修，做法并不统一。上檐前后檐为素筒瓦屋面，但大部分已垮塌，用石棉瓦遮盖，上檐山面及下檐仅翼角处存少量筒瓦，其余部分均为冷摊瓦屋面。筒瓦屋面的做法为，先在椽子上铺望瓦，望瓦上坐灰铺板瓦及筒瓦，勾头用瓦钉。屋脊为灰塑与烧制花纹砖相结合的做法，当沟、爪角、垂脊花板为灰塑，通脊砖、吻兽为烧制。

三、文字材料

（一）传世文献

雅安观音阁相关存世文献只有清乾隆四年（1739年）修、嘉庆十六年（1811年）补刻、光绪三十一年（1905年）重刻的《雅州府志》和民国十七年（1928年）石印本《雅安县志》两种。民国县志与清代府志记载大体相同，但传抄讹误增多，因此仍以府志为准。其中寺观志记载，观音阁“又名月心阁……国朝康熙四十四年（1705年），僧了悟重修，知州刘启和立碑记之”。艺文志收录的明正德年间许恩所撰《重修观音阁碑记》是关于观音阁早期历史最详尽的记录，该碑记作于明正德九年（1514年）或略晚，追述了观音阁在明天顺年间重建及正德年间改扩建的经过。当时，人们已不知道观音阁创建的年代和原有寺院名称，只是传说重建之前的梁上有“洪武甲子岁（1384年）建”的题记。天顺元年（1457年），住持妙能见殿宇凋落，便携徒弟圆正赴建昌卫（即今西昌）等地化缘，积累了一定的资金，后又得到雅州正千户刘通的支持，得以重建观音阁。至天顺五年（1461年），妙能去世，工程“尚有未备者”。时隔53年，圆正于正德八年（1513年），在山西商人贾钺的资助下，进行了改扩建，“更之以瓦，甃之以石”，两侧增建两厦，前后砌石台阶，正德九年（1514年）冬竣工。除这篇碑记外，当时还另立有捐资姓名碑。

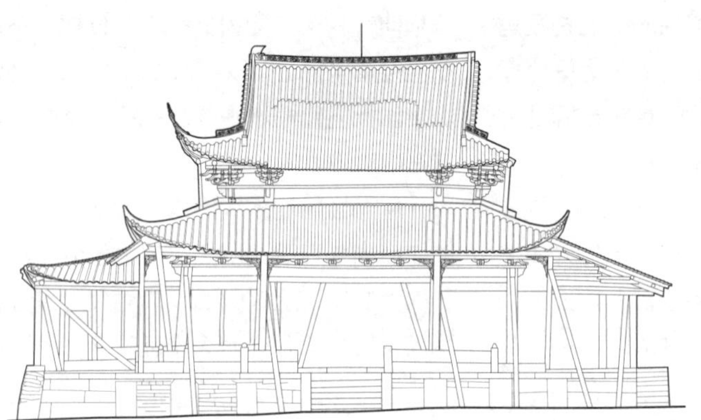

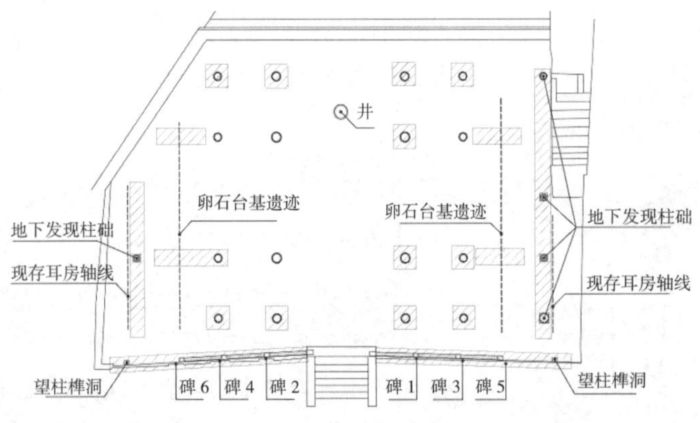

图4 观音阁修缮前正立面（上）
图5 台基调查平面图（下）

（二）碑刻

观音阁台基正面嵌有6块石碑，依年代先后，从中间向两侧一左一右交替排列，类似于昭穆制度，现按此顺序编为1~6号（图5）。

1号碑因石缝中长出小树，已完全风化，结合文献记载推测，可能是明正德年间举人许恩撰写的《重修观音阁碑记》。

2号碑风化较严重，首行存“万历甲辰”（1604年），末行存“大□□□□年春三月”等字，残存字口似为“明正德九”。据许恩碑记“别镌碑以记输财姓名”，可知正德年间还有一块记录功德名录的碑。2号碑可能是万历年重刻的正德功德名录碑。

3号碑风化严重，碑首残缺，末行存“皇清康熙四十四年岁次乙酉孟春”等字。与方志所载“康熙四十四年，僧了悟重修，知州刘启和立碑记之”吻合。此外在维修台阶时发现一块残碑，上有4个篆字，碑边缘的花纹与3号碑相同，推测是其碑首。

4号碑风化较严重，前四行为碑文，之后三行为官员题名，之后十余行小字为信众题名，末行“大□□□四十四年六月十九日立”，可能也是康熙四十四年的碑记。

图 6 “大明天顺”题记红外影像（摄于 2014 年）

5 号碑保存完好，施工中发现碑阴也有字，便将其整体取出，立于台基前。据碑文记载，乾隆年间，寺内有山门、前殿、观音阁等建筑，因信众要在观音阁内诵经，空间不足，在僧会正亨等人主持下，在阁两侧扩建两廊，将阁内罗汉像移至两廊。然而，两廊尚未竣工，就在乾隆三十三年（1768 年）发生了火灾，左廊、前殿、山门烧毁。至乾隆三十四年（1769 年），因资金有限，只完成了观音阁、前殿的培修。碑阴还详细记录了捐资的组织和个人，捐资金额和工程实际花费，以及参与工程的梓匠和石匠。

6 号碑保存较好，立于嘉庆四年（1799 年）十月，碑文记载当时重修后“檐牙焕彩，基址重新”，参与工程的有石匠和瓦匠。

（三）题记

四川现存的元明清时期寺观殿宇，往往会在木构件上墨书题记，正梁（即脊枋）下书颂词，靠前的看梁（即与正脊平行的屋内额或金枋）下书纪年，其他梁下书施主姓名等。通过红外三维激光扫描发现了观音阁脊枋下的颂词题记。然而最可能有纪年题记的一根屋内额严重糟朽，被木夹板和铁箍加固，落架后我们小心地移除了木夹板，通过红外摄影发现了“大明天顺……鼎新立”的题记，印证了文献中天顺年重建的记载（图 6、图 7）。

（四）其他文字材料

左缝前穿插枋上钉有一块木牌，刻有陈家彩装“满堂仙童、金龙二条”的题记，立于嘉庆四年（1799 年）十二月。

在几根檐柱内，发现了搓成条用来嵌补裂缝的报纸，为 1945 年 5 月 21 日和 23 日的《新新新闻》。在雅安雨城区博物馆，找到了民国雅安县长徐思执题写的“古观音阁”匾，而徐思执 1946 年即调任荥经。可知观音阁在 1945 年进行了维修，并请徐思执题匾。

瓦件当中，有一种规格最小、最轻薄的小青瓦上，模印有“观音阁”三字，推测为民国时期的瓦件。

在现场发现的石碑、题记、木刻、报纸、匾额等文字材料，丰富了雅安观音阁的文献记载，为研究观音阁建筑的营建历史，以及雅安当地宗教、社会、经济等情况提供了宝贵资料。

四、建筑调查

（一）台基

在修缮前的勘查中，我们已注意到殿内石板铺地叠压在早期柱础上的情况。又通过文献资料，知道观音阁主殿两侧在明代就建有两厦，但地面现存的两侧耳房明显是更晚的遗存。这些问题，都须要借施工的时机，调查建筑台基

图 7 带题记构件测绘图

来寻求解答。

设计要求拆除两侧耳房，并将主殿滴水线以外的地面降低，因此利用两山外侧铺地石板揭开的时机，沿前檐柱轴线向外探掘，首先在距左前角柱约4米处发现一个柱础，又陆续在左山面外侧发现一列柱础，右山面外侧约4米处也发现一个柱础。柱础大都为素面覆盆式，盆唇直径240~420mm不等，仅左后角一个为覆莲式，盆唇直径300mm。这些柱础与此次拆掉的耳房柱网不同，推测即为正德年间增建的两厦遗址。这些柱础形制、规格不一，可能经过后期更换，说明建筑持续使用时间较长（图5）。

由于防雷工程埋设接地电极的需要，在观音阁两侧各挖掘了2条沟。从沟的断面上发现，在两山外侧1.9米处各有一道与山面平行的卵石砌体，基本位于下檐滴水线下方。推测这些卵石是正德增建两厦以前的台基边界，即碑记中“左右接旧基各翼一厦”的“旧基”。

施工中，还挖掘了现存的大部分柱础，拆砌了台基正面条石。然后发现，地基后半部为红砂石基岩，前半部为人工回填土，原有柱础均为古镜式，后半部的柱础基本保持原位，前檐的柱础则下沉前倾，历史维修中，在原柱础上叠压了圆盘形柱础，并重新铺砌石板地面，覆盖了原有柱础，该石板铺地高于台基阶条石，抵至栏杆背面。之后地基继续沉降，地面及建筑构架整体前倾，形成了残损现状（图8）。

图8 台基断面示意图

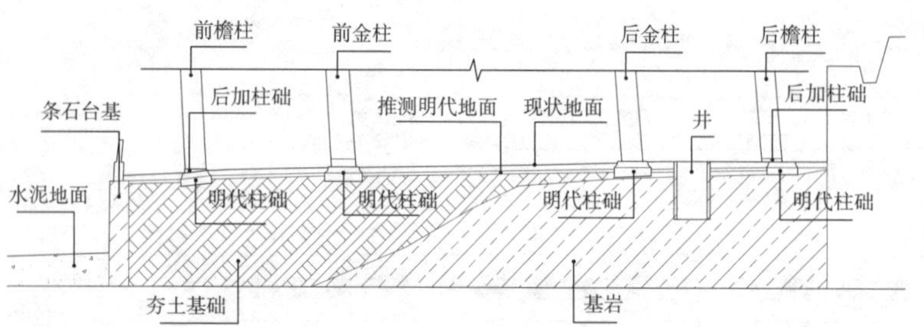

台基前的院落地面经后期抬升，西高东低，地表以上台基高度1.3米至1.7米不等，台基所嵌石碑底部被掩埋。根据挖出的5号碑的总高，及其上方阶条石的高度，可推算出被掩埋前的台基高2.1米。

（二）木构件材种鉴定

前期勘察阶段，我们在原构构件中采集了34个木材样本，由四川农业大学林学院做树种鉴定，样本包含柱、枋、梁、檩、垫板、斗栱等各类构件，试图了解观音阁中是否存在根据不同构件的受力特点选用不同木材的情况。经切片显微鉴定，这些木材样品全部为樟科楠属[⑤]。后来在修缮过程中，根据木材的宏观特征，也证实观音阁的原构构件全部为单一的楠木材种。同时也发现部分构件采用了杉木等其他木材，这些非楠木构件的榫卯做法、装饰做法、规格尺寸都与原构有差异，为后期更换构件，主要分布在后檐、翼角等部位，包括下檐后檐明间平身科斗栱、后檐右次间上额枋、上檐左前次间平板枋、上檐角科、上檐左后斜梁、所有大刀木和虾须、部分檩条、部分椽子等。

（三）大木节点构造

此次落架大修，有机会全面了解观音阁木结构内部构造。在观音阁中，水平构件与柱身相接，有透榫和半榫两类，安装时水平插入。透榫入榫处与构件等高，出榫则高度减半，因此又称大进小出榫。若无其他构件相碍，则减去上半，留下半（桃尖随梁与檐柱、小额枋与檐柱）；若同一高度有两根构件入柱，则一上一下（桃尖随梁与金柱、下层屋内额与金柱、小额枋与角柱、承椽枋与角瓜柱）；同一高度有三根构件的，则将构件高度三等分，45°方向构件留中间一份，另两构件各留上下一份（下檐桃尖梁与金柱）。还有的透榫在穿出柱子的出头上横开透眼，用木钉销住（下檐角梁与角瓜柱、脊枋与脊瓜柱）。半榫有两种情况：一种是两根水平构件相对入柱，在柱内会榫，一般与大进小出榫类似，只是榫头较短，在柱内上下搭接（承椽枋与檐瓜柱），只有下檐小额枋在山柱内会榫较特殊，在下出榫头下面伸出一段穿透柱子的榫舌，榫舌端部做成螳螂头状，相对的小额枋也在底面凿出相应的凹槽，但螳螂头两侧并未凸起卡在凹槽内，只是增加了摩擦面积（图9）；另一种是不起拉结作用的构件，只是简单的直榫，入柱少许（下槛、上槛、雀替、腰串、垫板）。

水平构件与柱头相接，有带袖肩燕尾榫和箍头榫两类，安装时从上落入。燕尾榫用于大额枋与檐柱和山柱、上额枋与上檐瓜柱、上层屋内额与金柱、金枋与金瓜柱、雀替丁头栱与金柱。箍头榫是榫身插入柱头，而榫头厚于榫身，箍住柱头无法水平移动，主要用于转角处，如大额枋与角柱、上额枋与角瓜柱、上檐斜桃尖梁与金柱等。此外五架梁、三架梁与柱交接也属于箍头榫，柱头开一字口，梁下半部按柱径宽度凿去两边，插入柱头，这种梁柱节点是四川地区元明时期建筑的普遍特点（图10）。

构件垂直叠摞主要有馒头榫、双榫、栽销三种方式。斗栱与柱头节点是在柱头上锯出方形馒头榫，榫头穿过平板枋，大斗底部凿海眼，套在馒头榫上。瓜柱与梁节点是在瓜柱底部按照梁的断面讨出弧线，中间开一字口让过角背，两侧出双榫，插入梁身开的两道槽内。其他水平构件叠摞都是采用栽销的方式，上下构件相对位置各凿不少于两个长方形小槽，插入木片销在一起，斗栱各层之间、檩条与垫板、角背与梁等部位都是如此。

水平构件对接，主要有燕尾榫、螳螂头榫、猪蹄叉三种形式。燕尾榫用于檩条对接和下檐平板枋对接，其中下檐平板枋每端同时做一阴一阳两个榫卯。螳螂头榫只用于上檐平板枋，而且是将榫头分作两半，中间让过柱头馒头榫，这种榫头过于纤细，此次修缮所见大都残损（图11）。猪蹄叉用于博风板的续接，只起拼接对位作用，不具有拉结作用。

水平构件十字搭交采用刻半榫，即两构件相交处分别刻去上半和下半，上下扣合在一起，用于平板枋、檩条转角处的搭交，以及斗栱构

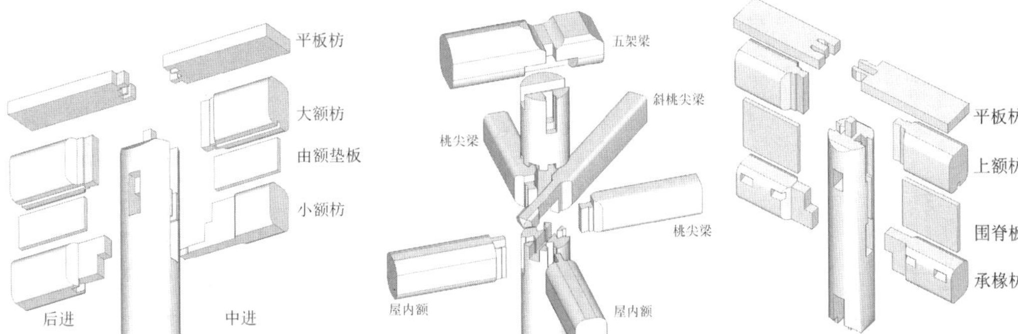

图9　左山后山柱柱头节点分解轴测图（左）
图10　左前金柱柱头节点分解轴测图（中）
图11　上檐柱柱头节点分解轴测图（右）

件交接等。其中斗栱出跳方向的构件都开口在下，并刻有子荫。

除榫卯结构外，铁钉也是传统木构建筑常用的连接、固定方式。观音阁中的传统铁钉均为方形断面。钉椽子用钉量最大，每椽 2 钉，钉长约 16 厘米。雀替尖端用钉一枚。隔架科雀替两端各用钉一枚，底部另有一钉孔，说明其下原来还有荷叶墩之类的构件。大刀木与角梁间，除木制千斤销外，也用粗大的铁钉，我们采集了一件样品，长 47cm，宽 3cm，厚 2cm，与 1984 年峨眉山飞来殿角梁上发现的带铭文“铁昂栓”应属同类构件[⑥]。升头木一端钉在角梁侧面，一端钉在檩条上。山花板钉在踏脚木与草架穿枋上。博风板钉在椽子外侧，与檩条端头无连接关系。虾须一端钉在挑檐桁，一端钉在大刀木上。吊檐板钉在椽飞头。

（四）墙体与门窗调查

观音阁原有墙体和门窗均已不存，仅存栱眼壁。根据柱子、小额枋、上槛等构件上残留的痕迹，可以推想出其始建状态及后期改易的情况。

栱眼壁为竹编壁做法，其骨架由竹篾编成，即《营造法式》中所谓“竹编道”，竹编道两面涂草拌泥，表面再抹灰。栱眼壁拆除后可见平板枋上有竹片压痕，正心枋及正心栱下有竹片尖戳痕，且只有这一次安装痕迹，也没有安装栱眼壁板的开槽，说明原构即为竹编壁做法。

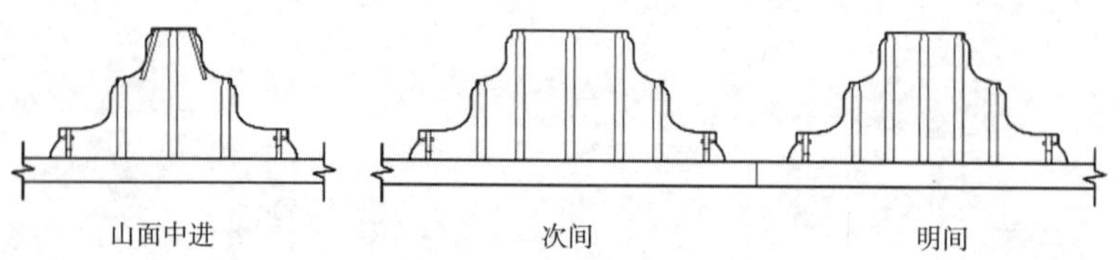

图 12　下檐栱眼壁经篾排布示意图

竹编道为纵经横纬，经篾宽 25~30mm，纬篾宽 10~15mm。根据攒当大小，每栱眼壁用经篾 3 或 5 根。正心瓜栱下、贴近大斗处则立竹管 1 根，竹管直径约 20mm，侧面开方孔，以竹钉穿过方孔钉在大斗上。由于栱眼壁边缘不规则，这些竖直的经篾还不足以固定纬篾的两端，因此还有斜向的辅助经篾，篾宽与纬篾相当。纬篾穿插编织于经篾之间（图 12）。

竹编道上抹草拌泥。上下檐的涂泥有明显差别，上檐含草秸很多，松散易碎，下檐则较坚实。由于上檐部分平板枋曾经更换过，所以一定有部分编壁也重新制作了，涂泥的差异可能就是这时形成的。竹编壁的抹灰面上曾写有文字，上檐为墨书，下檐为朱书，后被白灰覆盖。上檐前檐右次间原有一“啰”字，因观音阁像设主要依据《首楞严经》布置，推测原先上檐正面的 7 块栱眼壁中，除中间一块，其余写有《首楞严经》中的“悉怛多般怛啰”六字咒语。可惜调查人员注意到这一迹象时，大部分栱眼壁已被拆除，仅前檐下檐右次间清理出的“佛”字保存了下来。

在前后檐的次间和整个山面，都发现有编壁墙的痕迹。首先是小额枋底面，与平身科对应的位置，都有长约 20cm、宽约 4cm 的榫口，推测原有撑枋，竖立于小额枋和下槛之间，将开间分隔为 2 或 5 份。而且在柱子侧面的下槛与小额枋卯口之间，发现有一排槽口，其中前后檐槽口是圆形和狭长方形相间，山面则是方形和狭长方形相间，槽口间距约 30cm，狭长槽口长约 8cm，圆形和方形槽口宽约 4cm。推测这些槽口是安装竹编壁的经篾留下的，狭长槽口装竹片，圆形和方形槽口装圆竹，之后再编织竖向的纬篾（图 13、图 14）。这种只

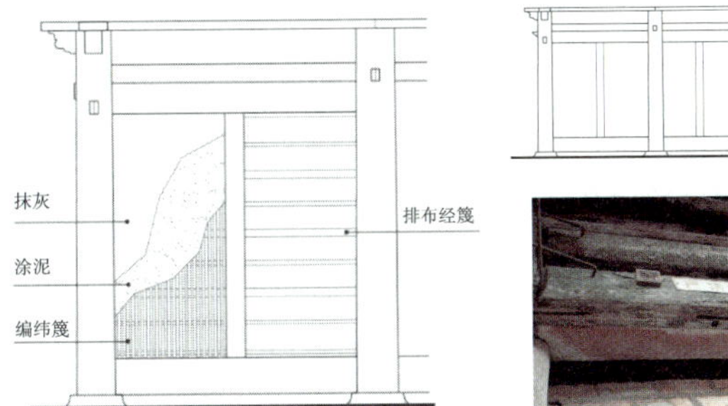

图 13 前檐次间编壁构造复原图（左）
图 14 山面编壁复原图（中上）
图 15 前檐次间小额枋底面痕迹（摄于 2012 年）（中下）
图 16 前檐次间后期改造复原图（右）

用撑枋分隔，四周没有另做木边框的编壁在四川其他元明时期建筑上较为常见，但内部竹编骨架的做法尚未见到相同的实例。四川目前通行的竹编做法与《营造法式》中的类似，大面积的编壁，一道经篾要用 3 片竹篾，而且没有用圆竹的，因此目前推测的观音阁编壁做法还需要其他实例验证。

两山面的编壁可能是在清乾隆年间拓建左右回廊，移出罗汉像时被拆除。前檐次间的编壁则经过后期的改造。前檐小额枋底面，除了安装小额枋的卯口外，还有一组痕迹，为一排 4 个狭长的凹槽，其中中间两个凹槽后面还有圆孔（图 15）。推测两边的凹槽安装过抱框，抱框之间连一道腰串，腰串上立两根撑枋，中间开窗，两侧为编壁，为清代常见做法（图 16）。

前后檐明间大额枋下均有上槛，上槛的底面、侧面有大量不同时期的卯口、钉孔等痕迹，目前尚无法确定各痕迹的形成过程，只能大概分辨出在较晚近的时期，前檐为三开六扇门，后檐为单开双扇门。

图 17 右后金柱编壁痕迹（摄于 2014 年）

殿内两根后金柱下部朝明间一侧有一宽 7.5cm、高 18cm、深 8cm 的榫口，下皮距柱底 80 多厘米，推测原安装有腰串。腰串与下层额串榫口之间，分布有圆形和长方形交替排列的槽口，圆槽口直径约 4cm，长方槽口宽约 2cm、高约 9cm，各槽口中心间距约 36cm，推测原为编壁墙（图 17）。从受力上来说，腰串下面应该还有支撑，但柱脚没有发现下槛痕迹，或许是柱脚曾被锯短，或许是腰串下以砖石砌筑的佛坛作为支撑。

（五）椽子调查分析

椽子是了解屋面做法变化的重要线索。雅安观音阁现存椽子断面为扁长方形，椽、飞之间残存望板，翼角平行布椽，板瓦冷摊铺在椽子之间。用料主要有明代原构的楠木椽和后期更换的杉木椽，还有少量用其他构件改做的椽子。我们测量了 5 根保存较好的原构椽子，其中 1、2 号为山面下檐椽，3~5 号为翼角椽。

1 号椽子，长 2985mm，厚 75~80mm，宽 115mm，椽尾砍为与承椽枋椽碗相应的梯形，根据椽尾形状可判断椽子原始的上下面。椽子上有 6 个贯穿上下面的钉孔，2 个位于椽尾（其中一个从椽尾锯开豁口，现场木工说这样可防止钉钉子时椽子劈裂），2 个位于正心桁位置，2 个位于挑檐桁位置，每处位置的 2 个钉孔钉入方向相反（图 18）。这些钉孔说明该椽子曾经上下翻面使用一次，翻面之后椽尾未插入椽碗，而是搭在承椽枋上，位置略向后错，因此翻面后的钉孔位置略靠前，加之翻面后椽头被锯成与地面垂直的斜面以钉吊檐板，出檐势必有所减小（图 19）。椽子上表面有 7 个、下表面有 10 个未穿透椽身的钉孔，应为钉飞子及望板的钉孔，这种钉孔绝大部分位于椽子前段，可能大多是钉飞子的，说明飞子更换过多次。

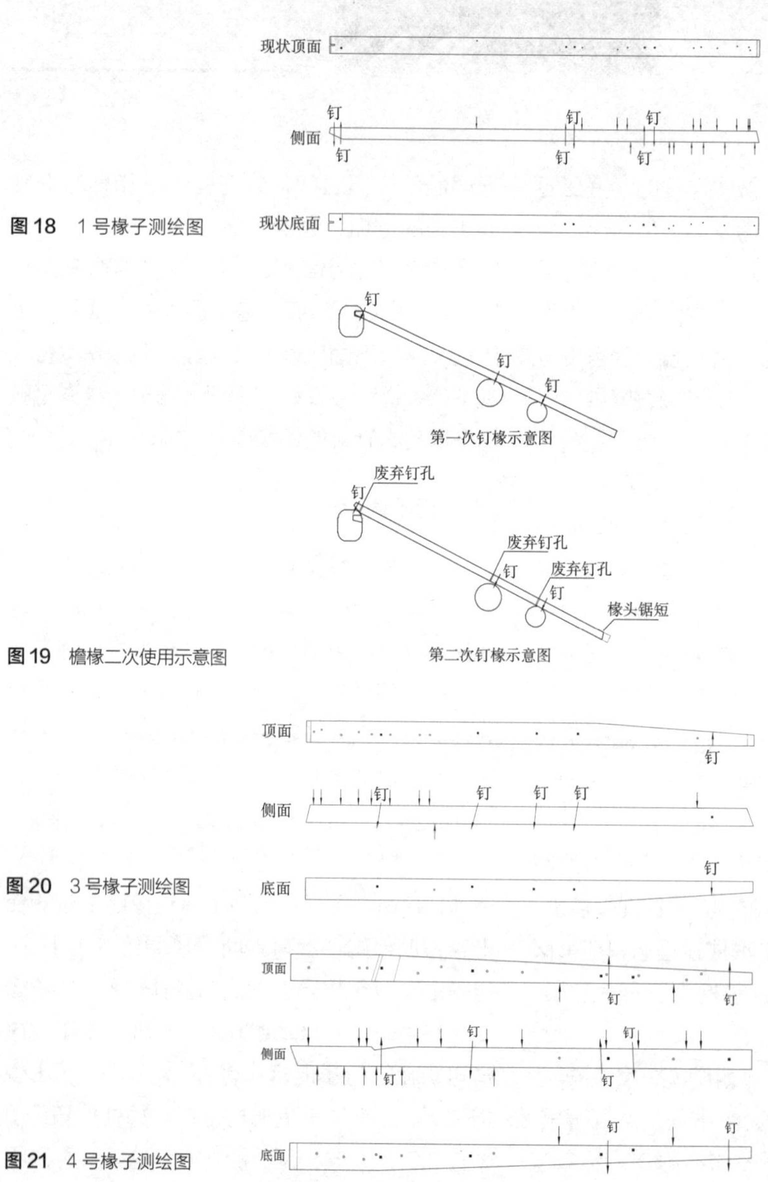

图 18 1 号椽子测绘图

图 19 檐椽二次使用示意图

图 20 3 号椽子测绘图

图 21 4 号椽子测绘图

2 号椽子，长 3035mm，厚 75~80mm，椽尾做法与 1 号椽子相同。椽子上有 6 个贯穿上下面的钉孔，1 个位于椽尾，2 个位于正心桁位置，2 个位于挑檐桁位置，1 个位于挑檐桁外。上表面有 5 个、下表面有 7 个未穿透椽身的钉孔。该椽子反映的信息与 1 号椽子基本一致。

3 号椽子，长 2410mm，厚 92mm，宽 112mm，椽后段逐渐收窄至 57mm。椽子上有 4 个贯穿上下面的钉孔，均为从上表面钉入，及 1 个贯穿侧面的钉孔，未穿透椽身的钉孔大都位于前段上表面（图 20）。推测 3 号椽子钉过两次。第一次是作为放射形布椽的翼角椽，1 枚钉子钉在正心桁上，1 枚钉子从侧面钉在其他翼角椽上。第二次是作为平行布椽的翼角椽，没有翻面，向前移动，1 枚钉子钉在正心桁上，1 枚钉在虾须上，并锯平了椽头。

4 号椽子，长 2065mm，厚 85mm，宽 115mm，椽后段逐渐收窄至 50mm，椽子上有 4 个贯穿上下面的钉孔，其中 2 个从上表面钉入，2 个从下表面钉入。侧面有 2 个贯穿的钉孔，及 2 个未穿透的钉孔（图 21）。可以判断 4 号椽子钉过两次。第一次是作为放射形布椽的翼角椽，2 枚钉子钉在正心桁和挑檐桁的升头木上，2 枚钉子从侧面钉在其他翼角椽上。第二次是作为平行布椽的翼角椽，上下翻面使用，1 枚钉子钉在正心桁上，1 枚钉子钉在虾须上，与虾须相交的位置挖了一道槽，并锯齐了椽头以钉吊檐板。

图 22 5 号椽子测绘图

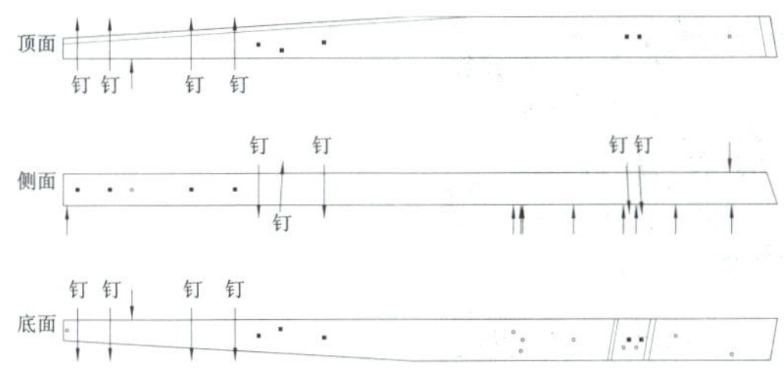

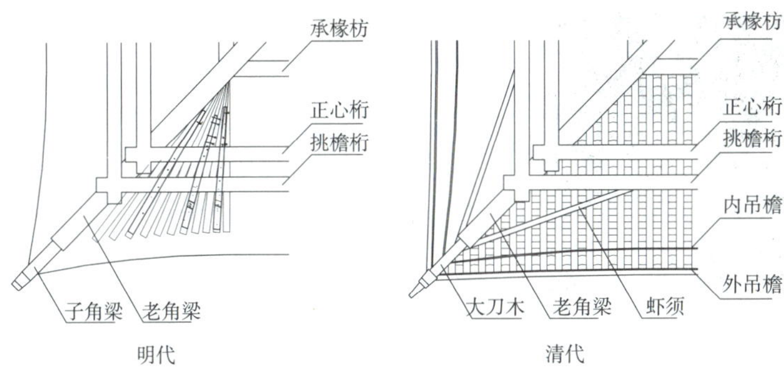

图 23 翼角椽构造变化示意图

5 号椽子，长 1970mm，厚 85mm，宽 112mm，椽后段逐渐收窄至 55mm，椽子上有 5 个贯穿上下面的钉孔和 4 个贯穿侧面的钉孔，椽子前段与虾须相交处开槽（图 22）。推测 5 号椽子钉过 3 次。第一次为放射形翼角椽，上下面钉 1 个钉子，侧面钉 4 个钉子。第二次为平行布椽的翼角椽，上下翻面，用 2 个钉子钉在桁条和虾须上。第三次向翼角端头平移，椽子略向下移动，用 2 个钉子钉在桁条和虾须上。

图 24 观音阁部分瓦件（摄于 2012、2014 年）

龙纹勾头

与天无极勾头

凤纹滴水

观音阁铭文瓦

这几根翼角椽的发现，证明雅安观音阁翼角曾经为放射形布椽，椽子上必须钉望板，望板上再铺瓦，瓦垄和椽子不会一一对应。后期重修中，翼角变为平行布椽，檐椽从承椽枋椽椀中抽出，缩小椽间距后，钉在承椽枋上，铺瓦方式改为椽子上直接铺望瓦或板瓦，瓦垄和椽子一一对应（图 23）。

（六）瓦件调查

此次修缮前，观音阁的屋面上檐前后坡为筒瓦屋面，上檐两山及下檐为板瓦屋面，上下檐翼角都存少量筒瓦。筒瓦长 305mm（不含瓦脖），宽 155mm，高 80mm，厚 20mm，重 2.6kg，瓦内残留的灰为石灰掺碎瓦片。板瓦有多种规格，最大的长 330mm，大头宽 240mm、厚 22mm，小头宽 210mm、厚 20mm，重 3.6kg。其次长 305mm，大头宽 230mm、厚 17mm，小头宽 190mm、厚 15mm，重 2.1kg。还有长 280mm、240mm、200mm 的，更为轻薄。其中部分 200mm 的小青瓦上戳印有“观音阁”字样。檐口保存有多种勾滴瓦，其中绝大部分是龙纹勾头配凤纹滴水，瓦质坚厚，勾头瓦上有瓦钉。其次是仿汉“与天无极”勾头瓦，仅分布于翼角处且翼角处皆为此种勾头，瓦质极轻薄。“与天无极”勾头有意识地复古，“观音阁”铭文瓦有意识地记录，同时两者是所有瓦件中规格最小最轻薄的，很可能是已有初步保护古物观念的民国时期所造（图 24）。

（七）特殊现象分析

调查发现，观音阁木作存在错活及做法不统一的情况。如大小额枋、平板枋等构件交

图 25 下檐左后角构件叠压关系（摄于 2014 年）（左）

图 26 下檐右后角构件叠压关系（摄于 2014 年）（右）

图 27 左后角科错活（摄于 2014 年）（左）

图 28 右后角科错活（摄于 2014 年）（右）

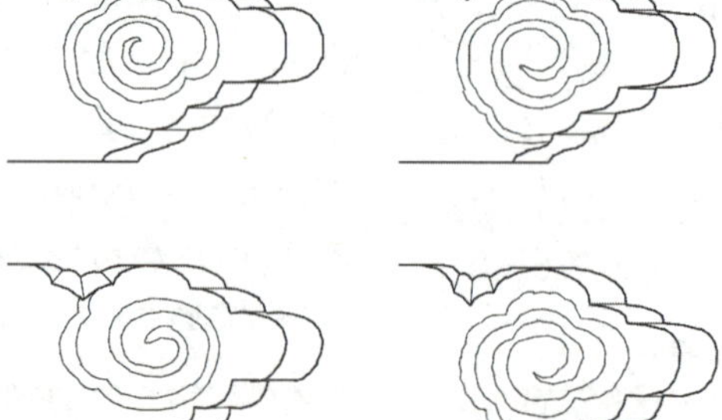

图 29 麻叶头的 4 种样式

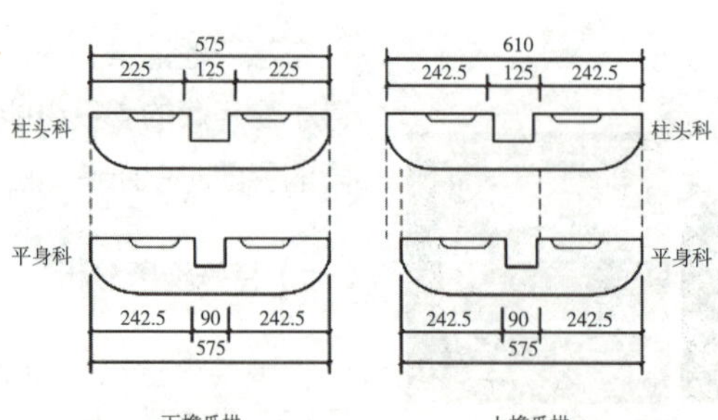

图 30 上下檐瓜栱长度比较图

角处的叠压顺序，按官式做法的规矩，应该山面构件压在檐面构件上，但观音阁全不按此规矩，甚至下檐左后角和右后角的小额枋的叠压顺序相反，这可能是由于加工角柱时误将两根角柱的开口做成了完全一样的，而非对称的（图 25、图 26）。

下檐角科斗栱存在两处错活。一是左后角科外拽万栱的栱眼刻到了栱身内侧，二是右后角科外拽万栱上的角昂开口处有两道方向错误的锯痕，但后来还是改正了（图 27、图 28）。角科构件的叠放次序也有错乱，大部分构件为正压闹，但也有闹压正的情况。

三幅云、麻叶头等带雕饰构件，纹样有细微差别，下檐斗栱的麻叶头有 4 种类型，里三幅云有 3 种类型，外三幅云有 4 种类型，不同类型在空间分布上无任何规律，很可能是不同工匠的个人差异（图 29）。

这些现象说明天顺重建观音阁的施工组织可能不太严密，各工匠之间缺乏统一标准，且容易出现错活。

此外，上下檐构件之间存在一些外观不易察觉的差异。①平板枋榫卯不同。下檐用阴阳燕尾榫，上檐用螳螂头榫。②栱眼壁抹泥配比不同。下檐抹泥掺有较多麻刀，而上檐抹泥掺有大量草秸。③斗栱横栱长度算法不同。下檐柱头科与平身科横栱总长度相等，上檐柱头科与平身科横栱自昂侧面伸出长度相等（图 30）。这些差异已不能用一支施工队中的个人差异来解释，可能存在时代差异，结合文献综合考虑，上檐的部分结构可能是正德年间才建造的。

观音阁上额枋的霸王拳上都有一块缺口，据平武报恩寺万佛阁的同类做法，这种缺口是为围脊合角吻所留，说明观音阁原有脊饰为官

图 31 观音阁上额枋霸王拳缺口（摄于 2014 年）（左上）

图 32 平武报恩寺万佛阁上额枋与合角吻（摄于 2010 年）（左下）

图 33 右缝前檐柱彩画（摄于 2014 年）（右）

式风格的烧制脊（图 31、图 32）。

五、建筑装饰与陈设

雅安观音阁原有宗教功能早已改变，殿内陈设、塑像已全部不存。此次调查，还发现了部分彩画、塑像的痕迹，结合文献记载，可以部分还原观音阁的建筑装饰与陈设。

（一）彩画痕迹

部分檐柱的室内一侧发现了明代缠枝西番莲彩画，以右缝前檐柱保存最好，铲除后期漆皮后，露出明代彩画，彩画直接绘制在木材表面，用黑白两色勾画轮廓，后期被土红灰覆盖（图 33）。右山上檐围脊板和瓜柱上局部残存彩画痕迹，轮廓线略凸起于木材表面，似为沥粉。少数斗栱残存青绿彩画痕迹。平板枋、大额枋、金柱上段、上檐穿插枋等构件也残留有彩画线条轮廓。

（二）像设痕迹

雅安观音阁内现已无任何像设，但在构件上发现众多与像设相关的痕迹，结合文献记载及佛教经典，可以大致推想出观音阁的像设情况。

据历代碑记，天顺年间重建观音阁时“中塑观音佛像，列立二十四天神，即坐二十五圆通阿罗汉，维饬四壁之上有诸天二十四。殿之中甃石为炉，绕金龙，左右钟鼓。后壁立塑南海救苦大士，下以寒泉之出，遂成一井，名曰龙井。”正德年间“左右接旧基各翼一厦，以寓钟鼓”。清乾隆年间“开拓阁之左右，翼以回廊，移阿罗汉趺坐其中”。嘉庆四年彩装“满堂仙童、金龙二条”。

其中“二十五圆通”出自《楞严经》，佛祖开导阿难，让座下的菩萨、罗汉们介绍自己修行成就的法门（即圆通），有二十五位罗汉、菩萨依次讲述了自己的圆通。《楞严经》第五章为前二十四圆通，第二十五圆通单独占第六章，是观世音菩萨讲述其耳根圆通，并呈现出千手千眼的妙容⑦。

据此经典，观音阁内主尊当为千手观音像，其余的二十四位菩萨及罗汉列坐两侧。主尊的位置可以从室内地面铺装推测，明间的前半部分地面铺砌规整，由条石板围成框，框内用方石板斜铺。框的后端正中有一块较大的整石板，应为礼拜处，从这里再往后 3 排条石板，铺地就渐渐不规整了，其中还有椀花结带浮雕的须弥座束腰残石嵌在地里，说明后部的这一区域是原来佛坛所在位置，佛坛形式应为石砌须弥座。主尊的样式可能与平武报恩寺大悲殿内的千手观音立像接近。其余的二十四圆通坐像，

图 34 左山中进额枋悬塑痕迹（上）

图 35 前檐明间平板枋与大额枋悬塑痕迹（下）

图 36 右山后桃尖随梁上痕迹（摄于 2014 年）

于清乾隆年间移至两廊，已无迹可寻。二十四天神立像也没有留下任何痕迹，如果殿内两侧同时布置二十四圆通和二十四天神，估计塑像的体量应小于真人尺度。

四壁上塑二十四诸天、前金柱塑盘龙、梁架上塑仙童是四川明代寺院常见的布置，在许多木构件上都发现了相关的痕迹。

在大小额枋朝向室内的一侧，可发现一些浅色印痕，在红外摄影下更为清晰，印痕形状不甚规则，纵跨大小额枋，有些能分辨出带有弯曲向上的飘带形痕迹，这些印痕是没有被深色油漆覆盖的，其分布也很规律，次间每套额枋有 2 块，山面中进则有 5 块，位置都对应着斗栱之间的空隙，这样的痕迹共 26 块。这些印痕之间，还有一些纵长方形的小块印痕（图 34）。印痕以外的深色区域还发现有云纹彩绘痕迹。可以推测这些印痕即文献中的“四壁之上有诸天二十四”的悬塑痕迹，弯曲向上的飘带形痕迹是彩云的尾部，塑像为立于彩云上降下的姿态，大小额枋上还绘满了祥云背景，长方形印痕则是榜题痕迹，一般会写明捐资塑像的人名、祈愿及塑像的内容。然而，痕迹的数量有 26 个，可能是其他眷属、部众或童子之类。悬塑的固定，未发现在木构件上插木桩的痕迹，可能采用了铁链拉结的方式。

在前檐明间平板枋上表面，殿内一侧 5 个攒当处，都发现有 2 个并列的方形榫洞，榫口边长约 3cm，深约 4cm，间距约 7cm，有的洞内还有残留的木桩，大额枋的相应位置上，有 5 处浅色印痕，其中第 2 和第 4 印痕处还有一方形榫洞（图 35）。可以推测这些也是悬塑痕迹，这 5 尊塑像与之前的 26 尊不同，应该是通过平板枋上的木桩来固定的，由于明间没有小额枋，像的位置也会略偏高，尺度可能更小。悬塑的题材已不可考，可能也是眷属、部众或童子之类。

观音阁的 4 根顺桃尖随梁枋上，都发现了 2 个并列的方形榫洞，榫口长 6cm，宽 4cm，间距 6cm，榫洞位于随梁枋上表面中央偏中

图 37 右缝下层屋内额悬塑痕迹

进一侧，同侧枋侧面有飘带形彩绘，其中右山后随梁枋对侧发现钉有一个铁环（图 36）。可以推测这是 4 尊童子悬塑，童子足部通过木桩固定在随梁枋上，身体略向前倾，背部通过铁链拉结到随梁枋后面，肩披天衣垂至随梁枋上用彩绘形式表现。

左右缝金柱之间的下层屋内额上，靠明间一侧的中央偏下处有一矩形榫洞，榫洞周围有浅色印痕，应该也是悬塑留下的痕迹（图 37）。在后金柱间的下层屋内额背面、部分大额枋的外侧，也有类似的矩形榫洞，但并未发现有印痕，其位置或在较隐蔽处，或在室外，并不适合安装悬塑，这些榫洞的用途尚不明确。

图 38 左前金柱盘龙痕迹（摄于 2014 年）

在 2 根前金柱上则留有明显的盘龙印痕及木桩榫口（图 38）。根据四川地区其他实例，龙头应朝向殿内主尊的方向。结合现存痕迹，我们推测龙的姿态为，龙头向殿内主尊方向，身体先向后上盘绕至随梁枋高度与金柱接触，接着向下弯折又转而向上，向前经挑尖梁与随梁枋之间绕过金柱盘旋向上，尾部达到下层屋内额的高度。

“殿之中甃石为炉”指殿内正中有石砌香炉，这是四川明代寺院常见配置，现存有不少实例。香炉一般平面呈方形或圆形有多层带雕饰的石构件累砌而成。

后壁立塑南海观音应与新津观音寺观音殿后壁悬塑类似，以大海为背景，海中伸出鳌头，观音立于鳌头上。雅安观音阁的南海观音像下面还有一口水井，这种配置在四川也较流行，信众往往将井水奉为可以治病的神水。

根据以上文献、实例及遗存痕迹，我们尝试还原了在观音阁殿内礼拜位置所能看到的像设场景图。殿内主尊为千手观音像，立于须弥座佛坛上，观音前有石砌香炉。殿两侧靠墙有两排佛坛，下层为二十四圆通坐像，上层为二十四天神立像。四周额枋上有悬塑二十四诸天。桃尖随梁、屋内额等处还有悬塑的童子等（图 39）。

六、修建历史还原

通过现场调查发现的遗迹遗痕，结合文献记载，我们尝试还原了雅安观音阁营建、维修、改造的过程。

至迟在明洪武十七年（1384 年），雅安城南月心山下已经修建有一座观音阁，阁内有一口泉眼。至明天顺元年（1457 年），原有建筑已残损严重，住持妙能决定重建观音阁，和徒弟圆正远赴建昌卫（今西昌市）一带募集资金，又在雅州正千户刘通的支持下，召集众多工匠重建观音阁。此次营建，采用楠木建造，观音阁只有主殿三间，台基两侧边缘至主殿两山檐下为止。主体结构外观形制上为四川地区明代中期的典型样式，大木作加工上没有形成

图 39 雅安观音阁像设复原示意图

完备的规矩，构件的位置与搭交顺序间关系不固定，雕饰性构件在大体样式的框架下存在不同工匠的个人发挥。殿内依据《首楞严经》以千手观音为主尊，配以二十五圆通，又塑有南海观音、二十四诸天、盘龙、仙童等像，布置有香炉、钟、鼓等陈设，南海观音像前还依泉眼凿成井，这些像设几乎充满了室内空间，只留下狭小的礼拜空间。天顺五年（1461 年），妙能圆寂，观音阁工程停滞，上檐的部分结构及屋顶可能暂时采用了较简陋的做法（如茅草屋面、树皮屋面等）。

五十三年后的正德八年（1513 年），圆正遇到山西商人贾钺资助，继续完善观音阁工程，上檐结构及瓦屋面得以完工，同时还拓宽了台基两侧，加建了两厦，并将殿内钟鼓移入两厦。这时的建筑工艺在平板枋的榫卯、斗栱栱长的确定等方面与天顺年间的营建有所差异。此次工程于明正德九年（1514 年）竣工，这时的观音阁，老角梁上出子角梁，翼角放射形布椽，椽上满铺望板，素筒瓦屋面，围脊用合角吻，梁柱斗栱遍施无地仗彩画，墙体采用无边框的竹编抹泥墙。

康熙四十四年（1705 年），僧人了悟重修观音阁，知州刘启和立碑。此次重修是明末清初长期战乱后的第一次维修，可能是一次规模较大的工程，明清之间的重大改变可能此时已经发生。木料不再使用楠木，而是采用柏木、杉木等木材。建筑的屋面全部更换，子角梁改为大刀木，并增加了虾须，椽子从承椽枋的椽碗中抽出，翻面使用，椽间距缩小，翼角椽改为平行布椽，椽子上直接铺瓦。

乾隆年间，随着佛教进一步世俗化，观音阁的使用功能除了单纯礼拜塑像外，还增加了信众集体诵经的需求，此时明代加建的两厦已不存。乾隆三十三年（1768 年），住僧与信众在观音阁两侧加建两廊，并将殿内罗汉像移至两廊，以使正殿宽敞，室内打通为五间，原山面编壁墙被拆除。然而尚未完工就发生了火灾，左廊、前殿、山门被烧毁，住持远赴打箭炉（今康定）募化资金，只修复了上殿（即观音阁）和前殿，山门、左廊尚未修复。

嘉庆四年（1799 年）又有一次维修，工程至少包括石作、瓦作及塑像的彩装。现存石砌台基中所嵌碑记，年代最晚的即嘉庆四年，因此台基可能就是此次重砌的。原有柱础沉降后用石盘垫高，应不晚于此次维修。

民国三十四年（1945 年），观音阁作为古迹得到维修，由县长徐思执题写了“古观音阁”匾额。修缮中使用的瓦件，戳印有“观音阁”铭文，翼角是修缮的重点部位，翼角勾头瓦全部更换为仿汉代瓦当样式的瓦件。维修中还用当时最常见的报纸《新新新闻》搓成纸条，用来嵌补柱子的裂缝。

新中国成立后，观音阁改为商业局车队，

原山门位置修建了木结构仓库，前殿位置被填平，使院落地面整体抬高，将观音阁台基底部埋入地下。20 世纪 80 年代，观音阁尚保存较完好。1993 年，李直祥先生绘制了一套测绘图，是观音阁现存最早的测绘资料。2002 年，观音阁屋面垮塌，严重倾斜，雅安市博物馆进行了临时支护。2014 年 3 月，雅安观音阁开始落架大修。2015 年 2 月，文物本体保护、防雷、消防工程全部竣工。

七、结语

雅安观音阁 2014 年的落架大修工程，是一次难得的机会，使我们能够较全面地调查其建筑内部构造和遗留下来的历史痕迹。调查的方法首先是通过拆解、挖掘、清理，使遗物遗迹暴露出来，再经过观察，用测绘、影像、文字等形式记录下来，最后综合所有的记录信息，分析得出结论，部分还原出观音阁在各历史时期的营建过程。这些历史信息在修缮工程中会大量损失，因此翔实的调查记录是迫切的和必须的，在此，特别感谢业主单位雅安市博物馆及施工单位泉州刺桐古建公司的理解、支持和帮助，使雅安观音阁在众多同类古建筑中受到特别的对待，让我们能够在施工中持续的调查研究。

注释：

① （乾隆）雅州府志 // 中国地方志集成四川府县志辑第 63 册 [Z]. 成都：巴蜀书社，1992.

② 大刀木是四川古建筑翼角起戗的木构件。

③ 虾须是为了承托平行排布的翼角椽，而在挑檐檩与大刀木之间钉的呈现翼角曲线的木构件。

④ 挂枋是四川穿斗式建筑中，檩条下方拉结柱头的构件。

⑤ 齐锦秋，肖辉 . 木材树种鉴定结论报告 [R]. 雅安：四川农业大学林学院，2012. 所有样品均具有以下微观特征：“散孔材；导管横切面为圆形及卵圆形，单管孔及短径复管孔（通常 2~3 个）；轴向薄壁组织环管状，或似翼状；油细胞或黏液细胞甚多；具分割木纤维。木射线非叠生。单列射线较少，多列射线通常有 2~3 个细胞；射线组织异性 Ⅱ 及 Ⅲ 型。射线细胞内树胶丰富，油细胞或黏液细胞数多。胞间道缺如。”

⑥ 魏奕雄 . 峨眉山飞来殿 [J]. 中共乐山市委党校学报，2011，135（2）：96.

⑦ （唐）般刺密谛 译 . 大佛顶如来密因修证了义诸菩萨万行首楞严经 [Z]. 大正新修大藏经第十九册 . 台北：新文丰出版公司，1972. 卷六，“其中或现一首三首五首七首九首十一首，如是乃至一百八首，千首万首，八万四千烁迦罗首。二臂四臂六臂八臂十臂十二臂，十四十六十八二十至二十四，如是乃至一百八臂，千臂万臂，八万四千母陀罗臂。二目三目四目九目，如是乃至一百八目，千目万目，八万四千清净宝目。或慈或威，或定或慧，救护众生，得大自在。”

不识不用：
石灰砌砖古法之洞察

Unknown，Unloved：
Insights in the Historic Use of Lime Mortar in Brickwork

Koenraad VAN BALEN

摘要：建筑考古为研究人员和遗产专家提供了可能对当今社会有益的启示。在中国和欧洲，建筑考古在砖石结构中的应用使我们面临新的挑战。历史文献记载已经了这类砌体结构的耐久性。

长期以来的现代建筑技术，特别是硅酸盐水泥和混凝土的发展，使建筑和文物部门的技术人员对石灰砂浆的具体做法及其对建筑长久寿命所做出的贡献视而不见。在“坚固”（维特鲁维的建筑三要素之一，公元前 1 世纪）中所表达的强度和刚度被理解为确保一个稳定、有力和坚固的结构。在 20 世纪，强度和刚度仍旧指导着工程师和建筑师的培养，并导致了硅酸盐水泥和混凝土的使用。这些强度和刚度原则是现代范式下的工程学基础，但在研究古代砌体结构上，它们导致建筑工程技术人员的“短视”。

用石灰浆体砌筑的大量优秀历史砌体通常呈现良好的耐久性，本研究源于对这一现象的思考与疑问。研究结果显示，石灰浆体的所谓“弱点”反而解释了它所粘含的砌体结构的耐久性。这一研究成果不仅有助于保护历史建筑，而且还有助于改进新的砖石建筑技术。历史证据以及所取得的科学知识证明了传统技术和工艺的重要性。它增加了更多的理由来保护砖石砌体遗产，不仅因为它的外观和相关的遗产价值，还有对深嵌在历史砖石砌体中的“无形”遗产的尊重。

关键词：石灰砂浆；砖砌体；预防性保护

作者简介：
Koenraad.VAN BALEN，University of Leuven（KU Leuven），Civil Engineering Department；director of the Raymond Lemaire International Centre for Conservation，PRECO-M_3OS UNESCO chair.

Abstract：Building archaeology informs researchers and heritage specialists with insights that society today may benefit from. In the Chinese and European contexts，building archaeology confronts us with unforeseen properties of brick masonry structures. Documentation and studies of those structures evidence their longevity and durability. Historic and technical insights in traditional brick and masonry construction shed light on characteristics and properties of bricks and mortar that explain such durability.

For a long time modern construction technology，particularly the development of Portland Cement and concrete，has blinded technicians in the construction and heritage sector to understand the particular behaviour of lime mortar and its contribution to longevity of structures made of it. Strength and stiffness as expressed in *firmitas*（one of the three components of architecture according to Vitruvius，1st century B.C.）was understood to guarantee a stable，strong and firm (masonry) construction. Strength and stiffness have guided the education of engineers and architects still in the 20th century and led to the use of Portland Cement and concrete. The principles that are the basis of the modern paradigm explains the 'short-sightedness' of construction technicians in understanding historic masonry.

Research started with questioning the obvious durability of often remarkable historic masonry structures made with lime mortar. It has revealed that the so called 'weakness' of lime mortar explains the durability of masonry made with it. The insights gained are not only valuable for the preservation of historic fabric but have also helped to improve the technology for new masonry structures. The historical evidences as well as the gained scientific knowledge demonstrate the importance of traditional technologies and craftsmanship. It adds more arguments to preserve brick masonry heritage not only for its appearance and the related heritage values, but also for valuing the 'intangible' heritage that is embedded in historic brick masonry.

Keywords: Lime mortar; Brick masonry; Preventive conservation

Introduction

Building archaeology confronts researchers and heritage specialists with insights that present society may benefit from. Both in Chinese and European contexts, building archaeology confronts the professionals with unforeseen properties of brick masonry structures. Documentation and studies of those structures show evidence of their longevity and durability. Historic and technical insights in traditional brick and masonry construction shed light on characteristics and properties of bricks and mortar that explain such durability. Those insight are valuable for the preservation of heritage as well as for the development of novel sustainable construction methods.

At first this contribution will explain the context that allowed the development of brick masonry and mortar technology in Belgium. In the second part novel insights are developed on the behaviour of masonry with the understanding of the contribution of lime mortar. The insights have been inspired by the respectful understanding of the behaviour of long lasting brick structures. They help not only to value and preserve brick masonry heritage but also help to critically review today's models used to explain the mechanical behaviour of brick masonry. Finally an integrated and preventive approach to the preservation of historic brick masonry is proposed.

The Making of Brickwork in Ancient Time: bricks, mortars; evidenced durability

As Belgium has been part of the Roman Empire (27 B.C.-395 A.D.), Roman civilisation had an influence on the way its society was organised. As an example, the impact of Roman Law on the way legislation is being conceived and developed in Western Europa, can be referred to. Similarly this civilisation contributed to the development of local and adapted construction technologies. This is the case for brick masonry, which required technology for the production and use of bricks and lime mortar.

Roman construction technology is well documented. One of the major sources of information are the *Ten Books on Architecture* by the Roman architect and engineer Marcus Vitruvius Pollio (c. 80-70 B.C. to 15 B.C.).[1] In those books Vitruvius refers to the three essential components of architectural values: *utilitas* (function), *firmitas* (strength) and *venustas* (beauty). The books also contain a vast amount of information on building materials, construction technology and design, amongst others on brick masonry. In the 15th century, humanists rediscovered Vitruvius' writings, which influenced the architectural treatises of Renaissance architects such as Leon Battista Alberti (1404-1472).

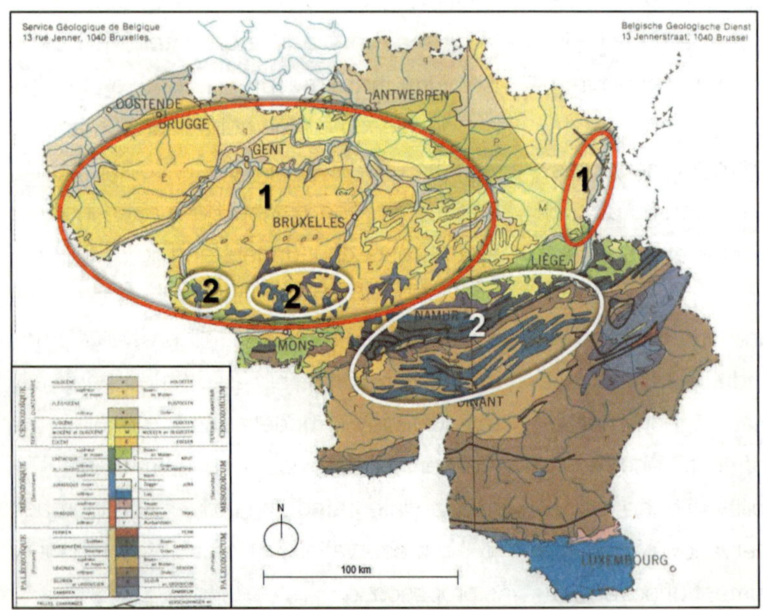

Fig.1 Geological map of Belgium locating the regions with (1) high concentration of clay, (2) limestone extraction for lime production [© Geological Survey of Belgium].

Since Roman times in Western Europe vast constructions as churches, abbeys, castles and palaces, both in rural and urban contexts, were constructed with bricks and lime mortar. This technology developed alongside half-timber construction in the majority of the rural areas. A consequence of urbanisation in the Low Countries was the use of appropriate building materials. Rural timber frame constructions using thatched roofs and timber, when placed alongside in streets, created a risk for fire. As early as from the 13th century, urban regulations on fire pushed the conversion of thatched roofs and timber walls towards more fire resistant materials as bricks and stone masonry, and roofs covered with slates and tiles. This transformation gradually lead to an overall 'petrification' of architecture in towns and later in rural environment too.

The geological context in Belgium provided the necessary resources for construction materials in that transition. The geological conditions provided clay for bricks and tiles, stone and lime stone for the production of lime and later Portland cement [Fig. 1]. As the underground provided the raw materials for the production of brick and lime for mortar, both industrial activities developed a strong tradition in Belgium. Even today, the roots of several international companies go back to the 19th-century industrial revolution. Before the industrialisation, the production was local, thus more decentralised and depending on the availability of local materials and fuel.

A continuous variation of raw materials based on a gradation of clay versus limestone fraction leads to a continuity of 'industrial' products going from ceramics until lime [Fig. 2]. Each of those 'mixed' raw materials would require different firing and other production techniques to produce the related industrial products. Within this scheme, the production of bricks and binders can be positioned requiring different clay versus limestone fractions. Improving firing technologies — kiln construction, control of firing temperature, availability of fuel, etc. — was required in order to be able to increase temperatures and allow the production of special ceramics as well as hydraulic binders like Portland cement. At lower temperatures, however, hydraulic binders were produced using 'natural' materials as *pozzolana* or crushed bricks. Mixed with lime, it allowed to make water-resistant constructions ad could harden under water, thus using hydraulic binders.

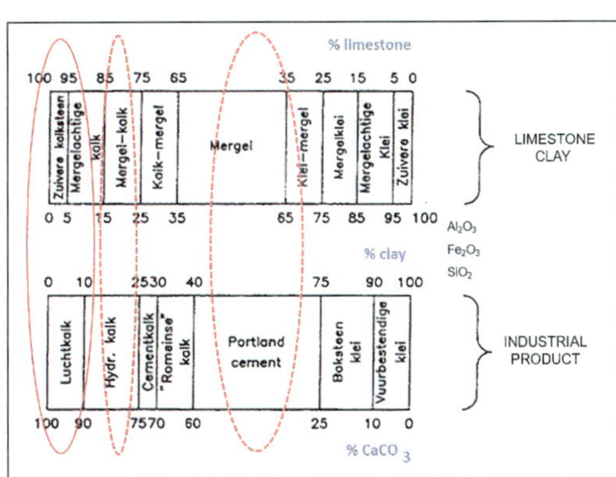

Fig.2 Lime-Clay / Industrial Products, binders on a row (from lime to clay), a continuum with increasing hydraulicity that drops again at the end. Each type of binder with specific raw materials is produced according to specific process (a.o. T°) [adapted from: K. Van Balen, *Karbonatatie van kalkmortel en haar invloed op het gedrag van historisch metselwerk* (*Carbonation of lime mortar and its influence on the behaviour of historical masonry*), doctoral dissertation, University of Leuven, Faculty of Engineering Science, 1991].

Historic understanding of lime mortar

Until the 19th century the possibility to increase temperature in local kilns and later in industrial kilns was a driving force in the production of binders and bricks. The required temperatures for brick and lime production were rather similar, what allowed to produce lime mortar and bricks when craftsmanship, raw materials and fuel were locally available. Quality control on the selection of raw materials was often based on a direct appreciation

Fig.3 Composition of lime mortar by Vitruvius (1st century B.C.) [© K. Van Balen, 1991].

Overview of mortars (Vitruvius, 1st century B.C.)		
binder	aggregate	water
1 part (vol.)	3 parts quarry sand	15% – 20 %
1 part (vol.)	2 parts river sand	15% – 20 %
1 part (vol.)	2 parts river sand + 1 part crushed bricks (tiles)	15% – 20 %
1 part (vol.)	2 parts of *pozzolana*	15% – 20 %

of the materials on the final product. However, this allowed variations that are difficult to understand from a today's scientific point of view. Within certain margins the 'pollution' of lime stone by clayish components (AlO, FeO, SiO, etc.) would not have a negative impact on the properties of the lime produced from it. Today's chemical analysis based on cement technologies, however, often wrongly attribute some of those components to the presence of cement.

The design of mortar for various types of application depended on the way the lime was slaked, how the sand was mixed up with the lime: from dry to 'wet' applications. Aside of that, the type of sand and their grain size distribution defined the use and also the mixing proportions: sand from quarries or from river. Yet a lot of that knowledge was available in Roman time as evidenced by Vitruvius [Fig. 3] and the descriptions of Cato the Elder (234-149 B.C.) on the best location for constructing a lime kiln [Fig. 4].

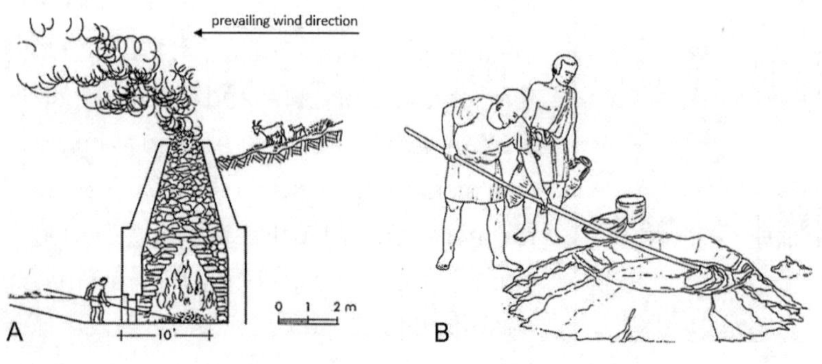

Fig.4 Roman techniques: (A) lime kiln according to the description of Cato the Elder; (B) mixing lime mortar [© J.-P. Adam, *La construction romaine*, Paris: Picard, 1984].

Lime mortar technology

Both historical sources and (building) archaeological evidences have contributed to the understanding of the production processes of lime for construction. The survival of many historic buildings proves to today's society the durability and behaviour of brickwork made with lime mortar. It is remarkable how in the early 21st century, after two centuries of technological development allowed to create large kilns able to heat materials up to 1500℃, lime mortar still remains unknown and unloved by architects and engineers. It seems that modernity had shifted the proof of concept from empirical evidence towards laboratory evidence up to the point that architects and engineers got blinded for the durability proven by history in the real world.

Lacking the models to understand the behaviour of ancient masonry, modernity promoted the development of concrete and the cement lobby pushed the professional world towards the use of cement and the replacement of lime mortar by cement mortar. After several decades, this choice proved not always to be more durable [Fig. 5].

Fig.5 Leuven, Great Beguinage, 17th-century houses. Left: example of well-preserved historic brick masonry. Right: example of integration of new architecture in historical context. Restored masonry with lime mortar pointing [© K. Van Balen].

Reviewing the Behaviour of Lime Mortar

It is important to notice that 'modern' perception by engineers and architects is based on the 'paradigm' that strong materials are required for making strong masonry. Such perception has complicated the understanding on how historical construction materials can contribute to strength and durability. This paradigm along with the reliability on the proof of concept in laboratories only — which on itself has no demonstrative history — , has led to the gradual replacement of lime based mortars by cement mortars. The latter were perceived as stronger and more tested in laboratories, thus better. Practice has shown that in many cases cement mortars compared to lime-based mortars had lower durability and that their resilience to deformation, for instance, is much less.

The lime mortar research carried out at the University of Leuven, Raymond Lemaire International Centre for Conservation (RLICC) and the Civil Engineering Department, was based on a respectful understanding of the behaviour of historic structures. How understand the durability of historic structures that could not be explained by so-far known (mechanical) models? The research started from understanding history and heritage values that acknowledge the history of technology. This research inspired by cultural heritage led to the development of an innovative understanding of the role of (weak) mortars, a model that is also helpful for new constructions. History so helps developing a sustainable future.

Why is masonry with lime mortar durable and is it that deformable without 'breaking'?

Research at the University of Leuven has studied the tri-axial behaviour of different types of mortar and masonry. This complex matter required a lot of engineering research and newly developed test procedures to come up with a new model that explains the mechanical behaviour of masonry with lime mortar. Explaining all technical details would make this contribution too long,

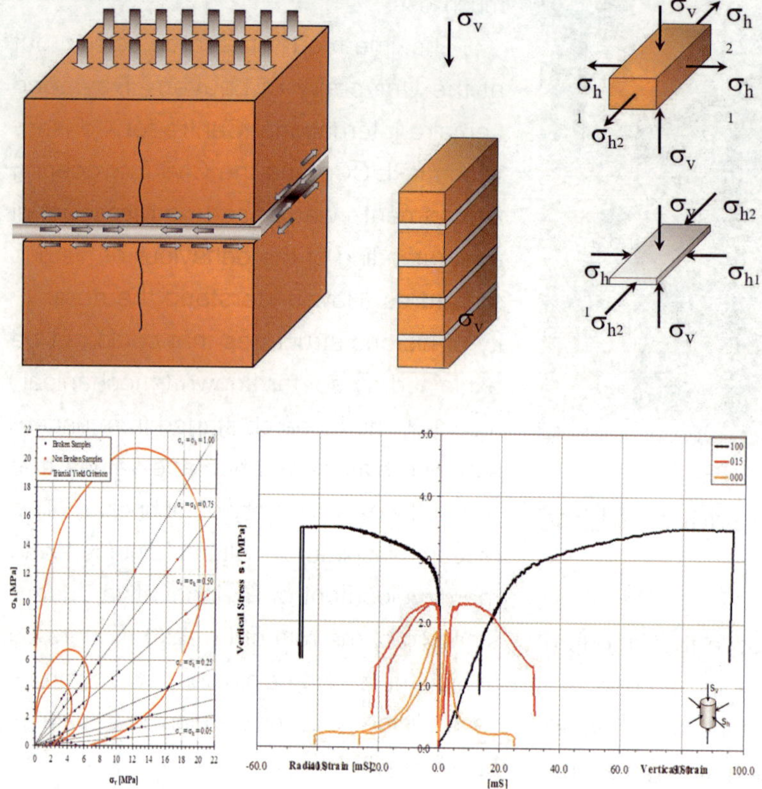

Fig.6 Triaxial stress states of (lime) mortar and bricks in masonry [© Hayen, R. e.a., 2009]. (upper)

Fig.7 Tri-axial tests on different types of mortar: lime mortar, hydraulic lime mortar and cement mortar [© Hayen, R., e.a., 2009]. (down)

but the essence is explained in the following lines.

The usual stress state of bricks and mortar in a (historic) masonry composite: usually the stiffness of the brick is higher than that of the mortar [Fig. 6]. Mortars, in general, are subjected to tri-axial compression, bricks are subjected to mono directional compression stresses and perpendicular to this to bi-axial tensile stresses. Most models that use that concept consider those materials to behave (linearly) elastic with a perfect adhesion between mortar joints and bricks. In a simplified way they assume mortar and brick to behave as rubber. But let for the same simplification assume that mortar rather behaves as a 'sponge' which has the possibility to reduce its pore volume when subjected to tri-axial compression. It can be visualised as how we squeeze a sponge in a hand.

The (horizontal) tensile stresses in the bricks result from a reaction of the bricks to the horizontal expansion induced in the mortar by pushing on it. These reaction stresses are induced by the friction between mortar and bricks, the friction that avoids the mortar to be squeezed out from in between the bricks [Fig. 7]. When the load increases each mortar will see its behaviour changing from a brittle to a shear band collapse mechanisms and further to a pore collapse mechanism when the horizontal confinement stresses reach 15% versus 25% of the (vertical) stresses in the mortar.[2] At the latter stress state mortar will behave as a sponge, which means that it can collapse its pores, considering the bricks can provide the necessary resistance to induce the confinement. This is the case until the tensile stresses in the bricks reach the level that the brick will crack. Thanks to the pore collapse the increase of tensile stresses in the bricks will gradually reduce as the mortar is not pushed out anymore but collapses in itself. If so, the mortar will deform and so does the

Fig.8 Leuven, Park Abbey, 18th-century coach house: deformability of historic masonry [© K. Van Balen].

masonry without cracking of the masonry, the latter is induced by the cracking of the bricks.

Our research shows that, despite the limited tensile strength of bricks, lime mortar will have reached a confinement stress that allows to induce a pore collapse mechanism in it, thus allowing for deformation without breaking of the masonry. In case of cement mortar, a similar behaviour could be reached with bricks that have a much higher tensile strength than bricks usually have. It means that the bricks will start cracking when the mortar is still in its brittle or shear band collapse mechanism. It also means that the cement mortar is still in a phase in which it will increase the horizontal stresses, yet unable to limit the latter by collapsing in itself. Cement mortar or alike will (compared to lime mortar) behave rather as a rubber at the same load on masonry, which has as a consequence that the tensile stresses in the brick will increase until the bricks crack, and so does the masonry. This results in a sudden and brittle failure of the masonry!

The new 'model' explains better what we see in historic buildings: cement and lime mortar in essence behave similarly, but the transition from shear bands to pore collapse mechanism happens 'earlier' in lime mortar than in cement mortar. Therefore, the tensile stresses in the bricks will be limited at a lower level in case of lime mortar. This explains why lime mortar makes masonry more deformable, why lime mortar contributes to durability and longevity of masonry as we can see in historic structures [Fig. 8]. The improved model can help 'engineers' to be more confident, to accept the 'lower standard compressive strength' or 'weakness' of lime mortar. For instance, it helps to understand how Gothic masonry structures, thanks to that deformability, were able to balance forces between vaults and flying buttresses over a rather long period of time.

Valuing and Repairing Historic Brick Masonry

Conservation of heritage structures requires an understanding of their heritage values, an understanding about ways to preserve them and principles on which their

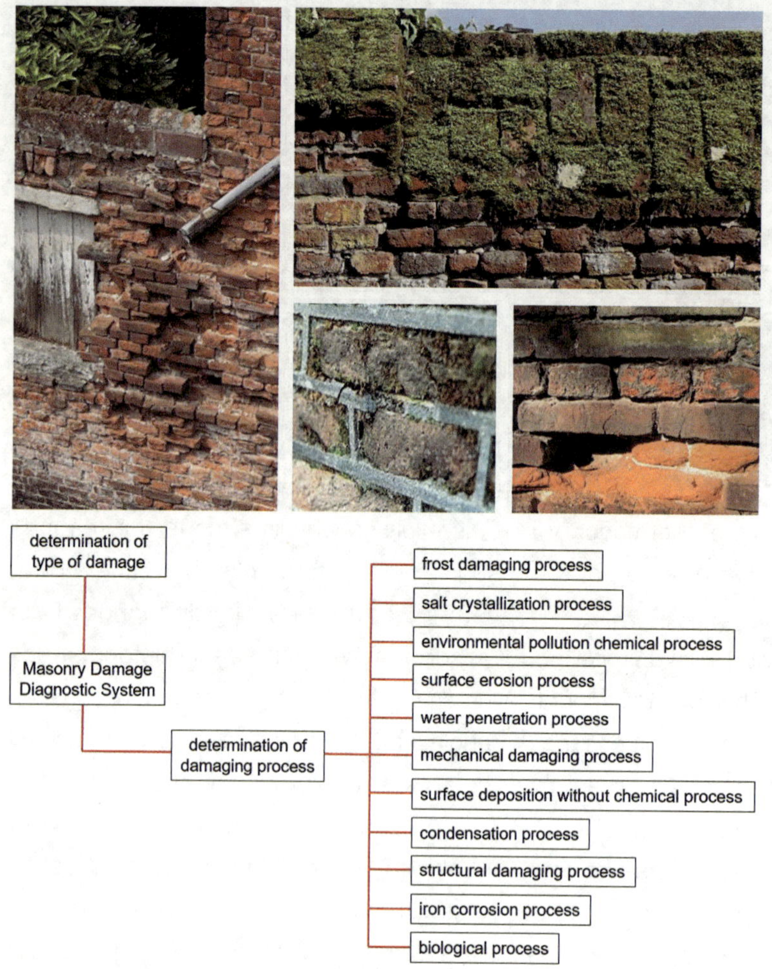

Fig.9 Brick Masonry Damage Atlas and relation with the MDDS expert system with reference to the different damaging mechanisms [© K. Van Balen e.a., 1999].

conservation can be approached. Understanding the heritage values of brick masonry structures is a source of inspiration and a stock of solutions for future sustainable development.

The PRECOM³OS UNESCO chair on 'Preventive Conservation, Monitoring and Maintenance of Monuments and Sites' hosted at the Raymond Lemaire International Centre for Conservation (RLICC),[3] University of Leuven, has contributed a lot since 2009 to develop a preventive conservation strategy for historic buildings.[4] The chair aims at identifying research and educational activities in the field of preventive conservation, maintenance and monitoring of monuments and sites, so as to contribute to: 1) Identifying the particularities of preservation policies and practices; 2) Developing new appropriate tools and techniques to improve preventive preservation strategies; 3) Developing legal frameworks, policies and exemplary field applications considering the variety of cultural and social contexts.

This approach was yet initiated somehow through the development of a Masonry Damage Diagnostic System (MDDS) in the 1990s, which looked into the relationship between damage and the mechanisms that caused them [Fig. 9]. The MDDS was developed as a decision support system, which started from analysing and documenting damages in brick masonry using a brick masonry damage atlas as a book,[5] and as a software tool.[6] Taking the condition assessment as a starting point, a set of damaging mechanisms were examined to help the user of the system to understand the causes of the damages. The approach was developed having in mind the importance of monitoring the state of

ASPECTS 相 / DIMENSIONS 度	artistic 艺术性	historic 历史性	social 社会性	scientific 科学性
form & design 形式与设计				
materials & substance 材料与物质				
use & function 使用与功能				
tradition, techniques & workmanship 传统，技术与匠艺				
locations & setting 地域性与环境				
spirit & feeling 精神与感觉				

Fig.10 Nara Grid: an evaluation scheme based on the Nara Document on Authenticity [© K. Van Balen, 2008].

conservation as a basis for condition assessment as well as for a maintenance approach to conservation. This practice existed at that time yet in the Netherlands and in Flanders (Belgium) and was supported by organisations like 'Monuments Watch' (*Monumentenwacht*) .[7]

In 2008, the 'Nara Grid' was developed as a tool to articulate the Nara Document on Authenticity (ICOMOS 1994) into an scheme that would allow to identify and to value built cultural heritage[8] [Fig. 10]. The latter allowed to integrate aspects that have been mentioned before. Intangible values as 'knowledge' could be integrated in the value assessment and thus also in the means to preserve them.

When addressing interventions and preservation strategies, similarly the different layers that represent those values have to be preserved and can be instrumental to the preservation itself. In *From Conservation Principles to Materialization (Or the other way around: how is materialization guided by principles?)* [9], I explained that when considering the activities on the ground, the reality is created through preservation activities of which the final outcome is influenced by many factors. Most of those parameters result from the complex context in which implementations are carried out. Hence, the conclusions were: 1) that in-between conservation principles and execution, different dialectic layers exist, and 2) that dictating principles without consideration of that reality thus create illusions. At the same time the complexity calls for the active involvement of that reality in the process. This means that local communities and local craftsmanship should be involved, which are also a form of intangible heritage.

In the European Pointing project which resulted in a valuable contribution to the RILEM committee on repair of ancient mortar joints, [10] heritage valuing and damage assessment methods were developed. These methods are connected with maintenance and prevention as well as with an integrated approach to preservation that includes the importance of craftsmanship.

But also from this research a connection was made between understanding and valuing cultural heritage with insights for sustainability of new constructions. In his doctoral dissertation Roel Hendrickx has shown the discrepancy between standardised tests that measure workability of mortar and the feeling by construction professionals as masons.[11] That discrepancy was not systematic but also depended on the type of binders. Uncritical use of the standardised tests — for example in the case of a comparison of cement and lime based mortar — resulted in an inappropriate dosage of water or wrong mixing procedures in case of lime mortar. This finding also supported the understanding that many standards, which (unintentionally) were designed based on Portland cement properties, were not sufficiently clear to what extend they are biased by those properties and were presented to be valid for other binders, as lime for example. The research eventually developed an alternative measuring technique that measures workability in a reliably for various types of binders, Portland cement and lime alike. This research did 1) elucidate the importance of craftsmanship in construction in general, 2) demonstrate how a critical reflection on today's practices based on understanding historical sustainable construction techniques can help to improve today's building practices.

Conclusion

The geological and historical context as well as the understanding of the alignment of different raw materials in combination with technological development help to explain the long tradition in using brick masonry with lime mortar in Belgium. The predominant use of lime mortar in historic constructions until the 20th century posed a problem for many technicians in the 20th century as they were blinded by their quest for strength and stiffness. These principles, which were the basis of the modern paradigm, were responsible for their 'short-sightedness' to understand historic masonry.

Research on the obvious durability of often remarkable historic masonry structures made with lime mortar has revealed that the 'weakness' of lime mortar explains the durability of masonry made with it. The insights gained are not only valuable for the preservation of historic fabric but have also helped to improve the technology for new masonry structures. The historical evidences and also the scientific knowledge demonstrate the importance of traditional technologies and (historic) craftsmanship. It adds more arguments to preserve the brick masonry heritage for its appearance and the related heritage values as well as for valuing the 'intangible' heritage that is embedded in historic brick masonry.

Notes

① Latin title: *De Architectura.* There are many translations and commented editions, notably: Vitruvius, *Ten Books on Architecture*, translated by Ingrid D. Rowland and illustrated by Thomas Noble Howe, Cambridge University Press, 1999.

② Hayen, R.; Van Balen, Koenraad; Van Gemert, Dionys, 'Triaxial interaction of natural stone, brick and mortar in masonry constructions', in Scheremans, Luc (ed.), *Building Materials and Building Technology to Preserve the Built Heritage*, WTA International PhD symposium Leuven, 8-9 October 2009, Pfaffenhofen: WTA Schriftenreihe, 2009, p. 333-352.

③ https: //set.kuleuven.be/rlicc/research/precomos (accessed 2018.04.15).

④ Van Balen, Koenraad, 'Preventive Conservation of Historic Buildings', *International Journal for Restoration of Buildings and Monuments*, 21, 2015, p. 99-104.

⑤ Franke, L.; Schumann, I.; van Hees, Rob; van der Klugt, L.; Naldini, S.; Binda, L.; Baronio, G.; Van Balen, Koenraad; Mateus, J., *Damage Atlas*, *Classification of Damage Patterns Found in Brick Masonry*, *Protection and Conservation of European Cultural Heritage*, Research report ñ 8, vol.2, Stuttgart: Frauenhofer IRB Verlag, 1998.

⑥ Van Balen, Koenraad; Mateus, J.; Binda, L.; Baronio, G.; van Hees, Rob; Naldini, S.; van der Klugt, L.; Schumann, I.; Franke, L., *Scientific Background of the Damage Atlas and the Masonry Damage Diagnostic System*, *Protection and Conservation of European Cultural Heritage*, Research report n ° 8, vol.1, Luxemburg: Office for Official Publications of the European Communities, 1999.

⑦ See http: //www.monumentenwacht.be/en (accessed 2018.04.14).

⑧ Van Balen, Koenraad, 'The Nara Grid: An Evaluation Scheme Based on the Nara Document on Authenticity', *APT Bulletin. The Journal of Preservation Technology*, 39 (2-3), 2008, p. 39-45. Nara Document on Authenticity, see: https: //whc.unesco.org/archive/nara94.htm (last consulted 2018.04.14).

⑨ Van Balen, Koen, 'From Conservation Principles to Materialization (Or the other way around: how is materialization guided by principles?)', in: Van Gemert, Dionys (ed.), *Consolidation of Masonry*, 1, Karlsruhe: Aedification Publishers, 2003, p. 135-144.

⑩ Van Balen, Koenraad; Bicer-Simsir, Beril; Binda, Luigia; Bläuer, Christine; Elsen, Jan; Groot, Caspar; Hansen, E.; van Hees, Rob; Henriques, F.; Hughes, J.; Toumbakari, Eleni-Eva; von Konow, T.; Lindqvist, J.; Maurenbrecher, P.; Middendorf, B.; Papayianni, I.; Simon, S.; Stefanidou, M.; Subercaseaux, M.; Tedeschi, C.; Thomson, M.; Valek, Jan; Valluzi, M.; Vanhellemont, Yves; Veiga, R., 'Performance and repair requirements for repointing mortars, Testing of repair mortars for historic masonry', in: Valek, Jan; Groot, Caspar; Hughes, John (eds), *Historic Mortars Conference HMC2010 and RILEM TC 203-RHM*, Prague, Czech Republic; 22-24 September 2010, Prague: RILEM Publications, 2010, p. 1349-1352.

⑪ Hendrickx, Roel; Van Balen, Koenraad; Van Gemert, Dionys, 'The Workability of Masonry Mortar Assessed by Masons', *International Journal for Restoration of Buildings and Monuments*, 15/1, 2009, p. 39-50; Van Balen, Koenraad; Hendrickx, Roel, 'Preservation of Workmanship or Workmanship for Preservation', in: D'Ayala, Dina; Fodde, Enrico (eds), *6th International Conference on Structural Analysis of Historical Constructions*: *Preserving Safety and Significance*, International Conference on Structural Analysis of Historical Constructions; Bath; 2-4 July 2008, London: CRC Press, 2008, p. 3-12.

附录

附录 1：北京大学文物建筑专业与中国建筑考古学

徐怡涛

非常高兴有这样一天，我们能够聚集在一起。如果要说办会感言的话，我想简单地讲一下北京大学文物建筑专业从 1999 年正式招生以来到现在的经历。我于 1999 年来到北大攻读博士学位，师从宿白先生。当时，北大文物建筑专业本科专业刚刚成立，没有专职的专业教师，主要靠外聘清华、北建大等学校的老师开展教学。为了培养专职教师队伍进行文物建筑专业教学与学科建设，所以从读博开始，我就参与了这个专业的教学工作，从 27 岁一直做到现在，17 年过去了。

回顾专业这些年来的发展，我们主要做了两件事情：一是建设文物建筑教学体系；二是开展建筑考古学研究。我们带出了一批优秀的学生，今天在座的人中，我很高兴地看到，有一些北大文物建筑专业的毕业生来参会。他们从北大毕业后，现在中国、日本及美国等国家的相关研究机构中从事本专业的研究工作。对我来讲，我视人才培养为最大成果，是比个人所获得的任何学术成果都更重要的成就。北大招收了中国最优秀的学生，但是，最好的学生往往不愿意从事不能被社会广泛认可的专业。就国内来讲，在经济高速发展的年代，从事历史相关研究，对于很多学生来讲，可能会影响到他的自我实现以及在现代社会中的认同。但非常令人高兴的是，我们看到，我们的教学能够让中国最优秀的学生以文物建筑研究、保护和利用这种“冷门专业”作为他们毕生的工作，我觉得这是我们十多年工作的最大成果。

我们一直在反思，为什么他们能留下来？我认为其中最关键的原因和我们今天会议的焦点——建筑考古学相关：我们将建筑考古学的研究与教学紧密结合，让学生找在学习过程中找到了研究的乐趣，他们在学习研究中，发现文物建筑的价值，逐步了解其所学所做对国家、对人类文化的贡献和意义，他们继而认识到，在文化遗产事业中，个人生命的价值能和文化遗产融为一体，通过他们的研究、通过他们的努力、通过他们的坚持，可以让文化遗产的价值得以揭示，并得到世人的承认，进而使文化遗产得到尊重和保护，他们的生命，也因融入文化遗产得以永恒。

这样的认知，首先源自我自己的亲身体会。我在中国很多省份做过田野调查，曾经有一位山西的文物干部非常支持我们的教学科研工作，但当我们在该地区的研究取得了一定成果，想要向他汇报时，得到他不幸患癌症去世的消息。这件事情对我产生了很大触动。我曾应北大校友会之约，写过一篇名为“宿命的求索”的文章，介绍我们专业的历史，其中便提到了这件事。每当我看到或想起这座我们在他家乡发现的一处北宋建筑时，就会想到这位山西的同志，我常对学生讲起这件事：在我看来，这处北宋建筑的价值，并不仅仅存在于形制、结构、年代等客观因素之中，我希望我的学生们能更深切地认识到，文物建筑所连缀的历史的意义——在我们这个时代，依然有人为保护建筑遗产而默默奉献，甚至付出生命，这种行为增加了文物建筑的价值，因为我们的建筑，必将烙印上她所经历的一切，我们的后代通过这些文物建筑可以认识到，在我们这个时代，对历史、文化和乡情的尊重，虽如丝缕，并未断绝。

我和鲁汶大学高曼士教授的合作，也正是基于这样的理念。我感动于这位外国教授对中国的文化遗产的付出，我们在一起交谈时，能感受到彼此学术理念的共鸣，刚才高曼士教授所讲的，对于建筑考古学科发展的思考，正是支撑我们这些年来，得以在建筑考古学领域不断合作进取的学术共识。我想，本次会议的宗旨，就是让国内外有志于建筑考古学的学者都能达成共识，一起来实现建筑考古学的终极目标——让全人类的建筑遗产得到科学的认知，完善的保护和合理的呈现，让建筑见证历史，让历史照亮建筑。

附录 2：
2016 中欧建筑考古国际学术研讨会议程 · 主论坛

考古学的多样面：如何处理考古发掘前后的遗址——以土耳其萨迦拉索斯遗址为例

Marc WAELKENS　鲁汶大学考古系　荣休教授

北京城明代诸内门研究

晋宏逵　故宫研究院古建筑研究所　研究员

事物的生命：建筑复写性的调查与保护的应用

Carolina DI BIASE　米兰理工大学建筑系　教授

周原凤雏三号建筑的形制与性质

雷兴山　北京大学考古文博学院　教授

近年中国建筑史研究动态概览——以 2009 至 2014 年为例

王贵祥　清华大学建筑学院　教授

天堂的象征与其建造的挑战：意大利早期现代穹顶的建筑考古调查

史林姆（Hermann SCHLIMME）维也纳技术大学　教授

马普艺术史研究所

辽上京皇城西山坡建筑遗址

汪盈　中国社科院考古研究所　助理研究员

董新林　中国社科院考古研究所　研究员

跟随夏洛克 · 福尔摩斯的脚步：英国遗产实践的勘察传统

Adam MENUGE　剑桥大学建筑系　教授

几何宇宙与嵩岳寺塔平面

梅晨曦（Tracy Miller）范德堡大学　副教授

建筑考古：从田野到保护

Elke NAGEL　慕尼黑工业大学　博士生

舍“圆”用“方”——中国城市形态的历史选择

韦正　北京大学考古文博学院　教授

青年论坛分场一总结报告

吴葱　天津大学建筑学院　教授

青年论坛分场二总结报告

徐怡涛　北京大学考古文博学院　副教授

北京大学中国考古学研究中心

西安老牛坡建筑遗址

郭明　四川省文物考古研究所　助理研究员

未知，缺爱：洞见砖砌体中石灰砂浆具有历史意义的使用

库恩（Koen VAN BALEN）鲁汶大学建筑系　教授

雷蒙德 · 勒麦尔国际保护中心主任

万荣稷王庙建筑考古研究

徐怡涛　北京大学考古文博学院　副教授

北京大学中国考古学研究中心

初论喜仁龙对北京建筑遗产的贡献

刘临安　北京建筑大学建筑学院　教授

杜彬　北京建筑大学建筑学院　博士生

文化遗产保护的战时合作：罗伯茨委员会 1944 年至 1945 年在华活动与影响

左拉拉　美国海军学院　助理教授

近代化与本土化——鼓浪屿近代建筑的发展（1840-1949）

钱毅　北方工业大学建筑学院　副教授

砖与树轮：13、14 世纪比利时佛兰德斯砖建筑的测年与评估

Vincent DEBONNE　鲁汶大学　博士生　弗莱明遗产研究所

南宋园林遗产研究综述

鲍沁星　浙江农林大学风景园林与建筑学院　副教授

钢铁遗产的结构建筑学：学会接纳他者

Werner LORENZ　勃兰登堡工业大学　教授

明清官式建筑和玺彩画形制分期研究

曹振伟　故宫博物院　助理研究员

西夏陵所体现的亚欧大陆文化交流与融合

陈同滨　中国建筑设计院有限公司　研究员

李　敏　中国建筑设计院有限公司　副研究员

刘翔宇　中国建筑设计院有限公司　建筑师

晋南宋金元建筑之横栱装饰形象研究

徐新云　中国建筑设计院有限公司　建筑师

人造天穹：中国教堂中的哥特拱顶

高曼士　鲁汶大学建筑系　教授

雷蒙德·勒麦尔国际保护中心

青年论坛分场三总结报告

刘畅　清华大学建筑学院　教授

青年论坛分场四总结报告

钱毅　北方工业大学建筑学院　副教授

从建筑考古探索保护比利时和卢森堡近代早期建筑——重温 15-16 世纪那些“消逝”的古迹

Krista DE JONGE　鲁汶大学建筑系　教授

雷蒙德·勒麦尔国际保护中心

石窟寺的外部连接空间：龟兹为例

魏正中 北京大学考古文博学院 教授

明长城砖砌空心敌台的建筑特点与类型学分析——以“蓟州镇”与“真保镇”为中心

张依萌 中国文化遗产研究院 助理研究员

如龙桥精细测绘：作为技术史研究手段的建筑考古学

刘妍 慕尼黑工业大学 博士候选人

鼓浪屿日本领事馆之建筑分析与研究

张光玮 北京国文琰文化遗产保护中心 博士

从屯田到守边——以玉门关为例谈经济与军事双重因素下的汉长城体系

王琳峰 中国建筑设计院有限公司 副研究员

宋金时期晋东南墓葬仿木构建筑史料研究

俞莉娜 早稻田大学创造理工学研究科 博士生

徐怡涛 北京大学考古文博学院 副教授

北京大学中国考古学研究中心

雅安观音阁修缮工程中的调查研究

赵元祥 成都文物考古研究所 工程师

李林东 成都文物考古研究所 工程师

蔡宇琨 成都文物考古研究所 工程师

有形的阿姆斯特丹黄金时代：建筑考古和保护

Gabri VAN TUSSENBROEK 阿姆斯特丹大学 教授

中国砖石拱券技术源流的考古学研究

杨哲峰 北京大学考古文博学院 教授

圆明园武陵春色桃花洞遗址调查

张凤梧 天津大学建筑学院 讲师

显示或是隐藏？ 16-20 世纪法国图卢兹砖墙

Val¨|rie NÈGRE 法国巴黎拉维莱特建筑学院 教授

古迹：中国古代方志中所体现的文化遗产观念探析

吴葱 天津大学建筑学院 教授

Annex 2: Conference papers of the Sino-Europe Building Architecture Forum 2016 · Main Forum

The Many Faces of Archaeology: How to Deal with a Monumental Site Before, During and After Excavations: Sagalassos (SW Turkey)
Marc WAELKENS, Professor Emeritus, University of Leuven, Department of Archaeology

Study on the Inner Gates in the City of Ming Beijing
JIN Hongkui, Professor, Institute of Architectural Heritage, Academy of the Palace Museum

The Life of Things: Investigating Architectural Palimpsests towards Conservation
Carolina DI BIASE, Professor, Politecnico di Milano, Dipartimento di Architettura e Studi Urbani

The Style and Characteristic of the Building No.3 at Fengchu, Zhouyuan
LEI Xingshan, Professor, School of Archaeology and Museology, Peking University

Reviews on the Studies of Chinese Architectural History in Recent Years: from 2009 to 2014
WANG Guixiang, Professor, School of Architecture, Tsinghua University

Symbol for Heaven and Construction Challenge: Domes in Early Modern Italy Investigated through Building Archeology
Hermann SCHLIMME, Professor, Vienna Technical University / Bibliotheca Hertziana, Max Planck Institute for Art History (Rome)

Xishanpo (West Hillside) Building Site of the Imperial City of Shangjing (the Upper Capital) of the Liao Dynasty
WANG Ying, Assistant Research Scientist, Institute of Archaeology, Chinese Academy of Social Sciences
DONG Xinlin, Professor, Institute of Archaeology, Chinese Academy of Social Sciences

In the Footsteps of Sherlock Holmes: The Investigative Tradition in UK Heritage Practice
Adam MENUGE, Professor, University of Cambridge, Department of Architecture

Geometry, Cosmology, and the Plan of the Songyuesi Pagoda
Tracy Miller, Associate Professor, Vanderbilt University

Building Archaeology (Bauforschung): From Scientific Fieldwork to Conservation
Elke NAGEL, Doctor-Ing, Technische Universität München, Institute for Building History, Building Archaeology and Heritage Conservation

Replacing 'Circle' with 'Square': The Historic Adoption of Urban Form in China
WEI Zheng, Professor, School of Archaeology & Museology, Peking University

Report on the Youth Forum I on the Evening of the Day Before
WU Cong, Professor, School of Architecture, Tianjin University

Report on the Youth Forum II on the Evening of the Day Before
Xu Yitao, Associate Professor, School of Archaeology & Museology, Peking University / Center for Chinese Archaeology of Peking University

Archaeological Building Site of Laoniupo, Xi'an
GUO Ming, Assistant Researcher, Sichuan Institute of Historic Relic Archaeology and Research

Unknown, Unloved: Insights in the Historic Use of Lime Mortar in Brick Masonry
Koen VAN BALEN, Professor, University of Leuven, Department of Construction / Director of Raymond Lemaire International Centre for Conservation, UNESCO Chair on Preventive Conservation

Building Archaelogicial Resarch on the Jiwang Temple in Wanrong, Shanxi
Xu Yitao, Associate Professor, School of Archaeology & Museology, Peking University / Center for Chinese Archaeology of Peking University

Osvald Siren's Contribution to the Preservation of Architectural Culture in Beijing
LIU Lin'an, Professor, Beijing University of Civil Engineering and Architecture
DU Bin, Pdoctoral student, Beijing University of Civil Engineering and Architecture

Wartime Collaboration on Preserving the Cultural Heritage: History of the Roberts Commission in China 1944-1945
ZUO Lala, Assistant Professor, United States Naval Academy

YU Lina, Doctoral Student, *Waseda* University
Xu Yitao, Associate Professor, School of Archaeology & Museology, Peking University / Center for Chinese Archaeology of Peking University

An Investigation during the Restoration of the Guanyin Pavilion at Ya'an, Sichuan
ZHAO Yuanxiang, Engineer, Chengdu Cultural Heritage and Archaeology Research Institute
LI Lindong, Engineer, Chengdu Cultural Heritage and Archaeology Research Institute
CAI Yukun, Engineer, Chengdu Cultural Heritage and Archaeology Research Institute

The Tangible Golden Age of Amsterdam (1585–1700): Building Archaeology and Preservation
Gabri VAN TUSSENBROEK, Professor, University of Amsterdam, Department of Art History

An Archaeological Study on the Origin and Development of Brick-and-Stone Arching Technology in China
YANG Zhefeng, Professor, School of Archaeology & Museology, Peking University

A Survey of the Taohuadong Site at Wuling Chunse, Yuanmingyuan (The Old Summer Palace)
ZHANG Fengwu, Lecturer, School of Architecture, Tianjin University

Showing or Hiding Bricks? Brick Walls in Toulouse (France) from the 16th to the 20th Century
Val¨¦rie NÈGRE, Professor, École nationale supérieure d'architecture Paris La Villette

Ancient Traces: Traditional Chinese Conception of Cultural Heritage Rediscovered in Local Records
WU Cong, Professor, School of Architecture, Tianjin University

Concluding Speech
SUN Hua, Professor, School of Archaeology & Museology, Peking University

附录 3:
2016 中欧建筑考古国际学术研讨会议程 · 青年论坛

“全面采集、典型再现”文物建筑测绘方法新论——以景福宫文物建筑测绘为例
李东遥、徐丹、何蓓洁 天津大学

清代皇家建筑内檐装修现状记录方法初探
荣幸、何蓓洁 天津大学

景山寿皇殿石质文物数字化初探——以石狮为例
周悦煌 天津大学

紫禁城排水系统设计理念研究
张雅平、曹萍 故宫博物院

由无锡惠山祠堂群顾可久祠堂修缮前后形制变化反映的实际建筑遗产保护问题
朱琨、朱蕾 天津大学

故宫景福宫调查研究报告
肖芳芳 天津大学
庄立新 故宫博物院

觉苑寺壁画彩塑数字化勘察测绘工程前期研究
段牛斗 中央美术学院
祁娜、王泽昊 北京国文琰文化遗产保护中心

文物建筑四维空间投影测绘方法初探
尚劲宇、张剑葳、徐怡涛 北京大学

古桥解体：泰顺文兴桥建筑史与技术史研究
周淼 东南大学

绘画资料中所见的宋代建筑外檐装修
李若水 北京联合大学

南宋临安城恭圣仁烈皇后宅复原研究
王端正 西安建筑科技大学

南宋临安恭圣仁烈杨皇后宅遗址的复原研究
袁怡雅 中国建筑设计院有限公司

唐代皇家藏书楼建筑在都城中的空间位置分析
刘虹 西南科技大学

殷周金文中的建筑史料述略
李敏 北京大学考古文博学院、中国建筑设计院有限公司

曾侯乙墓一号陪葬坑出土“帷帐”的复原研究
张昌平、李雪婷 武汉大学历史学院

游仙寺石碑中的高平李家
李竞扬 天津大学

北京西郊极乐寺史考
郭勉 北京大学元培学院

圆明园西洋楼养雀笼的数字复原理论

Sadiq Javer，朴文子　北京数字圆明科技文化有限公司

明初京师地区城址类型与城池兴筑历程

段智钧　北京工业大学建筑与城市规划学院

赵娜冬　天津大学建筑学院

内蒙古藏传佛教建筑殿堂空间分类与特征研究

韩瑛、李新飞　内蒙古工业大学建筑学院

隆福寺行宫复原研究

朱蕾　天津大学

张恒媛　山东大学

谒清东陵行宫初探

朱蕾、陈书砚　天津大学

鸠摩罗什舍利塔建造背景与艺术特征初探

喻梦哲　西安建筑科技大学

西安唐小雁塔塔身南北向券门两侧方形小“塔”做法源流考

李双双　西安建筑科技大学

故宫宝蕴楼屋面“海狸尾瓦”来源寻踪

杨菁　天津大学

吴伟　故宫博物院

李程远　天津大学

拉萨色拉寺建筑遗产存续：历史身份重塑与再生

孙新飞、郭建伟　同济大学

土山湾宝塔的投影：木样、废墟与中华想象

杨兆凯　北京大学考古文博学院

中华民国临时参议院旧址研究

高钢　东南大学

沈阳老城区红砖建筑研究

刘思铎　沈阳建筑大学

台湾庙宇屋顶形制差异探析

邱琼仪　北京大学元培学院

建筑考古与公众文化遗产保护实践——北京林开謩、陈宝琛旧居的调查研究与文物认定

崔金泽　比利时鲁汶大学

颐和园排云门—佛香阁区域因山构室理法初探

戈祎迎、赵小燕、刘晓明　北京林业大学

浅谈布鲁日英国修道院的保护研究及其启示

赵东旭　清华大学、雷蒙德·勒麦尔国际保护中心

Annex 3: Conference papers of the Sino-Europe Building Architecture Forum 2016 · Youth Forum

A New Survey Method of 'Comprehensive Collection，Representing the Typical' for Traditional Architectural: Using Jingfu Palace as an Example
LI Dongyao，*XU Dan*，*HE Beijie*，Tianjin University

Methods of Documenting the Decoration in Imperial Architecture of the Qing Dynasty
RONG Xing，*HE Beijie*，Tianjin University

The Digitalization of Stone Cultural Relics in Shouhuang Hall of Jingshan Hill
ZHOU Yuehuang，Tianjin University

The Designing Theory of the Sewerage System in the Forbidden City
ZHANG Yaping，*Cao Ping*，The Palace Museum

Preservation Issues of Architectural Heritage: the Change of Style Resulted from the Restoration Project of Gu Kejiu Ancestral Hall in Wuxi
ZHU Kun，*ZHU Lei*，Tianjin University

A Research Investigation of Jingfu Palace in the Forbidden City
XIAO Fangfang，Tianjin University
ZHUANG Lixin，The Palace Museum

A Pre-Survey Study for the Digitalization of Murals and Statues in Jueyuansi
DUAN Niu'dou，China Central Academy Of Fine Arts
QI Na，*WANG Zehao*，Beijing Guowenyan Cultural Heritage Conservation Center Ltd

Theories and Methodologies of Detailed Architectural Survey
SHANG Jinyu，*ZHANG Jianwei*，*XU Yitao*，Peking University

Deconstruction of Ancient Bridge: Research on History of Architecture and Technique of Timber Arch Bridge Wenxingqiao in Taishun，Zhejiang
ZHOU Miao，Southeast University

Exterior Eave Decoration of Song Architecture in Paintings
LI Ruoshui，*Beijing* Union University

The Reconstruction of Empress Yang's Residence in Lin'an of the Southern Song
WANG Duanzheng，Xi'an University of Architecture and Technology

The Reconstruction of the Site of Empress

Yang's Residence in Lin'an of the Southern Song
YUAN Yiya, China Architecture Design Academy CO. LTD.

A Space Position Analysis of the Royal Library Building in Capital in the Tang Dynasty
LIU Hong, Southwest University of Science and Technology

Architectural History in the Bronze Inscriptions of China (16–8 Century BC.)
LI Min, School of Archaeology and Museology, Peking University / China Architecture Design Academy CO. LTD.

Reconstruction of the 'Canopy' Discovered from the Burying Pit of Marquis Zeng's Tomb
ZHANG Changping, LI Xueting, History School, Wuhan University

The Li Family of Gaoping in a Stele Inscription of Youxiansi
LI Jingyang, Tianjin University

A History of Jilesi, Beijing
GUO Mian, Yuanpei School, Peking University

Theories Regarding the Digital Reconstruction of The Aviary in the Western Buildings Area at Yuanmingyuan
Sadiq Javer, Wenzi Piao, Beijing Re -Yuanmingyuan Company Limited, Beijing, China

Types of Urban Sites and the Course of Town Planning in the Imperial Capital Area of the Early Ming Dynasty
DUAN Zhiju, ZHAO Nadong, School of Architecture and Urban Planning, Beijing University of Technology

Spatial Types and Characteristics of Tibetan Buddhist Architecture in Inner Mongolia
Han Ying, Li Xinfei, School of Architecture, Inner Mongolian University of Technology

The Imperial Secondary Residence in Longfusi
ZHU Lei, Tianjin University
ZHANG Hengyuan, Shandong University

A Visit to the Temporary Imperial Residence in the Eastern Mausoleums of the Qing Dynasty
ZHU Le, CHEN Shuyan, Tianjin University

A Preliminary Study on the Building Background